CONTEMPORARY

INSTRUCTOR'S GUIDE

reading

basics

A REAL-WORLD APPROACH TO LITERACY

McGraw Hill Education

Bothell, WA • Chicago, IL • Columbus, OH • New York, NY

Image Credits: **Cover** Lisa Fukshansky/The McGraw-Hill Companies

mheonline.com

 **Education**

Send all inquiries to:
Contemporary/McGraw-Hill
130 East Randolph Street, Suite 400
Chicago, IL 60601

ISBN: 978-0-07-659136-7
MHID: 0-07-659136-0

Printed in the United States of America.

3 4 5 6 7 8 9 QDB 15 14 13 12

The **McGraw-Hill** Companies

Contents

Intermediate 1 Reader

Intermediate 2 Reader

Advanced Reader

reading

basics

PART 1: PROGRAM OVERVIEW

Program Summary

Reading Basics aligns closely with the current research and practices of evidence-based reading instruction (EBRI) to inform instruction. Current research emphasizes four essential components of reading: alphabetics (phonics and word analysis), vocabulary, fluency, and comprehension. We will discuss major points of EBRI in the next section.

Reading Basics is designed for adult basic education learners who want to improve their reading ability for a variety of reasons, such as succeeding in their daily lives, improving their workplace skills, and/or passing various standard assessments. For example, learners may want to handle everyday reading tasks more easily, get a new job or a promotion, or attain their GED® credentials. Still others are English Language Learners who are interested in furthering their skills in both reading and communicating.

To serve these diverse learners, the program is divided into four levels: Introductory, Intermediate 1, Intermediate 2, and Advanced. Each book in *Reading Basics* encompasses a range of reading grade levels.

Book	Reading Level
Introductory	1.6–3.9
Intermediate 1	3.6–6.9
Intermediate 2	6.6–8.9
Advanced	8.6–12.9

These levels correspond to the reading levels in standard assessments. You can use these tests to diagnose, evaluate, and place students in the appropriate level of the program. The goal is to place students into a level in which they feel sufficiently challenged but can also experience success.

Program Components

The *Reading Basics* program has the following components:
- Four *Student Editions (Introductory, Intermediate 1, Intermediate 2, Advanced)*
- Four *Readers (Introductory, Intermediate 1, Intermediate 2, Advanced)*
- One *Instructor's Guide* covering all four levels
- A website with additional resources including MP3 recordings of all the articles in the *Readers*

Student Editions

Each *Student Edition* provides direct instruction and practice in reading skills, workplace skills, vocabulary, and alphabetics. In all four levels, the *Student Edition* is organized into three units, each consisting of six or seven eight-page lessons.

In each lesson, the Introduce page presents the targeted reading skill and provides an opportunity for you to model the skill for students. The Practice page offers students the chance to practice the reading skill, and the Apply page allows them to apply it in a different way. The Check Up page assesses students' understanding of the skill, using a multiple-choice format. These Practice, Apply, and Check Up questions are similar to those in standard assessments and will help prepare students for those tests.

Next comes the Workplace Skill page, which exposes students to the types of documents they might encounter in the workplace. Students practice the reading skill by applying it to the workplace document. The Write for Work section builds on the workplace skill and allows students to further apply the reading skill. They also practice the kinds of writing they will be expected to do in the workplace.

Lessons 1 through 5 of each unit include a Reading Extension that gives students the opportunity to apply the lesson reading skill to an article in the corresponding lesson of the *Reader*. Students answer multiple-choice and open-ended questions related to the reading skill.

Four lessons of each book include a Workplace Extension instead of a Reading Extension. Here, students read a scenario about a particular situation that takes place in a work environment. Students are asked to think about the situation and answer questions about what the characters did or should have done.

The Explore Words section focuses on alphabetics and vocabulary development. Instruction covers a variety of word analysis and vocabulary skills, such as word endings, prefixes, synonyms, and homophones. The final section of the lesson features five academic vocabulary words that students will have previously encountered in the lesson. Each unit concludes with a Unit Assessment that checks understanding of the unit skills taught.

Readers

The four reading levels of the *Readers* correspond to the four reading levels of the *Student Editions*. The level in each Reader, as in the *Student Edition*, advances over the course of three units. The *Readers* contain high-interest, nonfiction articles on a variety of topics, such as disasters, UFOs, monsters, adventure, survival, and ghosts. In each article, vocabulary words appear in boldface type and are also defined in the margin.

Each *Reader* also contains a Before You Read section that presents a reading strategy, such as previewing, to prepare students for reading and to make them more conscious readers. A consistent set of comprehension and critical-thinking exercises follows each article. The first three exercises are Recognize and Recall Details, Find the Main Idea, and Summarize and Paraphrase. The next three exercises assist students in thinking about what they have read and how it relates to their own experience. These exercises are Make Inferences, Recognize Author's Effect and Intentions, and Evaluate and Create.

Instructor's Guide

This guide is divided into three parts: *Program Overview, Student Editions*, and *Readers*.
- Part 1, *Program Overview*, provides:
    - o A summary of the *Reading Basics* program
    - o Research and practices of evidence-based reading instruction (EBRI)
    - o A description of the target audience
    - o A discussion of workplace literacy
    - o A description of the various components of the program to help you successfully implement *Reading Basics* in your classroom
    - o A description of how to use blogs to integrate technology in the classroom
- Part 2, *Student Editions*, includes:
    - o A lesson plan for each lesson in the *Student Editions*
    - o Workplace Skill Activity sheets
    - o Answer Keys for all the exercises, Unit Assessments, and Workplace Skill Activity sheets
- Part 3, *Readers*, includes:
    - o A lesson plan for each lesson in the *Readers*
    - o Unit Assessments
    - o Language Development Activities
    - o Answer Keys for exercises, Unit Assessments, and Graphic Organizer activities

Reading Basics Website

You and your students will have access to *Reading Basics* online resources by going to www.mhereadingbasics.com. There you will find:

- **MP3 recordings** All the articles in all the *Readers* have been recorded for students to play or download. The recordings provide modeled fluency and read-along support.
- **Graphic Organizers** You can download a variety of graphic organizers that correspond to the Graphic Organizer activity in each lesson plan for the *Reader*. (The *Reader* lesson plans are in Part 3 of this guide).
- **TABE® correlations** You can download a TABE Correlations Chart for each level of the *Reading Basics* program. These charts correlate the skills taught in *Reading Basics* to those assessed in TABE (Test of Adult Basic Education). The chart also lists the pages in the *Student Editions* and the *Readers* where each TABE skill is practiced.
- **Language Development** Language Development Self-Assessment Sheets, Activity Sheets, and their answer keys are included.
- **A link to *PassKey*** *PassKey* is an online reading program where students can get additional practice in reading skills (see below).

PassKey

This online program provides instruction and guided feedback for students who need extra help with comprehension, vocabulary, and word analysis skills. Lessons start at reading grade level 1.6 and continue all the way to 12.9. The levels have been correlated to the four *Reading Basics* instructional levels. For further customization, direct students toward lessons in another level. For example, if students frequently have difficulty reading sight words, you may want them to use the sight word lesson, which appears only in the Introductory level.

Reading Basics	**Reading Level**	*PassKey*
Introductory	1.6–3.9	Levels 1 & 2
Intermediate 1	3.6–6.9	Levels 2 & 3
Intermediate 2	6.6–8.9	Levels 3 & 4
Advanced	8.6–12.9	Levels 4 & 5

Assessments

Reading Basics contains a number of assessments to help you diagnose students' needs and monitor progress. Once students have been placed in a level of the program, have them take the Pretest in the *Student Edition* to which they have been assigned. The Pretest assesses all the reading skills taught in the level as well as many vocabulary and alphabetics skills. When your students have finished the Pretest, use the Answer Key and Evaluation Chart on pages 11–12 of the *Student Edition* to determine which skills your students need to target for improvement.

Each lesson in the *Student Edition* contains a Check Up page. This page generally consists of one or more reading passages or graphics followed by questions designed to test the target reading skill. These pages allow you to monitor student understanding as you teach each lesson. Each unit in the *Student Edition* ends with a Unit Assessment that tests the unit reading, vocabulary, and alphabetics skills. Reading skills are tested using passages as well as graphics and realistic workplace documents. At the end of each *Student Edition* is a Posttest, which covers reading, vocabulary, and alphabetics skills taught in all the units. Use the Answer Key and Evaluation Chart on pages 199–200 to determine if students need to review any skills.

In Part 3 of this guide, there are Unit Assessments for all the units in the *Readers*. Each Unit Assessment presents a passage followed by 10 questions that move from concrete to more abstract, following the order of Anderson's taxonomy.

How the Program Components Work Together

The components of this program are designed to work together. Each component reinforces the others as the four components of reading are taught and students develop into skilled readers. Below is a sample Pacing Chart for a class that meets on a four-class cycle and that uses all the components of the program. The chart shows you how you can put the pieces together to create a strong lesson. Feel free to adapt it to fit your class schedule. For example, if your classes meet on a five-class cycle, you may add some instruction. If your classes meet on a three-class cycle, you will need two weeks to complete the lesson. If your classes meet on a two-class cycle, you will need two weeks to complete the lesson, and you may need to consolidate some instruction. Allow one day each for Pretest, Posttest, and Unit Assessment. Students work on their own with *PassKey* modules as needed.

Four-class Cycle Pacing Chart

The following abbreviations are used in the chart:

SE	*Student Edition*	IG/SE	*Student Edition* lesson plan in this guide	IG	*Instructor's Guide*
RDR	*Reader*	IG/RDR	*Reader* lesson plan in this guide	Web	*Reading Basics* Website

Day	Program Component	Component of Reading	Topic/Activity
1	SE	Comprehension	Reading Skill: "Introduce"
	SE	Alphabetics/Vocabulary	"Explore Words"—one topic
	IG/SE	Comprehension/Vocabulary	"Comprehension," "Academic Vocabulary"
	IG/RDR	Comprehension/Vocabulary	"Summary," "Build Vocabulary," "Activate Prior Knowledge," "Build Background," "Preview and Predict,"
	RDR	Comprehension/Vocabulary	"Before You Read"
	Web	Fluency	Play MP3 recording as students read along.
	IG/RDR	Comprehension	"Differentiated Instruction," "English Language Learners"

Day	Program Component	Component of Reading	Topic/Activity
2	SE	Comprehension	Reading Skill: Review, "Practice"
	SE	Alphabetics/Vocabulary	"Explore Words"—one topic
	SE	Comprehension	"Workplace Skill" passage and questions
	IG/SE	Fluency	Fluency strategy
	RDR	Comprehension/Vocabulary	Relate SE reading skill to article
	IG/RDR, Web	Comprehension	Graphic organizer

Day	Program Component	Component of Reading	Topic/Activity
3	SE	Comprehension	Reading Skill: Review, "Apply"
	SE	Alphabetics/Vocabulary	"Explore Words"—one topic
	IG/SE	Alphabetics/Vocabulary	"Alphabetics," "Vocabulary"
	SE	Comprehension	"Write for Work"
	RDR	Fluency	"Timed Reading"
	IG/RDR	Comprehension	"Respond to the Article"
	RDR	Comprehension/Vocabulary	"Comprehension and Critical Thinking Skills" exercises A–C
	IG/RDR, Web	Alphabetics/Comprehension/Vocabulary	"Language Development Activity"

Day	Program Component	Component of Reading	Topic/Activity
4	SE	Comprehension	Reading Skill: Review, "Check Up"
	SE	Alphabetics/Vocabulary	"Explore Words"—one topic
	SE	Comprehension	"Reading or Workplace Extension"
	RDR	Fluency	"Words-per-Minute" and reading-speed graph
	RDR	Comprehension/Vocabulary	"Comprehension and Critical Thinking Skills" activities D–F
	IG/SE	Comprehension/Fluency/Vocabulary	"Workplace Skill Activity"

Evidence-Based Reading Instruction (EBRI) in *Reading Basics*

Reading Basics aligns to the four components of reading essential to EBRI: alphabetics, fluency, vocabulary, and comprehension. *Reading Basics* provides instruction and practice in each of these components. Students study alphabetics, practice fluency by reading aloud passages and workplace documents, and learn to apply comprehension skills and strategies to a variety of texts. They also study and practice vocabulary skills and academic vocabulary and learn words important to understanding the articles in the *Readers*.

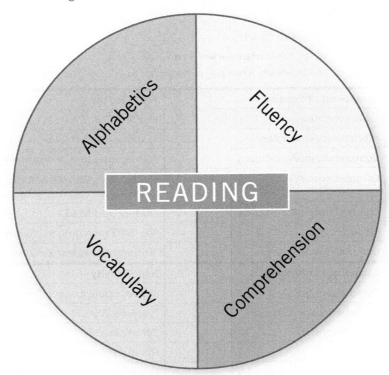

Reading Basics also aligns to practices of EBRI, which emphasize the importance of
- Providing direct, explicit, and relevant instruction
- Monitoring and assessing student progress and diagnosing student needs
- Including differentiated support
- Engaging learners in relevant instruction
- Improving fluency

Direct, Explicit, and Relevant Instructions

Research supports the idea that learners benefit from direct and explicit instruction. The teacher explains and models the skill or concept and provides guided practice. Students then practice or apply the skill independently or in groups as the teacher monitors their efforts. In *Reading Basics*, instruction for each of the four components of reading is designed around the principles of direct and explicit instruction.

Comprehension

Each *Student Edition* lesson provides an example for modeling the targeted reading skill and a passage or graphic for guided practice. Your students then have the opportunity to practice and apply the reading skill independently and in small groups. They will also apply the skill to a workplace document and, in most lessons, to an article in the *Reader*. Exercises at the end of each article in the *Reader* provide practice in a variety of comprehension and critical reading skills.

Comprehension strategies, introduced in the lesson plans in Part 2 of this *Instructor's Guide*, include a combination of monitoring and fix-up strategies, such as asking questions, clarifying meaning, making connections, and rereading or reading more slowly. Model how to use each strategy by thinking aloud as you apply it to a passage or graphic in the *Student Edition*.

Vocabulary

In each lesson plan in Part 2, you will find context sentences for preteaching five academic vocabulary words that students will encounter in the *Student Edition* lesson. Then, in the Explore Words section of the *Student Edition*, your students will complete a practice activity using these same words to reinforce meaning. This section also provides instruction and practice with synonyms, antonyms, multiple-meaning words, context clues, and other vocabulary skills.

Each lesson plan in Part 3 of this *Instructor's Guide* also provides you with an activity for preteaching selected vocabulary from the articles in the *Reader*. This activity not only builds vocabulary but also sets your students up for better comprehension when they come across those words in the article.

Alphabetics

The *Student Edition* presents direct instruction and practice for phonics and word analysis skills, such as syllable division and patterns, prefixes, suffixes, base words, and roots. The lesson plans in Part 2 of this *Instructor's Guide* provide additional examples, which you can use to model skills and provide guided practice.

Fluency

The lesson plans in Part 2 of this *Instructor's Guide* include fluency strategies that students can apply to passages or instructional text in the *Student Edition* and to the articles in the *Reader*. Model each strategy for students. Also encourage students to go to www.mhereadingbasics.com to play or download MP3 recordings of the articles so they can listen to good examples of fluent reading.

Monitoring and Assessment

EBRI research shows that assessment plays an important role in the success of a student's involvement in a reading program. Assessment tools allow you to diagnose a student's needs before, during, and after instruction.

Diagnostic Reading Assessment

You can use various assessments to gather information about students' levels of achievement in reading and to identify their strengths and weaknesses.

Once you've determined if a student should work in the Introductory, Intermediate 1, Intermediate 2, or Advanced level, administer the Pretest in the *Student Edition*. Results from this test will either confirm that a student has been assigned to the appropriate level for his or her ability or that he or she should be switched to a different level. The Evaluation Chart will help you further analyze the results to identify particular areas of strength and weakness.

Continuous Monitoring

As students progress through the *Reader* and *Student Edition*, there are numerous opportunities to monitor their progress. Classroom observation is an informal assessment tool that can help you gain insight into students' progress and pinpoint any areas of weakness. As students work through each lesson, note which students struggle with fluency, comprehension, vocabulary, or alphabetics.

Each *Student Edition* lesson includes Introduce, Practice, Apply, and Check Up sections, allowing you to monitor a student's progress along the way. Comprehension and critical reading skills are assessed after reading each article in the *Reader*. In addition, students complete graphic organizers, another tool that helps teachers monitor student understanding of the reading skill. This ongoing assessment helps you check for increased mastery of these skills on a continuous basis, instead of waiting until students complete each unit or each reading level.

You can monitor fluency with timed readings of articles in the *Reader*. Students can fill in the Words-per-Minute table. Then they can chart their reading times on the Plotting Your Progress graph, which allows them to track their reading-speed progress over time. See page 11 of this *Instructor's Guide* for a variety of fluency strategies. On these pages you will also find a fluency scale to help guide your continuous assessment of students' fluency progress.

Summative Assessment

While continuous assessment opportunities can provide you with valuable information, summative assessment information is equally beneficial. Each unit of the *Reader* and *Student Edition* concludes with a Unit Assessment. These tests check your students' progress with the comprehension skills they practiced throughout the unit. The results of such assessments help you determine if a student is ready to progress to the next unit or if additional work is needed in a particular skill area.

Posttests, which come at the end of each *Student Edition* level, test your students' understanding of comprehension, vocabulary, and alphabetics. The results will help you decide whether a particular student needs further practice in any of the skills.

Differentiated Instruction

Teachers who are effective in the classroom tend to use differentiated instruction almost instinctively. These teachers understand the individual needs of their students, are sensitive to them, and strive to identify the best possible methods to help each student learn in a way that best suits him or her.

Research has long shown that there are differences among students in the ways they receive, process, and demonstrate learning. For example, some students learn best by listening, while others benefit from viewing the material. Some students process and retain information best through discussion, others by taking notes, still others by making charts or diagrams. To demonstrate learning, some students need extra time before replying in class or when taking a test. Some learners can show what they know in multiple-choice tests, while others are more comfortable using more open-ended formats.

Howard Gardner, a well-respected professor in the field of education, has proposed the theory that learners have multiple intelligences through which they gain and demonstrate knowledge. The eight intelligences are linguistic, visual-spatial, interpersonal, naturalist, musical, logical-mathematical, bodily-kinesthetic, and intrapersonal. Helping students to become aware of their particular learning styles, strengths, and interests can facilitate learning and build self-esteem. For adult learners especially, understanding these strengths can be helpful in thinking about career goals.

Because of all these differences, many educators support the concept of differentiated instruction. In a differentiated classroom, teachers customize the ways they deliver content, the ways students are invited to process the content, and the ways in which students demonstrate their understanding of the content. The teacher considers each learner's readiness, interests, learning style, and language ability.

Many proponents of differentiated instruction advocate the use of partner and small-group activities. Students learn from one another and can participate at their own level. For example, pairing English Language Learners (ELLs) with English speakers can provide the extra language support and modeling that ELLs need to succeed. Group work also provides opportunities for individual students to show leadership and even to coach their peers in their particular areas of strength. In addition, while most students are working in pairs or small groups, the teacher is able to provide extra help for those who need it.

Differentiated Instruction in *Reading Basics*

In *Reading Basics*, the four levels of instruction—Introductory, Intermediate 1, Intermediate 2, and Advanced—allow you to assign each student to reading material that matches his or her readiness level. The Pretest at the beginning of each *Student Edition* will help you confirm whether students have been placed in the correct level. In all levels, you will find that opportunities for differentiated instruction have been incorporated into the program.

The *Reader* lesson plans in Part 3 of this *Instructor's Guide* include Differentiated Instruction and English Language Learners support. Each of these sections provides an alternate activity or approach to teach the targeted reading comprehension skill or strategy. Many of the activities offer partner or small-group work. Such groupings encourage those who are strong in one area to participate with confidence, while others can experience a new approach to learning without feeling pressured to produce immediately. The Graphic Organizer section gives learners a different way to process the information they have read in the article and to demonstrate their understanding. It is particularly helpful for visual learners.

Workplace Skill Activities in Part 2 of this guide suggest partner or small-group work followed by class discussion and sharing. Many of these activities involve role-play as well, which allows students to demonstrate understanding in a different way, using interpersonal, bodily-kinesthetic, and linguistic intelligences.

The Language Development Activities provided in Part 3 of this guide also incorporate the principles of differentiated instruction. While these activities are differentiated for ELLs, all students will benefit from participating in different ways. The teacher begins by addressing the class as a whole. Next, students are often split into smaller groups, allowing them to feel supported by their peers and to contribute to the extent they feel comfortable. Student participation ranges from listening attentively to sharing ideas to playing a specific role in a group task.

Reading Basics integrates technology to help you differentiate instruction. Students whose level of fluency impedes comprehension can go to www.mhereadingbasics.com to play or download recordings of the *Reader* articles. At the same site, students who need extra help with comprehension, vocabulary, and word analysis skills can access *PassKey* for online instruction and guided feedback.

Reading Basics helps you meet the diverse needs of the adult learners in your classroom. It also offers a variety of ways for students to process instruction and to demonstrate their understanding of the materials.

Learner Engagement and Relevance of Instruction

There are few things more challenging for the educator than attempting to reach students who have "turned out the lights" on learning. Research shows that the more engaged, or active, students are in their learning, the greater the retention of information learned and the more likely students are to pursue further studies. What does active learning look like? Active learners are involved in small-group work, role-playing, workplace simulations, and class discussions, to name a few possibilities. In other words, students are active participants in their own learning.

Throughout *Reading Basics*, the instruction provides for individual, partner, and small-group learning opportunities. Many students enjoy collaborative activities and find small groups a supportive way to learn.

The Workplace Skill, Write for Work, and Workplace Extension activities in the *Student Edition* offer practice with workplace documents and scenarios that students will find particularly relevant to their lives. Using their reading and writing skills for real-world purposes can be particularly motivating.

In addition, the *Instructor's Guide* for each level includes Workplace Skill Activities (see pages 48–50, 82–84, 116–118, 150–152) and Language Development Activities (see pages 187–189, 216–218, 245–247, 274–276) that provide opportunities for role-playing and other forms of partner and group work. These kinds of meaningful interactions help to keep students focused and engaged.

Reading Basics also gives students tools to help them become more independent learners. Self-monitoring and fix-up strategies help students become aware of reading problems and ways to solve them. Learning to recognize difficult words, such as multiple-meaning words, builds student awareness of words that might confuse them when they read. Learning syllable patterns can help students decode multisyllabic words.

Many adult learners who return to the classroom are self-motivated and eager to succeed. Others enroll because employment advancement is dependent upon successful completion of coursework. Still, it is not uncommon for students to begin their journey full of enthusiasm only to feel the excitement fizzle. One way for teachers to combat this is to make learner engagement and relevance a priority in their classrooms. Take time to get to know your students—their interests, strengths, and career goals—and strive to make connections to their lives whenever possible.

Developing Fluency

Fluency is one of the most important components of reading. Fluent readers read with appropriate pace, intonation, and phrasing. To develop fluency, it is important that students hear examples of fluent reading and have many opportunities to practice. As their fluency improves, students are better able to focus on comprehending the text instead of decoding individual words.

Fluency practice calls on students to integrate many reading abilities into one activity: the oral reading of text. Having students do a lot of reading at an appropriate level—with a teacher, tutor, or peer supporting them and helping them self-monitor—is a good way for students to practice their way to competence. When you provide fluency practice in your classroom, you give students the opportunity to develop and demonstrate their reading skills.

Fluency Strategies in *Reading Basics*

Students practice fluency using articles in the *Reader* and passages or instructional text in the *Student Edition*. Each *Reader* includes a Words-per-Minute table and a reading-speed graph where students can record their reading times and monitor their progress. Students can also visit www.mhereadingbasics.com to play or download the recordings of the articles from the *Reader*. These recordings provide excellent modeling of smooth, accurate, and expressive oral reading. You may also wish to model fluent reading by reading aloud to the students several times a week.

Each lesson plan for the *Student Edition* suggests one of the fluency techniques described below for use with instructional text or passages. These techniques can be used with other appropriate materials to improve fluency.

- **Echo Reading** Read a sentence from one of the passages aloud. Have students echo you by reading the sentence with the same speed and expression.
- **Partner Reading** Have partners read aloud to one another or at the same time. Encourage students to offer each other support and correction. Circulate to offer guidance as needed.
- **Collaborative Reading** Have each student in a group take a turn reading one or more lines of text. Correct pronunciation and phrasing as needed by modeling.
- **Repeated Reading** Lead a group of students in reading a passage aloud several times until the reading sounds smooth and consistent.
- **Marked Phrase Reading** Mark a passage with phrase boundaries, showing how words should be grouped for meaning and emphasis, and distribute copies to students. Read the text aloud as students follow along. Then have students join you in reading the text.

Assessing Fluency

An easy way to determine if a student needs fluency practice is to listen to him or her read aloud. As the student reads a passage aloud, observe and record reading accuracy, rate, and the number of pauses and repetitions. If you wish, use the following Fluency Scale:

3	Student reads smoothly and pauses at the boundaries of meaningful phrases and clauses, few or no errors or repetitions
2	Student reads with some pauses in phrasing, some errors or repetitions
1	Student's reading is choppy and uneven, frequent repetitions, pauses to sound out words, mispronunciations
0	Student reads word by word, continual repetitions, pauses or stops to sound out words, many mispronunciations

Characteristics of the Adult Learner

Adult students include learners with varied backgrounds and experiences. Some learners speak English as their first language, and others are literate in a language other than English. Their common goal is to become better readers, but the reasons behind this goal vary. Some students may want to earn high-school equivalency certificates, while others may need to improve their skills in order to succeed in their jobs or to advance in the workplace.

When teaching adult learners to read, it is important to keep in mind that these students are not children. Their cognitive abilities and life experiences provide a rich base from which to build. Because their cognitive abilities are in step with their chronological age, adult learners should not be taught how to read using the same materials that are used with children. While reading passages, for example, need to be at a low reading level, the topics should be of high interest to the adult learner.

Barriers to Learning

All learners need to experience success in order to build self-confidence. The reality is that many adult learners face obstacles that work against them in their pursuit to become better readers. Many adults are ashamed and embarrassed that they cannot read well. Overcoming memories of past failures is one challenge. Lack of support from spouses or other family members might be another obstacle. Praise, encouragement, and patience will go a long way in reassuring adult learners that they can succeed.

Strategies for Teaching ELL Students

English Language Learners (ELLs) are a subgroup of adult students who want to improve their reading skills. These students have the added obstacle of a limited oral vocabulary in English. If they do not understand the meaning of a spoken word, they will probably not be able to comprehend the written form of the word. Cultural differences pose another potential challenge for ELL students. Certain topics that seem basic to most English-speaking readers' understanding may present difficulties in comprehension for ELL students. *Reading Basics* provides support for these students in a variety of ways.

Comprehension Support
The *Reader* lesson plans in Part 3 of this guide suggest different ways to set up your students for success. Students need explicit instruction in how to ask questions before, during, and after reading an article. The Before Reading section includes prompts to help you guide students in asking questions, activating prior knowledge, previewing the article and making predictions about it, and encouraging class discussion. The Build Background section also provides you with additional information that you may share with students.

Each *Reader* lesson plan also includes activities to support Differentiated Instruction and English Language Learners. These activities provide an alternative way for your students to practice the targeted reading comprehension skill or strategy. Skills and strategies include asking questions, visualizing, identifying sequence, identifying cause and effect, making inferences, predicting, and determining word meanings from context. Many of these alternative activities involve partner or small-group work. Pairing an ELL student with an English speaker can be very effective.

Each lesson plan for the *Student Edition* includes suggestions for modeling and explaining the targeted reading skill as well as a monitoring or fix-up strategy, such as asking questions, clarifying meaning, making connections, rereading, or reading more slowly. You can model the use of the suggested strategy by thinking aloud as you read a passage in the *Student Edition* lesson. Encourage your students to apply the strategy to the passages or instructional text in the *Student Edition* as they read. These strategies are particularly helpful for ELLs and other striving readers.

Vocabulary and Alphabetics Support

Repeatedly hearing and seeing new words, especially within different contexts, improves vocabulary acquisition. The *Student Edition* lesson plans in Part 2 of this *Instructor's Guide* include sentences that you can use to preteach the academic vocabulary words that your students will encounter in the *Student Edition* lesson. The Explore Words section at the end of the *Student Edition* lesson provides an activity for practice and reinforcement. The lesson plans also include examples for modeling many of the phonics, word analysis, and vocabulary skills taught in the Explore Words sections.

Each lesson plan in Part 3 of this guide includes an activity that you can use to preteach vocabulary important to the understanding of the *Reader* article. Before discussing meaning, write each word on the board and read it aloud. These same vocabulary words are glossed in the margin of the articles at points of use.

Language Development Activities

Reading Basics provides three Language Development Activities for each level. These activities develop areas of language in which ELL students often require extra support—multiple-meaning words, multiword verbs, vocabulary, syntax, idioms, parts of speech, and prefixes/suffixes—in a multilevel, differentiated instructional format. The activities are completed by the entire class. Opportunities for participation within each activity are differentiated to provide students with different avenues for expressing what they know. A self-assessement form and downloadable activity sheets that are included with some of the lessons can be found at www.mhereadingbasics.com.

After each activity, students fill out a self-assessment form in which they check off statements that describe their involvement. The assessment forms help the student and the teacher monitor progress over time and plan future instruction and participation. The blank activity sheets may also be used as quizzes.

The Language Development Activities serve both beginning and experienced teachers. The instructions are highly explicit; they are designed for teachers with little ELL experience, but they can be modified to fit any teacher's delivery style. Activities may also be used as models with which you can generate additional activities.

Additional strategies for working with ELL students include the following:

- **Visual Aids** Whenever possible, use visual aids, such as maps or photos, to clarify meaning and support learning.
- **Sufficient Wait Time** Pause after asking a question to allow all students time to think about and formulate their answers before responding. ELL students in particular may need extra time to translate their answer from their first language into English or to find the proper words.
- **Modeling Spoken Language** During lesson discussions, it is best not to correct students' spoken language. Instead, simply restate what was said, or ask a related question. If a student says, for example, "Last night I no sleep well," you might say, "Oh no, you didn't sleep well!" or ask, "Why didn't you sleep well?" Encourage students to answer or repeat.
- **Skim and Scan** In addition to the comprehension skills and strategies taught in *Reading Basics*, you might teach the prereading strategy of skimming and scanning. These strategies help students preview material before they begin to read. Encourage students to ask questions about any unfamiliar words or phrases.

Reading Challenges and Suggested Techniques

Research has shown that some readers are unaware that they have comprehension difficulties because they do not realize that they are missing something. If readers are struggling to decode individual words, they may not be giving much thought to the meaning of the words as they relate to each other. Another cause of a breakdown in comprehension is a difficulty in making inferences to "fill in the holes" left by writers. The focus on alphabetics, comprehension, fluency, and vocabulary in *Reading Basics* will help these readers. Still, even the most motivated learners may encounter reading challenges because of other areas that need attention.

Vision

While issues with vision do not "cause" learning disabilities, they can interfere with the learning process. Poor eye-muscle coordination can make it difficult for a student to focus on fine print. Students who often fidget, blink and squint, hold a book very close, or lose their place on the page might be experiencing a problem with focus. Taking frequent breaks and routinely looking away from the printed page can help.

Hearing and Memory

Some students cannot hear or distinguish certain sounds, making it difficult to match sound-to-letter correspondences. For ELL students, interference from a first language may make it difficult to hear and reproduce certain speech sounds in English. Those with memory issues may exhibit difficulty following oral directions. Breaking down directions into shorter steps and using visual clues as often as possible may prove beneficial to these students.

Gross- and Fine-Motor Coordination

Although *Reading Basics* is a reading program, it does include writing activities to support reading comprehension. Students with motor-control difficulties may find it less fatiguing to complete assignments by using a computer and printing out their work. You might also consider accommodating students by permitting oral responses to some of the activities.

Paying Attention

Students who have trouble attending to tasks for long periods of time might have attention issues. Helpful strategies include working in small blocks of time and taking frequent breaks.

Reading Disabilities

Reading disabilities typically include one or more of the following characteristics: difficulty with visual memory, phonological processing (including sounds of letters and word parts), and comprehension of oral and written materials as well as weakness in vocabulary and grammar. Difficulty in any of these areas can impede fluency. It is important to be aware of where the breakdown occurs in the reading process and to gear instruction to areas of strength while reinforcing areas of weakness. Useful strategies include chunking information, providing visual aids, and allowing sufficient wait time for processing and response.

Lack of Confidence

Treating adult students with respect is the key to inviting their successful participation. Many adult learners have struggled to succeed in their education. It is understandable, therefore, that they may be sensitive to criticism and to the possibility of experiencing yet another failure. Encouragement and the acknowledgment of the skills and abilities your adult students do possess will help motivate these learners to return to class on a regular basis. One simple way to do this is by making an effort to end your lessons on a positive note.

Workplace Literacy

Adult learners are most interested in learning something when they believe it will be useful. Therefore, focusing on workplace literacy can be particularly motivating when teaching reading skills. Adult learners also bring varied work and life experiences to the classroom. Encouraging your students to share these experiences will help them feel respected and more engaged in learning. Connecting new instruction to prior knowledge and experience will also help your students learn.

The importance of acquiring good reading skills extends well beyond the classroom setting. Many adult learners need to improve their reading skills in order to get a job, succeed in the one they have, or advance in the workplace. In today's workplace, people are expected to be able to coordinate and communicate through written text. The ability to comprehend both written and graphic materials has also become increasingly important.

The Needs of the Workforce

An overwhelming majority of data from recent reports on basic skills education and the workforce indicates that the current worker supply is not meeting the workforce demand. This shortage is due to a combination of an increasing skill base needed for the new and replacement jobs of the emerging knowledge-based economy and the simultaneous decline in the basic skill levels of the workers seeking to fill those jobs.

According to a 2006 American Community study by the U.S. Census Bureau, about 88 million of the 150 million adults ages 18–64 in the current workforce have at least one educational barrier that prevents them from entering the knowledge-based economy. With a current high school dropout rate of approximately 7,000 students per day, the number of adults underprepared to join this emerging high-skills economy is increasing. At the same time, nearly twice as many new and replacement jobs in the next decade will require a postsecondary credential or college degree. With more than 93 million adults scoring at the lower levels of national assessments of functional literacy skills, most of these adults are not prepared to master the postsecondary education or training needed to gain family-sustaining employment. An estimated 65 percent of the 2020 workforce is already beyond the reach of our educational system.

Today's employers want to know that their employees can read, understand, and use written information. Productivity, efficiency, and even safety in the workplace can depend upon the adequacy of literacy skills. For example:

- Factory workers who cannot read warnings can jeopardize workplace safety.
- Hospital food-service workers with reading deficiencies cannot heed instructions for critical diet or fasting requirements for patients.
- Employees who have difficulty following oral and written instructions can interfere with the workflow moving smoothly, thereby causing costly mistakes.

There are two main types of reading-related skills needed in the workplace—reading for information and locating information.

- **Reading for information**: Employees must be able to read job-related documents that are mostly text. Documents, such as company handbooks or health-care policies, provide general information about the job. Sets of procedures or memos might provide specific information for particular tasks. Other possible documents include:
  - o Memos, letters, and e-mails
  - o Bulletin board notices
  - o Manuals

- **Locating information:** Employees must be able to read and use a workplace graphic, such as a chart, diagram, or table. For example, they might include relevant data from the chart in a report or use information from the chart to make a work-related decision.

Literacy on the job includes not only reading and writing but also problem-solving, listening, and communicating. Professional and interpersonal skills, such as the following, are also important:

- Being punctual; having a good attendance record
- Being cooperative, respectful; having a pleasant attitude
- Practicing teamwork
- Being proactive; taking positive initiatives
- Setting priorities and meeting deadlines
- Displaying neatness and organization in the workspace and in the work itself
- Respecting the communal environment
- Expressing oneself clearly and appropriately, both formally and informally
- Negotiating with supervisors and coworkers
- Responding appropriately to criticism
- Resolving conflicts

Knowing how to behave appropriately and effectively in the workplace can help adult learners get, keep, or advance in a job. It may also increase their productivity.

Workplace Skill Instruction in *Reading Basics*

Reading Basics provides teachers with multiple opportunities to help students practice a variety of workplace skills that will help them succeed.

Workplace Skill

Each lesson in the *Student Edition* includes a Workplace Skill feature that relates to the lesson's reading skill and that introduces students to a type of document commonly used in the workplace or in job searches. The inclusion of documents from a wide range of job settings allows students to identify with jobs they are already familiar with and gain exposure to jobs they have yet to experience.

Write for Work

The Write for Work feature in the *Student Edition* builds on the Workplace Skill activity. It consists of a writing task that students might do in the workplace, such as write an e-mail or summarize information for a report.

Workplace Extension

Four lessons in each *Student Edition* have a Workplace Extension instead of a Reading Extension. Interpersonal and professional skills are introduced and explored in this feature.

Workplace Skill Activities

In Part 2 of this guide, you will find three Workplace Skill Activities for each level—one per unit. In these activities, students collaborate with one another to explore the kinds of skills taught in the Workplace Extension feature described above. Like the Workplace Extension, most of these activities begin with a description of a workplace situation. Here, however, students interact with the scenario in some way. For example, they might first read about an unhappy customer and then work with a partner to analyze the situation and role-play the parts of the customer and the vendor. These engaging activities allow students to work as a team as they develop important skills for success in the workplace.

How to Use the *Student Editions*

Each of the four *Student Editions* is organized in the same way, regardless of level. All books are divided into three units. The first unit is made up of seven lessons, and the second and third units have six lessons apiece. Each eight-page lesson follows the same pattern: Reading Comprehension Skill, Workplace Skill, Reading or Workplace Extension, and Explore Words.

In Part 2 of this *Instructor's Guide,* you will find a one-page lesson plan for each lesson in the *Student Edition.* The Reading Skill section of the lesson plan provides suggestions for explaining and modeling the reading skill, tips for guided practice, and ideas for presenting the Practice, Apply, and Check Up exercises. The Comprehension section describes a reading strategy for use with the *Student Edition* lesson, and in many lessons, the article in the *Reader* as well. In addition, the Fluency section describes a fluency strategy for students to apply. The Alphabetics section provides instructional tips and examples for modeling phonics, word analysis, spelling, and vocabulary skills with Explore Words activities. The Vocabulary section provides context sentences for preteaching the academic vocabulary words in the lesson. The Application section provides suggestions for use with the Workplace Skill and Write for Work sections and for the Workplace Extension, if applicable. Finally, the lesson plan includes a reference to *PassKey,* an online resource for reviewing many of the skills in the *Student Edition* lessons. Answers to questions in the Student Edition lessons, Unit Assessments, and the Workplace Skill Activity sheets appear in the Answer Keys in this part of the guide.

Reading Comprehension Skills

Introduce

The reading comprehension skills taught in this program are correlated to those tested in standard assessments. The Introduce page in the *Student Edition* presents the lesson reading skill and consists primarily of instruction that explains the skill to the students. Following this instruction is a short example that you can use to model instruction. The page concludes with a brief exercise for guided practice.

Everything in the *Student Edition—* instruction and reading passages—is written within the reading level range set for each book and unit. This ensures that students are working with material that challenges them yet allows them to achieve success.

While each *Student Edition* has the same number of lessons and follows the same unit structure, the same skills are not taught at every level. As students advance from one level of the program to the next, reading level and vocabulary choice become increasingly more difficult, and some skills are taught in a more complex way.

Practice, Apply, and Check Up

The Introduce page in each lesson of the *Student Edition* is followed by the Practice, Apply, and Check Up pages. These activities help you monitor students' progress as they work through the lesson and toward mastery of the reading skill.

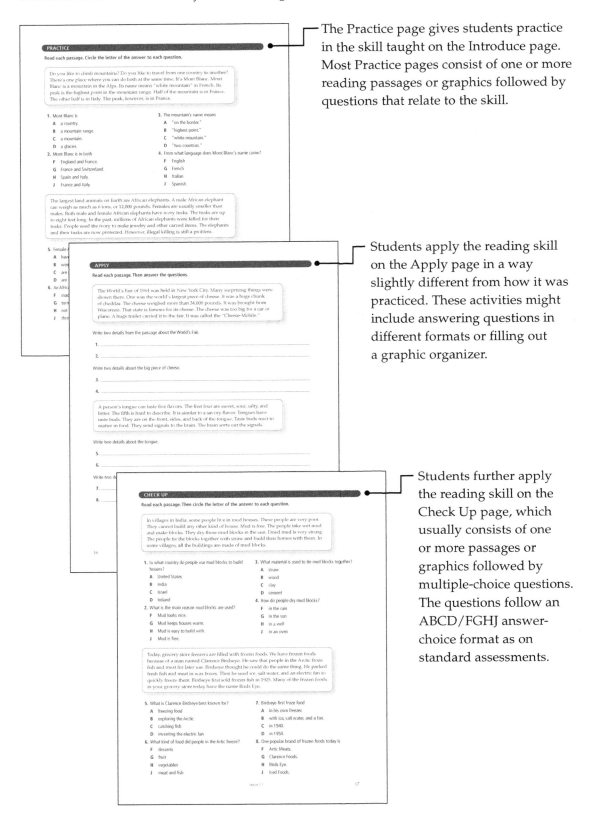

The Practice page gives students practice in the skill taught on the Introduce page. Most Practice pages consist of one or more reading passages or graphics followed by questions that relate to the skill.

Students apply the reading skill on the Apply page in a way slightly different from how it was practiced. These activities might include answering questions in different formats or filling out a graphic organizer.

Students further apply the reading skill on the Check Up page, which usually consists of one or more passages or graphics followed by multiple-choice questions. The questions follow an ABCD/FGHJ answer-choice format as on standard assessments.

Workplace Skill

This feature introduces, explains, and practices a workplace skill that relates to the lesson's reading skill. The workplace skills taught are those that people use when they read, write, and use text in order to do a job. There are two main types of skills taught in the workplace section of the lesson—reading for information and locating information.

- Reading for information: Students read a workplace document that is mostly text. They apply the reading skill by answering questions about the document they read.
- Locating information: Students examine a workplace graphic, such as a chart. They use the reading skill and their knowledge of graphic information to answer questions about the item.

This feature also introduces documents commonly used in the workplace or in job searches, such as these:

- Memos, letters, and e-mails
- Employment ads
- Bulletin-board notices
- Manuals and procedural documents
- Company handbooks and policies
- Diagrams, forms, charts, and graphs

The documents represent a wide range of job sectors, such as health, education, food services, manufacturing, and sales. Students who work in a particular sector will find the material particularly meaningful. For others, the exposure to different settings might open up new avenues for job and career exploration.

Students read the document and then apply the lesson reading skill to answer questions. In some exercises, additional questions are included to address skills that will further help students when they encounter similar documents in the workplace. For example, students might be asked to locate specific information on a chart or graph or to use context clues to figure out the meaning of a difficult word.

As students progress through the different program levels, they will notice that vocabulary and sentence structures used in the workplace documents become increasingly complex.

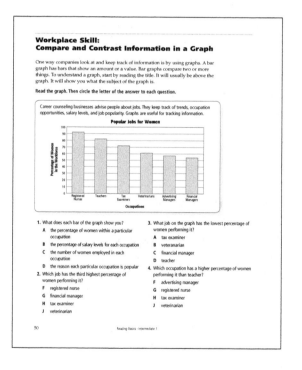

Write for Work/Reading Extension/ Workplace Extension

Write for Work ─────────────

The Write for Work activity appears at the top of both the Reading Extension and Workplace Extension pages and builds on the Workplace Skill page. The feature presents a realistic workplace situation that requires students to write. They might need to create a document similar to the one on the Workplace Skill page or to again apply the reading skill to the document and write up their results. Some activities include drafting an e-mail or memo or writing instructions.

Reading Extension ─────────────

Fifteen of the 19 lessons in each level of the *Student Edition* have a Reading Extension activity that follows Write for Work. Each Reading Extension activity relates directly to a specific article in the *Reader*. Students should read and/or listen to the article before beginning the Reading Extension section. The activity consists of a number of multiple-choice and open-ended questions that allow students to apply the reading skill taught in the *Student Edition* lesson to the article in the *Reader*.

Workplace Extension ─────────────

In four of the lessons in each *Student Edition* (Lessons 1.6, 1.7, 2.6, and 3.6), students will find a Workplace Extension activity instead of a Reading Extension activity. This activity helps students practice skills that are valuable in the workplace, such as taking responsibility, maintaining a positive attitude, and getting along with coworkers. In each activity, students read a workplace scenario and answer questions that ask them to consider how the characters in the scenario behaved, what the characters could have done differently, or what they should do next.

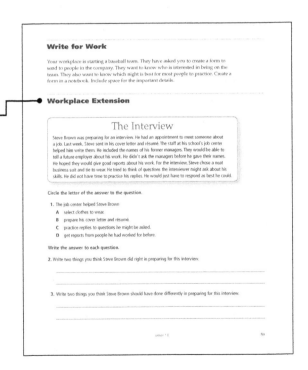

Explore Words

Two of the four components found to be important in EBRI—alphabetics and vocabulary development—are the focus of the concluding section of each lesson. In the Introductory and Intermediate 1 levels, one or more sets of exercises focus on phonetic elements. The other exercises focus on vocabulary, spelling, and word analysis. Synonyms, antonyms, context clues, homophones, and word endings are among the topics covered. In the Intermediate 2 and Advanced levels, the emphasis is on vocabulary, spelling, and word analysis.

The last activity of each Explore Words section reviews five academic vocabulary words, which are drawn from both the instructional page and the reading passages in the *Student Edition*. The words are presented and used in context within the lesson and then further defined and practiced in the Academic Vocabulary activity. As in the other sections of the lesson, the Explore Words exercises increase in difficulty as students progress through each book and advance from level to level.

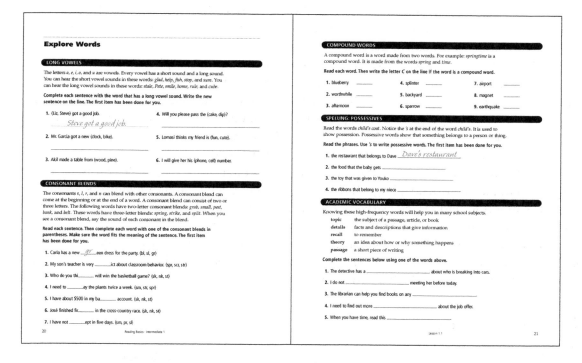

Unit Review and Assessment

Each unit ends with an eight-page Unit Review and Assessment. The first page reviews all the reading skills taught in the unit. The following assessment pages check mastery of these reading skills, using questions related to passages, workplace documents, and other kinds of items from the unit. The final assessment page tests the vocabulary and alphabetics skills taught in the unit.

How to Use the Readers

The four *Readers* in *Reading Basics* increase in difficulty from level to level and from unit to unit, in tandem with the *Student Editions*. The *Readers* provide a practical, effective, engaging set of materials that can help students develop comprehension, fluency, vocabulary, and critical thinking skills.

Everything in the *Reader*—instruction, articles, and exercises—is written within the reading-level range set for each book and unit. This ensures that students are working with material that challenges them yet allows them to achieve success.

Each of the four *Readers* is organized in the same way, regardless of instructional level. All books are divided into three units, each of which contains five articles. Each article has a title page, a Before You Read section, and glossed vocabulary. Reading comprehension and critical thinking exercises follow the article.

You may want to begin by introducing your students to the content and format of the *Reader* you are using. Examine the *Reader* together and discuss how it is organized. Read through the Contents list with the class to provide an overview of the various topics that will be covered within the articles of the *Reader*.

In Part 3 of this *Instructor's Guide* you will find a one-page lesson plan for each lesson in the *Reader*. Each lesson plan contains a summary of the article and activities to conduct before, during, and after reading. The Before Reading section contains activities to build vocabulary, activate prior knowledge, preview and predict, and build background. The During Reading section reinforces reading comprehension skills and strategies. The After Reading section provides a means for monitoring comprehension and critical thinking by inviting students to respond to the article in a handwritten journal or in a blog (see pages 25–26 of this guide). The Differentiated Instruction, English Language Learners, and Graphic Organizers sections provide support for individual learners and can be used at any point during the lesson plan. Part 3 also contains three Unit Assessments for each level of the *Reader*. These tests offer students another opportunity to demonstrate mastery of comprehension and critical thinking skills. Answers to exercises in the *Reader*, Unit Assessments, and Graphic Organizer activities appear in the Answer Keys in this part of the guide.

Lesson Opener

The first page of each lesson always includes the title of the article, a photograph or illustration, and a caption. Have students study the visual and read the title and caption in order to make predictions. Record students' predictions and revisit them after students read the article. Revisiting predictions gives students an opportunity to confirm their predictions or to discover any clues they may have missed the first time.

Unit 1 · Lesson 1.5

High-rise Window Washers: A Bird's-eye View

High-rise window washers, such as this Chicago man, take great risks to do their jobs.

33

Before You Read

This section appears either on the lesson-opener page or on the second page of the article. Each Before You Read section addresses one of these reading strategies in relation to the photograph or illustration and caption:

- Use prior knowledge
- Predict
- Preview
- Build background
- Make connections
- Clarify

Model the use of each strategy by thinking aloud as you apply it to the caption or other section of the article. Help students use the first four strategies before they read. Encourage them to continue to make connections and clarify as they read.

Audio Icon

You can play or download an MP3 recording of each article from the *Reading Basics* website for use with students. For the first reading, you may want to have students listen as they follow along in their text. Listening to good examples of fluent reading will help students develop their own fluency.

Glosses in the Margin

Vocabulary important to understanding the article is boldface in the text and defined in the margin. The lesson plan in the *Instructor's Guide* provides an activity that allows you to preteach these words. As students encounter each vocabulary word in the article, have them review the definition and think about how the word is used in context.

Humanitarian Aid Workers: Comfort Under Fire

Aid workers provide humanitarian aid in regions of the world undergoing civil strife. They have helped to open schools and health clinics in Afghanistan.

Before You Read
Predict

Make a reasoned guess about what will happen in the article. Then check whether it happens. To help you predict:

- look at the photograph.
- read the title and the photo caption.
- skim the article quickly to get a general idea of what it is about.

9

Before You Read
Build Background Knowledge

When you don't know much about a topic, you can look for information about it before you read. For this article, for example, you can:

- do research in the library or on the Internet to find information about the sinking of the *Titanic*.
- discuss the movie *Titanic* with classmates.

Death on the Unsinkable Titanic

1   "The safest ship afloat." "A seagoing hotel!" "Unsinkable!" These were the descriptions that writers used in newspaper articles about the *Titanic*, the largest ship ever constructed at that time.

2   In April 1912 the *Titanic* was sailing from Southampton, England, to New York City on its first voyage. The captain of the British ship was E. J. Smith, a veteran of many years of transatlantic service. Smith wanted to prove that the *Titanic* was not only the world's most **luxurious** ship but also the fastest. To achieve that goal, Smith held the *Titanic* to a speedy 22 knots for the majority of the voyage.

3   The *Titanic* was equipped with the very latest wireless equipment, which it used to communicate with other ships. The *Titanic's* wireless operators had received warnings from two neighboring ships that they had seen several icebergs, but in spite of the warnings, Captain Smith maintained a speed of 22 knots.

4   One of the ship's lookouts, Fred Fleet, peered ahead from his position high atop the mast. In the distance he spotted a huge bulk looming in *Titanic's* path—an iceberg! Fleet struck three bells—the signal for something dead ahead. First Officer Murdoch, on watch on the bridge, ordered the ship to turn *hard-a-starboard*. At almost the same instant, Murdoch

luxurious
rich and splendid

60   Reading Basics · Intermediate 2 Reader

Comprehension and Critical Thinking Skills

Comprehension and Critical Thinking Skills exercises appear at the end of each article. The exercises, which progress from concrete to abstract following Anderson's taxonomy, cover these skills: Recognize and Recall Details, Find the Main Idea, Summarize and Paraphrase, Make Inferences, Recognize Author's Effect and Intentions, and Evaluate and Create. Students will find directions at the beginning of each exercise. Before students begin the exercises, make sure they understand how to respond to the different types of questions and activities. When they have finished, go over their responses with them, using the answers provided in the Answer Keys.

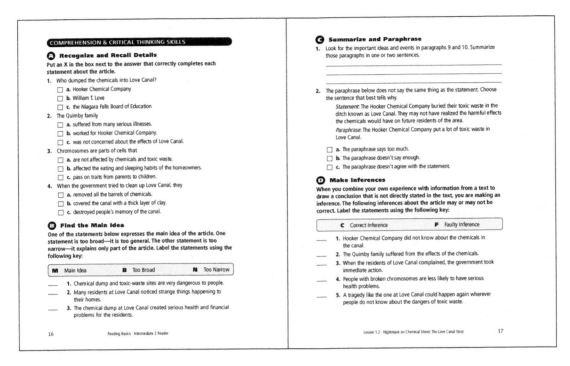

Words-per-Minute Table and Graph for Plotting Your Progress

A Words-per-Minute table and a graph for plotting reading speed appear at the end of each *Reader*. Students time their reading of each article and use the table to determine their reading speed. They then chart their reading speed on the graph, which allows them to track their progress over time.

How to Use Blogs to Integrate Technology in the Classroom

Teachers have picked up on the creative use of Internet technology and put the blog to work in the classroom. The blog can be a powerful and effective technology tool for students and teachers alike.

What Is a Blog?

A blog is a web publishing tool that allows authors to quickly and easily self-publish text, artwork, links to other blogs or websites, and a whole array of other content.

Blogs are set up like conventional websites, with navigation links and other standard website features. A blog is different from a typical website in that the primary content is comprised of a daily or scheduled posting. Blog postings are primarily text entries, similar to a diary or journal, which include a posting date. They include subsequent comments made by people other than the author. Postings are often short and frequently updated. They appear in reverse chronological order and can include archived entries. Blog postings may also include video and other media.

Blogs work well for students because they can be worked on at virtually any time and in any place with an Internet-enabled computer. Hence, they can be used by teachers to create a classroom that extends beyond the boundaries of the school.

User-friendly Technology

Blogs are surprisingly easy to use. They require minimum technical knowledge and are quickly and easily created and maintained. Unlike many traditional websites, they are flexible in design and can be changed relatively easily. Best of all, students will find them convenient and accessible via home or library computers.

Educational Benefits of Blogs

In addition to providing teachers with an excellent tool for communicating with students, there are numerous educational benefits of blogs. Blogs are
- motivators to students, especially those who otherwise might not become participants in classrooms
- excellent opportunities for students to read and write
- effective forums for collaboration and discussion
- powerful tools to enable scaffolded learning or mentoring to occur

Using the Blog in the Classroom

As an educational tool, blogs may be integrated in a multifaceted manner to accommodate all learners. Blogs can serve at least four basic functions.
1. **Classroom Management** Class blogs can serve as a portal to foster a community of learners. As they are easy to create and update efficiently, they can be used to inform students of class requirements or to post handouts, notices, and homework assignments. They can also act as a question-and-answer board.

2. **Collaboration** Blogs provide a space where teachers and students can work to further develop writing or other skills with the advantage of an instant audience. Teachers can offer instructional tips, and students can practice and benefit from peer review. Blogs also make online mentoring possible. For example, a class of native English-speaking students can help a class of ELL students develop more confidence in their writing skills. Students can also participate in cooperative learning activities that require them to relay research findings, ideas, or suggestions.

3. **Discussions** A class blog opens the opportunity for students to discuss topics outside of the classroom. With a blog, every person has an equal opportunity to share his or her thoughts and opinions. Students have time to react to ideas and reflect on learning. Teachers can also use a blog to bring together a group of knowledgeable individuals with whom students can network and conference for a given unit of study.

4. **Student Portfolios** Blogs present, organize, and protect student work as digital portfolios. As older entries are archived, developing skills and progress may be analyzed more conveniently. Additionally, as students realize their efforts will be published, they are typically more motivated to produce better writing. Teachers and peers may conference with a student individually on a developing work, and expert or peer mentoring advice can be easily kept for future reference.

Blog Risks to Consider

Schools often have guidelines and acceptable use policies (AUPs) regarding the use of school-wide computer networks and the Internet. These terms and conditions identify acceptable online behavior and access privileges. Policies regarding the displaying of any student work must be adhered to strictly.

Blogs, like other websites, may be viewed publicly. Students must be trained on issues regarding access, privacy, security, and free expression. Since blogs have no publisher, producer, or editor, students must carefully consider the content of postings to avoid anything defamatory, libelous, or infringing upon the rights of others.

Blogs are created by individuals for various and assorted purposes. Content should be recognized as the opinion of the blogger, and, therefore, may not necessarily be factual.

Preparing Students for Blogging

- Teach students safe, acceptable, and sensible behavior as online authors and readers.
- Review policies and guidelines pertaining to student access.
- Teach the nonposting rules of no complete names, e-mail accounts, or references that reveal location.
- Set clear expectations regarding tone, respect, and consequences.

Steps for Getting Started on Blogs

There are a number of free blogging tools available.

1. Go to one of the available free blogging sites.
2. Provide the necessary information requested (user name, password).
3. Create a title for your blog.
4. Accept terms and select a template.
5. Publish!

CONTEMPORARY

reading
basics

PART 2: STUDENT EDITIONS

reading
basics

A REAL-WORLD APPROACH TO LITERACY

McGraw Hill

Lesson Plan Introductory Student Edition

Unit 1 Lesson 1.1 pages 14–21

Introduce

READING SKILL

Recognize and Recall Details

Explain/Model: Explain that it is important to read attentively in order to recognize and recall specific details. Then have students read aloud the passage about Antonio and the one about the stone wall. Model recognizing details that would be important to remember.

Guided Practice: Have students read the boxed passage. Then work with them to complete the task given in the directions. Discuss why the responses given after the passage are correct. Ask students to give you two other details they recall from reading the passage.

Teach Lesson Skills

Practice: Have students read the passages about Mont Blanc and the African elephants. After reading each passage, discuss the answers to the questions and have students point out the details in the passage that support their answers.

Apply: After students answer the questions, have them read their responses aloud to the class. Encourage them to show classmates where they found the details in the passages.

Check Up: Have students work in small groups to read the passages and answer the questions. Then check each group's responses with those of other groups in the class.

COMPREHENSION

Set a Purpose for Reading: Encourage students to set a purpose for reading. Provide self-questioning models, such as *What do I hope to learn? What do the directions tell me to look for? What will happen next?* By setting a purpose and then evaluating whether they achieved the purpose, students consciously monitor their own comprehension. They can also discuss the purpose they have determined with a peer or a teacher.

Reading Extension

📖 Encourage students to read "A Young Man Speaks Out" on page 1 of the *Introductory Reader*. Use this as an opportunity to teach reading strategies and the lesson reading skill.

ALPHABETICS

Explore Words

Short Vowels: Write these words on the board and read them with students, emphasizing the short vowel sound: *print, flopped, tent, band, stuff.* Ask volunteers to circle the letter that stands for the short vowel sound.

Consonant Blends: List these blends vertically on the board and read them with students: *bl, dr, pl, sp, st.* Then finish writing each word and read it together with the students: *blink, drag, plane, spill, stamp.*

Spelling: Possessives: Remind students that *'s* is used to show that something belongs to someone. Use names of students and objects from the classroom, such as these: *the chair belonging to Tiara/Tiara's chair, the pencil of Sam/Sam's pencil.* Have students suggest other examples.

VOCABULARY

Academic Vocabulary/Tier 2

topic details recall describe passage

Before students complete the activity, write the academic vocabulary words and definitions on the board. Discuss each word's meaning with students. Then write the sentences below on the board. Read each sentence aloud and discuss it with students.

1. I chose an unusual *topic* for my research report.
2. The newspaper article includes *details* about the new mayor.
3. My sister and I *recall* the first day of school differently.
4. My assignment is to *describe* a park.
5. Have you read the *passage* about how honeybees communicate?

FLUENCY

Echo Reading: Read a sentence from one of the passages aloud. Then have students echo you by reading the same sentence and trying to read with the same speed and expression as you do.

Invite students to do a timed reading of "A Young Man Speaks Out." Afterwards, have them enter their times on the Words-per-Minute table on page 121 and chart their reading speed on page 122 of the *Introductory Reader*.

📶 Encourage students to listen to "A Young Man Speaks Out." Go to **www.mhereadingbasics.com** to play or download the recording. The recording provides modeled fluency and read-along support.

APPLICATION

Workplace Skill:

Find Details in an Employee Memo

Have students read the memo. Remind them that a memo is a workplace document that sends a message to one or more persons. Point out that although there may be a lot of information in a memo, the memo's format can help make it easier to find certain details. For example, there is always a section at the top of a memo that tells the date, the subject, and the names of the sender and the recipient. After students answer the questions, have them start a list of important details that need to be included in a good memo. This list will come in handy when they do the Write for Work activity.

Write for Work

Remind students which important details are needed in a good memo. Tell them to read the instructions for this task carefully to be sure they include all the requested information. Encourage them to share their work with a classmate and ask one another for suggestions about ways to make the memo clearer.

PASSKEY

💻 Go to **www.mhereadingbasics.com** and click on the *PassKey* link. Customize instruction for your class using modules from Reading/Language Arts, Levels 1 & 2.

Lesson Plan Introductory Student Edition

Unit 1 Lesson 1.2 pages 22–29

Introduce

READING SKILL
Understand Stated Concepts

Explain/Model: Explain that stated information can be found directly in the passage. Concepts that are not stated cannot be found in the passage. Then have students read aloud the passage about New Orleans. Model finding the stated concepts in the passage.

Guided Practice: Have students read the boxed passage. Encourage students to highlight or make margin notes about the stated concepts as they read. Then work with them to complete the task given in the directions. Discuss why the response given after the passage is correct.

Teach Lesson Skills

Practice: Have students look for facts that are stated directly as they read the passages about trilobites, the Japanese New Year, and fish. Discuss the answers to the questions and have students point out places in the passages where the information is directly stated.

Apply: After students answer the questions, have them read their responses aloud to the class. Encourage them to show classmates where they found the stated information in the passages.

Check Up: Have students work in small groups to read the passages and answer the questions. Then check each group's responses with those of other groups in the class.

COMPREHENSION
Clarify Meaning: Encourage students to actively clarify meaning as they read. Provide self-questioning models, such as *What clues can I find in other sentences to help me understand this word? Does this word resemble any other words I have learned? Can I find someone to ask about this?* When students proactively try to clarify meaning, they consciously monitor their own comprehension.

Reading Extension
Encourage students to read "Alone across the Atlantic" on page 9 of the *Introductory Reader*. Use this as an opportunity to teach reading strategies and the lesson reading skill.

ALPHABETICS
Explore Words

Consonant Pairs: Write these consonant pairs vertically on the board: *ch, th, ch, th*. Then finish writing each word and read it together with the students: *chin, thin, lunch, bath*. Then write *then* on the board, read it, and point out that the *th* in this word has a hard sound.

Spelling: Contractions: Remind students that the apostrophe in a contraction stands in for the missing letter: Write these words and contraction pairs: *did not/didn't, you are/you're, we will/we'll*. Have volunteers identify the missing letter in each pair.

Antonyms: Remind students that antonyms are words with opposite meanings. Give these examples: *up/down, tall/short*. Then ask students to share additional examples with the class..

VOCABULARY
Academic Vocabulary/Tier 2

stated concept directly notes legal

Before students complete the activity, write the academic vocabulary words and definitions on the board. Discuss each word's meaning with students. Then write the sentences below on the board. Read each sentence aloud and discuss it with students.

1. The instructions *stated* that the button on the left is the one to press.
2. We are learning about the *concept* of supply and demand in social studies.
3. The e-mail told us *directly* which step to do first.
4. The students took *notes* as their teacher explained the project.
5. When you are 18, it is *legal* to vote.

FLUENCY
Partner Reading: Have partners read aloud to one another and/or read aloud at the same time. Encourage them to offer support and correction to one another. Circulate to offer guidance as needed.

Invite students to do a timed reading of "Alone across the Atlantic." Afterwards, have them enter their times on the Words-per-Minute table on page 121 and chart their reading speed on page 122 of the *Introductory Reader*.

Encourage students to listen to "Alone across the Atlantic." Go to **www.mhereadingbasics.com** to play or download the recording. The recording provides modeled fluency and read-along support.

APPLICATION
Workplace Skill:
Identify Stated Concepts in a Procedural Document
Have students read the procedural document. Explain that a procedural document tells how to do something. Explain that steps are usually stated directly, but readers will also need to apply their knowledge, experience, and common sense to figure out steps that are not directly stated. For example, a procedural document may explain how to use a copier but not tell the user to turn on the copier. After students answer the questions, have them begin a list of steps for using a small appliance. They can revisit the list for the Write for Work activity.

Write for Work
Remind students that a good procedural document tells all the steps needed to complete a task. Tell them to read the instructions for this task carefully to be sure they include all the steps. Encourage classmates to share their work and discuss ways to make the steps clearer or add any steps or rules that are needed.

PASSKEY
Go to **www.mhereadingbasics.com** and click on the *PassKey* link. Customize instruction for your class using modules from Reading/Language Arts, Levels 1 & 2.

Lesson Plan Introductory Student Edition

Introduce

READING SKILL
Draw Conclusions

Explain/Model: Explain that to draw conclusions, we combine what we already know with new information. Then have students read aloud the passage about the hurricane. Model drawing a valid conclusion and an invalid conclusion.

Guided Practice: Have students read the boxed passage. Then work with them to complete the task given in the directions. Discuss why the responses given after the passage are valid or invalid. Ask students to give an example of another valid conclusion they can draw.

Teach Lesson Skills

Practice: Have students read the passages about the discovery of coffee and the ways different animals release heat. Tell them to think about what the text states and what they already know as they read about these topics. Remind them that for a conclusion to be valid, they must be able to support it with specific information from the text. Discuss the answers to the questions and have students explain how they arrived at their conclusions. Have them point to the specific information in the text that helped them recognize the valid conclusions.

Apply: After students answer the questions, have them read their responses aloud to the class. Encourage them to show classmates the text information they used to draw conclusions or to decide whether a conclusion was valid or invalid.

Check Up: Have students work in small groups to read the passage and answer the questions. Then check each group's responses with those of other groups in the class.

COMPREHENSION
Use Prior Knowledge: Encourage students to think about what they already know before they read. To get students started, provide self-questioning models, such as *Have I read about this topic before? Does this sound familiar?* When students can create a context or framework of known information in which to place new information, they consciously monitor their own comprehension.

Reading Extension
📖 Encourage students to read "Flight to Freedom" on page 17 of the *Introductory Reader*. Use this as an opportunity to teach reading strategies and the lesson reading skill.

ALPHABETICS
Explore Words

Long Vowels with Silent *e*: Write these words and read them with students: *tap, pin, not, pan*. Then model adding the silent *e* to each word. Have students read the new words, noting how the silent *e* changes the vowel sound from short to long.

Compound Words: List these compound words on the board: *sunshine, steamboat, railroad, snowman, eyeball, backyard*. Invite volunteers to identify the separate words that make up each compound word.

Context Clues: Write this example and have students tell which word helped them figure out the meaning of the underlined word: *He used to be clumsy, but now he is agile.* Identify the two words as antonyms.

VOCABULARY
Academic Vocabulary/Tier 2

conclusions conclude valid invalid supported

Before students complete the activity, write the words and definitions on the board. Discuss each word's meaning with students. Then write the sentences below on the board. Read each sentence aloud and discuss it with students.

1. What *conclusions* did you come to about the hats after comparing their prices?
2. I can *conclude* from the piles of books in my friend's room that she likes to read.
3. Being sick is a *valid* reason for absence.
4. There are no facts to back up that conclusion, so it is *invalid*.
5. She *supported* her answer with examples.

FLUENCY
Collaborative Reading: Gather in a group. Have each student read one or more lines of a passage and then pass the text to the next student. Supply pronunciation and phrasing corrections as needed.

Invite students to do a timed reading of "Flight to Freedom." Afterwards, have them enter their times on the Words-per-Minute table on page 121 and chart their reading speed on page 122 of the *Introductory Reader*.

🔊 Encourage students to listen to "Flight to Freedom." Go to **www.mhreadingbasics.com** to play or download the recording. The recording provides modeled fluency and read-along support.

APPLICATION
Workplace Skill:
Draw Conclusions from a Chart
Remind students that a chart is a visual way to present information. Point out features, such as column heads, that explain what kind of information the chart gives. Tell students that charts just give basic facts and figures. Readers have to use what they already know to draw conclusions about how the information applies to them or their job.

Write for Work
Have students list things people should and should not do in a job interview. Then remind students to use what they know about good interview etiquette to draw conclusions about why their friend did not get the job. Explain that the advice they give should address the things their friend could have done to make a better impression. Have classmates share advice and discuss ways to make it stronger.

PASSKEY
📘 Go to **www.mhreadingbasics.com** and click on the *PassKey* link. Customize instruction for your class using modules from Reading/Language Arts, Levels 1 & 2.

Lesson Plan Introductory Student Edition

Unit 1 Lesson 1.4 pages 38–45

Introduce

READING SKILL
Summarize and Paraphrase

Explain/Model: Explain that when we summarize, we tell only the most important ideas, but when we paraphrase, we include all the information in our own words. Have students read aloud the passage about the orchestra conductor. Model identifying the most important ideas. Then have students read aloud the paraphrase. Point out details in the paraphrase that are not included in the summary.

Guided Practice: Have students read the boxed passage. Then work with them to complete the task given in the directions. Discuss why the responses given after the passage are correct. Help students discuss the differences between the summary and the paraphrase.

Teach Lesson Skills

Practice: Have students read the passages about the Gorgons and pigs. Tell them to think about which details they would include in a summary and how they would paraphrase each passage if they were retelling it to a friend. Discuss the answers to the questions and have students explain why each correct answer is the best choice.

Apply: After students answer the questions, have them read their paraphrases and summary aloud to the class. Ask them to explain how they put each paraphrase into their own words and how they decided which ideas to include in the summary.

Check Up: Have students work in small groups to read the passages and answer the questions. Then check each group's responses with those of other groups in the class.

COMPREHENSION
Reread/Read More Slowly: Encourage students to become aware of the pace at which they read. Offer self-questioning models, such as *Did I read this passage too quickly? Does reading again help me understand better? Does reading more slowly help me retain information?* When students actively consider the manner in which they are reading, they consciously monitor their own comprehension.

Reading Extension
📖 Encourage students to read "The Heroes of Flight 93" on page 25 of the *Introductory Reader*. Use this as an opportunity to teach reading strategies and the lesson reading skill.

ALPHABETICS
Explore Words

Consonant Pairs: Write the consonant pairs *wr*, *gn*, and *kn* on the board. Say the sound that each pair stands for and have students identify the silent letter. Then write *wr*, *gn*, and *kn* in one column and *at*, *ap*, and *ow* in another column. Have students draw a line from each consonant pair to the ending that completes a word. *(wrap, gnat, know)*

Spelling: Possessives: Model forming singular possessives, using phrases such as *the backpack of Paul/Paul's backpack* and *the hat belonging to Maria/Maria's hat.*

Spelling: Plurals: Review the rules for adding -*s* and -*es*, and model making *car* and *lunch* plural. Have students make *dish, bowl, fox,* and *cake* plural.

VOCABULARY
Academic Vocabulary/Tier 2

summarize summary paraphrase reinforce relevant

Before students complete the activity, write the academic vocabulary words and definitions on the board. Discuss each word's meaning with students. Then write the sentences below on the board. Read each sentence aloud and discuss it with students.

1. *Summarize* the plot in a few sentences.
2. Her *summary* of the movie made me want to see it.
3. *Paraphrase* any information you use in your report, and give credit to the author.
4. Our teacher gives homework to *reinforce* what we learn in class.
5. I enjoy books that are *relevant* to my life.

FLUENCY
Repeated Reading: Lead a group to read the same passage aloud together several times. As the leader, emphasize accuracy and phrasing until the group reading sounds smooth and consistent.

Invite students to do a timed reading of "The Heroes of Flight 93." Afterwards, have them enter their times on the Words-per-Minute table on page 121 and chart their reading speed on page 122 of the *Introductory Reader*.

📶 Encourage students to listen to "The Heroes of Flight 93." Go to **www.mhereadingbasics.com** to play or download the recording. The recording provides modeled fluency and read-along support.

APPLICATION
Workplace Skill:

Summarize and Paraphrase a Want Ad

Have students read the want ad. Remind them that a want ad describes an available job. Point out that taking notes that summarize important information about the job, such as the experience needed, responsibilities, hours, pay, and contact information, can help them select and apply for jobs. After students answer the questions, have partners practice retelling the hints for reading a want ad. This retelling will help them do the Write for Work activity.

Write for Work
Remind students that a paraphrase retells all the information in a text or passage in a simpler way. Tell them to restate the hints in their own words. Ask classmates to share their work and check that their paraphrases include all the information. Then have them share their summaries of ads with a partner.

PASSKEY
💻 Go to **www.mhereadingbasics.com** and click on the *PassKey* link. Customize instruction for your class using modules from Reading/Language Arts, Levels 1 & 2.

Introduce

READING SKILL

Recognize Character Traits

Explain/Model: Explain that authors use different methods to show what the characters and people they are writing about are like. Then have students read aloud the passage about Alma. Model identifying some things Alma says and does that show she is hardworking. Invite students to share other things that Alma might do that would show she is hardworking.

Guided Practice: Have students read the boxed passage. Then work with them to complete the task given in the directions. Discuss why the response given after the passage is correct.

Teach Lesson Skills

Practice: Have students read the passages about William Sidis and Midas. Tell them to think about what Sidis and Midas do and what their actions say about them. Discuss the answers to the questions and have students point out words or actions that support their answers.

Apply: After students answer the questions, have them read their responses aloud to the class. Encourage them to explain how they selected character traits for each person.

Check Up: Have students work in small groups to read the passages and answer the questions. Then check each group's responses with those of other groups in the class.

COMPREHENSION

Make Connections: Encourage students to make connections as they read. Provide self-questioning models, such as *Have I learned something about this topic before? What was the context? Have I had any experiences in my own life that relate to this topic?* When students relate what they are reading to their own lives and educational experience, they consciously monitor their own comprehension.

Reading Extension

Encourage students to read "Seeing for the First Time" on page 33 of the *Introductory Reader*. Use this as an opportunity to teach reading strategies and the lesson reading skill.

ALPHABETICS

Explore Words

Hard and Soft *c* and *g*: Explain that *c* can stand for /k/ or /s/. When *c* is followed by *e, i,* or *y,* it usually makes the /s/ sound, as in *sip.* Write *candy, cell phone, city, cone,* and *cycle.* Read the words aloud and have students raise their hand when they hear words in which the *c* stands for the /s/ sound. Follow the same steps to introduce the two sounds of *g:* /g/ and /j/. Use the words *gem, gum, gymnastics, goat,* and *golf.*

Multiple-meaning Words: Tell students that some words have more than one meaning. The way the word is used in a sentence can help them figure out the meaning. Have students discuss the meaning of *cool* in each of these sentences: *Myra's sunglasses make her look cool. Sam put on a jacket because it was cool outside.*

VOCABULARY

Academic Vocabulary/Tier 2

characters   traits   consistently   clues   determine

Before students complete the activity, write the academic vocabulary words and definitions on the board. Discuss each word's meaning with students. Then write the sentences below on the board. Read each sentence aloud and discuss it with students.

1. Carlos enjoys reading about *characters* who are good at sports.
2. What *traits* do most good teachers have?
3. Laura *consistently* does her homework well.
4. The activities a person likes to do can give you *clues* about what he or she is like.
5. Marni checked the weather to help her *determine* what outfit to wear.

FLUENCY

Partner Reading: Have partners read aloud to one another and/or read aloud at the same time. Encourage them to offer support and correction to one another. Circulate to offer guidance as needed.

Invite students to do a timed reading of "Seeing for the First Time." Afterwards, have them enter their times on the Words-per-Minute table on page 121 and chart their reading speed on page 122 of the *Introductory Reader.*

Encourage students to listen to "Seeing for the First Time." Go to **www.mhereadingbasics.com** to play or download the recording. The recording provides modeled fluency and read-along support.

APPLICATION

Workplace Skill:

Identify Character Traits for a Job Placement

Have students read the description of Carmela Rodriguez and study the want ads. Remind them that want ads describe jobs and the qualities and qualifications an applicant needs. Point out that people are more likely to be hired and be happy in a position if the position is a good match for their skills, personality, and work experience. After students answer the questions, have them list character traits a person needs to be a good child-care worker. This list will come in handy when they do the Write for Work activity.

Write for Work

Remind students to think about the skills and personality one would need to be a good child-care helper. Tell them to be sure they include both traits and an explanation of their choices. Encourage them to share their work with a classmate and compare the traits they chose.

PASSKEY

Go to **www.mhereadingbasics.com** and click on the *PassKey* link. Customize instruction for your class using modules from Reading/Language Arts, Levels 1 & 2.

Lesson Plan Introductory Student Edition

Introduce

READING SKILL

Use Forms

Explain/Model: Explain that when completing a form, it is important to read the entire form and understand what you need to do before even picking up a pen to complete the form. Then have students read aloud the steps for completing a form. Suggest that students picture themselves following each step.

Guided Practice: Have students read the boxed library card application. Then work with them to complete the task given in the directions. Discuss why the response provided is correct. Ask students to tell what information they would need to write to complete the form.

Teach Lesson Skills

Practice: Have students read the interlibrary loan request form. Remind them to read the form completely and carefully. Discuss the answers to the questions and have students point out the specific instructions on the form that support their answers.

Apply: After students answer the questions, have them read their responses aloud to the class. Encourage them to show classmates where on the form they found the information to answer the questions.

Check Up: Have students work in small groups to read the form and answer the questions. Then check each group's responses with those of other groups in the class.

COMPREHENSION

Understand Author's Purpose: Encourage students to consider the author's purpose as they read. Provide self-questioning models, such as *Why did the author decide to write this? What does the author want me to know?* By examining the author's purpose, students can better analyze their own reaction to the writing and consciously monitor their own comprehension.

ALPHABETICS	VOCABULARY	FLUENCY
Explore Words	**Academic Vocabulary/Tier 2**	**Marked Phrase Reading:** Mark a passage with phrase boundaries, showing how words should be grouped for meaning and emphasis. Read the passage aloud, having students follow along, and then read aloud together with students.
Consonant Pairs *ck, ng*: Write *ck* and *ng*, pronounce them, and remind students that sometimes two consonants stand for one sound. Model adding *ck* or *ng* to *cli-*, *bri-*, and *lu-*. Then read the words aloud with students.	form previous headings complete apply	
	Before students complete the activity, write the academic vocabulary words and definitions on the board. Discuss each word's meaning with students. Then write the sentences below on the board. Read each sentence aloud and discuss it with students.	
Synonyms and Antonyms: Remind students that synonyms are words with similar meanings. Antonyms are words with opposite meanings. Have students give synonyms and antonyms for these words: *simple (easy/hard), big (large/small), tired (weary/energetic).*	1. I had to fill out a *form* to get a credit card.	
	2. Before I moved to Florida, my *previous* home was in California.	
	3. The *headings* were in bold print above each section of the article.	
Vowel Combinations: Write these words: *pain, ray, clear, peel, boat.* Read each word aloud and have students identify the letters that stand for the long vowel sound.	4. Please use a pen to *complete* the form.	
	5. I want to *apply* for a job at this company.	

APPLICATION	Write for Work	Workplace Extension
Workplace Skill:	Have students list information that would be good to include on a form to find out who is interested in joining a company baseball team. Tell them to read the instructions for this task carefully to be sure their forms include the requested information. Encourage them to share their work with a classmate and discuss other possible information to add to the form.	Remind students that the workplace requires them to behave in a professional manner. Have them review the passage about Steve Brown's preparations for an interview. Ask students what will be the first impression Steve makes. Have partners answer the questions and share their responses with the class.
Fill Out an Employee Record Form		
Have students read the form. Remind them that forms ask for facts and information. Point out that reading a form completely and gathering any necessary information before completing it will make the process faster and simpler. Remind students that forms are a simple way of tracking information.		

PASSKEY

🔲 Go to **www.mhereadingbasics.com** and click on the *PassKey* link. Customize instruction for your class using modules from Reading/Language Arts, Levels 1 & 2.

Lesson Plan Introductory Student Edition

Introduce

READING SKILL

Use Correct Spelling

Explain/Model: Explain that learning common spelling patterns and rules can improve spelling, which allows for more effective communication. Then have students read aloud the rules and patterns. Discuss each example and ask students to suggest additional ones.

Guided Practice: Have students read the sentences. Then work with them to complete the task given in the directions. Encourage them to refer to the spelling rules and patterns if necessary. Discuss why the responses given after the sentences are correct.

Teach Lesson Skills

Practice: Have students read the sentences and add the endings or choose the correct word. Tell them to think about what they know about spelling rules and patterns. Discuss the answers and have students tell how they added the endings or chose their answers.

Apply: After students complete each sentence or word, have them read their responses aloud to the class, spelling or writing the words. Encourage them to explain how they selected their answers or what rule they followed to add an ending.

Check Up: Have students work in small groups to read the passages and write the words. Then check each group's responses with those of other groups in the class.

COMPREHENSION

Clarify Meaning: Encourage students to actively clarify meaning as they read. Provide self-questioning models, such as *What clues can I find in other sentences to help me understand this word? Does this word resemble any other words I have learned? Can I find someone to ask about this?* When students proactively try to clarify meaning, they consciously monitor their own comprehension.

ALPHABETICS

Explore Words

Long *i* and Long *e*, Spelled *-y*: Write these words and read them with students, telling them to pay attention to the final sound: *why, shiny, lucky, pry, cry, money*. Then read the words again and have students raise their hands when they hear a word that ends with the long *i* sound. Follow the same process and use these words to introduce long *e sound*, spelled *-y*: *fry, lady, hungry, sty, my, thirsty*.

Prefixes *un-, re-*: Explain that the prefix *re-* means "again" and the prefix *un-* means "not." Write the following words on the board and have students use their knowledge of the prefixes to determine their meaning: *unusual, retake, reheat, unsafe.*

VOCABULARY

Academic Vocabulary/Tier 2

common   pattern   typically   examples   context

Before students complete the activity, write the academic vocabulary words and definitions on the board. Discuss each word's meaning with students. Then write the sentences below on the board. Read each sentence aloud and discuss it with students.

1. Cats and dogs are *common* pets.
2. Crying when they are hungry and when they wake up is a *pattern* for many babies.
3. We *typically* eat dinner at seven o'clock.
4. The teacher showed us some *examples* before we tried the problems on our own.
5. Desi looked for *context* in the sentence to help her figure out an unfamiliar word.

FLUENCY

Echo Reading: Read a sentence from the workplace skill e-mail aloud. Then have students echo you by reading the same sentence and trying to read with the same speed and expression as you do.

APPLICATION

Workplace Skill:

Use Correct Spelling in an E-mail

Remind students that work e-mails should be clear and free from spelling errors. Point out that spell-checker will not catch every error, so they should proofread their work carefully before hitting "send." After students read the e-mails and answer the questions, have them suggest other misspelled words that a spell-checker might not notice.

Write for Work

Remind students that correct spelling is an important part of workplace communication. Tell them to read the instructions for this task carefully to be sure they understand the purpose of the e-mail. After they write, encourage them to share their e-mails with a classmate and proofread each other's work for spelling errors.

Workplace Extension

Have students review the passage that describes how Julie Graham prepared to fill out a form. Discuss what she did to make filling out the form easier. For example, ask how calling ahead helped her. Have partners respond to the questions and share their responses with the class.

PASSKEY

Go to **www.mhreadingbasics.com** and click on the *PassKey* link. Customize instruction for your class using modules from Reading/Language Arts, Levels 1 & 2.

Lesson Plan Introductory Student Edition

Unit 2 Lesson 2.1 pages 78–85

Introduce

READING SKILL
Find the Main Idea

Explain/Model: Explain that the main idea of a passage can be stated or unstated. Then have students read aloud the passage about Michie. Point out that the main idea is stated in the first sentence and that all the other sentences support that idea. Next, ask students to read aloud the passage about lions. Explain what all the details have in common and model using this information to state the main idea.

Guided Practice: Have students read the boxed passage. Then work with them to complete the task given in the directions. Tell students to look for one sentence that gives the main idea of what the passage is about. Discuss why the responses given after the passage are correct.

Teach Lesson Skills

Practice: Have students read each passage and identify the sentence that tells the main idea. Remind them to think about what all the details have in common to help them find the main idea. Discuss the answers to the questions and have students share the main idea statements they wrote.

Apply: After students answer the questions, have them read their main ideas aloud to the class. Encourage them to explain how they used the details in the passage to determine the main idea.

Check Up: Have students work in small groups to read the passages and answer the questions. Then check each group's responses with those of other groups in the class.

COMPREHENSION

Clarify Meaning: Encourage students to actively clarify meaning as they read. Provide self-questioning models, such as *What clues can I find in other sentences to help me understand this word? Does this word resemble any other words I have learned? Can I find someone to ask about this?* When students proactively try to clarify meaning, they consciously monitor their own comprehension.

Reading Extension

Encourage students to read "Pigs to the Rescue" on page 41 of the *Introductory Reader.* Use this as an opportunity to teach reading strategies and the lesson reading skill.

ALPHABETICS
Explore Words

Synonyms: Remind students that synonyms are words with the same or similar meanings. Have students identify the two words in each set that are synonyms: *fast/slow/quick, tasty/delicious/terrible, sloppy/tidy/messy.*

Suffixes -er, -est: Remind students that -er is used to compare two things and -est is used to compare three or more things. Discuss these examples: *This cap is smaller than that one. That is the smallest cap of all.*

Spelling: Plurals: Review that plurals can be formed by adding -s or -es. Write *churches, papers, glasses, boxes,* and *books.* Have students identify the letter or letters that form each plural. Have volunteers form plurals of *wish, ax, can, duck,* and *class.*

VOCABULARY
Academic Vocabulary/Tier 2

identify imply restate paragraph vary

Before students complete the activity, write the academic vocabulary words and definitions on the board. Discuss each word's meaning with students. Then write the sentences below on the board. Read each sentence aloud and discuss it with students.

1. You can *identify* my brother by his hat.
2. I did not mean to *imply* that you were lying about that.
3. Please *restate* your phone number since I did not hear all of it.
4. Start a new *paragraph* for each new idea.
5. *Vary* your exercise routine to give your whole body a workout.

FLUENCY

Partner Reading: Have partners read aloud to one another and/or read aloud at the same time. Encourage them to offer support and correction to one another. Circulate to offer guidance as needed.

Invite students to do a timed reading of "Pigs to the Rescue." Afterwards, have them enter their times on the Words-per-Minute table on page 121 and chart their reading speed on page 122 of the *Introductory Reader.*

Encourage students to listen to "Pigs to the Rescue." Go to **www.mhereadingbasics.com** to play or download the recording. The recording provides modeled fluency and read-along support.

APPLICATION
Workplace Skill:
Find the Main Idea in a Mission Statement

Have students read the mission statement. Explain that a mission statement gives a company's purpose and goals. Looking for the main idea or ideas can help students better understand the company. Remind them that if the main idea is not directly stated, they will need to decide what the company wants them to know, based on the details given in the mission statement. After students answer the questions, have them brainstorm some ideas for a business. This brainstorming activity will come in handy when they do the Write for Work activity.

Write for Work

Have students choose an idea for a business and write a goal for this business. Tell students to read the instructions for this task to be sure they include all the information. Ask them to share their work with a classmate and to suggest details that could be added for clarity.

PASSKEY

Go to **www.mhereadingbasics.com** and click on the *PassKey* link. Customize instruction for your class using modules from Reading/Language Arts, Levels 1 & 2.

Introduce

READING SKILL
Identify Cause and Effect

Explain/Model: Explain that a cause is why something happens and an effect is what happens as a result. Then have students read aloud the sentence about four-leaf clovers. Point out that the word *because* signals a cause-and-effect relationship: the first part of the sentence gives the effect, and the second part tells the cause. Repeat the process for the sentences about Manuel.

Guided Practice: Have students read the boxed passage. Then work with them to complete the task given in the directions. Encourage students to ask themselves *what happened* and *why* as they look for words that signal causes and effects. Discuss the responses that follow the passage. Ask students to name the cause and effect in the final sentence of the boxed passage.

Practice: Have students read the cause-and-effect sentences. Tell them to look for signal words and to think about what happened and why. Discuss the answers to the questions and have students point out the signal words they used to help them identify causes and effects.

Apply: Have students complete the charts and share them with the class. Encourage students to point out any signal words they used to help them.

Check Up: Have students work in small groups to read the passages and answer the questions. Then check each group's responses with those of other groups in the class.

Teach Lesson Skills

COMPREHENSION

Ask Questions: Encourage students to ask themselves questions as they read. Provide questioning models that progress from concrete to abstract. For example, *What does this mean? Is this a main idea? Do I remember the order of important events?* By asking themselves questions, students consciously monitor their own comprehension. They can also ask questions of peers or a teacher to clarify understanding.

Reading Extension

📖 Encourage students to read "In the Line of Fire" on page 49 of the *Introductory Reader*. Use this as an opportunity to teach reading strategies and the lesson reading skill.

ALPHABETICS
Explore Words

Syllables: Review that a closed syllable ends in a consonant and usually has a short vowel sound. However, when a two-syllable word is made up of two closed syllables, the vowel in the second syllable usually stands for the schwa sound. Write these words on the board and model dividing them into *syllables: mel/on, dev/il, per/son, ban/dit.* Read the words aloud with students.

Spelling: Word Endings: Review that when you add endings to words that have closed syllables and end with a single consonant, it is usually necessary to double the final consonant. Model adding the ending *-ing* to *run* and *help.* Then have volunteers add *-er* and *-est* to *fast* and *hot.*

VOCABULARY
Academic Vocabulary/Tier 2

cause effect signal create technique

Before students complete the activity, write the academic vocabulary words and definitions on the board. Discuss each word's meaning with students. Then write the sentences below on the board. Read each sentence aloud and discuss it with students.

1. Hunger can *cause* your stomach to growl.
2. One *effect* of exercise is stronger muscles.
3. The team captain will hold up two fingers to *signal* a play.
4. Use your imagination to *create* the picture.
5. The basketball player practiced his shooting *technique*.

FLUENCY

Collaborative Reading: Gather in a group. Have each student read one or more lines of a passage and then pass the text to the next student. Supply pronunciation and phrasing corrections as needed.

Invite students to do a timed reading of "In the Line of Fire." Afterwards, have them enter their times on the Words-per-Minute table on page 121 and chart their reading speed on page 122 of the *Introductory Reader*.

🔊 Encourage students to listen to "In the Line of Fire." Go to **www.mhreadingbasics.com** to play or download the recording. The recording provides modeled fluency and read-along support.

APPLICATION
Workplace Skill:

Find Cause and Effect in a Safety Policy

Have students read the safety policy. Remind them that workplace documents such as policies have causes and effects. Not every workplace document will have signal words, so readers should ask themselves questions such as *Why do we have this rule? What can happen if I don't follow it?* After students answer the questions, have them make a cause-and-effect graphic organizer that shows the reasons for some of the rules at Johnson's Roofing and the effects of not following them. This list will come in handy for the Write for Work activity.

Write for Work

Remind students that a cause tells why something happens and an effect tells what happens. Tell them to read the instructions for this task carefully to be sure they include all the requested information. Encourage them to use signal words in their writing and to share their work with a classmate.

PASSKEY
💻 Go to **www.mhreadingbasics.com** and click on the *PassKey* link. Customize instruction for your class using modules from Reading/Language Arts, Levels 1 & 2.

Lesson Plan Introductory Student Edition

Unit 2 Lesson 2.3 pages 94–101

Introduce

READING SKILL

Use Consumer Materials

Explain/Model: Explain that many of the products and services that we consume, or buy, come with important papers. Have students read the second paragraph aloud. Ask them to give examples of warnings, labels, or instructions that have come with products or services they have bought. Have them describe how they used the information.

Guided Practice: Have students read the prescription label. Then work with them to complete the task given in the directions. Discuss why the responses given are correct.

Teach Lesson Skills

Practice: Have students read the medicine label. Tell them to read each detail on the label very carefully. Discuss the answers to the questions and have students point to the information on the label that supports their answers.

Apply: After students answer the questions, have them read their responses aloud to the class. Encourage them to show classmates where in the ad they found the information to answer each question.

Check Up: Have students work in small groups to read the beverage label and answer the questions. Then check each group's responses with those of other groups in the class.

COMPREHENSION

Set a Purpose for Reading: Encourage students to set a purpose for reading. Provide self-questioning models, such as *What do I hope to learn? What do the directions tell me to look for? What will happen next?* By setting a purpose and then evaluating whether they achieved the purpose, students consciously monitor their own comprehension. They can also discuss the purpose they have determined with a peer or a teacher.

Reading Extension

📖 Encourage students to read "How Fast Is Too Fast?" on page 57 of the *Introductory Reader*. Use this as an opportunity to teach reading strategies and the lesson reading skill.

ALPHABETICS

Explore Words

Syllables: Tell students that open syllables end in a vowel and have the long vowel sound. Silent *e* syllables end in silent *e* and also have the long vowel sound. Write these words: re/cent, i/rate, fi/nal, phone/book, fe/line. Draw a line between the syllables and have students identify open syllables and silent *e* syllables. Then have them read the words.

Spelling: Word Endings: Explain that when a word ends in silent *e*, the final *e* is usually dropped before the ending is added. When a word ends in -*y*, the *y* is usually changed to *i* before an ending is added. Model adding -*ed* and -*ing* to *dine* and *carry*. Then have students do the same for *state* and *deny*.

VOCABULARY

Academic Vocabulary/Tier 2

consumer   text   obvious   instructions   accompany

Before students complete the activity, write the academic vocabulary words and definitions on the board. Discuss each word's meaning with students. Then write the sentences below on the board. Read each sentence aloud and discuss it with students.

1. A *consumer* often shops for the best price.
2. The *text* under the photo is in small print.
3. The big sign on the door makes it *obvious* that no food is allowed in the store.
4. Read the *instructions* before you start the project.
5. My friend will *accompany* me to the party.

FLUENCY

Repeated Reading: Lead a group to read the same passage aloud together several times. As the leader, emphasize accuracy and phrasing until the group reading sounds smooth and consistent.

Invite students to do a timed reading of "How Fast Is Too Fast?" Afterwards, have them enter their times on the Words-per-Minute table on page 121 and chart their reading speed on page 122 of the *Introductory Reader*.

📶 Encourage students to listen to "How Fast Is Too Fast?" Go to **www.mhreadingbasics.com** to play or download the recording. The recording provides modeled fluency and read-along support.

APPLICATION

Workplace Skill:

Respond to a Consumer Complaint Letter

Have students read the complaint letter. Remind them that a complaint letter tells a company that a consumer is not happy with the product he or she purchased. Point out that a complaint letter states the problem, gives examples to describe the problem, and tells what the consumer wants the company to do to fix the problem. It is written in a formal style, so it should have a formal greeting and closing. After students answer the questions, have them brainstorm some ways the company could fix the problem for the consumer. This list will come in handy when they do the Write for Work activity.

Write for Work

Remind students that a response to a complaint letter should restate the problem and tell how the company plans to solve it. Tell them to read the instructions for this task to be sure they include all the requested information. Encourage them to read aloud their letters to classmates and discuss them.

PASSKEY

🔑 Go to **www.mhreadingbasics.com** and click on the *PassKey* link. Customize instruction for your class using modules from Reading/Language Arts, Levels 1 & 2.

Lesson Plan Introductory Student Edition

Introduce

READING SKILL
Identify Fact and Opinion

Explain/Model: Explain that facts can be proved, while opinions cannot. Have students read the pairs of facts and opinions. Model giving some facts and opinions about your favorite books or television shows. Then have students read aloud the statements about basketball and baseball. Point out words and details that can help you identify a statement as a fact or an opinion.

Guided Practice: Have students read the sentences. Then work with the students to complete the task given in the directions. Encourage students to look for words and details that signal an opinion or a fact. Discuss why the responses given are correct.

Practice: Have students read the sentences and decide whether they are facts or opinions. Tell them to look for words that signal opinions or to ask themselves whether each statement can be proved. Discuss the answers to the questions.

Apply: After students answer the questions, have them read their responses aloud to the class. Encourage them to point out words that helped them distinguish facts from opinions.

Check Up: Have students work in small groups to read the sentences and answer the questions. Then check each group's responses with those of other groups in the class.

Teach Lesson Skills

COMPREHENSION

Understand Author's Purpose: Encourage students to consider the author's purpose as they read. Provide self-questioning models, such as *Why did the author decide to write this? What does the author want me to know?* By examining the author's purpose, students can better analyze their own reaction to the writing and consciously monitor their own comprehension.

Reading Extension
Encourage students to read "The Mysteries of the Maya" on page 65 of the *Introductory Reader*. Use this as an opportunity to teach reading strategies and the lesson reading skill.

ALPHABETICS
Explore Words

Syllables: Review that closed syllables usually have the short vowel sound. Silent *e* syllables have the long vowel sound. Write the following syllables in two columns and have students match them to form words: 1. *hand, on, make;* 2. *up, line, made.* (*handmade, online, makeup*)

Multiple-meaning Words: Have students use these words in sentences that show their different meanings: *run, set, light, wave.*

Suffixes -less, -ful: Review that the suffix *-less* means "without" and the suffix *-ful* means "full of." Model adding both suffixes to *care* and *taste*, and discuss how the suffixes change the meaning of each base word.

VOCABULARY
Academic Vocabulary/Tier 2

fact opinion indicate evaluate verify

Before students complete the activity, write the academic vocabulary words and definitions on the board. Discuss each word's meaning with students. Then write the sentences below on the board. Read each sentence aloud and discuss it with students.

1. It is a *fact* that I was born in July.
2. In my *opinion*, a summer birthday is great.
3. The signs *indicate* that the road is closed.
4. The coach will *evaluate* all the players.
5. A good reporter will *verify* facts before putting them in an article.

FLUENCY

Echo Reading: Read a sentence from one of the passages aloud. Then have students echo you by reading the same sentence and trying to read with the same speed and expression as you do.

Invite students to do a timed reading of "The Mysteries of the Maya." Afterwards, have them enter their times on the Words-per-Minute table on page 121 and chart their reading speed on page 122 of the *Introductory Reader*.

Encourage students to listen to "The Mysteries of the Maya." Go to **www.mhreadingbasics.com** to play or download the recording. The recording provides modeled fluency and read-along support.

APPLICATION
Workplace Skill:
Find Fact and Opinion in a Business Survey

Have students read the survey. Remind them that a survey is a workplace document that requests facts and opinions about a product or service. Point out that when responding to survey questions, they should look for words that signal opinions or beliefs to help them understand whether a fact or an opinion is being requested. After students answer the questions, have them think about an experience they have had with a customer service department. Ask them to brainstorm a list of opinion words they could use to describe the experience. This list will come in handy when they do the Write for Work activity.

Write for Work

Remind students that facts include things like names, dates, and times. Tell students to read the instructions for this task carefully to be sure they include all requested information. Encourage them to share their work with a classmate to make sure there is a clear distinction between their facts and their opinions.

PASSKEY

Go to **www.mhreadingbasics.com** and click on the *PassKey* link. Customize instruction for your class using modules from Reading/Language Arts, Levels 1 & 2.

Lesson Plan Introductory Student Edition

Unit 2 Lesson 2.5 pages 110–117

Introduce

READING SKILL

Predict Outcomes

Explain/Model: Explain that when you read, you can use details from the passage and your own experience to predict what will happen next. Have students read aloud the passage about Gracia. Then model predicting what Gracia will do next.

Guided Practice: Have students read the boxed passage. Then work with them to complete the task given in the directions. Discuss why the responses given after the passage are correct. Ask students to make a prediction about what Li will do next.

Teach Lesson Skills

Practice: Have students read the passages. Tell them to use details from the passage and their own knowledge and experience to make predictions about the topic. Discuss the answers to the questions and have students share experiences that helped them make predictions.

Apply: After students answer the questions, have them read their responses aloud to the class. Encourage them to explain how they predicted the outcomes.

Check Up: Have students work in small groups to read the passages and answer the questions. Then check each group's responses with those of other groups in the class.

COMPREHENSION

Make Connections: Encourage students to make connections as they read. Provide self-questioning models, such as *Have I learned something about this topic before? What was the context? Have I had any experiences in my own life that relate to this topic?* When students relate what they are reading to their own lives and educational experience, they consciously monitor their own comprehension.

Reading Extension

📖 Encourage students to read "Journey to Saturn" on page 73 of the *Introductory Reader*. Use this as an opportunity to teach reading strategies and the lesson reading skill.

ALPHABETICS

Explore Words

Vowel Combinations: Write these words and read them with students, emphasizing the long vowel sound: *pain, play, peel, leap.* Ask volunteers to circle the letters that stand for the long vowel sound.

Consonant Pairs *wr, kn, gn*: Review the sounds of *wr, kn,* and *gn.* Then have volunteers add a consonant pair to these letters to form a word: *-ap, -ome, -ow, desi-, -ite.* Have students read the completed words aloud.

Synonyms: Remind students that synonyms are words that have the same or similar meanings. Write *mild, moist, cautious,* and *smart* on the board. Have volunteers suggest as many synonyms as they can for each word.

VOCABULARY

Academic Vocabulary/Tier 2

predict prior outcome adjust logical

Before students complete the activity, write the academic vocabulary words and definitions on the board. Discuss each word's meaning with students. Then write the sentences below on the board. Read each sentence aloud and discuss it with students.

1. The dark clouds help me *predict* it will rain.

2. *Prior* to becoming a principal, Dr. Jones was a teacher.

3. The *outcome* of the meeting is that plans for a community center will go forward.

4. Cruz can *adjust* the straps on his backpack.

5. April decided it would be *logical* to carpool to work.

FLUENCY

Marked Phrase Reading: Mark a passage with phrase boundaries, showing how words should be grouped for meaning and emphasis. Read the passage aloud, and then read aloud together with students.

Invite students to do a timed reading of "Journey to Saturn." Afterwards, have them enter their times on the Words-per-Minute table on page 121 and chart their reading speed on page 122 of the *Introductory Reader*.

🔊 Encourage students to listen to "Journey to Saturn." Go to **www.mhreadingbasics.com** to play or download the recording. The recording provides modeled fluency and read-along support.

APPLICATION

Workplace Skill:

Predict Outcomes from Employee Guidelines

Have students read the employee handbook section. Remind them that an employee handbook is a workplace document that provides guidelines for employees. Point out that making predictions about what will happen if an employee does certain things can help them better understand the reasons for the guidelines. After students answer the questions, have them make a two-column chart that lists times when it would and would not be acceptable to use a cell phone. This list will come in handy when they do the Write for Work activity.

Write for Work

Remind students that a letter or e-mail to a manager should be written in a professional tone. Tell them to read the instructions to be sure they include all the requested information. Encourage classmates to share their work and check that the suggestions are appropriate.

PASSKEY

🔘 Go to **www.mhreadingbasics.com** and click on the *PassKey* link. Customize instruction for your class using modules from Reading/Language Arts, Levels 1 & 2.

Lesson Plan Introductory Student Edition

Unit 2 Lesson 2.6 pages 118–125

Introduce	**READING SKILL** **Read Maps** **Explain /Model:** Have students read aloud the first paragraph. Discuss maps that you have found useful and have students talk about maps they have used in their lives. **Guided Practice:** Have students read the map. Then work with them to complete the task given in the directions. Model using the map scale if needed. Discuss why the responses given are correct.

Practice: Have students read the map. Tell them to use the key and the coordinates to answer the questions. Discuss the answers to the questions and have students demonstrate how they used the scale and coordinates to answer the questions.

Apply: After students answer the questions, have them read their responses aloud to the class. Encourage them to show classmates how they used the map to find the answers.

Check Up: Have students work in small groups to read the map and answer the questions. Then check each group's responses with those of other groups in the class.

COMPREHENSION

Visualize: Encourage students to use sensory imaging as a mental tool when they read. Provide useful self-questioning models, such as *What do I see in this photo? Does this diagram help me understand the text? Can I form a mental image of what the author is describing?* When students visualize what they are reading, they consciously monitor their own comprehension.

Teach Lesson Skills

ALPHABETICS

Explore Words

***r*-Controlled Vowels:** Read the following words aloud: *park, pick, pork, pack, perk, peach, purr.* Have students raise their hands when they hear a word with the *r*-controlled vowel sound.

Antonyms: Have students work with a partner to give antonyms for these words: *clean, strong, sweet, kind, boring.* Have one partner say a word and ask the other partner to say an antonym. Then have them switch roles.

Spelling: Homophones: Explain that homophones are words that sound the same but are spelled differently and have different meanings. Share these homophone pairs: *weak/week, pail/pale, red/read, close/clothes.* Discuss the meaning of each word and have volunteers use the words in sentences.

VOCABULARY

Academic Vocabulary/Tier 2

key physical feature symbol area

Before students complete the activity, write the academic vocabulary words and definitions on the board. Discuss each word's meaning with students. Then write the sentences below on the board. Read each sentence aloud and discuss it with students.

1. According to the *key* on this map, a box of popcorn stands for a place to buy snacks.
2. The *physical* map shows a nearby lake.
3. A sun roof is one *feature* you can get on a car.
4. The *symbol* for poison is a skull and crossbones.
5. The *area* of the park closest to the lake has picnic tables.

FLUENCY

Collaborative Reading: Gather in a group. Have each student read one or more lines of a passage and then pass the text to the next student. Supply pronunciation and phrasing corrections as needed.

APPLICATION

Workplace Skill:

Read a Store Map

Explain that a store map tells you where to find departments in a store. After students read the map and answer the questions, have them practice using the map with a partner to give directions from one part of the store to another. This activity will come in handy when they do the Write for Work activity.

Write for Work

Remind students that good directions give the simplest route from one point to another. Encourage them to read their directions aloud as a partner follows along with the map to check that the directions are clear and correct.

Workplace Extension

Remind students that the way they dress for work affects the way people perceive them. Have them review the passage about Chantal and her coworker Sharon. Discuss how Sharon's way of dressing might affect people's impression of her. Have partners discuss the questions and share their responses with the class.

PASSKEY

Go to **www.mhereadingbasics.com** and click on the *PassKey* link. Customize instruction for your class using modules from Reading/Language Arts, Levels 1 & 2.

Lesson Plan Introductory Student Edition

Unit 3 Lesson 3.1 pages 134–141

Introduce

READING SKILL

Identify Sequence

Explain/Model: Explain that writers use time order to show the order of events or steps. Then have students read aloud the passage about Manjira, paying attention to words that signal time order. Model describing Manjira's actions in order, using signal words. Then have students read the steps for using a fax machine. Point out that the steps must be done in a certain order for the machine to work.

Guided Practice: Have students read the boxed passage. Then work with them to complete the task given in the directions. Discuss why the responses given after the passage are correct. Ask volunteers to rewrite or retell the steps as numbered directions.

Teach Lesson Skills

Practice: Have students read the passages. Tell students to look for signal words that help them understand the order of steps or events. Discuss the answers to the questions and have students point out the signal words in the passages that helped them put the information in the correct order.

Apply: After students complete the graphic organizer, have them share their responses with the class. Encourage them to explain to classmates how they determined the correct order for the details.

Check Up: Have students work in small groups to read the passage and answer the questions. Then check each group's responses with those of other groups in the class.

COMPREHENSION

Look for Context Clues/Read On: Encourage students to look for context clues as they read. Investigating the context helps a reader to put words and paragraphs into a larger framework. Provide helpful self-questioning models, such as *What words surrounding this difficult word can help me understand it better? If I read a little farther, might I find additional clues that can help me understand?* When students proactively look for context clues, they consciously monitor their own comprehension.

Reading Extension

📖 Encourage students to read "Separate Lives" on page 81 of the *Introductory Reader*. Use this as an opportunity to teach reading strategies and the lesson reading skill.

ALPHABETICS

Explore Words

r-Controlled Vowels: Write these word pairs and have students identify the word in each pair with the *r*-controlled vowel: *fist/first, bird/bid, nut/nurse, turn/time.*

Letters *x* and *qu*: Write these words and read each one aloud: *exit, exhaust, axis, exert.* Have students tell whether the *x* stands for /ks/ or /gz/. Then write these words and read each one aloud: *quick, unique, boutique, quiet.* Have students tell whether the *qu* stands for /kw/ or /k/.

Context Clues: Write the following sentence: *We know Riva was contrite because she replaced the torn kite and said she was sorry.* Ask students to identify words that can help them define *contrite*.

VOCABULARY

Academic Vocabulary/Tier 2

sequence purpose relate order directions

Before students complete the activity, write the academic vocabulary words and definitions on the board. Discuss each word's meaning with students. Then write the sentences below on the board. Read each sentence aloud and discuss it with students.

1. Follow the steps in the correct *sequence*.
2. The *purpose* of the shopping trip was to buy new boots.
3. Celine enjoys reading books that *relate* to her life.
4. The students in the class lined up in *order* from shortest to tallest.
5. The *directions* at the top of the worksheet describe the activity.

FLUENCY

Echo Reading: Read a sentence from one of the passages aloud. Then have students echo you by reading the same sentence and trying to read with the same speed and expression as you do.

Invite students to do a timed reading of "Separate Lives." Afterwards, have them enter their times on the Words-per-Minute table on page 121 and chart their reading speed on page 122 of the *Introductory Reader*.

📶 Encourage students to listen to "Separate Lives." Go to **www.mhereadingbasics.com** to play or download the recording. The recording provides modeled fluency and read-along support.

APPLICATION

Workplace Skill:

Recognize Sequence in a Safety Procedure

Have students read the factory safety procedure. Remind them that procedures are steps for completing an activity or process. Signal words or numbers can help employees recognize the order of the steps or events. After students answer the questions, have them tell a partner how to use the fire extinguisher. This exercise will come in handy when they do the Write for Work activity.

Write for Work

Remind students that signal words can help them recognize what to do first, next, and last. Tell them to list the steps for using a fire extinguisher. Ask pairs of students to share their lists and check that all steps are included and clear.

PASSKEY

🖱 Go to **www.mhereadingbasics.com** and click on the *PassKey* link. Customize instruction for your class using modules from Reading/Language Arts, Levels 1 & 2.

Lesson Plan Introductory Student Edition

Introduce

READING SKILL
Compare and Contrast

Explain/Model: Explain that comparing means telling how things are alike and contrasting means telling how they are different. Point out the lists of words that writers use to signal comparison and contrast. Then have students read aloud the passage about plants, noting the signal words. Model explaining the contrast the writer is making in the paragraph.

Guided Practice: Have students read the boxed passage, noting ways that plants and animals are alike and different. Then work with students to complete the task given in the directions. Discuss why the responses given after the passage are correct. Ask students to tell two ways plants and animals are alike and two ways they are different.

Practice: Have students read the passages. Tell students to look for words that signal comparison and contrast. Discuss the answers to the questions and have students point out signal words in the passages.

Apply: After students complete the graphic organizer and answer the questions, have them read their responses aloud to the class. Encourage them to show classmates what signal words they used to determine similarities and differences.

Check Up: Have students work in small groups to read the passage and answer the questions. Then check each group's responses with those of other groups in the class.

Teach Lesson Skills

COMPREHENSION

Reread/Read More Slowly: Encourage students to become aware of the pace at which they read. Offer self-questioning models, such as *Did I read this passage too quickly? Does reading again help me understand better? Does reading more slowly help me retain information?* When students actively consider the manner in which they are reading, they consciously monitor their own comprehension.

Reading Extension

📖 Encourage students to read "Together Again after 50 Years" on page 89 of the *Introductory Reader*. Use this as an opportunity to teach reading strategies and the lesson reading skill.

ALPHABETICS
Explore Words

Long *i* and Long *o*: Review that the letter *i* alone can stand for the long *i* sound and the letter *o* alone can stand for the long *o* sound. Write *fin/find, boss/bolt, ring/grind,* and *cod/cold*. Have volunteers circle the word with the long vowel sound in each pair. Then read the words aloud together.

Spelling: Homophones: Write these homophone pairs: *whole/hole, weight/wait, bored/board*. Have students define each word. Then ask volunteers to use the words in sentences.

Vowel Combinations: Read aloud the examples with students, and challenge volunteers to provide other examples with the same spelling.

VOCABULARY
Academic Vocabulary/Tier 2

compare   contrast   respond   method   rare

Before students complete the activity, write the academic vocabulary words and definitions on the board. Discuss each word's meaning with students. Then write the sentences below on the board. Read each sentence aloud and discuss it with students.

1. Chin Ho test-drove three cars to *compare* them before choosing one.
2. Some people enjoy the *contrast* between sweet and sour in their food.
3. Isla will *respond* to her friend's e-mail tonight.
4. Boiling is one *method* of cooking potatoes.
5. The diamond is very valuable because it is so *rare*.

FLUENCY

Partner Reading: Have partners read aloud to one another and/or read aloud at the same time. Encourage them to offer support and correction to one another. Circulate to offer guidance as needed.

Invite students to do a timed reading of "Together Again after 50 Years." Afterwards, have them enter their times on the Words-per-Minute table on page 121 and chart their reading speed on page 122 of the *Introductory Reader*.

🔊 Encourage students to listen to "Together Again after 50 Years." Go to **www.mhreadingbasics.com** to play or download the recording. The recording provides modeled fluency and read-along support.

APPLICATION
Workplace Skill:
Compare and Contrast Information in a Table

Tell students that it is important to read the title and the column headings of a table before reading the data so that they know what is being compared or classified. After students read the table and answer the questions, have them make a list of which countries had the most jobs in each sector and which ones had the least. This information will be useful when they do the Write for Work activity.

Write for Work

Remind students to read the column heads so that they know what kind of information is being presented. Tell them to make sure that they compare and contrast the information for each sector. Encourage them to compare their answers with a partner to be sure that they interpreted the table correctly.

PASSKEY

💻 Go to **www.mhreadingbasics.com** and click on the *Passkey* link. Customize instruction for your class using modules from Reading/Language Arts, Levels 1 & 2.

Lesson Plan Introductory Student Edition

Unit 3 Lesson 3.3 pages 150–157

Introduce

READING SKILL

Identify Author's Purpose

Explain/Model: Explain the different purposes for writing, and point out that when reading a passage, asking questions can help students better understand what they read. *Why did the author write this? What did I learn?* Then have students read aloud the passage about butter. Model answering the sample questions to determine that the author's purpose is to explain how to make butter.

Guided Practice: Have students read the boxed passage. Then work with them to complete the task given in the directions. Discuss why the responses given after the passage are correct. Ask students to give one detail from the passage that shows that the purpose is to inform.

Teach Lesson Skills

Practice: Have students read the passages. Tell students to ask themselves questions as they read to help them determine the author's purpose. Discuss the answers to the questions and have students explain what information or details in the passages helped them determine each passage's purpose.

Apply: After students answer the questions, have them read their responses aloud to the class. Encourage them to show classmates the details or information that helped them determine and evaluate the purpose of each passage.

Check Up: Have students work in small groups to read the passages and answer the questions. Then check each group's responses with those of other groups in the class.

COMPREHENSION

Make Connections: Encourage students to make connections as they read. Provide self-questioning models, such as *Have I learned something about this topic before? What was the context? Have I had any experiences in my own life that relate to this topic?* When students relate what they are reading to their own lives and educational experience, they consciously monitor their own comprehension.

Reading Extension

Encourage students to read "A Special Kind of Horse Power" on page 97 in the *Introductory Reader*. Use this as an opportunity to teach reading strategies and the lesson reading skill.

ALPHABETICS

Explore Words

Vowel Combinations: Point out that the vowel pair *oi* usually appears in the middle of a word and the vowel pair *oy* usually appears at the end. Write *sp--l, t--, f--l*. Have students complete the words with the correct vowel pair.

Syllables: Write these words, with the slash indicating syllable division: *sta/ble, wob/ble, no/ble, lit/tle, can/dle*. Model identifying the first syllable as open or closed. Then blend the two syllables together to read the word aloud.

Prefixes *pre-, in-*: Write these words: *view, decisive, pay*. Have a volunteer add *pre-* or *in-* to each word and then tell what it means. *(preview, indecisive, prepay)*

VOCABULARY

Academic Vocabulary/Tier 2

events   intention   explain   minor   persuade

Before students complete the activity, write the academic vocabulary words and definitions on the board. Discuss each word's meaning with students. Then write the sentences below on the board. Read each sentence aloud and discuss it with students.

1. The fair has *events* for people of all ages.
2. It was never my *intention* to hurt your feelings.
3. Please *explain* these directions to me.
4. The *minor* character in the play had no lines.
5. Can I *persuade* you to share your recipe?

FLUENCY

Collaborative Reading: Gather in a group. Have each student read one or more lines of a passage and then pass the text to the next student. Supply pronunciation and phrasing corrections as needed.

Invite students to do a timed reading of "A Special Kind of Horse Power." Afterwards, have them enter their times on the Words-per-Minute table on page 121 and chart their reading speed on page 122 of the *Introductory Reader*.

Encourage students to listen to "A Special Kind of Horse Power." Go to **www.mhreadingbasics.com** to play or download the recording. The recording provides modeled fluency and read-along support.

APPLICATION

Workplace Skill:

Identify Author's Purpose in a Memo

Have students read the memo. Remind them that a memo is a workplace document that sends a message to one or more persons. Point out that the memo's format can make it easier to determine the author's purpose. For example, the subject line will often provide a clue to the purpose of the memo. After students answer the questions, have them start a list of important details that need to be included in a good memo. This list will come in handy when they do the Write for Work activity.

Write for Work

Remind students which important details are needed in a good memo. Tell them to read the instructions for this task carefully to be sure they include all the requested information. Encourage them to share their work with a classmate and ask one another for suggestions about ways to make the memo clearer.

PASSKEY

Go to **www.mhreadingbasics.com** and click on the *PassKey* link. Customize instruction for your class using modules from Reading/Language Arts, Levels 1 & 2.

Introduce

READING SKILL

Use Graphs

Explain/Model: Explain that when looking at a graph, it is important to first read the title and the axis labels carefully. Then have students read aloud these elements of the graph about the runners. Model figuring out how many runners there are in each age group.

Guided Practice: Have students read the graph about amendments to the Constitution. Then work with them to complete the task given in the directions. Discuss why the responses given about the graph are correct.

Practice: Have students read the graph about time used for soccer practice. Tell them to read the title and the axis labels to determine what information the graph shows. Discuss the answers to the questions and have students point to places on the graph that support their answers to the questions.

Apply: After students answer the questions, have them read their responses aloud to the class. Encourage them to show classmates where they found the information on the graphs to answer each question.

Check Up: Have students work in small groups to read the graphs and answer the questions. Then check each group's responses with those of other groups in the class.

Teach Lesson Skills

COMPREHENSION

Visualize: Encourage students to use sensory imaging as a mental tool when they read. Provide useful self-questioning models, such as *What do I see in this photo? Does this diagram help me understand the text? Can I form a mental image of what the author is describing?* When students visualize what they are reading, they consciously monitor their own comprehension.

Reading Extension

📖 Encourage students to read "Racing through the Pain" on page 105 of the *Introductory Reader*. Use this as an opportunity to teach reading strategies and the lesson reading skill.

ALPHABETICS

Explore Words

Vowel Combinations: Write these words and read them with students, emphasizing the vowel sound: *cause, paws, pounce, around, vow.* Ask volunteers to circle the letters that stand for the vowel sound.

Syllables: Write these words in two different ways: *ca/bin, cab/in; ra/ven, rav/en; li/mit, lim/it; bi/son, bis/on.* Pronounce the words both ways with students and have volunteers circle the word in each pair that is divided correctly.

Spelling: Suffixes *-able, -er.* Model adding suffixes: *excite + able, run + er, rely + able; taste + er; like + able.* Ask volunteers to point out any spelling changes. Then discuss the meaning of each new word.

VOCABULARY

Academic Vocabulary/Tier 2

graph   data   illustrate   label   estimate

Before students complete the activity, write the academic vocabulary words and definitions on the board. Discuss each word's meaning with students. Then write the sentences below on the board. Read each sentence aloud and discuss it with students.

1. The *graph* showed the most popular ice cream flavors.
2. The *data* shows that exercise and diet are important in helping people lose weight.
3. Shanira added a diagram to her report to *illustrate* the water cycle.
4. The *label* showed the soup ingredients.
5. I *estimate* that about 200 people attended the job fair.

FLUENCY

Repeated Reading: Lead a group to read the same passage aloud together several times. As the leader, emphasize accuracy and phrasing until the group reading sounds smooth and consistent.

Invite students to do a timed reading of "Racing through the Pain." Afterwards, have them enter their times on the Words-per-Minute table on page 121 and chart their reading speed on page 122 of the *Introductory Reader*.

🔊 Encourage students to listen to "Racing through the Pain." Go to **www.mhreadingbasics.com** to play or download the recording. The recording provides modeled fluency and read-along support.

APPLICATION

Workplace Skill:

Use Graphs in a Business Environment

Remind students that graphs are often used in business meetings, presentations, and documents to show and compare information in a clear, visual way. Point out that to understand what is being compared and contrasted, it is important to read the title and axis labels and to know the scale. After students read the graphs and answer the questions, have them list the four revenue categories and the percentages and dollar amounts for each. This list will come in handy when they do the Write for Work activity.

Write for Work

Remind students to use the title, labels, and data to interpret the graphs correctly. Tell them to make sure they include information for all four revenue categories. Encourage them to share their work with a classmate to double-check that they interpreted the graphs correctly.

PASSKEY

💻 Go to **www.mhreadingbasics.com** and click on the *PassKey* link. Customize instruction for your class using modules from Reading/Language Arts, Levels 1 & 2.

Lesson Plan Introductory Student Edition

Introduce

READING SKILL

Read Signs

Explain/Model: Point out that many of the signs we see in our everyday world have symbols and pictures. Have students look at the examples of signs in the middle of the page. Model using the pictures and letters to figure out the meaning of each sign.

Guided Practice: Have students look at the signs. Then work with students to complete the task given in the directions. Discuss why the responses given about the signs are correct. Ask students to give examples of other signs that commonly have the "no" symbol, such as "no smoking" signs.

Practice: Have students look at the signs. Tell them to think about what the pictures or symbols on each sign might mean. Discuss the answers to the questions and have students point out the details on the signs that support their answers.

Apply: After students answer the questions, have them read their responses aloud to the class. Encourage them to point out details on the signs that helped them answer the questions.

Check Up: Have students work in small groups to look at the signs and answer the questions. Then check each group's responses with those of other groups in the class.

Teach Lesson Skills

COMPREHENSION

Make Connections: Encourage students to make connections as they read. Provide self-questioning models, such as *Have I learned something about this topic before? What was the context? Have I had any experiences in my own life that relate to this topic?* When students relate what they are reading to their own lives and educational experience, they consciously monitor their own comprehension.

Reading Extension

Encourage students to read "In the Face of Danger" on page 113 of the *Introductory Reader*. Use this as an opportunity to teach reading strategies and the lesson reading skill.

ALPHABETICS

Explore Words

Vowel Combinations: Write these words and read them with students, emphasizing the vowel sound: *book, tool, look, cook, cool, school*. Ask which words have the vowel sound they hear in *took* and which have the vowel sound they hear in *pool*.

Base Words: Write these words: *unlikely, redo, careful, thoughtless*. Have volunteers underline the base words.

Spelling: Possessives: Remind students that *'s* is used to show that something belongs to someone or something and *s'* shows that it belongs to more than one person or thing. Discuss these example phrases: *the shoes of Keisha/Keisha's shoes, the boats of the two brothers/the two brothers' boats*.

VOCABULARY

Academic Vocabulary/Tier 2

communicate   concrete   abstract
correspond   examine

Before students complete the activity, write the academic vocabulary words and definitions on the board. Discuss each word's meaning with students. Then write the sentences below on the board. Read each sentence aloud and discuss it with students.

1. My aunt and I *communicate* by e-mail.
2. I need *concrete* details to plan the party.
3. What is the meaning of the *abstract* painting?
4. In a code, a number can *correspond* to a letter of the alphabet.
5. The doctor will *examine* Mia to find out why she has a cough.

FLUENCY

Marked Phrase Reading: Mark a passage with phrase boundaries, showing how words should be grouped for meaning and emphasis. Read the passage aloud, having students follow along, and then read aloud together with students.

Invite students to do a timed reading of "In the Face of Danger." Afterwards, have them enter their times on the Words-per-Minute table on page 121 and chart their reading speed on page 122 of the *Introductory Reader*.

Encourage students to listen to "In the Face of Danger." Go to **www.mhreadingbasics.com** to play or download the recording. The recording provides modeled fluency and read-along support.

APPLICATION

Workplace Skill:

Use Signs in the Workplace

Have students read the signs. Remind them that signs in the workplace help people do their jobs. They may provide directions, safety information, or specific instructions. Tell students to pay close attention to the information posted on signs in the workplace. After students answer the questions, have them start brainstorming signs that might be helpful in an office or other place of work. This list will come in handy when they do the Write for Work activity.

Write for Work

Remind students that signs can give safety information, directions, or show where things are located. Tell them to read the instructions for this task carefully to be sure they include all the information. Encourage them to share their work with a classmate to make sure they made a complete list of signs.

PASSKEY

Go to **www.mhreadingbasics.com** and click on the *PassKey* link. Customize instruction for your class using modules from Reading/Language Arts, Levels 1 & 2.

Lesson Plan Introductory Student Edition

Introduce

READING SKILL
Use a Dictionary

Explain/Model: Explain that online and print dictionaries are useful for checking the spelling, pronunciation, and meaning of words. Then point out that words in a dictionary are in the order of the alphabet, and use the lists of words on the page to review alphabetical order. Display a dictionary page and help students locate each of the guide words on the page.

Guided Practice: Have students read the words and guide words aloud. Then work with students to match the words with the guide words. Discuss why the responses given are correct. Ask students to explain how they used alphabetical order to match the words with the guide words.

Practice: Have students read the information about pronunciations and then write and match the pronunciations. Tell them to think about what the symbols in the pronunciations tell them about how to say the words. Discuss the answers to the questions and have students pronounce each word.

Apply: After students answer the questions, have them read their responses aloud to the class. Encourage them to point out the clues in each sentence that helped them choose the definitions.

Check Up: Have students work in small groups to answer the questions. Then check each group's responses with those of other groups in the class.

COMPREHENSION

Clarify Meaning: Encourage students to actively clarify meaning as they read. Provide self-questioning models, such as *What clues can I find in other sentences to help me understand this word? Does this word resemble any other words I have learned? Can I find someone to ask about this?* When students proactively try to clarify meaning, they consciously monitor their own comprehension.

Teach Lesson Skills

ALPHABETICS
Explore Words

Consonant Pairs: Write these words, underlining as shown: *thumb, knot, science, write, limb, know, scene.* Read the words aloud and ask students to identify the sound made by the underlined letters. Then have them identify the silent letter in each pair.

Spelling: Contractions: Write these contractions: *aren't, doesn't, wouldn't, we're, you're.* Have volunteers tell what words each contraction stands for. Then have them write contractions for *is not, could not,* and *they are.*

Multiple-Meaning Words: Help students identify different meanings for *feet, kind, show,* and *spring.* Then ask them to use the words in context sentences.

VOCABULARY
Academic Vocabulary/Tier 2

abbreviate arrange list define represent

Before students complete the activity, write the academic vocabulary words and definitions on the board. Discuss each word's meaning with students. Then write the sentences below on the board. Read each sentence aloud and discuss it with students.

1. You can *abbreviate* "Mister" by writing "Mr."

2. Arlene likes to *arrange* flowers in vases.

3. I try to *list* everything I need to buy at the store.

4. You can use other words in the sentence to help you *define* a word you don't understand.

5. Eagles *represent* freedom to many people.

FLUENCY
Collaborative Reading: Gather in a group. Have each student read one or more lines of a passage and then pass the text to the next student. Supply pronunciation and phrasing corrections as needed.

APPLICATION
Workplace Skill:

Use a Dictionary When Writing a Résumé

Have students read the résumé. Remind them that a résumé summarizes a person's skills and work experiences. Point out that using the right words in a résumé and spelling them correctly will help make a positive first impression, so it's wise to consult a dictionary to make sure all the words are correct. After students answer the questions, have them start a list of education, skills, and work experience they would include in their own résumé. This list will come in handy when they do the Write for Work activity.

Write for Work

Remind students that a good résumé includes information about a person's education, skills, and work experience. It should also include contact information so that the employer knows how to get in touch with the applicant. Tell students to read the instructions for this task carefully to be sure they include all the information. Encourage partners to proofread each other's work.

Workplace Extension

Remind students that a job that's right for them will most likely be one that matches their skills, experience, and interests. Have them review the passage about Jenny Rodriguez. Discuss how Jenny might go about starting to find a job in which she is interested. Have partners respond to the questions and share their responses with the class.

PASSKEY

Go to **www.mhereadingbasics.com** and click on the *PassKey* link. Customize instruction for your class using modules from Reading/Language Arts, Levels 1 & 2.

Unit 1 Workplace Skill Activity
Role-play Handling an Upset Customer

Working with customers is a big part of many jobs. Sometimes customers will be upset. They may not like a product. They may not like the help they got. Customers are important to a business. You will need to find a way to make them happy when they come to you with a problem.

Here are six steps for handling an upset customer:

1. Listen carefully. Make sure you understand the problem.
2. Respond to your customer's mood. If he or she is angry, acknowledge his or her anger.
3. Show your customer that you understand the problem. For example, say something like, "I understand that this mix-up is causing a problem for you."
4. Promise to try to fix the problem.
5. Explain how you will try to fix the problem.
6. Thank the customer for his or her business.

Read the passage about an unhappy customer. Work with a partner to answer the questions about his problem below the box. Then role-play the situation.

> Henry's check-engine light was on. He brought his car to Mr. Auto and waited while it was fixed. Then he paid the bill. On his way home, the check-engine light came back on. Now Henry is back at Mr. Auto. He is upset and wants his car fixed now.

1. What problem does Henry have?

   _____

2. What will you say to show you understand the problem?

   _____

3. What will you say to Henry about how you will fix the problem?

   _____

4. What will you say to thank Henry?

   _____

After you role-play, write about what happened.

_____

_____

_____

Unit 2 Workplace Skill Activity
Make a Flyer with Workplace Break-room Rules

At a job, you will work with others. You may have a personal space, such as a desk and a chair. You may have a computer of your own and desk items. However, you will also share public spaces and some supplies. One of these places is usually the break room or kitchen. When spaces or supplies are shared, you should do the following:

- Label things that belong to you.
- Ask before using other people's things.
- Put things back in the same place and in the same condition that you found them.
- Keep shared spaces clean and organized.

With a partner, list things people should and should not do when using the workplace break room or kitchen. Then use your list to make a flyer with rules that you can post in the break room or kitchen.

Do	Do Not

Name_____ Date _____

Unit 3 Workplace Skill Activity
Role-play Responding to a Request to Work Overtime

Supervisors will sometimes ask workers to put in overtime. Many workers like the chance to earn extra money. When overtime comes up unexpectedly, however, it can create scheduling conflicts.

Sometimes, an emergency situation arises at work. A worker is suddenly asked to cover a shift. A tight deadline must be met. Extra hours may be needed. Other times, a manager may just want to get ahead of schedule. When presented with a request to work overtime, the employee should weigh the needs of the business with his or her personal commitments.

Read the passage about an employee who is asked to work overtime. Work with a partner to answer the questions below the box. Then role-play the conversation between the employee and her boss.

> Prianka's boss, Gabe, asks her to stay a few hours late. He wants to get work done for next week's inventory. Prianka often likes to work overtime and make extra money. Today she has to pick up her children from school. They are not old enough to stay home by themselves. Prianka sometimes asks a neighbor to pick up her children. The neighbor, however, likes to plan ahead. Prianka would like to show her boss that she cares about her job. She also needs to take care of her children.

1. What is Prianka's problem?

   _____

2. Is the overtime request an emergency situation? Why or why not?

   _____

3. List three options Prianka has in this situation.

   _____

   _____

   _____

4. Choose the best option and explain why you chose it.

   _____

After you role-play, write about what happened.

   _____

   _____

Answer Key Introductory Student Edition

Unit 1 Lesson 1.1

Practice, page 15
1. C	3. C	5. C	7. D
2. J	4. G	6. F	8. G

Apply, page 16
Sample answers:
1. It was held in New York City.
2. It was held in 1964.
3. It weighed more than 34,000 pounds.
4. It was too big for a car or plane.
5. It can taste five flavors.
6. It has taste buds.
7. They react to matter in food.
8. They send signals to the brain.

Check Up, page 17
1. B	3. A	5. A	7. B
2. J	4. G	6. J	8. H

Workplace Skill, page 18
1. B	2. G

Write for Work, page 19
Check that students' writing follows this guideline: The memo is in a correct format and includes all of the key points needed to convey the message of the memo.

Reading Extension, page 19
1. B	2. G	3. C	4. G

5. *Sample answers:* You can't get it by hugging. You can't get it by kissing.
6. *Sample answers:* Nkosi wasn't afraid to speak out about AIDS. Nkosi fought to go to school.

Explore Words, page 20
Short Vowels
1. Jen	4. dropped
2. lap	5. run
3. wig	6. skip

Consonant Blends
2. gl	4. dr	6. st	8. nk
3. gr	5. nk	7. st	

Synonyms
1. sad, unhappy
2. small, little
3. shut, closed
4. speak, talk

Page 21
Spelling: Possessives
2. Farid's family
3. the professor's book
4. Grace's laptop
5. Tam's hat
6. Nuri's birthday
7. my uncle's car
8. the neighbor's mail
9. Lise's notebook
10. Yasir's sweater

Academic Vocabulary
1. recall	4. topic
2. passage	5. describe
3. details	

Unit 1 Lesson 1.2

Practice, page 23
1. stated	8. not stated
2. stated	9. stated
3. stated	10. not stated
4. not stated	11. stated
5. stated	12. not stated
6. stated	13. stated
7. stated	14. not stated

Apply, page 24
Sample answers:
1. They did not have sound. They did not tell a story.
2. not stated
3. *The Life of an American Fireman*
4. A runner got tackled and threw the ball.
5. Knute Rockne
6. not stated

Check Up, page 25
1. C	3. D	5. B
2. F	4. H	6. G

Workplace Skill, page 26
1. A	2. J

3. Call the copy service number, which is posted above the copier.

Write for Work, page 27
Check that the writing includes the following points: The writing contains a clear stated concept for how to use the appliance. The three rules support the stated concept.

Reading Extension, page 27
1. A	2. J	3. A

4. It caused sores to form on her skin.
5. in Barbados, in the West Indies

Explore Words, page 28
Short and Long Vowels
1. long	5. long
2. long	6. long
3. long	7. short
4. short	8. long

Consonant Pairs
2. ch	5. ch	8. th
3. th	6. th	9. ch
4. ch	7. ch	10. th

Page 29
Spelling: Contractions
1. it's	3. didn't
2. wasn't	4. let's

Antonyms
1. winter	3. tall
2. close	4. finish

Academic Vocabulary
1. directly	4. legal
2. notes	5. concept
3. stated	

Unit 1 Lesson 1.3

Practice, page 31
1. B
2. J
3. valid

Sample answers:
4. Birds rest in the warm parts of the day to keep cool.
5. Dogs and cats do not have as many ways to release heat as do birds.

Answer Key Introductory Student Edition

Apply, page 32
Sample answers:
1. A butterfly eats liquid foods.
2. People enjoyed watching London act.
3. They wanted to be like him.
4. If spiders suddenly disappeared, bugs might eat many of our crops.

Check Up, page 33
1. C   3. B   5. C
2. F   4. J

Workplace Skill, page 34
1. C   3. C
2. H   4. G

Write for Work, page 35
Check that the writing includes the following points: The writer understands that for an interview you should dress appropriately, arrive on time, and shut off your cell phone. The chart should separate things to do and things to avoid in separate columns or rows.

Reading Extension, page 35
1. B
2. J
3. *Sample answer:* She was frightened of getting caught.
4. *Sample answer:* He gave in to pressure from other people.

Explore Words, page 36
Long Vowels with Silent e
1. cane   4. ride
2. pale   5. grade
3. fine   6. plane

Consonant Pairs
1. ph   3. sh   5. wh
2. sh   4. wh   6. sh

Compound Words
2. bed   time
3. sun   flower
4. bath   tub
5. rain   coat
6. snow   storm
7. play   ground
8. wheel   chair

Page 37
Context Clues
1. necessary
2. emergency
3. simple; fancy
4. active; inactive

Academic Vocabulary
1. invalid   4. supported
2. conclude   5. conclusions
3. valid

Unit 1 Lesson 1.4

Practice, page 39
1. A   3. B
2. G   4. J

Apply, page 40
Sample answers:
1. Weeds in a garden are bad for plants. Weeds use up the water that plants need, and some can strangle plants.
2. The oldest diamond in the world was owned by the king of Persia in the 1700s. The king called it Kohinoor, which means "mountain of light."
3. Snakes use their tongues to smell. They stick out their tongues often, catching smells out of the air and bringing them to their mouths.
4. A servant named Nizam saved the king of India from drowning. The king was grateful and rewarded Nizam. He made him king for six hours.

Check Up, page 41
1. D
2. H
3. B

Workplace Skill, page 42
1. C
2. F

Write for Work, page 43
Check that the writing includes the following points: The writer has paraphrased the four hints in his or her own words and has included the main idea and some supporting detail. Then the writer has summarized five ads he or she has found.

Reading Extension, page 43
1. D
2. F
3. *Sample answer:* When Todd Beamer couldn't reach his family, he talked to a phone company official named Lisa Jefferson instead. He told her about the planned attack on the terrorists, and he asked her to tell his family he loved them.
4. *Sample answer:* Everyone on the plane died, but the passengers' brave actions saved hundreds of people on the ground from being killed.

Explore Words, page 44
Long Vowels
1. rode   4. slide
2. globe   5. code
3. tube   6. pine

Consonant Pairs
1. wr   4. kn
2. kn   5. kn
3. wr   6. gn

Spelling: Possessives
2. Yow's home
3. the teacher's story
4. the child's coat
5. Amari's sister

Page 45
Spelling: Plurals
1. actresses   9. passes
2. trucks   10. hoaxes
3. taxes   11. peaches
4. wishes   12. brushes
5. kitchens   13. wrenches
6. shampoos   14. subways
7. indexes   15. buses
8. skunks   16. classes

Academic Vocabulary
1. paraphrase   4. reinforce
2. summarize   5. summary
3. relevant

Unit 1 Lesson 1.5

Practice, page 47

1. C   3. D   5. B
2. F   4. G   6. H

Apply, page 48

Sample answers:

1. daring, helpful, brave, bold
2. daring, smart, brave, bold
3. creative, artistic
4. smart, creative
5. creative, smart, artistic
6. daring, wise, smart, brave, helpful
7. thoughtful
8. heroic
9. caring
10. angry
11. nurturing
12. thoughtful
13. timid
14. lazy

Check Up, page 49

1. B   3. A   5. A   7. B
2. G   4. F   6. H   8. F

Workplace Skill, page 50

1. B   2. J

Write for Work, page 51

Check that the writing includes the following points: The character traits should match the skill requirements for a child-care helper: responsible and patient, likes working with children and infants, experienced in child care.

Reading Extension, page 51

1. C   2. F   3. B
4. *Sample answer:* The strangers were kind, helpful, generous, and unselfish.

Explore Words, page 52

Hard and Soft c

1. hard   7. hard
2. hard   8. hard
3. hard   9. hard
4. soft   10. hard
5. soft   11. soft
6. soft   12. soft

Hard and Soft g

1. soft   7. hard
2. soft   8. hard
3. soft   9. hard
4. soft   10. soft
5. hard   11. hard
6. hard   12. soft

Compound Words

The following are compound words:

1. newspaper   8. wheelchair
2. ashtray   9. bedtime
3. basketball   11. moonbeam
6. baseball

Page 53

Multiple-meaning Words

1. a.   3. a.   5. a.
2. b.   4. b.   6. b.

Academic Vocabulary

1. determine
2. characters
3. traits
4. clues
5. consistently

Unit 1 Lesson 1.6

Practice, page 55

1. nothing
2. Taylor, Arlene
3. A
4. No; it is optional.

Apply, page 56

1. B
2. J
3. You should check one of the boxes to tell which computer course you want to take.
4. check or credit card
5. $95.00

Check Up, page 57

1. the month, day, and year you were born
2. the address of the place where you live now
3. the address of the place where you lived before your current address
4. when you have lived at your current address for less than two years
5. a ZIP code: that is, five numbers that stand for the area where you live
6. a person who owns and rents apartments to others

Workplace Skill, page 58

1. A
2. J
3. if you are not a U.S. citizen

Write for Work, page 59

Check that the writing includes the following points: The format indicates that the writer understands what a form is and its purpose. The form includes space for the required information.

Workplace Extension, page 59

1. B
2. *Sample answer:* He met with the staff at the job center to help him with his cover letter and résumé. He included a list of people he had worked for. He dressed in business attire.
3. *Sample answer:* He should have called his list of references to ask their permission and to let them know they might be called. He should have taken time to practice his responses to questions he might be asked.

Explore Words, page 60

Consonant pairs ck, ng

2. ng   4. ck   6. ck   8. ck
3. ng   5. ck   7. ng

Synonyms and Antonyms

1. A   3. S   5. A
2. S   4. A   6. A

Compound Words

1. birthday   5. blueberry
2. backpack   6. notebook
3. hairbrush   7. grasshopper
4. sunshine   8. bathtub

Page 61

Vowel Combinations
1. sail
2. peach
3. stone
4. coat
5. lame
6. played
7. rainy
8. feed
9. Spain
10. toast
11. jeans
12. sleep
13. tray
14. price
15. fade
16. road
17. peeled
18. note

Academic Vocabulary
1. previous
2. apply
3. form
4. complete
5. headings

Unit 1 Lesson 1.7

Practice, page 63
1. cried
2. tasty
3. married
4. tiring
5. saved
6. knife
7. gnaw
8. wrist
9. wreck
10. meat
11. plane
12. Where
13. son

Apply, page 64
1. sign
2. wrong
3. climb
4. hour
5. knee
6. buy
7. weak
8. right
9. rode
10. through
11. tried
12. bravest
13. merrily
14. giving
15. smoky
16. happier
17. copied
18. staler
19. cheerily
20. freezing
21. whining
22. craziest

Check Up, page 65
1. your
2. living
3. sea
4. pale
5. half
6. comb
7. raking
8. through
9. their
10. leaving
11. caring
12. their
13. loving
14. babies
15. Right
16. moving
17. see
18. made
19. They're
20. great

Workplace Skill, page 66
1. D
2. G
3. They can call the Human Resources Department or schedule an appointment online.

Write for Work, page 67
Check that all words are spelled correctly and that the language is appropriate for addressing coworkers.

Workplace Extension, page 67
1. C
2. G
3. *Sample answer:* She would not have been able to fill out the application at that time. She would have had to come back with the appropriate information.
4. *Sample answers:* passport, driver's license, utility bill

Explore Words, page 68
Long i, *Spelled* -y
The following words should be checked:
3. sky
4. spry
6. try
10. fry
12. pry

Long e, *Spelled* -y
The following words should be checked:
2. shiny
4. dusty
5. lobby
8. pretty
9. navy
11. ugly
12. many

Prefixes
Sample answers:
1. uncertain; I am uncertain about how he feels.
2. unknown; We will visit the tomb of the Unknown Soldier.
3. refill; It's time to refill the gas tank.
4. reread; You should reread something if you don't understand it the first time.

Page 69

Context Clues
Sample answers:
1. sleepy
2. bothered
3. build
4. signed up
5. sad
6. sent to another country
7. guess
8. leaves

Academic Vocabulary
1. context
2. common
3. typically
4. examples
5. pattern

Unit 1 Assessment

pages 71–76
1. B
2. F
3. A
4. J
5. B
6. J
7. C
8. J
9. B
10. G
11. A
12. H
13. D
14. G
15. C
16. H
17. B
18. J
19. A
20. G
21. A
22. H
23. D
24. H
25. B
26. F
27. D
28. G
29. D
30. H
31. B
32. F
33. C
34. J
35. A
36. G
37. B
38. H
39. B
40. J

Unit 1 Workplace Skill Activity

Sample answers:
1. Henry's car was supposedly fixed, but the same problem occurred when he left the repair shop.
2. I'm sorry the problem happened again. I understand how frustrated you must feel.
3. We will try again to fix the problem and make sure the car is working perfectly. You can wait here or we can give you a free rental car to use in the meantime. Then we'll call you.
4. Thank you for your patience. Your business means a lot to us.

After role-playing, the student playing Henry felt reassured by the answers the student playing the Mr. Auto employee gave.

Answer Key Introductory Student Edition

Unit 2 Lesson 2.1

Practice, page 79

1. Crows are clever birds.
2. Their name comes from the large claw of the male crab.
3. Ederle was the first woman to swim across the English Channel.
4. Angora rabbits are a valuable source of fine yarn.

Apply, page 80

Sample answers:

1. People and animals have many ways of communicating.
2. Animals' tails have many uses.
3. Birds eat many things in addition to seeds.
4. Vegans have a healthy diet without eating any animal products.

Check Up, page 81

1. D
2. F
3. C

Workplace Skill, page 82

1. B
2. J
3. Fresh and Fast will give fast and friendly service.

Write for Work, page 83

Check that students' writing follows these guidelines: The topic sentence clearly states the goal of the new company. The details help readers know more about the business.

Reading Extension, page 83

1. C
2. G
3. *Sample answer:* Even though potbellied pigs are different from regular pigs, Carder could not keep Iggy in the city.
4. detail; *sample answer:* Pam and Rick Abma's potbellied pig warned them that their house was on fire.

5. *Sample answer:* She knew Jo Ann was in trouble and was able to get her help, which saved Jo Ann's life.

Explore Words, page 84

Hard and Soft c *and* g

1. k
2. j
3. s
4. g
5. g
6. s
7. j
8. k

Synonyms

1. B
2. H
3. D
4. F

Suffixes -er, -est

1. -er
2. -est
3. -er
4. -est
5. -est
6. -er

page 85

Spelling: Plurals

1. candles
2. batches
3. books
4. cards
5. messes
6. boxes
7. pencils
8. classes
9. ducks
10. rashes
11. wishes
12. taxes
13. patches
14. bats
15. sandwiches
16. rings
17. sodas
18. tables
19. kittens
20. tunes

Academic Vocabulary

1. paragraph
2. identify
3. vary
4. imply
5. restate

Unit 2 Lesson 2.2

Practice, page 87

1. Cause: Hunters hide behind tall grass.
   Effect: Birds can't see them.
2. Cause: Fish swim in large groups.
   Effect: The fish can protect each other.
3. Cause: Tulips were rare in the 1500s.
   Effect: They were worth a lot of money.

4. Cause: The water in the lake froze over.
   Effect: People could walk across the lake.
5. Cause: The baby was crying.
   Effect: The father picked up the baby.
6. Cause: People's stomachs feel full.
   Effect: They stop eating.
7. Cause: It started to rain.
   Effect: The woman opened her umbrella.

Apply, page 88

1. The centers of the trunks of old trees make soft nests because they are rotten.
2. There are fewer than 10,000 groups of red-cockaded woodpeckers left.
3. People want to use pine wood.
4. Giraffes are tall and can see well.
5. The other animals run too.
6. There is less land for animals.
7. Condors are now a protected species.

Check Up, page 89

1. C
2. J
3. C
4. G

Workplace Skill, page 90

1. C
2. F
3. *Sample answer:* Don't try to carry too much equipment up the ladder at once. It is better to make two trips than to strain yourself or drop a heavy object.

Write for Work, page 91

Writers should clearly state three reasons company safety rules are good and include three effects that might happen if these rules are broken.

Answer Key Introductory Student Edition

Reading Extension, page 91

1. B
2. J
3. *Sample answers:* Many wounded men survived. The enemy was not able to use the machine gun against them.
4. *Sample answers:* Rascon's bravery; Rascon's army friends got the army to hear his case again.
5. *Sample answers:* Rascon saved Haffy's life. Haffy went on to get married and have children and grandchildren.

Explore Words, page 92

Consonant Pairs sh, th, ph, ck

1. th
2. sh
3. th
4. sh
5. ph
6. ck

Syllables

1. d. helmet
2. a. denim
3. b. lemon
4. c. onset
5. g. vivid
6. h. tidbit
7. e. campus
8. f. comic
9. 3
10. 1
11. 2
12. 4
13. 2
14. 3
15. 1
16. 4

page 93

Spelling: Word Endings

1. shipping
2. fairest
3. attending
4. scrubbed
5. sharpest
6. gladder
7. fishing
8. shocked
9. petted
10. highest
11. holding
12. poured
13. softer
14. tripped
15. eating
16. louder

Academic Vocabulary

1. cause
2. technique
3. create
4. effect
5. signal

Unit 2 Lesson 2.3

Practice, page 95

1. 10 days
2. Stop taking the drug and see a doctor.
3. You should ask a doctor whether the child should take the drug.
4. No: the label says you should keep this product away from excessive heat.

Apply, page 96

1. $235
2. $235
3. Yes and no: text messages are not included in the $29.99 plan, but 300 talk minutes are included.
4. Fill out the rebate form and mail it in.
5. No: the phone will not work with another company; it will only work with USATalk.
6. No: to get a discounted phone you need to sign up for a two-year contract.

Check Up, page 97

1. A
2. G
3. D
4. G
5. D

Workplace Skill, page 98

1. A
2. G
3. D
4. H

Write for Work, page 99

Check that the writing includes the following points: The letter states that the customer should have received a refund. The letter includes an apology and gives instructions to the customer about how to get the refund.

Reading Extension, page 99

1. B
2. J
3. *Sample answer:* The cars can come off of the track and hit people or objects.

4. *Sample answer:* Some people have weak blood vessels in their brains, which could start to bleed at any time (not only on a roller coaster).

Explore Words, page 100

Long Vowels

1. chute, rule
2. smoke, zone, rose
3. gripe, drive, nice
4. cute, fumes, music

Syllables

2. taco
3. canine
4. silo
5. migrate
6. female

Spelling: Word Endings

1. amused
2. preparing
3. luckier
4. thirstiest
5. funniest
6. finer

page 101

Prefixes pre-, mis-

1. misspell; spell incorrectly
2. preschool; before school
3. misunderstand; understand incorrectly
4. prepaid; paid in advance
5. predawn; before dawn
6. misheard; heard incorrectly
7. preapply; apply in advance

Academic Vocabulary

1. obvious
2. consumer
3. text
4. accompany
5. instructions

Unit 2 Lesson 2.4

Practice, page 103

1. fact
2. fact
3. fact
4. opinion
5. opinion
6. fact
7. opinion
8. fact
9. fact
10. opinion
11. B
12. H

Apply, page 104

1. F	5. F	8. O
2. F	6. O	9. F
3. F	7. F	10. O
4. O		

11. Red and yellow are colors.
12. Dogs and cats are mammals.
13. Jane Austen wrote the novel *Pride and Prejudice.*
14. Sewage and chemicals from factories cause water pollution
15. Paleontologists are people who hunt for and study fossils.
16. Tivoli Gardens is one of the world's oldest amusement parks.
17. A road map shows distance and direction.
18. Citizens of the United States have many rights.

Check Up, page 105

1. B	3. B	5. A
2. J	4. G	6. G

7. *Sample answers:* I am 27 years old. I have the best sisters and brother in the world.

Workplace Skill, page 106

1. C   2. J

Write for Work, page 107

Check that the writing includes three opinions and three facts, and that they are complete sentences. The facts should relate to or support the opinions in some way. Sample opinion: *The child-care center should be open late.* Sample fact: *Some employees get out of work late.*

Reading Extension, page 107

1. B
2. H
3. *Sample answer:* I think the Mayan calendars were their greatest accomplishment.
4. *Sample answer:* There were burn marks on buildings; the Maya cut down trees that had protected the soil from washing away.

5. *Opinion:* Their calendars were outstanding. *Facts will vary. Sample fact:* The Maya had 17 calendars in all.

Explore Words, page 108

Long e and i Spelled y
These words have the long e sound:
1. body
3. heavy
5. any
8. bunny
9. funny

Syllables
2. caveman
3. incline
4. refuse
5. fanfare
6. disgrace
7. profile
8. dictate

Multiple-meaning Words
1. b	3. b
2. b	4. a

page 109

Suffixes -less, -ful
1. forgetful
2. painless
3. flavorless
4. helpful
5. skinless
6. endless
7. thankful

Academic Vocabulary
1. opinion
2. fact
3. verify
4. indicate
5. evaluate

Unit 2 Lesson 2.5

Practice, page 111

1. C
2. F
3. A
4. H
5. B

Apply, page 112

Sample answers:
1. Ebo will search for his watch in the leaves and all around the yard.
2. Diego will see that the bread has burned.
3. Mr. Lee will not be able to find his way.
4. The cat will eat the tuna.

Check Up, page 113

1. B
2. F
3. C

Workplace Skill, page 114

1. C
2. H

Write for Work, page 115

Check that the writing includes the following points: The writer clearly understands the topic suggested. The suggestions are appropriate for the workplace. The tone of the e-mail or letter is appropriate.

Reading Extension, page 115

1. D
2. G
3. *Sample answer:* I predicted the probe would get information about Saturn.
4. *Sample answer:* The title tells me that the topic of the article is Saturn. I remember when the probe was launched.
5. *Sample answer:* It has no surface that someone could stand on, so a spacecraft couldn't land there, either.

Explore Words, page 116

Vowel Combinations
1. play	5. screamed
2. gray	6. jeep
3. tail	7. beach
4. pain	8. keep

Consonant Pairs wr, kn, gn
1. gn	3. gn	5. kn
2. kn	4. wr	6. wr

Answer Key Introductory Student Edition

Synonyms
1. clean
2. sweet
3. greet
4. wreck
5. scrape
6. peel

page 117

Spelling: Possessives
2. the cat's toy
3. the woman's skirt
4. the duck's feathers
5. the players' bats
6. the workers' computers
7. the teachers' rules
8. the parents' needs

Academic Vocabulary
1. outcome
2. prior
3. adjust
4. predict
5. logical

Unit 2 Lesson 2.6

Practice, page 119
1. Information
2. Fish Food Shop
3. Dolphin Show
4. The Fish Food Shop
5. Row A
6. Column 1
7. B3
8. A3
9. Shark Alley
10. Turtle Island

Apply, page 120
1. D	3. C	5. A	7. A
2. F	4. H	6. H	8. H

Check Up, page 121
1. Helena
2. state road
3. national interstate highway
4. about 20 miles
5. about 100 miles
6. E4
7. National Interstate Highway 90, State Road 200, and State Road 83
8. C1 Hamilton; B1 Missoula; C4 Helena; E4 Sheridan; F2 Jackson; B4 Wolf Creek

Workplace Skill, page 122
1. B   2. H

Write for Work, page 123
Check that the writing includes the following points: The writer should show knowledge of reading maps. The directions should be clear and concise. *Sample answer:* Go straight through the electrical and seasonal aisles. The lighting and ceiling fans department will be straight ahead of you.

Workplace Extension, page 123
1. C
2. J
3. *Sample answer:* Companies might have a dress-code policy so that their employees know what is appropriate to wear to work and what is not appropriate.
4. *Sample answer:* Chantal can say that she found a lot of useful information in the company's employee handbook, and she can recommend that Sharon read it. She can also tell Sharon that after reading the handbook, she can come to Chantal with any questions.

Explore Words, page 124
Vowel Combinations
1. ow
2. ie
3. oa
4. ue
5. oe

r-Controlled Vowels
1. mark
2. jar
3. smart
4. corner
5. worn
6. scar

Antonyms
Sample answers:
1. easy
2. tiny
3. forget
4. strong
5. right

page 125
Spelling: Homophones
2. knew, new
3. knows, nose
4. two, too
5. flower, flour
6. sun, son
7. eight, ate
8. blew, blue
9. pail, pale
10. wood, would
11. see, sea
12. tale, tail

Academic Vocabulary
1. area
2. physical
3. key
4. symbol
5. feature

Unit 2 Assessment

pages 127–132
1. A	10. F	19. C	28. G
2. G	11. B	20. H	29. A
3. B	12. G	21. C	30. F
4. H	13. C	22. F	31. A
5. D	14. G	23. B	32. J
6. F	15. C	24. H	33. C
7. D	16. G	25. B	34. F
8. G	17. B	26. H	35. C
9. D	18. F	27. D	36. G

Unit 2 Workplace Skill Activity

Sample answers:
Do: label all cans and containers that belong to you, clean the refrigerator every two weeks, wipe down counters, clean the microwave after use, wash all dishes at the end of the work day, wipe up spills and crumbs, make more coffee if the pot is empty

Do Not: put your food on top of someone else's, leave food in the refrigerator for more than three days, eat food or use utensils that do not belong to you unless they are meant to be shared, leave the break room when your food is in the microwave

Unit 3 Lesson 3.1

Practice, page 135

1.
   A 5
   B 1
   C 4
   D 2
   E 3
2.
   A 3
   B 1
   C 5
   D 2
   E 4
3.
   A 4
   B 1
   C 3
   D 2

Apply, page 136

1. Sand gets hot from the sun.
2. The sand heats the air directly above it.
3. The hot air rises.
4. The hot air pulls more air behind it.
5. The rising air pulls hot sand from the ground.
6. Air currents wrap around the rising air and spin around it.
7. The dust devil spins across the desert.

Check Up, page 137

1. D   4. G
2. F   5. A
3. D   6. G

Workplace Skill, page 138

1. B
2. F

Write for Work, page 139

Check that the writing includes the following points: The writer has written the steps in the correct sequence. Each step in the sequence is clear and understandable. Each step has been appropriately paraphrased and not copied.

Reading Extension, page 139

1. C
2. G
3. B
4. *Sample answer:* They used dolls that had been sewn together.
5. *Sample answer:* after they divided the girls' rib cage

Explore Words, page 140

r-Controlled Vowels
1. turkey
2. purse
3. nursing
4. word
5. merge
6. thirsty

Letters x and qu
1. gz   3. kw
2. ks   4. k

Context Clues
1. large boat
2. hate
3. comfort
4. healthy
5. kind of tree frog

Page 141

Synonyms and Antonyms
1. worried, calm
2. huge, tiny
3. flimsy, sturdy
4. silly, serious
5. made up, real

Academic Vocabulary
1. relate
2. purpose
3. directions
4. sequence
5. order

Unit 3 Lesson 3.2

Practice, page 143

1. Jake's Grill and Chez Paris
2. *Sample answers:* They both serve delicious food. They are both wonderful dining experiences.
3. *Sample answers:* but, on the other hand, in contrast, different

4. kangaroo rats and rat kangaroos
5. *Sample answers:* They are about a foot long. They hop on long back legs. Both have a head like a rat and a long tail.
6. *Sample answers:* The kangaroo rat has white fur, doesn't drink water, lives only in North America, and doesn't have a pouch. The rat kangaroo has brown fur, drinks water, lives in Australia, and has a pouch.

Apply, page 144

Marine Dolphins: mammal; home: oceans; size: up to 30 feet; types: 40; food: fish; sight: see well

River Dolphins: mammal; home: rivers; size: five to eight feet; types: seven; food: fish; sight: almost blind

1. although, on the other hand, but, like, different
2. *Sample answer:* Marine dolphins and river dolphins are both mammals, and they both eat fish. While marine dolphins live in the ocean and can be 30 feet long, river dolphins live in rivers and are only five to eight feet long.

Check Up, page 145

1. D
2. G
3. B
4. F
5. D
6. H

Workplace Skill, page 146

1. A
2. F

Write for Work, page 147

Check that the writing includes the following points: The writer shows the ability to gather information from a table. *Sample answer:* In 2006 Germany was leading in wind energy, while India was lagging behind. China was leading in solar thermal, while the United

States, Spain, and Germany were all lagging behind. Europe was leading in hydropower, although the United States was close behind. The United States was leading in geothermal energy, while Germany was lagging behind.

Reading Extension, page 147

1. C
2. H
3. A
4. *Sample answer:* They had families on the other side of the border.
5. *Sample answer:* Both Ryang and the public wanted Ryang to see his mother.

Explore Words, page 148

Long i and Long o
1. Most
2. sold
3. child
4. told
5. find
6. host

Spelling: Plurals
1. faxes
2. babies
3. leaves
4. bosses
5. peaches
6. wishes
7. chefs
8. lives

Spelling: Homophones
1. sea
2. roll
3. waist
4. to
5. would

Page 149

Vowel Combinations
1. oa
2. ue
3. ay
4. ee
5. ie
6. oe

7. ai
8. ay
9. ea
10. ue

Academic Vocabulary
1. respond
2. rare
3. compare
4. method
5. contrast

Unit 3 Lesson 3.3

Practice, page 151

1. B
2. J
3. D

Apply, page 152

Sample answers:
1. to inform readers about what to do and what not to do if they get burned
2. The author gives specific information about how to treat burns and when to see a doctor.
3. Yes, I have information about burns that I did not have before reading the passage.
4. to describe a small village
5. The passage has a lot of descriptive details.
6. Yes, I could visualize what the village looked and sounded like.

Check Up, page 153

1. B
2. H
3. A

Workplace Skill, page 154

1. B
2. F

Write for Work, page 155

Check that the writing includes the following points: The writer should use the correct memo format with date, subject, sender, receivers(s). The memo should

include key points that fellow employees need to know about the company meeting, such as time, date, and place.

Reading Extension, page 155

1. C
2. F
3. B
4. *Sample answer:* Riding a horse gives children with a brain injury and deaf children better balance. It lifts the spirits of all kinds of special-needs children.
5. *Sample answer:* I could pass on the information to someone who could benefit from it.

Explore Words, page 156

Vowel Combinations
1. point
2. choice
3. poisonous
4. destroy
5. spoiled
6. voyage
7. noise
8. annoy

Syllables
1. long
2. short
3. short
4. long
5. short
6. long

Page 157

Prefixes pre-, in-
1. predawn; before dawn
2. incomplete; not complete
3. prejudge; judge before
4. invisible; not visible
5. infrequent; not frequent
6. insane; not sane

Academic Vocabulary
1. minor
2. events
3. intention
4. explain
5. persuade

Answer Key Introductory Student Edition

Unit 3 Lesson 3.4

Practice, page 159
1. week 3
2. 10 hours
3. 15 hours
4. 25 hours
5. week 1 and week 4
6. week 4
7. week 3
8. week 2

Apply, page 160
1. 25%
2. train
3. D
4. graph B
5. H
6. line graph

Check Up, page 161
1. C	5. B
2. H	6. H
3. A	7. B
4. G	8. H

Workplace Skill, page 162
1. C	3. A
2. J	4. H

Write for Work, page 163
Check that the writing includes the following points: The writer is able to use the two graphs to detail the correct amount and percentage of revenue received for each category.

Reading Extension, page 163
1. B
2. J
3. D
4. F
5. She got parasites. She had to take a medicine that sheep take.

Explore Words, page 164
Vowel Combinations
1. spouse
2. awful
3. allow
4. sauce

Syllables
1. a	4. b
2. b	5. b
3. a	6. a

page 165
Spelling: Suffixes -able, -er
1. painter	5. breakable
2. adaptable	6. gardener
3. adorable	7. supplier
4. winner	8. drummer

Academic Vocabulary
1. data
2. estimate
3. label
4. illustrate
5. graph

Unit 3 Lesson 3.5

Practice, page 167
1. merge
2. fire hazard
3. divided highway
4. children playing
5. steep hill
6. signal ahead
7. deer crossing
8. bicycle route
9. slippery when wet
10. no smoking

Apply, page 168
1. I	6. H
2. F	7. B
3. A	8. C
4. E	9. D
5. G	

Check Up, page 169
1. C	6. H
2. J	7. B
3. D	8. J
4. H	9. B
5. B	10. G

Workplace Skill, page 170
1. C	5. A
2. D	6. E
3. B	7. F
4. H	8. G

Write for Work, page 171
Check that the list includes the following points: The list should include a good sample of the kinds of signs an office needs: Exit, No Smoking, In Case of Fire, Copy Room, Lunch Room, Restrooms, etc.

Reading Extension, page 171
1. B
2. J
3. A
4. *Sample answer:* She thought other people also did the right things too. She was only one of a few to get positive attention for it.
5. *Sample answer:* I think she did the right thing. She stood up for tolerance that day by saving McKeel.

Explore Words, page 172
Vowel Combinations
1. oo
2. aw
3. oi
4. oo

Base Words
1. sorrow
2. view
3. correct
4. cloud
5. visit
6. dream

Spelling: Possessives
1. my grandmother's garden
2. the travelers' hotel
3. the explorer's route
4. the artists' paintings

Page 173
Spelling: Word Endings
1. floods	6. correct
2. correct	7. correct
3. correct	8. banks
4. hopeless	9. correct
5. valuable	10. carried

Answer Key Introductory Student Edition

Academic Vocabulary
1. concrete
2. examine
3. correspond
4. abstract
5. communicate

Unit 3 Lesson 3.6

Practice, page 175

1. bŭt	14. invade
2. hərd	15. haze
3. strīk	16. bail
4. król	17. laugh
5. klēn	18. better
6. tīm	19. giraffe
7. tōd	20. jewel
8. brāk	21. dime
9. grēn	22. road
10. hól	23. bake
11. call	24. seen
12. cashier	25. fall
13. brook	

Apply, page 176

1. 3
2. 1
3. 2
4. 3
5. 1
6. 2
7. 2
8. 4
9. 1

Check Up, page 177

1. C	6. H
2. H	7. A
3. B	8. J
4. G	9. C
5. A	10. F

Workplace Skill, page 178

1. D
2. G

Write for Work, page 179

Check that the writing includes the following points: The résumé is written in a correct format. Level of education and work history are included.

Workplace Extension, page 179

1. A
2. G
3. *Sample answer:* A job as a writer could be a good choice for Jenny. She earned good grades in English. She volunteered to write articles for her school newspaper. She also worked after school at a local newspaper.

Explore Words, page 180

r-Controlled Vowels

1. ar	3. ir
2. ar	4. ur

Consonant Pairs

1. sign	4. scent
2. gnaw	5. comb
3. wrap	6. knock

Spelling: Contractions
1. couldn't
2. you're
3. isn't
4. aren't

Page 181

Multiple-meaning Words

1. a	4. a
2. b	5. a
3. b	6. b

Academic Vocabulary
1. arrange
2. represent
3. list
4. abbreviate
5. define

Unit 3 Assessment

Pages 183–188

1. A	10. G
2. G	11. A
3. C	12. H
4. H	13. B
5. A	14. F
6. H	15. D
7. B	16. J
8. H	17. A
9. A	18. H

19. D	28. J
20. H	29. B
21. B	30. H
22. F	31. A
23. C	32. J
24. J	33. C
25. D	34. H
26. F	35. B
27. A	36. G

Unit 3 Workplace Skill Activity

Sample answers:
1. Prianka would like to work extra hours for her boss, but she cannot do so today because of child care needs.
2. The situation does not seem like an emergency. There are at least several days before inventory happens.
3. She could just say that she can't work extra hours today. She could ask her neighbor to pick up her children and watch them today. She could suggest that she work late another time when she has had a chance to arrange for child care beforehand.
4. The third option is the best one since it meets the needs of both her family and her boss. It also allows her to show her dedication and good attitude.

After the role play: I played Prianka's boss. My partner played Prianka, and presented her solution to the dilemma in a very reasonable and appropriate way. We were able to work together to arrange for her to work late the following day.

Lesson Plan Intermediate 1 Student Edition

Unit 1 Lesson 1.1 pages 14–21

Introduce

READING SKILL
Recognize and Recall Details
Explain/Model: Explain that it is important to read attentively in order to recognize and recall specific details. Then have students read aloud the paragraph about silver. Model recognizing details that would be important to remember about the topic.

Guided Practice: Have students read the boxed passage. Then work with them to complete the task given in the directions. Discuss why the response given after the passage is correct. Ask students to give you two details they recall from reading the passage.

Teach Lesson Skills

Practice: Have students read the passage about collecting shells. Tell them to think about what the details have in common and which information does not belong. Discuss the answers to the questions and have students point out the details that support their answers.

Apply: After students answer the questions, have them read their responses aloud to the class. Encourage them to show classmates where they found the details in the passages.

Check Up: Have students work in small groups to read the passage and answer the questions. Then check each group's responses with those of other groups in the class.

COMPREHENSION
Set a Purpose for Reading: Encourage students to set a purpose for reading. Provide self-questioning models, such as *What do I hope to learn? What do the directions tell me to look for? What will happen next?* By setting a purpose and then evaluating whether they have achieved the purpose, students consciously monitor their own comprehension. They can also discuss the purpose they have determined with a peer or a teacher.

Reading Extension
Encourage students to read "The Man-Eaters of Tsavo" on page 1 of the *Intermediate 1 Reader.* Use this as an opportunity to teach reading strategies and the lesson reading skill.

ALPHABETICS
Explore Words
Consonant Blends: List these blends vertically and read them with students: *gr, sm, st, nk, pt, spr, str, spl.* Then finish writing each word and read it together: *grill, smooth, stuck, junk, wept, spread, stretch, splash.* Have volunteers underline the consonant blend in each word.

Compound Words: Have students combine these words to form compound words: *team, base, work, box, lunch, ball. (teamwork, baseball, lunchbox)*

Spelling: Possessives: Use names and examples from the classroom, such as these, to model the skill: *the coat belonging to Keisha/Keisha's coat, the book belonging to the teacher/the teacher's book.*

VOCABULARY
Academic Vocabulary/Tier 2
topic details recall theory passage

Before students complete the activity, write the academic vocabulary words and definitions on the board. Discuss each word's meaning with students. Then write the sentences below on the board. Read each sentence aloud and discuss it with students.

1. The *topic* of my speech is "How To Fold a Towel."
2. The magazine article included lots of *details* about the actor's life.
3. I can't *recall* what I had for lunch yesterday.
4. Mom has a *theory* about why all our plants are dying.
5. We discussed a *passage* from the first chapter of the novel.

FLUENCY
Echo Reading: Read a sentence from one of the passages aloud. Then have students echo you by reading the same sentence and trying to read with the same speed and expression as you do.

Invite students to do a timed reading of "The Man-Eaters of Tsavo." Afterwards, have them enter their times on the Words-per-Minute table on page 121 and chart their reading speed on page 122 of the *Intermediate 1 Reader.*

Encourage students to listen to "The Man-Eaters of Tsavo." Go to **www.mhereadingbasics.com** to play or download the recording. The recording provides modeled fluency and read-along support.

APPLICATION
Workplace Skill:
Locate and Recall Details in a Job Description
Remind students that a job description gives facts about an available job opportunity. Tell students that they should first scan a job description for key information, such as title, hours, and salary. Then they should look for bold or underlined information. Scanning for details can help them judge whether the position might be right for them. If it is, they can read more closely. After students read the job description and answer the questions, have them make a two-column chart labeled *Pros* and *Cons.* Have them sort details about the job into these categories. This chart will come in handy when they do the Write for Work activity.

Write for Work
Remind students that they should support their opinions with reasons and details. Tell them to read the instructions for this task carefully to be sure they include all the requested information. Encourage them to share their work with a classmate to make sure they clearly supported their main idea with details.

PASSKEY
Go to **www.mhereadingbasics.com** and click on the *PassKey* link. Customize instruction for your class using modules from Reading/Language Arts, Levels 2 & 3.

Lesson Plan Intermediate 1 Student Edition

Unit 1 Lesson 1.2 pages 22–29

Introduce

READING SKILL

Understand Stated Concepts

Explain/Model: Explain that it is important to pay attention to stated concepts during reading. Have students read aloud the passage about Amelia. Model for students how stated concepts in the passage help you determine how long Amelia has lived in New York City.

Guided Practice: Have students read the boxed passage. Encourage them to highlight or make margin notes as they read. Then work with them to complete the task given in the directions. Discuss why the response given after the passage is correct. Ask students to give you another important stated concept that they noted while reading.

Practice: Have students read the passages about Harvard and hummingbirds. Tell them to underline or highlight stated concepts as they read. Discuss the answers to the questions and have students point out the stated concepts in the passages that support their answers.

Apply: After students answer the questions, have them read their responses aloud to the class. Encourage them to show classmates where they found the stated concepts that helped them answer the questions.

Check Up: Have students work in small groups to read the passage and answer the questions. Then check each group's responses with those of other groups in the class.

Teach Lesson Skills

COMPREHENSION

Reread/Read More Slowly: Encourage students to become aware of the pace at which they read. Offer self-questioning models, such as *Did I read this passage too quickly? Does reading it again help me understand better? Does reading more slowly help me retain information?* When students actively consider the manner in which they are reading, they consciously monitor their own comprehension.

Reading Extension

📖 Encourage students to read "Doctors (and Nurses) Without Borders" on page 10 of the *Intermediate 1 Reader*. Use this as an opportunity to teach reading strategies and the lesson reading skill.

ALPHABETICS

Explore Words

Suffix -able: Work with students to complete these examples and then define the words: *market + able*; *agree + able*.

Spelling: Contractions: Write these words and contraction pairs on the board: *does not/doesn't, are not/aren't*. Have students identify the missing letter in each contraction and then use the contraction in a sentence.

Syllables: Review that a closed syllable ends in a consonant and usually has a short-vowel sound. An open syllable usually has a long-vowel sound. When a two-syllable word is made up of two closed syllables, the vowel in the second syllable usually stands for the schwa sound or the short-*i* sound. Use these words to discuss syllable types and vowel sounds: *rib/bon, ba/sic, pen/cil*.

VOCABULARY

Academic Vocabulary/Tier 2

stated   concept   directly   margin   notes

Before students complete the activity, write the academic vocabulary words and definitions on the board. Discuss each word's meaning with students. Then write the sentences below on the board. Read each sentence aloud and discuss it with students.

1. The instructions *stated* that we should turn off the power first.
2. You can spend too much if you have no *concept* of money.
3. The coach spoke *directly* to each player.
4. Put a check mark in the *margin* next to each key word.
5. I made *notes* to help me remember ideas.

FLUENCY

Partner Reading: Have partners read aloud to one another and/or read aloud at the same time. Encourage them to offer support and correction to one another. Circulate to offer guidance as needed.

Invite students to do a timed reading of "Doctors (and Nurses) Without Borders." Afterwards, have them enter their times on the Words-per-Minute table on page 121 and chart their reading speed on page 122 of the *Intermediate 1 Reader*.

📶 Encourage students to listen to "Doctors (and Nurses) Without Borders." Go to **www.mhereadingbasics.com** to play or download the recording. The recording provides modeled fluency and read-along support.

APPLICATION

Workplace Skill:

Find Stated Concepts in a Mission Statement

Have students read the mission statement. Remind them that a mission statement describes a company's purpose and focus. Point out that important ideas in a mission statement are often stated directly in a topic sentence. Details give more information about the stated concepts. After students answer the questions, have them brainstorm ideas for a business they would like to start. Ask them to list some goals and standards for the business they choose. This activity will come in handy when they do the Write for Work activity.

Write for Work

Remind students that a company mission statement should state goals and standards of the business. Tell students to make sure they include all the requested information. Encourage partners to share their work and suggest ways to make their mission statements clearer and more effective.

PASSKEY

💻 Go to **www.mhereadingbasics.com** and click on the *PassKey* link. Customize instruction for your class using modules from Reading/Language Arts, Levels 2 & 3.

Lesson Plan Intermediate 1 Student Edition

Unit 1 Lesson 1.3 pages 30–37

Introduce

READING SKILL

Draw Conclusions

Explain/Model: Explain that since authors do not always state their ideas directly, we often need to draw conclusions using what we already know and information in the text. After students read aloud the passage about fish, model drawing a conclusion, such as "Whales are not fish."

Guided Practice: Have students read the boxed passage. Then work with them to complete the task given in the directions. Discuss why the response given after the passage is correct. Ask students to point to specific facts that support the conclusion.

Teach Lesson Skills

Practice: Have students read the passages. Tell them to think about what they already know and what information is given in the passages to help them draw conclusions. Discuss the answers to the questions and have students point out facts that support their answers.

Apply: After students answer the questions, have them read their conclusions aloud to the class. Encourage them to explain how they used what they already knew and information in the passages to draw their conclusions.

Check Up: Have students work in small groups to read the passage and answer the questions. Then check each group's responses with those of other groups in the class.

COMPREHENSION

Use Prior Knowledge: Encourage students to think about what they already know before they read. To get students started, provide self-questioning models, such as *Have I read about this topic before? Does this sound familiar?* When students can create a context or framework of known information in which to place new information, they consciously monitor their own comprehension.

Reading Extension

Encourage students to read "The Truth about the Tasaday" on page 18 of the *Intermediate 1 Reader.* Use this as an opportunity to teach reading strategies and the lesson reading skill.

ALPHABETICS

Explore Words

Syllables: Write *locate* on the board, and point out that the open syllable *lo* and the silent-*e* syllable *cate* both have a long-vowel sound. Before students complete the exercise, have volunteers read aloud each syllable. Ask them to identify open, closed, and silent-*e* syllables.

Prefixes *sub-, in-*: Write these words: *subzero, inconsiderate, insufficient.* Have volunteers circle the prefixes. Discuss the meanings as a class.

Synonyms: Have students name synonyms for the following words: *tasty, relaxed, boast, laugh. (yummy, calm, brag, giggle)*

VOCABULARY

Academic Vocabulary/Tier 2

evidence   conclude   valid   frequently   supported

Before students complete the activity, write the academic vocabulary words and definitions on the board. Discuss each word's meaning with students. Then write the sentences below on the board. Read each sentence aloud and discuss it with students.

1. The police found *evidence* at the scene.
2. The locked doors led us to *conclude* that the restaurant was closed.
3. I had to agree with her because her point was *valid.*
4. Sanjay *frequently* plays soccer on Mondays.
5. We *supported* the cause by donating time and money.

FLUENCY

Collaborative Reading: Gather in a group. Have each student read one or more lines of a passage and then pass the text to the next student. Supply pronunciation and phrasing corrections as needed.

Invite students to do a timed reading of "The Truth about the Tasaday." Afterwards, have them enter their times on the Words-per-Minute table on page 121 and chart their reading speed on page 122 of the *Intermediate 1 Reader.*

Encourage students to listen to "The Truth about the Tasaday." Go to **www.mhereadingbasics.com** to play or download the recording. The recording provides modeled fluency and read-along support.

APPLICATION

Workplace Skill:

Draw Conclusions from a Business Ad

Have students read the business ad. Remind them that an ad is a persuasive message that uses words like *best, must,* and *everyone* to convince people to buy or do something. Readers must look for facts and use their knowledge and experience to help them draw their own conclusions about what is being advertised. After students answer the questions, have them think of a product they would like to sell or a service they would like to provide. Have them list persuasive words or phrases about the product or service that show what makes it special. This list will come in handy when they do the Write for Work activity.

Write for Work

Remind students of the purpose of an ad and information that is usually included in an ad. Tell them to make sure to include all the requested information in their own ad. Encourage them to share their ad with a classmate and ask one another for suggestions about ways to make the ad more persuasive or effective.

PASSKEY

Go to **www.mhereadingbasics.com** and click on the *PassKey* link. Customize instruction for your class using modules from Reading/Language Arts, Levels 2 & 3.

Lesson Plan Intermediate 1 Student Edition

Intermediate 1 Student Edition

Introduce

READING SKILL
Summarize and Paraphrase

Explain/Model: Tell students that when they summarize a passage, they need to convey only the most important ideas and details. When they paraphrase, they need to restate the text in their own words and use simpler language. After students read aloud the passage about scorpions, model the decision-making process that might have gone into creating the summary and paraphrase.

Guided Practice: Have students read the boxed passage. Then work with them to complete the task given in the directions. Discuss why the responses given after the passage are correct. Ask students to summarize or paraphrase the passage in a slightly different way.

Teach Lesson Skills

Practice: Have students read the passages about Japan and paprika. Tell them to think about which important ideas would be in a summary and which details would be in a paraphrase. Discuss the answers to the questions and have students explain how they chose their answers.

Apply: Have students read aloud their summaries and paraphrases. Encourage them to explain how they identified the most important ideas and details to include in a summary.

Check Up: Have students work in small groups to read and answer the questions. Then check each group's responses with those of other groups in the class.

COMPREHENSION
Understand Author's Purpose: Encourage students to consider the author's purpose as they read. Provide self-questioning models, such as *Why did the author decide to write this? What does the author want me to know?* By examining the author's purpose, students can better analyze their own reaction to the writing and consciously monitor their own comprehension.

Reading Extension
Encourage students to read "Near Death on the Football Field" on page 26 of the *Intermediate 1 Reader*. Use this as an opportunity to teach reading strategies and the lesson reading skill.

ALPHABETICS
Explore Words

Hard and Soft *g*: Write *gift, gem, gym, gas, gold*, and *gist*. Read them aloud and have students raise their hands when they hear the soft *g* sound.

Syllables: Explain that a closed syllable ends in a consonant and usually has a short vowel sound. In silent-*e* syllables, the vowel stands for its long sound. Write these words and help students identify the vowel sound in each syllable: *hot/cake, ex/cite, com/bine*. Read aloud the words with students.

Antonyms: Write these words and have students suggest an antonym or antonyms for each: *nervous, sad, down, exciting. (calm, happy, up, boring)*

VOCABULARY
Academic Vocabulary/Tier 2

summary   paraphrase   reinforce   result
exclude

Before students complete the activity, write the academic vocabulary words and definitions on the board. Discuss each word's meaning with students. Then write the sentences below on the board. Read each sentence aloud and discuss it with students.

1. The TV guide gave a *summary* of the show.
2. Be sure to *paraphrase* the information before you put it in your report.
3. The homework helped *reinforce* the lesson.
4. The *result* of the game will be in the newspaper tomorrow.
5. Trevor was careful not to *exclude* Maria from the conversation.

FLUENCY
Repeated Reading: Lead a group to read the same passage aloud together several times. As the leader, emphasize accuracy and phrasing until the group reading sounds smooth and consistent.

Invite students to do a timed reading of "Near Death on the Football Field." Afterwards, have them enter their times on the Words-per-Minute table on page 121 and chart their reading speed on page 122 of the *Intermediate 1 Reader*.

Encourage students to listen to "Near Death on the Football Field." Go to **www.mhereadingbasics.com** to play or download the recording. The recording provides modeled fluency and read-along support.

APPLICATION
Workplace Skill:

Summarize and Paraphrase an Article

Have students read the article. Remind them that to summarize, they retell just the main ideas. To paraphrase, they should restate the sentences in their own words. After students answer the questions, have them underline the main idea of one of the paragraphs. Then have them circle a paragraph they want to put in their own words. This will come in handy when they do the Write for Work activity.

Write for Work
Remind students that a summary should be one or two sentences. A paraphrase is about as long as the original text. Encourage partners to share their summaries and paraphrases to make sure they captured the important ideas in the summary and restated all the details in their paraphrase in their own words.

PASSKEY
Go to **www.mhereadingbasics.com** and click on the *PassKey* link. Customize instruction for your class using modules from Reading/Language Arts, Levels 2 & 3.

Introduce

READING SKILL

Compare and Contrast

Explain/Model: Explain that writers often use clue words and phrases to signal comparison and contrast. Read aloud the boxed words with students. Then model comparing apples and oranges, using clue words and details from the chart.

Guided Practice: Have students read the boxed passage. Then work with them to complete the task given in the directions. Encourage students to use the clue words or phrases to help them understand how the planets are alike and different. Discuss why the responses given after the passage are correct. Ask students to tell you one way Earth and Venus are alike and one way they are different.

Teach Lesson Skills

Practice: Have students read the sentences and decide whether each one compares or contrasts. Tell them to look for clue words or phrases. Discuss the answers and have students point out the clue words or phrases that support their answers.

Apply: After students write their sentences, have them read them aloud to the class. Encourage them to point out the clue word or phrase in each sentence that shows how the things being compared and contrasted are alike or different.

Check Up: Have students work in small groups to read the passage and answer the questions. Then check each group's responses with those of other groups in the class.

COMPREHENSION

Look for Context Clues/Read On: Encourage students to look for context clues as they read. Investigating the context helps a reader to put words and paragraphs into a larger framework. Provide helpful self-questioning models, such as *What words surrounding this difficult word can help me understand it better? If I read a little farther, might I find additional clues that can help me understand?* When students proactively look for context clues, they consciously monitor their own comprehension.

Reading Extension

Encourage students to read "The Mysterious Life of Twins" on page 34 of the *Intermediate 1 Reader*. Use this as an opportunity to teach reading strategies and the lesson reading skill.

ALPHABETICS

Explore Words

The Letter *x*: Write the words *ax, exit, wax, six,* and *exhaust,* and read them together. Then have students sort the words into two groups according to the sound of the *x.*

Spelling: Plurals: Remind students that the ending *-es* is usually added to words that end in *s, ss, x,* or *ch.* Write the words *box, kitten, class, patch, cake,* and *eye.* Have students underline the final letter of each word and then form the plural.

Word Endings *-er, -est*: Remind students that *-er* is used to compare two things and *-est* is used to compare three or more things. Discuss these examples, and have students add their own: *This pencil is longer than that one. Jean's backpack is the lightest of all.*

VOCABULARY

Academic Vocabulary/Tier 2

compare contrast clue organize similar

Before students complete the activity, write the academic vocabulary words and definitions on the board. Discuss each word's meaning with students. Then write the sentences below on the board. Read each sentence aloud and discuss it with students.

1. Let's *compare* the prices of the items.
2. Ivan sprinkles sugar on lemons because he likes the *contrast* between sweet and sour.
3. Grass stains on the child's pants were a *clue* that he had been playing outside.
4. To find things easily, *organize* your desk.
5. The two black cats look very *similar,* only their owner can tell them apart.

FLUENCY

Marked Phrase Reading: Mark a passage with phrase boundaries, showing how words should be grouped for meaning and emphasis. Read the passage aloud, having students follow along, and then read aloud together with students.

Invite students to do a timed reading of "The Mysterious Life of Twins." Afterwards, have them enter their times on the Words-per-Minute table on page 121 and chart their reading speed on page 122 of the *Intermediate 1 Reader.*

Encourage students to listen to "The Mysterious Life of Twins." Go to **www.mhereadingbasics.com** to play or download the recording. The recording provides modeled fluency and read-along support.

APPLICATION

Workplace Skill:

Compare and Contrast Information in a Graph

Remind students that a graph is a visual way to compare and contrast information at a glance. Point out that the title of the graph and the labels on the *x* and *y* axes help them understand the information that is being compared and contrasted. After students read the graph and answer the questions, have them state in their own words what the graph shows. Then have them tell a partner how they might use this information if they were a female entering the workforce. This activity will come in handy when they do the Write for Work activity.

Write for Work

Remind students to read the instructions for this task carefully to be sure they include all the requested information. Encourage them to share their work with a classmate to make sure that they've clearly stated what information the graph shows and how they might use it.

PASSKEY

Go to **www.mhereadingbasics.com** and click on the *PassKey* link. Customize instruction for your class using modules from Reading/Language Arts, Levels 2 & 3.

Lesson Plan Intermediate 1 Student Edition

Unit 1 Lesson 1.6 pages 54–61

Introduce

READING SKILL
Use Forms

Explain/Model: Explain that it is important to read directions carefully and completely before filling out a form. Model the process by showing students how you would fill out a particular school form. Have students describe some kinds of forms they have filled out.

Guided Practice: Have students read the form. Then work with them to complete the task given in the directions. Encourage students to think about what they need to do in each section. Discuss why the responses given after the passage are correct.

Teach Lesson Skills

Practice: Have students read the form. Tell them to make sure they understand all directions. Discuss the answers to the questions and have students point out the parts of the form that helped them determine the answers.

Apply: After students answer the questions, have them read their responses aloud to the class. Encourage them to explain how they figured out any new or unfamiliar terms.

Check Up: Have students work in small groups to study the form and answer the questions. Then check each group's responses with those of other groups in the class.

COMPREHENSION
Clarify Meaning: Encourage students to actively clarify meaning as they read. Provide self-questioning models, such as *What clues can I find in other sentences to help me understand this word? Does this word resemble any other words I have learned? Can I find someone to ask about this?* When students proactively try to clarify meaning, they consciously monitor their own comprehension.

ALPHABETICS
Explore Words

Consonant Pairs *wr, kn, gn*: Write the consonant pairs *wr, gn,* and *kn*. Say the sound that each pair stands for and have students identify the silent letter. Then write *wr, gn,* and *kn* in one column and *ome, ight,* and *ite* in another. Have students match pairs and endings to form words. (*gnome, knight, write*)

Long *e* Spelled *-y*: Write these word pairs and read them with students: *curly/cry, try/icy, why/dewy, kindly/fly.* Have students circle the word in each pair with the long *e* sound.

Context Clues: Write this example and have students figure out the meaning of the underlined word: *Snakes are <u>venomous</u>. They inject their poison with their fangs.*

VOCABULARY
Academic Vocabulary/Tier 2

form survey medical abbreviate clarify

Before students complete the activity, write the academic vocabulary words and definitions on the board. Discuss each word's meaning with students. Then write the sentences below on the board. Read each sentence aloud and discuss it with students.

1. Inez filled out a *form* to have her paycheck directly deposited into her bank account.

2. We took a *survey* to find out how many people use the recycling center.

3. An ambulance came for a *medical* emergency.

4. The way to *abbreviate* Texas is TX.

5. Does the e-mail *clarify* the meeting time?

FLUENCY
Echo Reading: Read a sentence from one of the passages aloud. Then have students echo you by reading the same sentence and trying to read with the same speed and expression as you do.

APPLICATION
Workplace Skill:

Use a Job Application Form

Have students read the job application form. Remind students that a job application provides employers with the information they need to decide whom they will interview for a job opening. Discuss the importance of filling out an application form accurately. Point out that reading the form before filling it out can help them complete it correctly. After students answer the questions, have them reread the form from start to finish. This will help them prepare to do the Write for Work activity.

Write for Work
Remind students that it is important for them to fill out a job application correctly so that employers can determine if they are a good fit for the position. Tell them to read the form carefully to be sure they have included all the requested information. Encourage classmates to share completed forms and check each other's work for accuracy and completeness.

Workplace Extension
Remind students that the workplace requires them to be flexible and adaptable. Have them discuss Jamal's problem and what he can do to show that he will be a good employee. Even though he is new to the job, what responsibilities does Jamal have to Mr. Gregor and to customers? Have partners discuss the questions and share their responses with the class.

PASSKEY
Go to **www.mhereadingbasics.com** and click on the *PassKey* link. Customize instruction for your class using modules from Reading/Language Arts, Levels 2 & 3.

Lesson Plan Intermediate 1 Student Edition

Unit 1 Lesson 1.7 pages 62–69

Introduce

READING SKILL
Find the Main Idea

Explain/Model: Explain that when reading a passage, it is important to identify the main idea and think about how each detail supports it. Have students read aloud the passage about whales. Then discuss the main idea, pointing out that it is not stated in a topic sentence.

Guided Practice: Have students read the boxed passage. Then work with them to complete the task given in the directions. Discuss why the responses given after the passage are correct. Ask students to tell you another way they could state the main idea in their own words.

Teach Lesson Skills

Practice: Have students read each passage and identify the main idea. Tell them to think about what the details have in common. Discuss the answers to the questions and have students point out the details in each passage that helped them determine the main idea.

Apply: After students write their main ideas and details, have them read their responses aloud to the class. Encourage them to explain how they determined the main ideas and how the details they chose support them.

Check Up: Have students work in small groups to read the passage and answer the questions. Then check each group's responses with those of other groups in the class.

COMPREHENSION

Visualize: Encourage students to use sensory imaging as a mental tool when they read. Provide useful self-questioning models, such as *What do I see in this photo? Does this diagram help me understand the text? Can I form a mental image of what the author is describing?* When students visualize what they are reading, they consciously monitor their own comprehension.

ALPHABETICS
Explore Words

Consonant Pair *sc*: Write the following words and read them aloud: *scoot, scene, scan, descent, scientist, scum.* Have students hold up one finger if *sc* stands for one sound and two fingers if it stands for two sounds.

Long *i* Spelled -*y*: Write these words and read them aloud. Have students identify the words in which the *y* stands for the long *i* sound: *dusty, sleepy, cry, sty, furry, fry, fly.*

Multiple-meaning Words: Write on the board: *We will leave to go camping at first light. We will take only what we need to keep our packs light.* Help students figure out the meaning of *light* in each sentence. Then have them suggest other words with more than one meaning.

VOCABULARY
Academic Vocabulary/Tier 2

point   example   identify   examine   relationship

Before students complete the activity, write the academic vocabulary words and definitions on the board. Discuss each word's meaning with students. Then write the sentences below on the board. Read each sentence aloud and discuss it with students.

1. After Yee explained why she was upset, I could see her *point.*
2. "Belling the Cat" is an *example* of a fable.
3. My dog wears tags on his collar to *identify* him.
4. The doctor will *examine* my painful arm.
5. There is a *relationship* between texting while driving and accidents.

FLUENCY

Collaborative Reading: Gather in a group. Have each student read one or more lines of a passage and then pass the text to the next student. Supply pronunciation and phrasing corrections as needed.

APPLICATION
Workplace Skill:

Find the Main Idea in an Article

Have students read the article. Remind them that the title often generally states the main idea of the whole article. Point out that paragraphs within the article often have a topic sentence that states the main idea of the paragraph and is supported by details. After students answer the questions, have them start a list of pros and cons about working for the government. This list will come in handy when they do the Write for Work activity.

Write for Work

Remind students to read the instructions for this task carefully to be sure they include all the requested information. Encourage them to share their work with a classmate and compare their lists of benefits and things they wouldn't like.

Workplace Extension

Remind students that an education is essential to getting ahead in almost any field or job they choose. Have them review the passage about Lewis Payne's conversation with his boss. Discuss what Lewis's boss wants him to do and why. Have partners discuss the questions and share their responses with the class.

PASSKEY

Go to **www.mhereadingbasics.com** and click on the *PassKey* link. Customize instruction for your class using modules from Reading/Language Arts, Levels 2 & 3.

Intermediate 1 Student Edition

Introduce

READING SKILL
Identify Sequence

Explain/Model: Tell students that passages explaining events, processes, or procedures often include words that signal order, such as *first* and *last*. Have students read aloud the paragraph about Tahir. Point out the clue words and explain how they help you understand the order of Tahir's actions. Next, have students read the steps for baking cookies and retell them in order.

Guided Practice: Have students read the boxed passage. Then work with them to complete the task given in the directions. Discuss why the responses given after the passage are correct.

Teach Lesson Skills

Practice: Have students read the passage about Amelia Earhart. Tell them to look for clue words that show the sequence of events. Discuss the answers to the questions and have students point out the clue words that helped them recognize the order of events in Earhart's life.

Apply: After students list the steps, have them read their responses aloud to the class. Encourage them to show classmates the clue words that helped them write the steps in order.

Check Up: Have students work in small groups to read the passage and answer the questions. Then check each group's responses with those of other groups in the class.

COMPREHENSION
Set a Purpose for Reading: Encourage students to set a purpose for reading. Provide self-questioning models, such as *What do I hope to learn? What do the directions tell me to look for? What will happen next?* By setting a purpose and then evaluating whether they have achieved the purpose, students consciously monitor their own comprehension. They can also discuss the purpose they have determined with a peer or a teacher.

Reading Extension
📖 Encourage students to read "Mummies" on page 41 of the *Intermediate 1 Reader*. Use this as an opportunity to teach reading strategies and the lesson reading skill.

ALPHABETICS
Explore Words

Syllables: Use the syllables *sim* and *pa* to review closed and open syllables, and introduce consonant + *le* syllables, such as -*ple*, and -*gle*. Explain that when dividing a word into syllables, the consonant + -*le* usually stays together. Then write these words and divide them into syllables: *sim/ple, pa/per, wig/gle, bu/gle*. Read the words aloud with students. Ask volunteers to tell whether the first syllable in each word is open or closed.

Synonyms: Write these words on the board and have students work in pairs to list as many synonyms as they can for each word: *shake, dirty, trash. (rattle, filthy, garbage)*

VOCABULARY
Academic Vocabulary/Tier 2

sequence obtain section submit application

Before students complete the activity, write the academic vocabulary words and definitions on the board. Discuss each word's meaning with students. Then write the sentences below on the board. Read each sentence aloud and discuss it with students.

1. The teacher showed the *sequence* of steps to the dancers.
2. In order to check out books at the library, you must first *obtain* a library card.
3. The bookstore has a large magazine *section*.
4. Kim will *submit* the report to his boss.
5. Fill out an *application* for a credit card.

FLUENCY
Echo Reading: Read a sentence from one of the passages aloud. Then have students echo you by reading the same sentence and trying to read with the same speed and expression as you do.

Invite students to do a timed reading of "Mummies." Afterwards, have them enter their times on the Words-per-Minute table on page 121 and chart their reading speed on page 122 of the *Intermediate 1 Reader*.

📶 Encourage students to listen to "Mummies." Go to **www.mhreadingbasics.com** to play or download the recording. The recording provides modeled fluency and read-along support.

APPLICATION
Workplace Skill:

Follow a Sequence of Events for a Customer Return

Have students read the procedure for processing a return. Explain that procedures are step-by-step instructions for completing a task. Point out that numbers or clue words such as *first, next, then*, and *finally* can help them understand the order in which to perform the steps. After students answer the questions, have them tell a partner in their own words how to process an in-store customer return. This activity will come in handy when they do the Write for Work activity.

Write for Work
Remind students that restating a procedure in their own words is a good way to check their understanding. Tell them to make sure they retell each step in the procedure. Have partners check each other's work to verify that they retold each step accurately and completely.

PASSKEY
💻 Go to **www.mhreadingbasics.com** and click on the *PassKey* link. Customize instruction for your class using modules from Reading/Language Arts, Levels 2 & 3.

Introduce

READING SKILL

Use Supporting Evidence

Explain/Model: Encourage students to read attentively in order to recognize specific details that support main ideas, whether they are opinions or facts. Have students read aloud the passage about Tito. Model identifying details that support the stated opinion.

Guided Practice: Have students read the boxed passage. Then work with them to complete the task given in the directions. Discuss why the response given after the passage is correct. Have students explain how the fourth sentence supports the idea stated in the first sentence.

Teach Lesson Skills

Practice: Have students read the passages. Tell them to identify the main idea in each passage and decide which details support it and which do not. Discuss the answers and have students explain why the details they selected do not support the main idea.

Apply: After students answer the questions, have them read their responses aloud to the class. Encourage them to show classmates where they found the evidence to support the opinions.

Check Up: Have students work in small groups to read and answer the questions. Then check each group's responses with those of other groups in the class.

COMPREHENSION

Reread/Read More Slowly: Encourage students to become aware of the pace at which they read. Offer self-questioning models, such as *Did I read this passage too quickly? Does reading it again help me understand better? Does reading more slowly help me retain information?* When students actively consider the manner in which they are reading, they consciously monitor their own comprehension.

Reading Extension

📖 Encourage students to read "Escape from Iran" on page 49 of the *Intermediate 1 Reader.* Use this as an opportunity to teach reading strategies and the lesson reading skill.

ALPHABETICS

Explore Words

***r*-Controlled Vowels:** Write these word pairs and read them with students: *park/pack, string/stir, free/first, scream/scar.* Have students identify each word with an *r*-controlled vowel.

Antonyms: Write the words *near, full,* and *proud* in one column. Write *empty, far,* and *embarrassed* in another column. Have students match the antonyms.

Compound Words: Model forming compound words by writing and solving these word problems: *tree + house, earth + worm, head + ache, book + shelf.* Have volunteers put together the meanings of the individual words to give definitions for the compound words.

VOCABULARY

Academic Vocabulary/Tier 2

judge support include enhance argument

Before students complete the activity, write the academic vocabulary words and definitions on the board. Discuss each word's meaning with students. Then write the sentences below on the board. Read each sentence aloud and discuss it with students.

1. The director had to *judge* which actor would be best for the part.
2. Fans *support* the team by going to games.
3. The meeting will *include* community leaders and members of the community.
4. Salt can *enhance* the taste of food.
5. Ken made a strong *argument* against using cell phones while driving.

FLUENCY

Partner Reading: Have partners read aloud to one another and/or read aloud at the same time. Encourage them to offer support and correction to one another. Circulate to offer guidance as needed.

Invite students to do a timed reading of "Escape from Iran." Afterwards, have them enter their times on the Words-per-Minute table on page 121 and chart their reading speed on page 122 of the *Intermediate 1 Reader.*

📶 Encourage students to listen to "Escape from Iran." Go to **www.mhereadingbasics.com** to play or download the recording. The recording provides modeled fluency and read-along support.

APPLICATION

Workplace Skill:

Find Supporting Details in a Project Start-up Procedure

Have students read the project start-up procedures. Remind them that procedures explain how a project, task, or assignment should be handled. Point out that looking for the main idea and supporting details will help them better understand the procedures from start to finish. After students answer the questions, have them jot down the main idea of the procedures and give some supporting details. This list will come in handy when they do the Write for Work activity.

Write for Work

Remind students that supporting details give more information about the main idea. Tell them to read the instructions carefully to be sure they include all the requested information. Have partners check each other's work to make sure they identified the main idea and gave three supporting details.

PASSKEY

💻 Go to **www.mhereadingbasics.com** and click on the *PassKey* link. Customize instruction for your class using modules from Reading/Language Arts, Levels 2 & 3.

Introduce

READING SKILL

Identify Style Techniques

Explain/Model: Explain that how an author uses sentence structure and language contributes to his or her special style. Have students read aloud the passages about Monifa. Point out the words, sentences, and punctuation that contribute to the writing style in each passage.

Guided Practice: Have students read the boxed passage. Then work with them to complete the task given in the directions. Discuss why the responses given after the passage are correct. Ask students to describe the author's style in one or two words, such as *spare* and *suspenseful*.

Teach Lesson Skills

Practice: Have students read the author descriptions and match each author with the passage he or she most likely wrote. Discuss the answers and have students point out words or sentences in the passage that support their answers.

Apply: Have students read the passages and identify the style techniques. Encourage them to show classmates specific words or sentences that helped them identify the author's style.

Check Up: Have students work in small groups to read the passages and answer the questions. Then check each group's responses with those of other groups in the class.

COMPREHENSION

Understand Author's Purpose: Encourage students to consider the author's purpose as they read. Provide self-questioning models, such as *Why did the author decide to write this? What does the author want me to know?* By examining the author's purpose, students can better analyze their own reaction to the writing and consciously monitor their own comprehension.

Reading Extension

📖 Encourage students to read "Alone at Sea" on page 57 of the *Intermediate 1 Reader*. Use this as an opportunity to teach reading strategies and the lesson reading skill.

ALPHABETICS

Explore Words

Vowel Combinations: Write these words and read them with students, emphasizing the long-vowel sound: *toast, woe, blow, pie, lied, cue, hue*. Ask volunteers to circle the letters that stand for the long-vowel sound.

Spelling: Word Endings: Model adding endings to these words: *fake + ing, wet + er, fast + est, tug + ed*. Have students point out spelling changes made to base words.

Syllables: Write these examples and pronounce them both ways with students: *shi/ver* or *shiv/er, ro/bot* or *rob/ot, dra/gon* or *drag/on*. Have students tell which word in each pair is divided correctly and whether the first syllable is open or closed.

VOCABULARY

Academic Vocabulary/Tier 2

style communicate technique emphasis highlight

Before students complete the activity, write the academic vocabulary words and definitions on the board. Discuss each word's meaning with students. Then write the sentences below on the board. Read each sentence aloud and discuss it with students.

1. The writer's *style* was easy to understand.
2. E-mail is one way people *communicate*.
3. Use this *technique* for organizing coupons.
4. The coach put *emphasis* on the players working together as a team.
5. Nestor made sure to *highlight* his past work experience in his cover letter.

FLUENCY

Collaborative Reading: Gather in a group. Have each student read one or more lines of a passage and then pass the text to the next student. Supply pronunciation and phrasing corrections as needed.

Invite students to do a timed reading of "Alone at Sea." Afterwards, have them enter their times on the Words-per-Minute table on page 121 and chart their reading speed on page 122 of the *Intermediate 1 Reader*.

🔊 Encourage students to listen to "Alone at Sea." Go to **www.mhreadingbasics.com** to play or download the recording. The recording provides modeled fluency and read-along support.

APPLICATION

Workplace Skill:

Identify Style Techniques in E-mails

Have students read the e-mails. Remind them that most business communications are written in a formal style. Writers avoid casual language, such as slang, abbreviations, and contractions. Point out that e-mails between coworkers can be less formal but they should still be professional. After students answer the questions, have them make a two-column chart and label one column *formal* and one column *informal*. Have them list appropriate uses for each kind of communication. This list will be useful for the Write for Work activity.

Write for Work

Remind students that when they want to show that they are serious, professional, and qualified, they should use a formal writing style. Encourage them to share their work with a classmate to make sure their letter uses a formal and professional style from beginning to end.

PASSKEY

💻 Go to **www.mhreadingbasics.com** and click on the *PassKey* link. Customize instruction for your class using modules from Reading/Language Arts, Levels 2 & 3.

Introduce

READING SKILL

Make Generalizations

Explain/Model: Explain that passages sometimes include generalizations, or general statements. Readers recognize generalizations and also make them by using information in the passage and their own knowledge. Have students read the passage about dog parks. Discuss the generalization in the passage and point out that a logical generalization makes sense and is supported by information in the passage.

Guided Practice: Have students read the boxed passage. Then work with them to complete the task given in the directions. Discuss why the response given after the passage is correct. Ask students to identify some words that signaled the generalization.

Teach Lesson Skills

Practice: Have students read the passages. Tell them to look for specific facts and details that can lead them to a logical conclusion. Discuss the answers to the questions and have students point out the details in the passages that support their answers.

Apply: After students answer the questions, have them read their generalizations aloud to the class. Encourage them to show classmates the information and details they used to make their generalizations.

Check Up: Have students work in small groups to read the passages and answer the questions. Then check each group's responses with those of other groups in the class.

COMPREHENSION

Use Prior Knowledge: Encourage students to think about what they already know before they read. To get students started, provide self-questioning models, such as *Have I read about this topic before? Does this sound familiar?* When students can create a context or framework of known information in which to place new information, they consciously monitor their own comprehension.

Reading Extension

📖 Encourage students to read "Night Killers" on page 65 of the *Intermediate 1 Reader.* Use this as an opportunity to teach reading strategies and the lesson reading skill.

ALPHABETICS

Explore Words

Hard and Soft *c* and *g*: Write these words and read them with students: *gum, gem, camp, cent, pigeon, price.* Have students tell whether the *g* or *c* in each word is hard or soft.

Prefixes *pre-, pro-*: Have volunteers underline the prefix in each word: *prewrite, promarket, proactive, preview.* Then discuss the meaning of each word.

Spelling: Possessives: Use examples such as these to model forming singular and plural possessive forms: *the camper's tent, the campers' tents; the firefighter's uniform, the firefighters' uniforms.* Have students suggest other examples.

VOCABULARY

Academic Vocabulary/Tier 2

general applies events specific logical

Before students complete the activity, write the academic vocabulary words and definitions on the board. Discuss each word's meaning with students. Then write the sentences below on the board. Read each sentence aloud and discuss it with students.

1. We will be in the *general* area of downtown, but I can't give you any more information.
2. The discount *applies* to the large pizza only.
3. The community center plans many *events.*
4. I need *specific* instructions to do this task.
5. Since Inez and Tony live and work near one other, it is *logical* for them to carpool.

FLUENCY

Repeated Reading: Lead a group to read the same passage aloud together several times. As the leader, emphasize accuracy and phrasing until the group reading sounds smooth and consistent.

Invite students to do a timed reading of "Night Killers." Afterwards, have them enter their times on the Words-per-Minute table on page 121 and chart their reading speed on page 122 of the *Intermediate 1 Reader.*

📶 Encourage students to listen to "Night Killers." Go to **www.mhereadingbasics.com** to play or download the recording. The recording provides modeled fluency and read-along support.

APPLICATION

Workplace Skill:

Make Generalizations from a Salary Table

Remind students that a table is a visual comparison of data. Point out that students should read the table's title, column headings, and small print first to understand what information is being compared. Then they can compare the data to arrive at logical generalizations about the information. After students read the table and answer the questions, have them tell a partner what they notice about the salaries of computer science teachers in different cities. This activity will come in handy when they do the Write for Work activity.

Write for Work

Tell students that to make generalizations about information in the table, they should compare two or more sets of data. Encourage students to use words such as *most, usually*, and *typically* in their generalizations. Have partners check each other's generalizations to make sure they are logical.

PASSKEY

🔑 Go to **www.mhereadingbasics.com** and click on the *PassKey* link. Customize instruction for your class using modules from Reading/Language Arts, Levels 2 & 3.

Lesson Plan Intermediate 1 Student Edition

Intermediate 1 Student Edition

Introduce

READING SKILL

Recognize Author's Purpose, Effect, and Intention

Explain/Model: Tell students that thinking about why an author wrote a passage and what the author wants them to know can improve their comprehension. Have students read aloud the passage about smoking. Point out the style techniques that the author uses.

Guided Practice: Have students read the boxed passage. Then work with them to complete the task given in the directions. Discuss why the responses given after the passage are correct. Ask students to identify style techniques that help create the welcoming effect.

Teach Lesson Skills

Practice: Have students read each passage. Tell them to think about why the author wrote the passage and what the author wanted readers to think, feel, know, or do. Discuss the answers and have students point out the details in the passages that support their answers.

Apply: After students answer the questions, have them read their responses aloud to the class. Encourage them to show classmates which words or details helped them determine the author's purpose and intention.

Check Up: Have students work in small groups to read the passages and answer the questions. Then check each group's responses with those of other groups in the class.

COMPREHENSION

Clarify Meaning: Encourage students to actively clarify meaning as they read. Provide self-questioning models, such as *What clues can I find in other sentences to help me understand this word? Does this word resemble any other words I have learned? Can I find someone to ask about this?* When students proactively try to clarify meaning, they consciously monitor their own comprehension.

Reading Extension

 Encourage students to read "Escape to Freedom" on page 73 of the *Intermediate 1 Reader*. Use this as an opportunity to teach reading strategies and the lesson reading skill.

ALPHABETICS

Explore Words

Long e and Long i Spelled -y: Write *daisy, apply, intensify, every, pry,* and *swiftly*. Read the words aloud with students. Have them sort the words into two categories: long *e* and long *i*.

Suffixes -ful, -ness: Write the following base words: *thought, sweet, mean, help, ill*. Have students choose -ful or -ness to add to each word. Write the new words and discuss their meanings.

Context Clues: Write these sentences and model using context clues to determine the meaning of the underlined words: *The room was filled to capacity. It could not hold any more people. The crowd gave the actors a standing ovation. The applause was loud.*

VOCABULARY

Academic Vocabulary/Tier 2

convey intention purpose describe persuade

Before students complete the activity, write the academic vocabulary words and definitions on the board. Discuss each word's meaning with students. Then write the sentences below on the board. Read each sentence aloud and discuss it with students.

1. Please *convey* this message to your boss.
2. My *intention* is to go to the gym after work.
3. The *purpose* of the meeting was to choose carpeting for the new office.
4. Can you *describe* what you are wearing so it will be easy for me to spot you in the crowd?
5. Izi tried to *persuade* Mac to see the movie.

FLUENCY

Marked Phrase Reading: Mark a passage with phrase boundaries, showing how words should be grouped for meaning and emphasis. Read the passage aloud, having students follow along, and then read aloud together with students.

Invite students to do a timed reading of "Escape to Freedom." Afterwards, have them enter their times on the Words-per-Minute table on page 121 and chart their reading speed on page 122 of the *Intermediate 1 Reader*.

Encourage students to listen to "Escape to Freedom." Go to **www.mhereadingbasics.com** to play or download the recording. The recording provides modeled fluency and read-along support.

APPLICATION

Workplace Skill:

Understand Author's Purpose in an Employee Memo

Have students read the memo. Remind them that a memo is a workplace document that sends a message to one or more persons. Point out that a memo's format can make it easier to determine the author's purpose. For example, the subject line often provides a clue to the purpose and intention of the memo. After students answer the questions, have them start a list of important details that need to be included in a memo for a company picnic. This list will come in handy when they do the Write for Work activity.

Write for Work

Remind students which important details are needed in a good memo. Tell them to read the instructions for this task carefully to be sure they include all the requested information. Encourage classmates to share their work and suggest ways to make the memo clearer.

PASSKEY

Go to **www.mhereadingbasics.com** and click on the *PassKey* link. Customize instruction for your class using modules from Reading/Language Arts, Levels 2 & 3.

Lesson Plan Intermediate 1 Student Edition

Unit 2 Lesson 2.6 pages 118–125

Introduce

READING SKILL

Read Graphs

Explain /Model: Preview the lesson with students, pointing out examples of bar graphs, circle graphs, and line graphs. Point out the horizontal and vertical axes that provide information on the bar graphs and line graphs. Have students look at the bar graph about dogs at a park on a given day. Model for students how you can tell which day had the most dogs and which day had the least dogs.

Guided Practice: Have students look at the graph on the right. Then work with them to complete the task given in the directions. Encourage students to use the lengths of the bars to help them. Discuss why the responses given after the graph are correct. Ask students to estimate the length of the Ohio and the Snake rivers.

Teach Lesson Skills

Practice: Have students look at the circle graph about budgets. Tell them to read the labels and percentages to help them interpret the graph. Discuss the answers to the questions and have students point out sections of the graph that support their answers.

Apply: After students answer the questions about the line graph, have them read their responses aloud to the class. Encourage them to demonstrate reading the graph to show how they answered each question.

Check Up: Have students work in small groups to read the bar graph and answer the questions. Then check each group's responses with those of other groups in the class.

COMPREHENSION

Visualize: Encourage students to use sensory imaging as a mental tool when they read. Provide useful self-questioning models, such as *What do I see in this photo? Does this diagram help me understand the text? Can I form a mental image of what the author is describing?* When students visualize what they are reading, they consciously monitor their own comprehension.

ALPHABETICS

Explore Words

Base Words: Review that base words can stand alone and have meaning. Write these words: *thoughtful, helped, review, unkind, colder, repayment.* Ask students to identify the base word in each word. Underline it as they say it.

Spelling: Plurals: Model forming the plurals of these words: *search, glass, coat, puppy, battery.* Have students point out any spelling changes you made.

Spelling: Contractions: Write these phrases: *he will, would not, does not, we are, she is, I will, do not.* Have students write the contraction for each. Then have volunteers use the contractions in sentences.

VOCABULARY

Academic Vocabulary/Tier 2

graph data illustrate label estimate

Before students complete the activity, write the academic vocabulary words and definitions on the board. Discuss each word's meaning with students. Then write the sentences below on the board. Read each sentence aloud and discuss it with students.

1. The bar *graph* showed the average temperatures.

2. Researchers collect *data* about safety records.

3. A pie chart can *illustrate* how I spend my free time.

4. The *label* on the soup can gives information about ingredients and nutrition.

5. I *estimate* that it will take about five minutes to walk to your house from my house.

FLUENCY

Collaborative Reading: Gather in a group. Have each student read one or more lines of a passage and then pass the text to the next student. Supply pronunciation and phrasing corrections as needed.

APPLICATION

Workplace Skill:

Use a Sales Graph

Remind students that businesses often use graphs to show information. Point out that by following the path of the line on the line graph, they can see how a value rises and falls over a period of time. After students read the graph and answer the questions, have them explain to a partner what they noticed about milk sales during 2006. Were they steady, or were there big rises or falls? This activity will come in handy when they do the Write for Work activity.

Write for Work

Ask students to follow the ups and downs of the line graph to note how milk sales rose and fell during 2006. Then have them put that information into their own words. Encourage them to share their work with a classmate to make sure they accurately explained what happened to milk sales throughout the year.

Workplace Extension

Remind students that presentations require practice and preparation. The speaker must appear knowledgeable, have correct information, and be prepared to answer any questions. Have partners answer the questions and share their responses with the class.

PASSKEY

Go to **www.mhereadingbasics.com** and click on the *PassKey* link. Customize instruction for your class using modules from Reading/Language Arts, Levels 2 & 3.

Intermediate 1 Student Edition

Introduce

READING SKILL
Predict Outcomes

Explain/Model: Explain that when we read, we often make predictions about what will happen based on clues in the text and our own experience. After students read aloud the bulleted points, model the process of predicting outcomes, using the example about Tom. Point out that if you were to discover that Tom had just read about boxes filled with dangerous substances, you might need to adjust your prediction.

Guided Practice: Have students read the boxed passage and work with a partner to complete the task given in the directions. Discuss why the responses given after the passage are correct.

Teach Lesson Skills

Practice: Have students read the passages and make predictions. Tell them to use text information and their prior knowledge to make predictions. Discuss the answers and have students share information in the passages and from personal experience to support their answers.

Apply: After students answer the questions, have them read their responses aloud to the class. Encourage them to share specific text clues and things they know from experience that helped them make their predictions.

Check Up: Have students work in small groups to read the passages and answer the questions. Then check each group's responses with those of other groups in the class.

COMPREHENSION
Use Prior Knowledge: Encourage students to think about what they already know before they read. To get students started, provide self-questioning models, such as *Have I read about this topic before? Does this sound familiar?* When students can create a context or framework of known information in which to place new information, they consciously monitor their own comprehension.

Reading Extension
Encourage students to read "A Horrible Way to Die" on page 81 of the *Intermediate 1 Reader*. Use this as an opportunity to teach reading strategies and the lesson reading skill.

ALPHABETICS
Explore Words
Vowel Combinations: Write these words on the board and read them aloud: *drain/stray/strap, boat/blow/cow, wild/pill/fried, seal/brief/bread, fuel/full/mule.* Ask volunteers to circle the letters that stand for the vowel sound in each word. Then have students identify which words in each set have the same vowel sound.

Syllables: Write these examples and pronounce them both ways with students: *sil/ent* or *si/lent, ba/sic* or *bas/ic, ro/bin* or *rob/in.* Have students tell which word in each pair is divided correctly and whether the first syllable is open or closed.

VOCABULARY
Academic Vocabulary/Tier 2

predict outcome prior adjust reveal

Before students complete the activity, write the academic vocabulary words and definitions on the board. Discuss each word's meaning with students. Then write the sentences below on the board. Read each sentence aloud and discuss it with students.

1. On Friday, the sportscaster will *predict* who he thinks will win Saturday's game.
2. Don't tell me the *outcome* of the soccer match because I plan to watch it on TV.
3. Marla had no *prior* experience as a salesperson, but she was eager to learn.
4. I have to *adjust* to a new schedule.
5. The biography will *reveal* many of the famous actor's secrets.

FLUENCY
Echo Reading: Read a sentence from one of the passages aloud. Then have students echo you by reading the same sentence and trying to read with the same speed and expression as you do.

Invite students to do a timed reading of "A Horrible Way to Die." Afterwards, have them enter their times on the Words-per-Minute table on page 121 and chart their reading speed on page 122 of the *Intermediate 1 Reader*.

Encourage students to listen to "A Horrible Way to Die." Go to **www.mhereadingbasics.com** to play or download the recording. The recording provides modeled fluency and read-along support.

APPLICATION
Workplace Skill:
Use a Diagram to Predict Outcomes

Have students look at the diagram. Remind them that diagrams are plans, sketches, or outlines that show how to put something together or how something works. Point out that studying the picture and reading the label that goes with it will help students understand the information the diagram shows. After students answer the questions, have them summarize the information in the diagram to a partner. This activity will come in handy when they do the Write for Work activity.

Write for Work
Remind students that a summary retells the most important ideas and details of a passage. Tell them to write a brief summary of the information in the diagram. Encourage them to share their work with a classmate to make sure they included all the main ideas and important details.

PASSKEY
Go to **www.mhereadingbasics.com** and click on the *PassKey* link. Customize instruction for your class using modules from Reading/Language Arts, Levels 2 & 3.

Lesson Plan Intermediate 1 Student Edition

Unit 3 Lesson 3.2 pages 142–149

Introduce

READING SKILL
Identify Cause and Effect

Explain/Model: Explain that a cause can have more than one effect and an effect can have more than one cause, and have students read the information in the cause-and-effect charts. Then point out the signal words and model using them to describe the effects of the doubling of world population and the causes of the possible extinction of Asian elephants.

Guided Practice: Have students read the boxed passage. Then work with them to complete the task given in the directions. Encourage students to pay attention to signal words and note that a cause can have more than one effect. Discuss why the responses given after the passage are correct. Ask students to give at least two effects of the electrical problem on the subway.

Teach Lesson Skills

Practice: Have students read the sentences and list causes and effects. Tell them to look for signal words and think about *what happened* and *why* as they read. Discuss student responses and have students point out the signal words in the sentences.

Apply: After students complete the graphic organizer with causes and effects, have them read their responses aloud to the class. Encourage them to share the signal words they used or questions they asked themselves to identify causes and effects.

Check Up: Have students work in small groups to read and answer the questions. Then check each group's responses with those of other groups in the class.

COMPREHENSION

Understand Author's Purpose: Encourage students to consider the author's purpose as they read. Provide self-questioning models, such as *Why did the author decide to write this? What does the author want me to know?* By examining the author's purpose, students can better analyze their own reaction to the writing and consciously monitor their own comprehension.

Reading Extension

Encourage students to read "A Shocking Experience" on page 89 of the *Intermediate 1 Reader*. Use this as an opportunity to teach reading strategies and the lesson reading skill.

ALPHABETICS
Explore Words

Silent Letters: Write these words and read them aloud: *wrap, align, knit, budget, batch.* Have students identify the silent letters.

Spelling: Homophones: Write these words: *weight, night, write, four.* Model identifying a homophone for *weight* and use the two words in sentences that demonstrate the two meanings. Then have students follow the same procedure for the other homophones.

Prefixes: *post-, re-, un-*: Write these base words: *date, set, kind, operation, view, usual.* Have students choose *post-, re-,* or *un-* to form words that mean *after the date, set again, not kind, after the operation, view again,* and *not usual.*

VOCABULARY
Academic Vocabulary/Tier 2

cause effect relate obvious determine

Before students complete the activity, write the academic vocabulary words and definitions on the board. Discuss each word's meaning with students. Then write the sentences below on the board. Read each sentence aloud and discuss it with students.

1. The official figured out the *cause* of the fire.
2. One *effect* of the storm was a loss of power.
3. In a paragraph, all the sentences should *relate* to the main idea.
4. Susana's frown made it *obvious* that something was wrong.
5. My sister's spice cake has a secret ingredient, but I can't *determine* what it is.

FLUENCY

Partner Reading: Have partners read aloud to one another and/or read aloud at the same time. Encourage them to offer support and correction to one another. Circulate to offer guidance as needed.

Invite students to do a timed reading of "A Shocking Experience." Afterwards, have them enter their times on the Words-per-Minute table on page 121 and chart their reading speed on page 122 of the *Intermediate 1 Reader*.

Encourage students to listen to "A Shocking Experience." Go to **www.mhreadingbasics.com** to play or download the recording. The recording provides modeled fluency and read-along support.

APPLICATION
Workplace Skill:
Identify Cause and Effect in a Policy

Have students read the policy. Remind them that a company policy is a set of guidelines for employee actions and behavior. Point out that looking for causes and effects as they read will help them understand the reasons for the guidelines and what effect they have on them as employees. After students answer the questions, have them make a cause-and-effect graphic organizer and list three causes and effects from the attendance policy. This graphic organizer will come in handy when they do the Write for Work activity.

Write for Work

Tell students to include the most important ideas from the attendance policy and make sure they stress the importance of good attendance. Encourage partners to share their work and suggest ways to make the memo or e-mail clearer.

PASSKEY

Go to **www.mhreadingbasics.com** and click on the *PassKey* link. Customize instruction for your class using modules from Reading/Language Arts, Levels 2 & 3.

Lesson Plan Intermediate 1 Student Edition

Unit 3 Lesson 3.3 pages 150–157

Introduce

READING SKILL

Understand Consumer Materials

Explain/Model: Explain that consumers use and purchase products and services. Discuss examples that a business might use, such as paper supplies or window-washing services. Then explain that it is important to carefully read consumer materials, such as product labels, instructions, and contracts. Have students look at the nutrition label and discuss why the information might be important.

Guided Practice: Have students read the label. Then work with them to complete the task given in the directions. Encourage students to pay attention to abbreviations and fine print so they can better understand all the information. Discuss why the responses given after the questions are correct. Ask students to explain how they would use the information on a nutrition label.

Teach Lesson Skills

Practice: Have students read the coupon and answer the questions. Tell them to pay attention to the small type and to the ways they are supposed to use the coupon. Discuss the answers and have students point out the information on the coupon that supports their answers.

Apply: After students answer the questions, have them read their responses aloud to the class. Encourage them to show classmates the parts of the chart where they found the information to answer each question.

Check Up: Have students work in small groups to read the passage and answer the questions. Then check each group's responses with those of other groups in the class.

COMPREHENSION

Set a Purpose for Reading: Encourage students to set a purpose for reading. Provide self-questioning models, such as *What do I hope to learn? What do the directions tell me to look for? What will happen next?* By setting a purpose and then evaluating whether they achieved the purpose, students consciously monitor their own comprehension. They can also discuss the purpose they have determined with a peer or a teacher.

Reading Extension

📖 Encourage students to read "Needles That Cure" on page 97 of the *Intermediate 1 Reader*. Use this as an opportunity to teach reading strategies and the lesson reading skill.

ALPHABETICS

Explore Words

Vowel Combinations: Write these words and read them aloud, emphasizing the sounds of *au, aw,* and *oo: pause, claw, cool, foot.* Point out that *au* and *aw* stand for the same sound, while *oo* stands for two different sounds.

Spelling: Contractions: Write *do not, will not, she is, we are,* and *would not.* Have students write the contractions for these words and use them in sentences.

Spelling: Word Endings: Model changing *run* to *running, tasty* to *tastier,* and *white* to *whitest.* Have students describe the spelling change you made to each word.

VOCABULARY

Academic Vocabulary/Tier 2

consume   instructions   purchase   transfer   annual

Before students complete the activity, write the academic vocabulary words and definitions on the board. Discuss each word's meaning with students. Then write the sentences below on the board. Read each sentence aloud and discuss it with students.

1. We *consume* a lot of paper at work.
2. To log on, review the *instructions*.
3. I need to *purchase* a new microwave.
4. Carmen has to *transfer* her wallet and keys from her old purse to her new one.
5. Kevin scheduled his *annual* checkup.

FLUENCY

Collaborative Reading: Gather in a group. Have each student read one or more lines of a passage and then pass the text to the next student. Supply pronunciation and phrasing corrections as needed.

Invite students to do a timed reading of "Needles That Cure." Afterwards, have them enter their times on the Words-per-Minute table on page 121 and chart their reading speed on page 122 of the *Intermediate I Reader*.

🔊 Encourage students to listen to "Needles That Cure." Go to **www.mhreadingbasics.com** to play or download the recording. The recording provides modeled fluency and read-along support.

APPLICATION

Workplace Skill:

Use an Employee Direct Deposit Sign-up Document

Have students look at the sign-up form. Remind them that in the workplace, they may be asked to fill out forms to sign up for a variety of employee benefits and services. Point out that scanning the headings and bold print will give them a general idea of the information needed to complete the form. Reading the small print will help them understand details, restrictions, and other important information. Review that they should always read a form completely from beginning to end *before* filling it out. After students answer the questions, have them start a list of documents they would need to attach in order to participate in the company's direct deposit option. This list will come in handy when they do the Write for Work activity.

Write for Work

Brainstorm with students a list of information a letter from a bank would need to include in order for a person to get direct deposit of his or her paycheck. Tell them to use a formal tone in the letter. Encourage partners to share letters to make sure they have clearly stated that the customer has an account and has permission to use the direct deposit option.

PASSKEY

💻 Go to **www.mhreadingbasics.com** and click on the *PassKey* link. Customize instruction for your class using modules from Reading/Language Arts, Levels 2 & 3.

Introduce

READING SKILL

Recognize Character Traits

Explain/Model: Tell students that when reading, they should pay attention to what the characters or real people do and say to figure out what they are like. Have students read aloud the sentences about Lu Chu. Then model identifying words and actions that show that Lu Chu is thoughtful, impatient, excited, and nervous.

Guided Practice: Have students read the boxed passage. Then work with them to complete the task given in the directions. Discuss why the response given after the passage is correct. Ask students to give examples of narration or dialogue the author could have used.

Practice: Have students read the passages. Tell them to pay close attention to the things the characters do and say. Discuss the answers to the questions and have students point out specific words or actions in the passages that support their answers.

Apply: After students write their descriptions, have them read the descriptions aloud to the class. Encourage them to show classmates things the characters did or said that helped them write their descriptions.

Check Up: Have students work in small groups to read the passage and answer the questions. Then check each group's responses with those of other groups in the class.

Teach Lesson Skills

COMPREHENSION

Make Connections: Encourage students to make connections as they read. Provide self-questioning models, such as *Have I learned something about this topic before? What was the context? Have I had any experiences in my own life that relate to this topic?* When students relate what they are reading to their own lives and educational experience, they consciously monitor their own comprehension.

Reading Extension

📖 Encourage students to read "Hanging from a Cliff" on page 105 of the *Intermediate 1 Reader.* Use this as an opportunity to teach reading strategies and the lesson reading skill.

ALPHABETICS

Explore Words

r-Controlled Vowels: Write these pairs of words: *pride/party, report/pantry, furnish/friendship, precise/personal.* Read the words with students and have them identify the word in each pair with the *r*-controlled vowel. Ask volunteers to circle the letters that stand for the vowel sound.

Suffixes -y, -en: Model matching the following words with their meanings to help students understand the effect of the suffix: *soften/become soft, golden/made of gold, snowy/characterized by snow.*

Multiple-meaning Words: Write *fair, light,* and *fire.* Have students brainstorm meanings. Then have them use the words in sentences that show their meaning.

VOCABULARY

Academic Vocabulary/Tier 2

characters traits exhibit distinguish genres

Before students complete the activity, write the academic vocabulary words and definitions on the board. Discuss each word's meaning with students. Then write the sentences below on the board. Read each sentence aloud and discuss it with students.

1. The *characters* on the show are funny.
2. Strength and determination are two *traits* that most athletes possess.
3. Maya will *exhibit* her singing ability at the talent show.
4. I could not *distinguish* between the twins.
5. My favorite *genres* are fiction and poetry.

FLUENCY

Repeated Reading: Lead a group to read the same passage aloud together several times. As the leader, emphasize accuracy and phrasing until the group reading sounds smooth and consistent.

Invite students to do a timed reading of "Hanging from a Cliff." Afterwards, have them enter their times on the Words-per-Minute table on page 121 and chart their reading speed on page 122 of the *Intermediate 1 Reader.*

📶 Encourage students to listen to "Hanging from a Cliff." Go to **www.mhereadingbasics.com** to play or download the recording. The recording provides modeled fluency and read-along support.

APPLICATION

Workplace Skill:

Compare Character Traits in a Planning Document

Have students read the planning document. Remind them that a planning document describes how to accomplish a task or achieve a goal. Point out that thinking about the goals and delivery methods that a supervisor describes can help them figure out what that supervisor's management style is like. After students answer the questions, have them start a two-column chart of things employees can do to keep a workplace lunchroom neat and clean on a daily and weekly basis. This chart will come in handy for the Write for Work activity.

Write for Work

Remind students that a planning document lists steps for achieving a goal. Tell them to read the instructions carefully to be sure they include all the requested information. Have partners share their work and suggest ways to make the planning document clearer.

PASSKEY

📖 Go to **www.mhereadingbasics.com** and click on the *PassKey* link. Customize instruction for your class using modules from Reading/Language Arts, Levels 2 & 3.

Lesson Plan Intermediate 1 Student Edition

Intermediate 1 Student Edition

Introduce

READING SKILL
Identify Fact and Opinion

Explain/Model: Explain that words such as *must, should, greater, fastest,* and *most* often signal opinions. Have students read aloud the facts and opinions about Joe DiMaggio and George Washington. Point out the use of the words *better* and *best*.

Guided Practice: Have students read the boxed passage. Then work with them to complete the task given in the directions. Encourage students to look for words that signal opinions and to think about which statements can be proved. Discuss why the responses given after the passage are correct. Ask students to restate one of the opinions as a fact.

Teach Lesson Skills

Practice: Have students read the statements and write them in the correct column of the graphic organizer. Tell them to think about which statements can be proved and which ones show what someone thinks or believes. Discuss their responses and have students explain how they distinguished between facts and opinions.

Apply: After students complete each item, have them read their responses aloud to the class. Encourage them to explain how they would use the resources they chose to prove the facts.

Check Up: Have students work in small groups to read and answer the questions. Then check each group's responses with those of other groups in the class.

COMPREHENSION
Reread/Read More Slowly: Encourage students to become aware of the pace at which they read. Offer self-questioning models, such as *Did I read this passage too quickly? Does reading it again help me understand better? Does reading more slowly help me retain information?* When students actively consider the manner in which they are reading, they consciously monitor their own comprehension.

Reading Extension
Encourage students to read "Killer Bees" on page 113 of the *Intermediate 1 Reader*. Use this as an opportunity to teach reading strategies and the lesson reading skill.

ALPHABETICS
Explore Words

Consonant Pairs: Write the following words: *timber, crumb, score, scenic*. Have students underline the consonant pair *sc* or *mb* in each word and tell whether it stands for one sound or two.

Syllables: Write these syllables: *cir, wig, pur, furn, gle, ple, ish, cle*. Review the syllable types and read them aloud. Then model combining the syllables to form *circle, wiggle, purple,* and *furnish*. Read aloud the words with students.

Base Words: Write these words: *retake, unwisely, preheat, careful, unlikely*. Have students underline each base word. Help students define each complete word.

VOCABULARY
Academic Vocabulary/Tier 2

fact   opinion   prove   viewpoint   signal

Before students complete the activity, write the academic vocabulary words and definitions on the board. Discuss each word's meaning with students. Then write the sentences below on the board. Read each sentence aloud and discuss it with students.

1. Check each *fact* to make sure it is correct.
2. In my *opinion*, the movie was too long.
3. Vaz gave an example to *prove* his point.
4. From a child's *viewpoint*, a cookie is a better snack than carrot sticks.
5. The librarian put a finger to her mouth to *signal* the students to stop talking.

FLUENCY
Marked Phrase Reading: Mark a passage with phrase boundaries, showing how words should be grouped for meaning and emphasis. Read the passage aloud, having students follow along, and then read aloud together with students.

Invite students to do a timed reading of "Killer Bees." Afterwards, have them enter their times on the Words-per-Minute table on page 121 and chart their reading speed on page 122 of the *Intermediate 1 Reader*.

Encourage students to listen to "Killer Bees." Go to **www.mhereadingbasics.com** to play or download the recording. The recording provides modeled fluency and read-along support.

APPLICATION
Workplace Skill:

Distinguish between Fact and Opinion in a Business Ad

Have students look at the ad. Remind them that ads are messages that try to persuade people to think or do something. Point out that distinguishing between facts and opinions can help readers make decisions about the product or service that is being advertised. After students answer the questions, have them list facts and opinions that they might use in an ad for a winter coat sale. This list will come in handy for the Write for Work activity.

Write for Work
Remind students that ads are a mix of facts and opinions. Point out that facts might include the date, time, location, and prices offered. Opinions are often expressed in persuasive language. Ask students to share their ads with a classmate and check that they have included necessary facts and persuasive language.

PASSKEY
Go to **www.mhereadingbasics.com** and click on the *PassKey* link. Customize instruction for your class using modules from Reading/Language Arts, Levels 2 & 3.

Introduce

READING SKILL

Use Indexes

Explain/Model: Tell students it is important to first scan an index to see how it is organized. Model how you would use the index to find information about air travel. Then ask them to tell when they have used indexes and why indexes are helpful.

Guided Practice: Work with students to use the index to complete the task given in the directions. Encourage students to pay attention to both the headings and subheadings within the index. Discuss why the responses given after the index are correct. Ask students to give additional examples of information that can be found in the book and on which pages it can be found.

Teach Lesson Skills

Practice: Have students read the magazine index. Tell them to scan the index headings first to see how the information is organized. Then have them read it in more detail. Discuss the answers to the questions and have students point out the index entry or entries that support their answers.

Apply: After students answer the questions, have them read their responses aloud to the class. Encourage them to show classmates where they found the answers in the index.

Check Up: Have students work in small groups to read the index and answer the questions. Then check each group's responses with those of other groups in the class.

COMPREHENSION

Clarify Meaning: Encourage students to actively clarify meaning as they read. Provide self-questioning models, such as *What clues can I find in other sentences to help me understand this word? Does this word resemble any other words I have learned? Can I find someone to ask about this?* When students proactively try to clarify meaning, they consciously monitor their own comprehension.

ALPHABETICS

Explore Words

The Schwa: Review the rules for syllable division, using *picnic* and *wagon*. Then write these words and read them aloud, emphasizing the stressed syllable: *regal, dollop, review.* Help students identify the schwa sound.

Prefixes *uni-, bi-, tri-*: Write the prefixes *uni-, bi-,* and *tri-* and the numbers 1, 2, and 3. Have students match the prefixes with the numbers. Then have them write a word for each prefix.

Spelling: Plurals: Model making the words *tent, beach, puppy, puff,* and *knife* plural. Have students identify any spelling changes. Then have them make the words *camp, bush, bunny, cuff,* and *life* plural.

VOCABULARY

Academic Vocabulary/Tier 2

index   subject   discuss   order   scan

Before students complete the activity, write the academic vocabulary words and definitions on the board. Discuss each word's meaning with students. Then write the sentences below on the board. Read each sentence aloud and discuss it with students.

1. The *index* shows that information about butterflies can be found on page 42.
2. The *subject* of today's lecture is about responsibility and reliability.
3. The boss held a meeting to *discuss* attendance issues.
4. List the last names in alphabetical *order.*
5. I always *scan* the headlines before I read a newspaper.

FLUENCY

Repeated Reading: Lead a group to read the same passage aloud together several times. As the leader, emphasize accuracy and phrasing until the group reading sounds smooth and consistent.

APPLICATION

Workplace Skill:

Use Indexes to Locate Information

Have students look at the index. Remind them that an index is an alphabetical list of names, topics, and terms that are mentioned in a book and the page numbers where they appear. Point out that using an index makes it quicker and easier to find specific information. After students answer the questions, have them make a list of steps for using an index. This list will come in handy when they do the Write for Work activity.

Write for Work

Tell students to make sure they have their coworker identify the problem and then use the index to find where information about it can be located in the manual. Suggest they briefly summarize the steps for using an index. Encourage them to share their work with a classmate and ask one another for suggestions about ways to make the e-mail clearer.

Workplace Extension

Remind students that people often choose careers based on their interests. They may need further education or training in order to pursue their chosen profession. Have them discuss why nutrition is a good match for Ryan's interests. Have partners respond to the questions and share their responses with the class.

PASSKEY

 Go to **www.mhereadingbasics.com** and click on the *PassKey* link. Customize instruction for your class using modules from Reading/Language Arts, Levels 2 & 3.

Name_____ Date _____

Unit 1 Workplace Skill Activity
Set Priorities to Create a Schedule

In many jobs, you will often have several assignments and need to decide what has to be done first. You may sometimes need to work with others to make decisions about priorities. For example, if someone is out sick, you might need to divide up work assignments differently.

Follow these guidelines for setting priorities:

- Review all the tasks that need to be done.
- Determine which tasks have the highest priority.
- Note if any tasks must be done by a certain time or before others.

Imagine that you work at a small animal shelter that houses dogs and cats. Each day certain tasks must be accomplished, and some tasks should be done more than once a day. Work with a partner to create a daily schedule.

1. There are two staff members, Carlos and Anne, who both work eight hours a day from 9 A.M.–5 P.M. They each take an hour lunch break at different times.

2. Rank the priority of each task by writing *high*, *medium*, or *low* in the second column.

Tasks	Priority
clean cages	
wash/fold towels	
feed animals	
restock food from closet	
organize files	
do paperwork	
walk dogs	

3. Then fill out a schedule for each employee and his or her responsibility for each work hour. Don't forget to include a lunch break!

Name	9–10 A.M.	10–11 A.M.	11 A.M.–Noon	Noon–1 P.M.
Carlos				
Anne				
	1–2 P.M.	2–3 P.M.	3–4 P.M.	4–5 P.M.
Carlos				
Anne				

Unit 2 Workplace Skill Activity
Role-play an Interview

Many jobs require an interview before you are hired. It is important to prepare for interviews by having ready answers to commonly asked questions.

Suppose you are a production line worker at a factory that manufactures hand and power tools. In the break room, you see this notice informing employees about a job opening.

Retail Specialist

Description: As a retail specialist you will spend time in various retail stores that sell our products. You will maintain product displays, help customers buy the right products for their needs, and increase sales.

Requirements: To be a good fit for this opportunity:
- You have a strong understanding of the product line.
- You have excellent communication skills.
- You work well on a team with individuals from various backgrounds.

In addition:
- You can lift heavy loads and climb up and down ladders.
- You enjoy working with your hands.
- You have a valid driver's license, your own vehicle, and proof of car insurance or have other reliable transportation.

Contact: Aurora Mendes, Human Resources Manager, Extension 837, for an interview.

The job description interests you, and you decide to schedule an interview.

Read the interview questions and jot down notes about how you might answer them. Practice asking and answering the questions aloud with a partner.

1. Why do you want this position?

   _____

2. What skills and experience make you right for this job?

   _____

3. How would you describe your ability to work as a member of a team?

   _____

4. What motivates you to do a good job?

   _____

5. What questions do you have about the job?

   _____

Unit 3 Workplace Skill Activity
Role-play Requesting to Leave Early

Most jobs have attendance policies and set schedules to make sure there is enough staff to meet business needs. A supervisor usually makes the schedule and communicates it to employees. Most attendance policies require you to do the following:

- Arrive at your scheduled start time ready to begin working.
- Work until designated stopping times, such as breaks, meal times, or the end of a shift.
- Call in advance if you are going to be tardy or absent.
- Submit a doctor's note if you are absent for medical reasons for more than five days.

Sometimes personal situations arise that conflict with your schedule. When this happens, you will need to request time off or ask your manager to adjust your schedule. It is helpful if you can suggest ways to make up your work or rearrange your schedule.

Read the passage about an employee's problem. Work with a partner to respond to the directions below the box. Then use your responses to role-play a meeting between the employee and her boss.

> Bettina Hernandez is a file clerk at an office. She is scheduled to work each week from 8 A.M. to 3 P.M. on Monday through Thursday and from 8 A.M. to noon on Saturday. Bettina has just found out that she needs to leave at 2 P.M. every Monday and Wednesday to pick up her daughter from school. She needs to ask her manager to adjust her schedule to accommodate this.

1. List three solutions Bettina might offer to her manager.

   _____

   _____

2. List two objections the manager might make and ways to overcome them.
   Possible Objections:

   _____

   _____

   Solutions to Possible Objections:

   _____

   _____

3. Choose one solution and explain why you chose it.

   _____

Answer Key Intermediate 1 Student Edition

Unit 1 Lesson 1.1

Practice, page 15
1. A
2. H
3. D
4. H
5. D

Apply, page 16
Sample answers:
1. Some molds are good.
2. Molds on food look like fuzz.
3. Unwanted mold can spoil a food's taste.
4. Some cheeses need mold to get their flavor.
5. Throw away expired food.
6. No one knows for sure where sea salt came from.
7. Sea salt may have come from rocks.
8. Water washed salt off the rocks.
9. Every gallon of seawater has about a quarter of a pound of salt.

Check Up, page 17
1. B
2. J
3. B
4. H
5. A

Workplace Skill, page 18
1. D
2. G

Write for Work, page 19
Check that the writing includes the following points: a main idea about why the writer would like or dislike being a maintenance worker and one or two details to support the main idea.

Reading Extension, page 19
1. B
2. F
3. C
4. G
5. A
6. H
7. *Sample answers:* It was huge. It was almost nine feet long. It was almost three and a half feet high. It took eight men to carry it.
8. *Sample answers:* He was in charge of the railroad project. He was a skilled hunter.

Explore Words, page 20
Long Vowels
2. bike
3. pine
4. cake
5. cute
6. phone

Consonant Blends
2. str
3. nk
4. spr
5. nk
6. st
7. sl

Page 21
Compound Words
The following are compounds:
1. blueberry
2. worthwhile
3. afternoon
5. backyard
7. airport
9. earthquake

Spelling: Possessives
2. the baby's food
3. Youko's toy
4. my niece's ribbons

Academic Vocabulary
1. theory
2. recall
3. topic
4. details
5. passage

Unit 1 Lesson 1.2

Practice, page 23
1. not stated
2. stated
3. not stated
4. B
5. F
6. A
7. J

Apply, page 24
Sample answers:
1. Lightning is a great spark caused by an electric current.
2. A bolt of lightning can kill a person or start a fire.
3. Lightning can occur within one cloud or between a cloud and Earth.
4. Tears keep eyes moist and help keep out dust. Without tears, we would go blind.
5. Tears come from glands that are behind the upper eyelids.
6. When we cry, we let out too many tears for the ducts to handle—so they overflow.
7. Tear ducts are drains in the inside corners of the eyes.

Check Up, page 25
1. C
2. F
3. B
4. G
5. C

Workplace Skill, page 26
1. C
2. H
3. A
4. G

Write for Work, page 27
Check that the writing includes the following points: a clearly stated key concept about the company and at least one goal to achieve it.

Reading Extension, page 27
1. B
2. F
3. B
4. F
5. *Sample answer:* They were very thankful for the help she gave them.
6. *Sample answers:* The house had no stove or refrigerator. Her bed was a mat on the floor.

Explore Words, page 28
Consonant Blends
1. thr
2. shr
3. shr
4. thr

Suffix -able
1. taxable; able to be taxed
2. comfortable; able to give comfort
3. dependable; able to be depended upon
4. refundable; able to be refunded

Spelling: Contractions
1. don't
2. didn't
3. shouldn't
4. wouldn't
5. couldn't
6. aren't

Page 29
Syllables
2. la/tex
3. ex/act
4. ho/tel
5. cab/in
6. be/gin
7. mu/sic
8. rob/in
9. ti/ger
10. pock/et
11. drag/on
12. tu/lip

Answer Key Intermediate 1 Student Edition

Academic Vocabulary
1. directly
2. stated
3. margin
4. concept
5. notes

Unit 1 Lesson 1.3

Practice, page 31
1. C
2. J
3. valid

Apply, page 32
Sample answers:
1. Birds are built to fly.
2. Birds have to learn how to fly.
3. Bigger birds can soar and glide longer than smaller birds.

Check Up, page 33
1. D
2. G
3. C
4. F
5. B

Workplace Skill, page 34
1. D
2. G
3. C
4. F

Write for Work, page 35
Check that the writing includes the following points: a description of a specific product or service and a statement about why this product or service is special or beneficial.

Reading Extension, page 35
1. D
2. G
3. B
4. F
5. *Sample answer:* Most people strongly believed that the Tasaday were a true Stone Age tribe. They didn't want to believe that the tribe could possibly be a hoax.
6. *Sample answer:* There are probably no Stone Age tribes still living today.

Explore Words, page 36
Hard and Soft c
1. hard
2. soft
3. hard
4. soft
5. hard
6. hard

Syllables
2. bu)tane
3. inside
4. hu)mane
5. unmade
6. ba)sis

Prefixes sub-, in-
1. subbasement
2. inexperienced
3. substandard
4. incomplete

Page 37
Synonyms
1. worried
2. ached
3. difficult
4. carpet
5. kettle
6. careless
7. excited
8. book

Academic Vocabulary
1. frequently
2. conclude
3. valid
4. supported
5. evidence

Unit 1 Lesson 1.4

Practice, page 39
1. C
2. G
3. A

Apply, page 40
Sample answers:
Summary: We hear because the eardrum, bones, and fluid behind them vibrate from sound waves. The vibration stimulates nerve endings in the fluid to send a message to the brain.
Paraphrase: The eardrum is a thin flap of skin inside the ear. It vibrates when sound hits it. It sends the vibrations on to three tiny bones that lie behind it. The moving bones cause liquid in a canal to shake. The moving liquid makes nerve cells send impulses to the brain. The brain senses the impulses as sound.

Check Up, page 41
1. C
2. F
3. B
4. G
5. B
6. F

Workplace Skill, page 42
1. A
2. H

Write for Work, page 43
Sample answers: Summary: If you have not graduated from high school, you can take the GED test. Passing the test is equal to a high school diploma, and it can help you get jobs.
Paraphrase: Most GED test questions are multiple choice. Depending on your state, you can take the test in one or two parts. It can take up to seven hours to take the test.

Reading Extension, page 43
1. D
2. F
3. *Sample answer:* Luck, good health, and a new medical treatment gave Brown a better chance to be able to walk again than many people with the same injury.
4. *Sample answer:* Reggie Brown can't play football or do anything else that would risk hurting his neck or his head, but he can do many things that the average person can do.

Explore Words, page 44
Hard and Soft g
1. hard
2. soft
3. soft
4. hard
5. hard
6. soft

Syllables
1. b
2. a
3. c
4. b
5. c
6. a

Spelling: Contractions
1. you're
2. you'll
3. we'll
4. they're
5. it's
6. I'm

Page 45
Antonyms
1. c
2. e
3. h
4. g
5. a
6. f
7. i
8. b
9. j
10. d

Answer Key Intermediate 1 Student Edition

Academic Vocabulary
1. exclude
2. summary
3. reinforce
4. paraphrase
5. result

Unit 1 Lesson 1.5

Practice, page 47
1. contrast; but
2. contrast; however
3. compare; like
4. compare; both
5. contrast; although
6. contrast; on the other hand
7. contrast; in contrast
8. contrast; unlike
9. compare; similarly
10. compare; in the same way
11. compare; as
12. contrast; but
13. contrast; unlike
14. compare; like
15. compare; both
16. contrast; better than
17. compare; both
18. contrast; but
19. compare; as well
20. compare; likewise

Apply, page 48
Sample answers:
1. Alike: The Rocky Mountains and Appalachian Mountains are in North America and rise far above surrounding land. Different: The Appalachians have rounded peaks, worn by erosion; in contrast, the younger Rocky Mountains have tall, sharp, ice-capped peaks.
2. Alike: Like a housefly, an ant is an insect with six legs. Different: Unlike houseflies, ants do not all have wings, and they live in organized communities.
3. Alike: A dance class and aerobics class both require people to move through a set of steps together to music. Different: People take a dance class to learn dance steps for pleasure or performance; on the other hand, aerobics students want to get fit.
4. Alike: Like the spoon, the fork is an eating tool with a flat handle. Different: A spoon has a bowl on the end; in contrast, a fork has sharp tines to spear food.
5. Alike: A pen and pencil are both writing tools. Different: Pencils write with graphite and can be erased, but pens write with ink and cannot be erased.

Check Up, page 49
1. B
2. J
3. C
4. F
5. B

Workplace Skill, page 50
1. A
2. H
3. C
4. G

Write for Work, page 51
Check that the writing includes a statement that the graph shows the percentages of six of the most popular jobs for women.

Reading Extension, page 51
1. D
2. H
3. B
4. *Sample answer:* Every set of twins had amazing similarities.
5. *Sample answer:* They both wore rectangular, wire-rimmed glasses.

Explore Words, page 52
The Letter x
1. ks
2. gz
3. gz
4. ks
5. gz
6. gz
7. ks
8. ks

Compound Words
1. bookmark
2. bookcase
3. checklist
4. checkbook

Spelling: Plurals
1. coupons
2. students
3. dishes
4. teachers
5. churches
6. dresses
7. taxes
8. buses

Page 53
Word Endings -er, -est
1. longer, longest
   Sample answers:
   The girl's hair was longer than the boy's hair.
   Takiko's hair was the longest in the class.
2. louder, loudest
   Sample answers:
   A Great Dane barks louder than a Chihuahua.
   Dillon bought the loudest alarm clock in the store.
3. smaller, smallest
   Sample answers: A baby is smaller than a toddler. Imelda bought the smallest cell phone in the store.
4. thicker, thickest
   Sample answers: Miko has thicker hair than her sister. Juanita wanted to find the thickest book in the library.

Academic Vocabulary
1. contrast
2. similar
3. clue
4. compare
5. organize

Unit 1 Lesson 1.6

Practice, page 55
1. Social Security number
2. $24,000
3. Diaz, Anna
4. D
5. G

Apply, page 56
1. It is the person applying for the insurance.
2. nothing, N/A, or not applicable
3. height and weight
4. circle the one that answers each question
5. the date the applicant (and/or spouse) last visited or talked to a doctor

Check Up, page 57
1. B
2. G
3. D

Answer Key Intermediate 1 Student Edition

Workplace Skill, page 58
1. C
2. F
3. B
4. F

Write for Work, page 59
The writer should attempt to fill out as much of the application form as possible.

Workplace Extension, page 59
1. D
2. G
3. *Sample answer:* Jamal should be polite with the customer and answer the question. If he cannot answer the question, he should get someone else in the store to help the customer.

Explore Words, page 60
Consonant Pairs wr, kn, gn
2. kn
3. wr
4. gn
5. wr
6. kn

Long e Spelled -y
1. study
2. ugly
3. any
4. family

Context Clues
1. tired
2. open waters that do not belong to any nation
3. stopped
4. no way to leave

Page 61
Spelling: Possessives
2. dogs'
3. hawk's
4. turkeys'
5. fox's
6. father's
7. girls'
8. twins'

Academic Vocabulary
1. survey
2. abbreviate
3. medical
4. form
5. clarify

Unit 1 Lesson 1.7

Practice, page 63
1. C
2. F
3. B

Apply, page 64
Sample answers:
1. *Main Idea:* In 2009 some people in Michigan made the world's largest slab of fudge.
2. *Detail:* It measured 8 feet by 36.3 feet and weighed 5,200 pounds.
3. *Main Idea:* Your foot falls asleep when it doesn't get enough blood because the blood vessels are blocked.
4. *Detail:* When you sit on your foot, you block off the blood vessels.
5. *Main Idea:* California condors are in danger of extinction.
6. *Detail:* Not many baby condors are born each year.

Check Up, page 65
1. C
2. H
3. A
4. H
5. C

Workplace Skill, page 66
1. D
2. F

Write for Work, page 67
Check that the writing includes a few advantages and disadvantages of working for the government.

Workplace Extension, page 67
1. C
2. J
3. *Sample answer:* He feels lucky that he got a job because he quit high school early.
4. *Sample answer:* To get a better job, Lewis needs to listen to his boss and go back to school.

Explore Words, page 68
Consonant Pair sc
1. two sounds
2. one sound
3. two sounds
4. two sounds
5. one sound
6. two sounds

Long i Spelled -y
1. pry
2. sky
3. apply
4. shy
5. try
6. cry

Context Clues
1. a
2. b
3. b
4. a

Page 69
Multiple-meaning Words
1. b
2. a
3. b
4. b
5. b
6. a
7. a
8. b

Academic Vocabulary
1. point
2. identify
3. examine
4. example
5. relationship

Unit 1 Assessment

Pages 71–76
1. B
2. F
3. C
4. J
5. A
6. G
7. C
8. J
9. A
10. H
11. B
12. J
13. C
14. G
15. D
16. F
17. D
18. F
19. C
20. F
21. D
22. G
23. C
24. F
25. C
26. H
27. D
28. H
29. A
30. J
31. A
32. F
33. C

Unit 1 Workplace Skill Activity
Answers should include priorities and a completed schedule reflecting those priorities.

Sample list of priorities:
High: feed animals, clean cages, walk dogs; **Medium:** restock food, wash/fold towels, do paperwork; **Low:** organize files
Schedules will vary but should include all the tasks in the list and reflect priorities assigned by students. Tasks, such as feeding the animals and walking the dogs, should appear more than once on the schedule.

Unit 2 Lesson 2.1

Practice, page 79
1. A
2. G
3. B
4. J
5. D

Apply, page 80
1. The inventor records the date the invention came to mind.
2. The inventor draws a sketch with a description of the idea.
3. The inventor has two witnesses sign the document.
4. The inventor submits an application to the patent office.
5. The patent office checks to see whether anyone else has submitted a patent for the same thing.
6. If the application is accepted, the patent office gives the invention a patent number.

Check Up, page 81
1. C
2. F
3. D
4. H

Workplace Skill, page 82
1. B
2. H

Write for Work, page 83
Check that the writing includes the following points: The steps are written in the writer's own words. Make sure that the sequence of steps has not changed and that the sequence is correct.

Reading Extension, page 83
1. A
2. J
3. D
4. H
5. *Sample answers:* then, once, during that time, by the end, next, finally, by the time
6. They wrapped the body with 20 layers of cloth.

Explore Words, page 84
Vowel Combinations
1. train
2. week
3. due
4. lie
5. paint
6. sweet

Syllables
1. cra / dle; open
2. ti / tle; open
3. sam / ple; closed
4. puz / zle; closed

Synonyms
1. C
2. G

Page 85
Spelling: Homophones
1. flour
2. sale
3. jeans
4. bored
5. whole
6. guessed
7. blew
8. pane
9. wrapper

Academic Vocabulary
1. sequence
2. application
3. section
4. obtain
5. submit

Unit 2 Lesson 2.2

Practice, page 87
1. A
2. H
3. B
4. F

Apply, page 88
Sample answers:
1. A Many workers do not interact with customers.
   B Dressing down makes employees happier.
   C Dressing down makes employees more productive.
2. A It is proven that animal therapy lowers blood pressure.
   B Animal therapy can decrease anxiety.
   C Dogs can make the sick and elderly feel useful.

Check Up, page 89
1. B
2. G
3. A
4. H
5. C
6. J
7. B

Workplace Skill, page 90
1. B
2. J

Write for Work, page 91
Check that the writing includes the following points: The main idea of the procedures is to provide guidance to employees about how to run a company project. Three details from the procedures should support that main idea.

Reading Extension, page 91
1. A
2. J
3. C
Sample answers:
4. They were angry that the Canadians had helped the Americans escape.
5. He opened an office and hired staff. He created a script for a fake movie.

Explore Words, page 92
r-Controlled Vowels
1. curb
2. scar
3. charge
4. skirt
5. short
6. market

Syllables
2. sta / ble; open
3. gos / sip; closed
4. can / dle; closed
5. in / sect; closed
6. ma / ple; open

Antonyms
1. deep, shallow
2. easy, hard
3. dead, alive
4. smooth, rough
5. stupid, smart
6. cruel, kind

Page 93

Compound Words
1. c; firefighter
2. f; beehive
3. a; bookbag
4. h; cardboard
5. g; countdown
6. e; applesauce
7. b; hairstyle
8. d; earthquake

Academic Vocabulary
1. judge
2. include
3. argument
4. support
5. enhance

Unit 2 Lesson 2.3

Practice, page 95
1. Writer B
2. Writer C
3. Writer A

Apply, page 96
1. descriptive details; punctuation for emphasis; long sentences
2. dialogue
3. action; descriptive details; punctuation for emphasis

Check Up, page 97
1. B
2. J
3. A
4. F

Workplace Skill, page 98
1. B
2. J

Write for Work, page 99
Check that the writing includes the following points: The writer understands the difference between a formal writing style and an informal writing style and when it is appropriate to use one or the other. The letter should be professional and formal in tone.

Reading Extension, page 99
1. A
2. J
3. A
4. G
5. *Sample answer using long sentences:* On December 23, 1952, Dr. Alain Bombard reached the West Indies after being at sea for 65 days and after sailing 2,750 miles. He had lost 56 pounds, but he was alive, he had proven his theory, and he had the unbroken seal on his emergency supplies to prove it!

Explore Words, page 100

Vowel Combinations
2. flies
3. goes
4. rescue
5. crow
6. true
7. died
8. value
9. cloak

Spelling: Homophones
1. horse
2. would
3. allowed
4. won
5. waste
6. stare

Spelling: Word Endings
1. attending
2. strongest
3. scared
4. digging
5. eraser
6. zigzagged

Page 101

Syllables
2. pi / lot; open
3. cra / zy; open
4. cab / in; closed
5. pro / gram; open
6. com / et; closed
7. rob / in; closed
8. car / ton; closed
9. sal / ad; closed
10. mel / on; closed
11. la / bor; open
12. be / low; open
13. pil / grim; closed
14. bro / ken; open

Academic Vocabulary
1. technique
2. highlight
3. communicate
4. emphasis
5. style

Unit 2 Lesson 2.4

Practice, page 103
1. A
2. G
3. D

Apply, page 104
Sample answers:
1. is thinking about or playing soccer.
2. care for their pet very well.
3. are probably 50 to 60 years old.
4. reads books.

Check Up, page 105
1. C
2. F
3. A

Workplace Skill, page 106
1. B
2. H

Write for Work, page 107
Check that the writing includes the following points: The writer has provided sensible generalizations. *Sample answer:* Boston metropolitan area teachers are paid more than many teachers. Teachers in Los Angeles make more money than teachers in Bethesda through most of their careers.

Reading Extension, page 107
1. C
2. J
3. A
4. *Sample answer:* If you live in a cold climate, you don't have to worry about vampire bats.

Answer Key Intermediate 1 Student Edition

Explore Words, page 108

Hard and Soft c *and* g
1. hard
2. soft
3. hard
4. soft
5. hard
6. soft

Consonant Pairs kn, wr, gn
1. kn
2. gn
3. kn
4. gn
5. wr
6. wr
7. kn
8. kn
9. kn
10. wr
11. wr
12. gn

Prefixes pre-, pro-
1. shrunk earlier
2. in support of labor
3. heat before
4. in support of democracy

Page 109

Spelling: Possessives
2. the doctor's patients
3. the workers' lunches
4. my brother's car
5. my sisters' children
6. the carpenter's tools
7. the dogs' fleas
8. our families' support

Academic Vocabulary
1. events
2. logical
3. applies
4. specific
5. general

Unit 2 Lesson 2.5

Practice, page 111
1. to persuade people to help raise funds
2. The writer uses words such as *benefit, improve, safely,* and *important.*
3. to entertain with a story
4. suspense
5. to entertain with a story
6. to express mixed feelings

Apply, page 112
1. to describe sea horses
2. to make the information lively and engaging

3. *Sample answer:* the use of facts, questions, exclamation points, and description
4. to persuade the city council to put a stoplight on a certain corner
5. It conveys a sense that the issue is critical.
6. *Sample answer:* very dangerous, fatally, immediate, greatly reduce

Check Up, page 113
1. C
2. H
3. A
4. H

Workplace Skill, page 114
1. C
2. J

Write for Work, page 115
Check that the writing includes the following points: The writer should use the correct memo or e-mail format with date and subject. The memo should include key points that fellow employees need to know about the company picnic.

Reading Extension, page 115
1. D
2. G
3. C
4. *Sample answer:* It might help readers finish the selection on an upbeat note.
5. *Sample answer:* to add to the feeling of danger and suspense and to make readers aware of how much danger Douglass was in

Explore Words, page 116
Long e *and Long* i *Spelled* -y
1. long *i*
2. long *e*
3. long *e*
4. long *i*
5. long *e*
6. long *i*

Suffixes -ful, -ness
Sample answers:
1. careful
2. fondness
3. sickness
4. helpful
5. thoughtful
6. illness

Context Clues
Sample answers:
1. make
2. joining
3. not able
4. decay

Page 117

Spelling: Word Endings
1. greatness
2. freezing
3. thickest
4. cloudiness
5. copied
6. annoying
7. thankful
8. earliest
9. madder
10. bragged

Academic Vocabulary
1. intention
2. purpose
3. persuade
4. convey
5. describe

Unit 2 Lesson 2.6

Practice, page 119
1. the Jackson family budget
2. Each section represents a category of spending.
3. 8%
4. housing
5. transportation
6. miscellaneous
7. clothes
8. 70%

Apply, page 120
1. the temperature each hour from 6 A.M. to 1 P.M. on January 15
2. the time from 6 A.M. to 1 P.M.
3. temperature from 0°F to 50°F
4. 25°F
5. noon
6. between 9 A.M. and 10 A.M.
7. about 27°F
8. 9 A.M.

Answer Key Intermediate 1 Student Edition

Check Up, page 121
1. C
2. J
3. C
4. G
5. A
6. F

Workplace Skill, page 122
1. A
2. H
3. *Sample answer:* The table shows exact values. You can only estimate values on the graph. If you needed to know exactly how much milk was sold in a certain month, you could use the table.

Write for Work, page 123
Check that the writing includes the following points: The writer understands how the graph is organized and is able to clearly describe what is happening based on the information in the graph. The writing should note milk sales fluctuated by about 8 million gallons, except for June, when they took a strong downward dip.

Workplace Extension, page 123
1. B
2. J
3. *Sample answer:* There might be a technical problem with the computer slideshow of which she would not be aware.

Explore Words, page 124
Consonant Pairs sc, mb
1. s©ene
2. num®
3. com®
4. lim®
5. s©ent
6. s©ience

Base Words
1. way
2. laugh
3. cheer
4. cook
5. fast
6. play
7. strong
8. worry
9. kind
10. speed
11. try
12. eat

Spelling: Plurals
1. painters
2. butterflies
3. addresses
4. berries
5. watches
6. stories

Page 125
Spelling: Contractions
1. shouldn't
2. didn't
3. we'll
4. hasn't
5. they're
6. you're
7. couldn't
8. haven't
9. I've
10. they'll

Academic Vocabulary
1. illustrate
2. data
3. label
4. graph
5. estimate

Unit 2 Assessment

Pages 127–132
1. A		18. J	
2. J		19. B	
3. B		20. G	
4. H		21. C	
5. C		22. J	
6. G		23. B	
7. B		24. H	
8. F		25. D	
9. B		26. F	
10. J		27. B	
11. B		28. H	
12. H		29. C	
13. B		30. F	
14. F		31. B	
15. D		32. H	
16. H		33. A	
17. D		34. H	

Unit 2 Workplace Skill Activity
Sample answers:
1. I enjoy working with people.
2. I know our product line and have worked in sales in the past.
3. I am cooperative and like to do my part.
4. I have self-respect and want to advance myself.
5. What are the hours? Are there opportunities for advancement?

Answer Key Intermediate 1 Student Edition

Unit 3 Lesson 3.1

Practice, page 135
1. D
2. F
3. B

Apply, page 136
1. C
Sample answer: Thanh likes adventure, and he would find this a more exciting adventure than the others.
2. H
Sample answer: Efia will think that Naima won't mind, because she has not minded lending Efia clothes in the past.
3. B
Sample Answer: Jazmin is hot and thirsty, and these actions will cool her off and replace lost water.

Check Up, page 137
1. C
2. G
3. D

Workplace Skill, page 138
1. B
2. F

Write for Work, page 139
Check that the writing includes the following points: The summary is clear and shows that the writer understands how to read the diagram.

Reading Extension, page 139
1. B
2. F
3. C
4. *Sample answer:* I predicted that the runaways would spread the disease, and the outbreak would get even bigger.
5. *Sample answer:* I predicted that the disease would keep spreading.

Explore Words, page 140
Vowel Combinations
1. weekend
2. clueless
3. throw
4. day
5. tried
6. need

Syllables
2. in / dent, short
3. to / ken, long
4. do / nate, long

Context Clues
1. delicate
2. hungry
3. continue

Page 141
Synonyms and Antonyms
1. construct, destroy
2. chilly, hot
3. refuse, accept
4. silent, noisy
5. vacant, full

Academic Vocabulary
1. outcome
2. adjust
3. predict
4. prior
5. reveal

Unit 3 Lesson 3.2

Practice, page 143
1. Causes: The days grew shorter. The weather turned colder.
   Effect: The geese flew south.
2. Cause: The furnace stopped working.
   Effects: The pipes in the house froze. The houseplants died.
3. Cause: Heavy rain flooded the town.
   Effects: Houses were destroyed. Drinking water was scarce. People were evacuated.
4. Cause: I was the first thing the orphaned ducks saw when they hatched.
   Effects: The ducklings followed me everywhere. They thought I was their mother.
5. Cause: A big discount store opened outside town.
   Effects: Several small shops downtown lost business and failed. People have to shop at the discount store, which is impersonal and less convenient.

Apply, page 144
1. Earth is the ideal distance from the sun.
2. Water can exist in a liquid state.
3. Living things that need oxygen can thrive.
4. Earth is protected from the sun's harmful UV rays.
5. The moon's gravity affects Earth's axis.

Check Up, page 145
1. C
2. H
3. A
4. F
5. D
6. J

Workplace Skill, page 146
1. C
2. G

Write for Work, page 147
Check that the writing includes the following points: The writer understands the policy and understands the importance of why the policy has been established.

Reading Extension, page 147
1. D
2. H
3. B
4. *Sample answer:* High humidity and hot weather breed many violent storms.
5. *Sample answer:* He regained his sight. His hearing improved. He regrew some hair on his head.

Answer Key Intermediate 1 Student Edition

Explore Words, page 148

Vowel Combinations
1. ow
2. ou
3. oy
4. oi

Silent Letters
1. bridge
2. wrist
3. knots
4. gnat
5. patch
6. sign

Spelling: Homophones
1. knight, night
2. buy, by
3. chili, chilly
4. plain, plane
5. nose, knows

Page 149

Prefixes post-, re-, un-
1. replay
2. unhappy
3. rethink
4. postwar
5. repay
6. unknown
7. unfair
8. postgame
9. rewrite

Academic Vocabulary
1. cause
2. obvious
3. determine
4. effect
5. relate

Unit 3 Lesson 3.3

Practice, page 151

1. during checkout
2. No; the coupon is only valid if you buy $100 worth of full-priced items.
3. You will get to use it, but only on the $110 of full-priced items.
4. No; the coupon is not valid on prior purchases.
5. *Sample answer:* You must spend $100 on full-priced items and bring the coupon to the store. To purchase online, you must spend $100 on full-priced items and enter the code.

Apply, page 152

1. balances transferred from other credit cards
2. 3.9%
3. asterisk (*)
4. 12.99%–22.99%, depending on the prime rate
5. up to 23.99%
6. *Sample answer:* The credit card company doesn't want customers to recognize the high interest rates on purchases and cash advances.

Check Up, page 153

1. D   3. B
2. G   4. F

Workplace Skill, page 154

1. C
2. J

Write for Work, page 155

Check that the writing includes the following points: The letter uses formal language to certify that the employee has a bank account with this branch and permission to directly deposit.

Reading Extension, page 155

1. B   3. A
2. G
4. *Sample answer:* in a scientific journal
5. *Sample answers:* a phone book, the Internet, ads in the local newspaper

Explore Words, page 156

Vowel Combinations
1. au
2. aw
3. oo
4. oo

Long i and Long o
1. colt, kindest
2. unwind, wildness
3. most, boldness
4. grinder, scold

Spelling: Contractions
1. c; i
2. e; o
3. d; a
4. a; ha
5. b; o

Page 157

Spelling: Word Endings
1. madness
2. hiking
3. thinnest
4. happiness
5. spinning
6. helpful
7. carried
8. wider

Academic Vocabulary
1. instructions
2. transfer
3. consume
4. purchase
5. annual

Unit 3 Lesson 3.4

Practice, page 159

1. whiny and dependent
2. resentful and critical
3. generous and thoughtful
4. ambitious and hardworking

Apply, page 160

Sample answers:
1. Tim loves music and likes to listen to it on vinyl records.
2. Imari is hard working. He is a good baker who enjoys his job.
3. Vidraj is critical of others. He annoys people with his know-it-all personality.
4. Chelsea is very organized.

Check Up, page 161

1. B
2. F
3. C
4. J

Workplace Skill, page 162

1. A
2. G

Answer Key Intermediate 1 Student Edition

Write for Work, page 163

Check that the writing includes the following points: The writer understands the purpose of a planning document; the information provided will help employees in their efforts to keep the lunchroom and refrigerator clean.

Reading Extension, page 163

1. C
2. F
3. B
4. *Sample answers:* strong, brave, resourceful, determined
5. *Sample answers:* action, dialogue, narration, what other characters think of him

Explore Words, page 164

r-Controlled Vowels
1. target
2. hornet
3. curtain

Vowel Combinations
2. long *a*
3. long *e*
4. short *e*

Suffixes -y, -en
1. wooden
2. rainy
3. oily
4. weaken

Page 165

Multiple-meaning Words
1. a   5. b
2. a   6. b
3. b   7. b
4. a   8. a

Academic Vocabulary
1. exhibit
2. characters
3. distinguish
4. traits
5. genres

Unit 3 Lesson 3.5

Practice, page 167

Fact:
The Great Pyramid of Giza is about 450 feet high.

Egyptians used papyrus, a form of paper made from a tall water reed.

Egyptian pyramids served as royal tombs.

When a pharaoh died, he was buried with many treasures.

Egyptian bodies were mummified, or preserved in salt, dried out, and wrapped in cloth.

Opinion:
A pyramid is one of the most inspiring sights on Earth.

Ancient Egypt had one of the greatest civilizations of all time.

A mummy is spooky looking.

The modern way of preserving bodies is better than the ancient Egyptian method.

Apply, page 168

1. F; atlas or encyclopedia
2. F; encyclopedia
3. O
4. O
5. O
6. F; encyclopedia
7. F; newspaper
8. O
9. F; atlas or encyclopedia
10. O
11. F; newspaper

Check Up, page 169

1. B   4. G
2. H   5. A
3. D   6. J

Workplace Skill, page 170

1. C
2. F

Write for Work, page 171

Check that the writing includes the following points: The ad is written using a combination of fact and opinion. There is adequate and appropriate use of persuasive language.

Reading Extension, page 171

1. C
2. F
3. D
4. *Sample answer:* Killer bees will chase a person for a metric mile.
5. *Sample answer:* They are very dangerous.

Explore Words, page 172

Consonant Pairs
1. crumb
2. scissor
6. descend

Spelling: Possessives
1. your son's drums
2. my sisters' party
3. the driver's maps
4. my uncles' children

Syllables
2. tur)tle
3. var)nish
4. mainly
5. handle
6. skir)mish

Page 173

Base Words
1. suffix: est; base word: large
2. prefix: pre; ending: ing; base word: view
3. prefix: un; suffix: y; base word: luck
4. prefix: sub; ending: ed; base word: lease
5. prefix: un; suffix: able; base word: depend
6. prefix: pre; ending: ed; base word: stamp
7. prefix: un; suffix: ful; base word: help
8. prefix: re; suffix: able; base word: sell

Academic Vocabulary
1. opinion
2. prove
3. fact
4. viewpoint
5. signal

Unit 3 Lesson 3.6

Practice, page 175
1. three
2. salmon with dill
3. page 37
4. There are no carrot recipes.
5. two
6. spicy chicken salad
7. page 34
8. pepper and tomato salad, tomatoes with cheese
9. alphabetical

Apply, page 176
1. true
2. false; The picture is on page 220. Salvia is on page 32.
3. true
4. false; The northern forest is mentioned on page 95, but there is no picture.
5. false; It is a plant.

Check Up, page 177
1. B   4. F
2. G   5. C
3. C   6. J

Workplace Skill, page 178
1. A   3. C
2. H   4. F

Write for Work, page 179
Check that the writing includes the following points: The writer directs the coworker to determine what area of the fax machine is not working properly and directs the coworker to use the index of the fax machine manual to find the page reference that covers that specific area.

Workplace Extension, page 179
1. C
2. *Sample answer:* Ryan might look into working in computer support, electronics sales and repairs, or computer networks.

Explore Words, page 180
The Schwa
1. pupil, secret
2. cupid, regal
3. afraid, freedom
4. unit, frozen

Syllables
2. disbelief
3. inspected
4. glimmering
5. rekindle
6. preapprove

Prefixes uni-, bi-, tri-
1. tri
2. tri
3. bi
4. uni
5. bi

Page 181
Spelling: Plurals
1. giraffes
2. ladies
3. shelves
4. classes
5. benches
6. scruffs
7. selves
8. strawberries
9. taxes
10. proofs

Academic Vocabulary
1. subject
2. order
3. discuss
4. scan
5. index

Unit 3 Assessment

Pages 183–188
1. A	17. C
2. J	18. F
3. C	19. D
4. G	20. G
5. B	21. C
6. H	22. F
7. B	23. A
8. G	24. H
9. A	25. B
10. G	26. H
11. B	27. A
12. G	28. G
13. A	29. C
14. H	30. H
15. C	31. D
16. F	32. F

Unit 3 Workplace Skill Activity

Sample answers:
1. Come in one hour early on Mondays and Wednesdays. Work extra hours on Tuesdays, Thursdays, or Saturdays. Come in a half hour early Monday through Thursday.
2. *Possible Objection:* Bettina may not be available when work needs to be done on Monday and Wednesday afternoons. *Solution:* Bettina can create a place where people can leave tasks for her to accomplish when she comes in to work. *Possible Objection:* She may not have anything to do if she comes in early. *Solution:* Her manager could give her an ongoing project.
3. Students should choose a solution and solid reasons for why it would work.

Introduce

READING SKILL

Recognize and Recall Details

Explain/Model: Explain that it is important to read attentively in order to recognize and recall specific details. Have students read aloud the passage about the Nile River. Model locating descriptive details about the Nile.

Guided Practice: Have students read the boxed passage. Then work with them to complete the task given in the directions. Discuss why the responses given after the passage are correct. Ask students to give you two other details they recall from reading the passage.

Practice: Have students read the passages about beards. Tell them to think about *what, when,* and *why* as they read about this topic. Discuss the answers to the questions and have students point out the details in the passages that support their answers.

Apply: After students answer the questions, have them read their responses aloud to the class. Encourage them to show classmates where they found the details.

Check Up: Have students work in small groups to read the passage and answer the questions. Then check each group's responses with those of other groups in the class.

Teach Lesson Skills

COMPREHENSION

Set a Purpose for Reading: Encourage students to set a purpose for reading. Provide self-questioning models, such as *What do I hope to learn? What do the directions tell me to look for? What will happen next?* By setting a purpose and then evaluating whether they achieved the purpose, students consciously monitor their own comprehension. They can also discuss the purpose they have determined with a peer or a teacher.

Reading Extension

📖 Encourage students to read "King Kong" on page 1 of the *Intermediate 2 Reader.* Use this as an opportunity to teach reading strategies and the lesson reading skill.

ALPHABETICS

Explore Words

Compound Words: Write *bedroom, horseshoe, nighttime,* and *weekend* on the board. Draw a line between the two words that make up each compound word. Have volunteers define each compound word, using their understanding of the two words that comprise it.

Synonyms: List these words on the board: *cautious, scary, soothing,* and *dirty.* Have students name as many synonyms as they can for each word. You may want to have them use a thesaurus.

Prefixes *pre-, re-, sub-:* Write *preheat, review, rewrite, substandard, preview,* and *subzero.* Have volunteers circle the prefixes. Then discuss the meaning of each word.

VOCABULARY

Academic Vocabulary/Tier 2

detail subject recall passage clarify

Before students complete the activity, write the academic vocabulary words and definitions on the board. Discuss each word's meaning with students. Then write the sentences below on the board. Read each sentence aloud and discuss it with students.

1. The artist added *detail* to his drawing.
2. The *subject* of Kim's speech was recycling.
3. Ivan could not *recall* where he had put his keys.
4. We had to read a *passage* and then answer questions.
5. The teacher had to *clarify* the instructions because the class wasn't sure what to do.

FLUENCY

Echo Reading: Read a sentence from one of the passages aloud. Then have students echo you by reading the same sentence and trying to read with the same speed and expression as you do.

Invite students to do a timed reading of "King Kong." Afterwards, have them enter their times on the Words-per-Minute table on page 129 and chart their reading speed on page 130 of the *Intermediate 2 Reader.*

🔊 Encourage students to listen to "King Kong." Go to **www.mhreadingbasics.com** to play or download the recording. The recording provides modeled fluency and read-along support.

APPLICATION

Workplace Skill:

Locate Details in a Want Ad

Have students look at the want ad. Point out that they can first scan the ad for details, such as the job title, hours, salary, and experience needed. Then, if the position is a good match for them, they can read more closely for additional information about the job. After students answer the questions, have them summarize the main idea and important details about the job to a partner. This activity will come in handy when they do the Write for Work activity.

Write for Work

Tell students to read the instructions for this task to be sure they include all the requested information. Encourage them to share their work with a classmate to make sure they clearly stated basic information about the position, including what it is, what the hours are, and what benefits are included.

PASSKEY

💻 Go to **www.mhreadingbasics.com** and click on the *PassKey* link. Customize instruction for your class using modules from Reading/Language Arts, Levels 3 & 4.

Introduce

READING SKILL

Understand Stated Concepts

Explain/Model: Explain that it is important to pay attention to information that is directly stated in order to understand ideas and concepts. Then have students read aloud the passage about roundworms. Model how to find some stated concepts about roundworms.

Guided Practice: Have students read the boxed passage. Then work with them to complete the task given in the directions. Discuss why the responses given after the passage are correct. Ask students to tell you something they can infer, or figure out, about sand fleas from reading the stated information in the passage.

Teach Lesson Skills

Practice: Have students read the passage about ocean thermal energy conversion. Tell them to look for facts and information that are directly stated. Discuss the answers to the questions and have students point out stated concepts in the passage that support their answers.

Apply: After students write their facts, have them read the facts aloud to the class. Encourage them to show classmates where they found the facts in the passages.

Check Up: Have students work in small groups to read the passage and answer the questions. Then check each group's responses with those of other groups in the class.

COMPREHENSION

Reread/Read More Slowly: Encourage students to become aware of the pace at which they read. Offer self-questioning models, such as *Did I read this passage too quickly? Does reading it again help me understand better? Does reading more slowly help me retain information?* When students actively consider the manner in which they are reading, they consciously monitor their own comprehension.

Reading Extension

📖 Encourage students to read "Nightmare on Chemical Street: The Love Canal Story" on page 10 of the *Intermediate 2 Reader*. Use this as an opportunity to teach reading strategies and the lesson reading skill.

ALPHABETICS

Explore Words

Consonant Blends: List these blends vertically and read them with students: *br, sl, sk, nt, nd, scr, shr, thr.* Then write the following words next to the blends and read them together: *bright, sloppy, skate, bent, bend, scrub, shrew, throw.*

Spelling: Plurals: Write *bench, pass,* and *daisy.* Model making each of these words plural. Then have volunteers form the plural of *ranch, crash,* and *army.*

Antonyms: Model giving antonyms for *sleepy* and *full. (energetic, empty)* Then have students give antonyms for *fast, clean, simple, broken,* and *huge. (slow, dirty, complex, whole, small)*

VOCABULARY

Academic Vocabulary/Tier 2

distinguish imply directly state infer

Before students complete the activity, write the academic vocabulary words and definitions on the board. Discuss each word's meaning with students. Then write the sentences below on the board. Read each sentence aloud and discuss it with students.

1. It is hard to *distinguish* one twin from the other because the two of them look alike.
2. A frown can *imply* that someone is unhappy.
3. My sister asked me *directly* if I borrowed her dress without asking.
4. Please *state* your full name and address.
5. When my dog stands by the door, I can *infer* that he wants to go out.

FLUENCY

Partner Reading: Have partners read aloud to one another and/or read aloud at the same time. Encourage them to offer support and correction to one another. Circulate to offer guidance as needed.

Invite students to do a timed reading of "Nightmare on Chemical Street: The Love Canal Story." Afterwards, have them enter their times on the Words-per-Minute table on page 129 and chart their reading speed on page 130 of the *Intermediate 2 Reader*.

📡 Encourage students to listen to "Nightmare on Chemical Street: The Love Canal Story." Go to **www.mhereadingbasics.com** to play or download the recording. The recording provides modeled fluency and read-along support.

APPLICATION

Workplace Skill:

Understand Stated Concepts in a Policy

Have students look at the policy. Remind them that a policy is a workplace document that tells employees about the company's rules and procedures. Point out that the main concepts in a policy will often be stated directly in titles, headings, and topic sentences. They will usually be followed by details and examples that give more information. After students answer the questions, have them start a list of reasons why it is not a good idea to access the Internet for personal use at work. This list will come in handy when they do the Write for Work activity.

Write for Work

Remind students that when they communicate with coworkers, they should use a professional and respectful tone. Tell them to read the instructions for this task carefully to be sure they include all the requested information. Encourage them to share their work with a classmate.

PASSKEY

📘 Go to **www.mhereadingbasics.com** and click on the *PassKey* link. Customize instruction for your class using modules from Reading/Language Arts, Levels 3 & 4.

Lesson Plan Intermediate 2 Student Edition

Introduce

READING SKILL

Draw Conclusions

Explain/Model: Explain to students that they should use facts and their own experience to draw a valid conclusion. Then have them read the sentences about hiccups. Ask them to share their own experiences with hiccups and how this helped them draw a conclusion.

Guided Practice: Have students read the boxed passage. Then work with them to complete the task given in the directions. Discuss why the responses given after the passage are correct. Ask students to share another conclusion they could draw about Qin Shihuangdi.

Practice: Have students read the passage about earthquakes. Tell them to think about what the passage says and what they know as they read about this topic. Discuss the answers to the questions and have students explain how they drew their conclusions.

Apply: After students answer the questions, have them read their responses aloud to the class. Encourage them to explain how they drew each conclusion.

Check Up: Have students work in small groups to read the passages and answer the questions. Then check each group's responses with those of other groups in the class.

COMPREHENSION

Use Prior Knowledge: Encourage students to think about what they already know before they read. To get students started, provide self-questioning models, such as *Have I read about this topic before? Does this sound familiar?* When students can create a context or framework of known information in which to place new information, they consciously monitor their own comprehension.

Reading Extension

📖 Encourage students to read "An Encounter in New Guinea" on page 19 of the *Intermediate 2 Reader.* Use this as an opportunity to teach reading strategies and the lesson reading skill.

Teach Lesson Skills

ALPHABETICS

Explore Words

Syllables: Write *rib, bro, it, am, milk, cab, shake, ba,* and *line.* Help students sort the syllables into *closed, open,* and *silent* e. Review the syllable types as needed. Then have volunteers read each syllable and identify the vowel sound as long or short.

Suffixes -ness, -ment: Model adding suffixes: *kind + ness, excite + ment, weak + ness, resent + ment.* Work with students to determine the meaning of each word.

Spelling: Base Words and Endings: Write *fake/faked/faking, worry/worried/worrying, dip/dipped/dipping.* Help students identify the spelling rules they applied for each word.

VOCABULARY

Academic Vocabulary/Tier 2

conclusion   draw   valid   appropriate   always

Before students complete the activity, write the academic vocabulary words and definitions on the board. Discuss each word's meaning with students. Then write the sentences below on the board. Read each sentence aloud and discuss it with students.

1. We came to the *conclusion* that cookies taste better when they are warm.
2. Many people *draw* strength from friends.
3. You must enter a *valid* zip code to use the credit card at the gas station.
4. A suit is *appropriate* for an interview.
5. That dog *always* barks at the mail carrier.

FLUENCY

Collaborative Reading: Gather in a group. Have each student read one or more lines of a passsage and then pass the text to the next student. Supply pronunciation and phrasing corrections as needed.

Invite students to do a timed reading of "An Encounter in New Guinea." Afterwards, have them enter their times on the Words-per-Minute table on page 129 and chart their reading speed on page 130 of the *Intermediate 2 Reader.*

🔊 Encourage students to listen to "An Encounter in New Guinea." Go to **www.mhreadingbasics.com** to play or download the recording. The recording provides modeled fluency and read-along support.

APPLICATION

Workplace Skill:

Draw Conclusions from a Time-off Request Form

Have students look at the form. Remind them that a form is a workplace document that asks for information. Tell students to read the form completely before completing it so they can understand or draw conclusions about what kind of information is needed. After students answer the questions, have them think about a reason they might need time off from work. Ask them to read the form again with this reason in mind. This exercise will be helpful when they do the Write for Work activity.

Write for Work

Remind students that forms need to be filled out accurately and completely. Tell them to read the instructions for this task carefully to be sure they include all the requested information. Encourage them to share their work with a classmate to make sure all the necessary information has been provided.

PASSKEY

💻 Go to **www.mhreadingbasics.com** and click on the *PassKey* link. Customize instruction for your class using modules from Reading/Language Arts, Levels 3 & 4.

Intermediate 2 Student Edition

Introduce

READING SKILL

Summarize and Paraphrase

Explain/Model: Explain that it is necessary to read attentively to note the most important ideas and details. Then have students read aloud the passage about Texas's fight for independence. Point out ways in which the summary and paraphrase are alike and different.

Guided Practice: Have students read the boxed passage. Then work with them to complete the task given in the directions. Discuss why the response given after the passage is correct. Ask students to list which details weren't included in the summary and why.

Teach Lesson Skills

Practice: Have students read the passages. Tell them to think about what the passages are mostly about and how they could state the main ideas and details in their own words. Discuss the answers and have students explain how they chose the best summary and paraphrase.

Apply: After students answer the questions, have them read their responses aloud to the class. Ask them to explain which details they included in the paraphrase. Ask them to explain why they did not include these details in the summary.

Check Up: Have students work in small groups to read the passages and answer the questions. Then check each group's responses with those of other groups in the class.

COMPREHENSION

Ask Questions: Encourage students to ask themselves questions as they read. Provide questioning models that progress from concrete to abstract. For example, *What does this mean? Is this a main idea? Do I remember the order of important events?* By asking themselves questions, students consciously monitor their own comprehension. They can also ask questions of peers or a teacher to clarify understanding.

Reading Extension

📖 Encourage students to read "Ocean-born Mary" on page 26 of the *Intermediate 2 Reader*. Use this as an opportunity to teach reading strategies and the lesson reading skill.

ALPHABETICS

Explore Words

Hard and Soft *c* and *g*: Write these words and read them with students: *giant, game, cape, cent, girl, cone, recess, pigeon*. Ask students to raise their hand when they hear a word with the soft sound of *c* or *g*.

Suffixes -*y*, -*en*: Write these words and underline the suffix in each: *silky, leaden, greasy, moisten*. Read each word without and then with the suffix. Discuss how the suffix changed the meaning of the word.

Multiple-meaning Words: Work with students to list as many meanings as you can for *ring, table,* and *land*. Then ask volunteers to use the words in sentences that show their different meanings.

VOCABULARY

Academic Vocabulary/Tier 2

summary paraphrase brief include sustain

Before students complete the activity, write the academic vocabulary words and definitions on the board. Discuss each word's meaning with students. Then write the sentences below on the board. Read each sentence aloud and discuss it with students.

1. The back of the book has a plot *summary*.
2. This statement is a *paraphrase*, not the writer's exact words.
3. The boss kept the meeting *brief* so that employees could get right back to work.
4. Juan's party will *include* all of the team.
5. A snack can *sustain* you until dinnertime.

FLUENCY

Repeated Reading: Lead a group to read the same passage aloud together several times. As the leader, emphasize accuracy and phrasing, until the group reading sounds smooth and consistent

Invite students to do a timed reading of "Ocean-born Mary." Afterwards, have them enter their times on the Words-per-Minute table on page 129 and chart their reading speed on page 130 of the *Intermediate 2 Reader*.

📶 Encourage students to listen to "Ocean-born Mary." Go to **www.mhereadingbasics.com** to play or download the recording. The recording provides modeled fluency and read-along support.

APPLICATION

Workplace Skill:

Summarize and Paraphrase a Procedures Document

Have students look at the procedures document. Remind them that a procedures document explains how to do something. Tell them that to summarize a procedures document, they should restate only the most important ideas. Point out that important information may appear in headings or in boldface type within the document. To paraphrase, they should retell the information in their own words and in more detail. After students answer the questions, have them start a list of steps to apply for an internal position at Springhouse Care Center. This list will be helpful when they do the Write for Work activity.

Write for Work

Remind students that a summary includes just the most important information. Tell them to read the instructions for this task carefully to be sure they include all the requested information. Encourage them to share their work with a classmate to make sure they included all the main points and no unnecessary details.

PASSKEY

🔑 Go to **www.mhereadingbasics.com** and click on the *PassKey* link. Customize instruction for your class using modules from Reading/Language Arts, Levels 3 & 4.

Lesson Plan Intermediate 2 Student Edition

Unit 1 Lesson 1.5 pages 46–53

Introduce

READING SKILL
Identify Cause and Effect

Explain/Model: Explain that a cause is why something happens and an effect is what happens. Looking for signal words can help readers make connections between what happened and why. Have students read aloud the sentence about the sandwich shop. Model using the signal words to help you identify the cause and effect. Follow the same process to read and discuss the sentence about Shani.

Guided Practice: Have students read the boxed passage. Then work with them to complete the task given in the directions. Discuss why the response given after the passage is correct. Ask students to give you two effects of drakes losing their feathers.

Teach Lesson Skills

Practice: Have students read the passage about dolphins. Tell them to think about what happens and why as they read about this topic. Discuss the answers to the questions and have students point out the details in the passage that support their answers.

Apply: After students write their cause-and-effect sentences, have them read their sentences aloud to the class. Encourage them to identify the cause and effect in each sentence for the class.

Check Up: Have students work in small groups to read the passage and answer the questions. Then check each group's responses with those of other groups in the class.

COMPREHENSION
Look for Context Clues/Read On: Encourage students to look for context clues as they read. Investigating the context helps a reader to put words and paragraphs into a larger framework. Provide helpful self-questioning models, such as *What words surrounding this difficult word can help me understand it better? If I read a little farther, might I find additional clues that can help me understand?* When students proactively look for context clues, they consciously monitor their own comprehension.

Reading Extension
Encourage students to read "Custer's Last Stand: Battle of Little Bighorn" on page 34 of the *Intermediate 2 Reader*. Use this as an opportunity to teach reading strategies and the lesson reading skill.

ALPHABETICS
Explore Words
Base Words: Write the following words on the board: *repayment, misspelled, preheating.* Have volunteers circle the base word in each word and discuss the meaning of each word.

Syllables: Use *hat, go,* and *late* to review closed, open, and silent e syllables. Elicit other examples of these syllable types from students. Before students complete the items in the activity, check that they can identify the syllables and read them correctly.

Silent Consonants: Write these words and have students read them with you: *knight, gnu, scenic, sign, kneel.* Underline the consonant pairs and have students tell which letter is silent.

VOCABULARY
Academic Vocabulary/Tier 2
cause effect signal benefit examine

Before students complete the activity, write the academic vocabulary words and definitions on the board. Discuss each word's meaning with students. Then write the sentences below on the board. Read each sentence aloud and discuss it with students.

1. Bacteria are the *cause* of many sicknesses.
2. The swelling was an *effect* of her injury.
3. The quarterback gave a *signal* to call the play.
4. One *benefit* of flossing is healthier gums.
5. The doctor will *examine* the patient to make sure she is healthy.

FLUENCY
Echo Reading: Read a sentence from one of the passages aloud. Then have students echo you by reading the same sentence and trying to read with the same speed and expression as you do.

Invite students to do a timed reading of "Custer's Last Stand: Battle of Little Bighorn." Afterwards, have them enter their times on the Words-per-Minute table on page 129 and chart their reading speed on page 130 of the *Intermediate 2 Reader*.

Encourage students to listen to "Custer's Last Stand: Battle of Little Bighorn." Go to **www.mhereadingbasics.com** to play or download the recording. The recording provides modeled fluency and read-along support.

APPLICATION
Workplace Skill:
Recognize Cause and Effect in a Performance Assessment Form

Have students look at the assessment form. Remind them that an assessment form is a record of a worker's job performance. Thinking about how their work performance will affect their performance rating can help them better understand what is expected of them at the workplace. After students answer the questions, have them write examples of actions that would make someone an exemplary worker or a below average worker in each category. These examples will come in handy when they do the Write for Work activity.

Write for Work
Remind students that a performance review evaluates the employee's strengths and weaknesses and comes up with an overall rating. Tell them to make sure each job performance area is covered and an overall assessment and tips for improvement are given. Encourage them to share their evaluation with a classmate as if they were delivering a performance review.

PASSKEY
Go to **www.mhereadingbasics.com** and click on the *PassKey* link. Customize instruction for your class using modules from Reading/Language Arts, Levels 3 & 4.

Lesson Plan Intermediate 2 Student Edition

Intermediate 2 Student Edition

Introduce

READING SKILL
Identify Style Techniques

Explain/Model: Tell students that paying attention to sentence structure and length, word choice, and use of punctuation can help them determine the author's style. Then have students read aloud the passages about Aata. Ask them to describe each author's style and how it affects the writing.

Guided Practice: Have students read the boxed passage. Then work with them to complete the task given in the directions. Discuss why the responses given after the passage are correct. Ask students to tell why the style is appropriate for the author's purpose.

Teach Lesson Skills

Practice: Have students read the passages and match them with the authors. Tell them to note which style techniques are used in each passage. Discuss the answers to the questions and have students point out the techniques in each passage that support their answers.

Apply: After students identify the style techniques and continue the passages, have them read their responses aloud to the class. Encourage them to tell which style techniques they used and why.

Check Up: Have students work in small groups to read the passages and answer the questions. Then check each group's responses with those of other groups in the class.

COMPREHENSION

Visualize: Encourage students to use sensory imaging as a mental tool when they read. Provide useful self-questioning models, such as *What do I see in this photo? Does this diagram help me understand the text? Can I form a mental image of what the author is describing?* When students visualize what they are reading, they consciously monitor their own comprehension.

ALPHABETICS
Explore Words

r-Controlled Vowels: Write these word pairs on the board and read them aloud with students: *pool/poor, cave/carve, fun/fur, kennel/kernel.* Ask volunteers to circle the r-controlled vowel in each pair.

Base Words and Roots: Model distinguishing between a base word and a root with the words *retake* and *resist.* Then write *preview, misspell, prepare, retain.* Underline the base word or root in each word. Have students identify whether it is a base word or a root.

Syllables: List these syllables in a column: *gar, han, sta.* To the right of it, list these: *gle, dle, ple.* Read each row with students, forming a word (*gargle, handle, staple*).

VOCABULARY
Academic Vocabulary/Tier 2

style individual highlight structure communicate

Before students complete the activity, write the academic vocabulary words and definitions on the board. Discuss each word's meaning with students. Then write the sentences below on the board. Read each sentence aloud and discuss it with students.

1. I enjoyed the writer's *style.*
2. The clerk wrapped each *individual* plate separately.
3. In an interview, *highlight* your work experience.
4. The *structure* of the paragraph relies on cause and effect.
5. Text messaging is one way to *communicate.*

FLUENCY
Marked Phrase Reading: Mark a passage with phrase boundaries, showing how words should be grouped for meaning and emphasis. Read the passage aloud, having students follow along, and then read aloud together with students.

APPLICATION
Workplace Skill:
Understand Style Techniques in E-mails

Have students read the e-mails. Remind them that business communications should have a formal style that is polite, professional, and free from slang, abbreviations, and contractions. After students answer the questions, have them make a list of their qualifications for a job for which they would like to apply. This list will come in handy when they do the Write for Work activity.

Write for Work

Tell students to read the instructions for this task carefully to be sure they include all the requested information. Remind them to use a formal writing style and to avoid informal language, such as slang, abbreviations, and contractions. Ask them to read their work to a classmate to make sure it is written in an appropriate tone and style.

Workplace Extension

Have students review the passage and discuss what impression Savita will make at the interview. Is the language she uses to respond to Ms. Rockwell a good match for the language Ms. Rockwell uses to address her? Have partners respond to the questions together and share their responses in a class discussion.

PASSKEY
Go to **www.mhereadingbasics.com** and click on the *PassKey* link. Customize instruction for your class using modules from Reading/Language Arts, Levels 3 & 4.

Lesson Plan Intermediate 2 Student Edition

Unit 1 Lesson 1.7 pages 62–69

Introduce

READING SKILL
Find the Main Idea

Explain/Model: Explain that looking for a topic sentence or thinking about what all the details have in common can help readers identify main ideas. Then have students read aloud the passage about sledding. Model the process of identifying the main idea, which is stated in the second sentence. Use the passage about telescopes to model identifying an implied main idea.

Guided Practice: Have students read the boxed passage. Then work with them to complete the task given in the directions. Discuss why the response given after the passage is correct. Ask students to state the main idea of the passage in their own words.

Teach Lesson Skills

Practice: Have students read the passages. Tell them to look for the topic, a stated main idea, or details that can help them determine the main idea. Discuss the answers to the questions and have students point out main idea or detail sentences that support their answers.

Apply: After students write the main ideas, have them read their main idea statements aloud to the class. Encourage them to show classmates where they found the main idea or which details they used to determine an implied one.

Check Up: Have students work in small groups to read the passages and answer the questions. Then check each group's responses with those of other groups in the class.

COMPREHENSION

Understand Author's Purpose: Encourage students to consider the author's purpose as they read. Provide self-questioning models, such as *Why did the author decide to write this? What does the author want me to know?* By examining the author's purpose, students can better analyze their own reaction to the writing and consciously monitor their own comprehension.

ALPHABETICS
Explore Words

Vowel Combinations: Write these word sets and read them aloud: *wood/stood/pool, blow/plow/row, lawn/sauce/lane, boil/toy/bowl.* Help students identify the two words in each set with the same vowel sound.

Spelling: Word Endings -er, -est: Write these words: *silly, strange, fit, clear.* Model adding the -er and -est endings. Have students point out any spelling changes that were made.

Syllables: Model syllable division using *barber, juggle, wagon,* and *bison.* Explain that when two consonants come together in the middle of a two-syllable word, you divide between them. When only one consonant is in the middle, try dividing it both ways and pronounce the word to see which way is correct.

VOCABULARY
Academic Vocabulary/Tier 2

topic main determine develop overlap

Before students complete the activity, write the academic vocabulary words and definitions on the board. Discuss each word's meaning with students. Then write the sentences below on the board. Read each sentence aloud and discuss it with students.

1. The *topic* of her report is global warming.
2. The *main* road is closed because of an accident.
3. Silas checked the weather so he could *determine* what to wear.
4. My shoes caused me to *develop* blisters.
5. The shingles on the roof *overlap* one another.

FLUENCY
Partner Reading: Have partners read aloud to one another and/or read aloud at the same time. Encourage them to offer support and correction to one another. Circulate to offer guidance as needed.

APPLICATION
Workplace Skill:

Recognize Main Idea in an Employee Handbook

Have students look at the section from an employee handbook. Point out that most handbooks are organized into sections with headings and subheadings. The headings tell the topic or main idea, and the details that follow give more information about it. After students answer the questions, have them state the main idea of this section of the employee handbook in their own words. This statement will come in handy when they do the Write for Work activity.

Write for Work
Remind students that the main idea should sum up what the whole section is about. Tell them to read the instructions for this task carefully to be sure they include all the requested information. Encourage them to share their work with a classmate to make sure they clearly stated the main idea and supporting details.

Workplace Extension
Have students review the passage about Maya Rosini's decision to stay late to finish her work. Discuss what might have happened if Maya had left early. Have partners respond to the questions and share their responses with the class.

PASSKEY
Go to **www.mhereadingbasics.com** and click on the *PassKey* link. Customize instruction for your class using modules from Reading/Language Arts, Levels 3 & 4.

Introduce

READING SKILL

Identify Sequence

Explain/Model: Explain that paying attention to sequence, or the order in which things happen, helps readers understand how events relate to one another. Have students read aloud the passage about the "Candy Bombers." Ask them to point out signal words that help show the order of events.

Guided Practice: Have students read the boxed passage. Then work with them to complete the task given in the directions. Discuss why the responses given after the passage are correct. Ask students to point out the sequence words that helped them determine the sequence.

Teach Lesson Skills

Practice: Have students read the passage about using the self-timer button on a digital camera. Tell them to look for clue words such as *first, then,* and *next* as they read about this topic. Discuss the correct order, and have students point out the clue words they used.

Apply: Have students put the sentences in order and read them aloud to the class. Then ask them to share the words and dates that helped them put the events in time order.

Check Up: Have students work in small groups to read the passage and answer the questions. Then check each group's responses with those of other groups in the class.

COMPREHENSION

Set a Purpose for Reading: Encourage students to set a purpose for reading. Provide self-questioning models, such as *What do I hope to learn? What do the directions tell me to look for? What will happen next?* By setting a purpose and then evaluating whether they achieved the purpose, students consciously monitor their own comprehension. They can also discuss the purpose they have determined with a peer or a teacher.

Reading Extension

📖 Encourage students to read "Kim's Story: The Big Bubble" on page 42 of the *Intermediate 2 Reader*. Use this as an opportunity to teach reading strategies and the lesson reading skill.

ALPHABETICS

Explore Words

Prefixes *mis-, un-*: Write *friendly, treat, step,* and *wise* on the board. Have students decide whether to add the prefix *un-* or *mis-* to each word. Then have volunteers read the words aloud and give the words' meanings.

Synonyms: List these words: *inform, meddle,* and *reside.* Have students name as many synonyms as they can for each word. You may want to have them use a thesaurus.

Spelling: Word Endings: Model spelling rules by adding endings to these words: *invent + ed, damage + ing, submit + ing,* and *locate + ed.* Have volunteers point out any spelling changes.

VOCABULARY

Academic Vocabulary/Tier 2

sequence concept theme survey subsequent

Before students complete the activity, write the academic vocabulary words and definitions on the board. Discuss each word's meaning with students. Then write the sentences below on the board. Read each sentence aloud and discuss it with students.

1. Ida arranged her photos in *sequence* by date.
2. The *concept* for the new restaurant was based on 1950s diners.
3. What is the *theme* of the party?
4. The grocery store handed out a *survey* to find out how it could improve its service.
5. The *subsequent* books in the series were not as good as the first one.

FLUENCY

Echo Reading: Read a sentence from one of the passages aloud. Then have students echo you by reading the same sentence and trying to read with the same speed and expression as you do.

Invite students to do a timed reading of "Kim's Story: The Big Bubble." Afterwards, have them enter their times on the Words-per-Minute table on page 129 and chart their reading speed on page 130 of the *Intermediate 2 Reader*.

🔊 Encourage students to listen to "Kim's Story: The Big Bubble." Go to **www.mhereadingbasics.com** to play or download the recording. The recording provides modeled fluency and read-along support.

APPLICATION

Workplace Skill:

Use Sequence to Write a Résumé

Remind students that a résumé lists their qualifications for doing a job. Have them look at the instructions. Point out that the instructions explain how to write a résumé. Paying attention to the signal words can help them determine the correct way to organize their information when they write a résumé. After students answer the questions, have them retell to a partner the steps for writing a résumé. This activity will come in handy when they do the Write for Work activity.

Write for Work

Tell students to pay attention to the signal words in the instructions to help them write the information in the correct order on their résumé. Encourage them to share their work with a classmate to make sure their résumé includes all the necessary information in the correct sequence.

PASSKEY

📄 Go to **www.mhereadingbasics.com** and click on the *PassKey* link. Customize instruction for your class using modules from Reading/Language Arts, Levels 3 & 4.

Introduce

READING SKILL

Understand Consumer Materials

Explain/Model: Explain that it is important to carefully read consumer materials because they contain information needed in order to use or maintain products or services correctly. Then have students read aloud the information about coupons. Ask them to tell you how they use coupons in their everyday lives.

Guided Practice: Have students read the coupon. Then work with them to complete the task given in the directions. Discuss why the responses given are correct. Ask students to tell what they can get with this coupon and what they have to do to get it.

Practice: Have students read the excerpt from the car owner's manual. Tell them to use the headings to help them locate important information. Discuss the answers to the questions and have students point out information in the excerpt that supports their answers.

Apply: After students answer the questions, have them read their responses aloud to the class. Encourage them to show classmates where they found the information to answer the questions.

Check Up: Have students work in small groups to read the excerpt from the cough syrup label and answer the questions. Then check each group's responses with those of other groups in the class.

Teach Lesson Skills

COMPREHENSION

Clarify Meaning: Encourage students to actively clarify meaning as they read. Provide self-questioning models, such as *What clues can I find in other sentences to help me understand this word? Does this word resemble any other words I have learned? Can I find someone to ask about this?* When students proactively try to clarify meaning, they consciously monitor their own comprehension.

Reading Extension

Encourage students to read "Poison on the Drugstore Shelf" on page 50 of the *Intermediate 2 Reader*. Use this as an opportunity to teach reading strategies and the lesson reading skill.

ALPHABETICS

Explore Words

Suffixes -ive, -ish: Write these words: *child, destruct, distinct,* and *girl*. Have students decide whether to add *-ish* or *-ive* to each word. Discuss the meaning of each word.

Base Words and Roots: Write *predict, invisible, reheat,* and *unusual*. Underline the base word or root in each word. Have students tell whether it is a base word or root. Challenge them to suggest other words that share the same base word or root.

Context Clues: Write these sentences on the board: *Elena is quite vivacious. She is always laughing and smiling.* Have students use context clues to try to determine the meaning of *vivacious*.

VOCABULARY

Academic Vocabulary/Tier 2

consume instructions excerpt request specific

Before students complete the activity, write the academic vocabulary words and definitions on the board. Discuss each word's meaning with students. Then write the sentences below on the board. Read each sentence aloud and discuss it with students.

1. We can *consume* a gallon of milk in a week.
2. I followed the *instructions* to set my watch.
3. The magazine published an *excerpt* from the author's new book.
4. Carmen plans to *request* an extra shift.
5. Violet only likes a *specific* brand of soap.

FLUENCY

Partner Reading: Have partners read aloud to one another and/or read aloud at the same time. Encourage them to offer support and correction to one another. Circulate to offer guidance as needed.

Invite students to do a timed reading of "Poison on the Drugstore Shelf." Afterwards, have them enter their times on the Words-per-Minute table on page 129 and chart their reading speed on page 130 of the *Intermediate 2 Reader*.

Encourage students to listen to "Poison on the Drugstore Shelf." Go to **www.mhereadingbasics.com** to play or download the recording. The recording provides modeled fluency and read-along support.

APPLICATION

Workplace Skill:

Use Consumer Materials: Waiver of Group Health Coverage Form

Have students read the waiver. Explain that a waiver is a written statement that shows a person is giving up a right or a privilege or is free from responsibility for an action. Point out that it is important for people to read waivers carefully, including any small print, to make sure they understand what they are signing. After students answer the questions, have them make a list of consumer documents they use and how they use them. This list will come in handy when they do the Write for Work activity.

Write for Work

Tell students to read the instructions for this task carefully to be sure they include all the requested information. Encourage them to share their work with a classmate to be sure the purpose is clear and the information is complete.

PASSKEY

Go to **www.mhereadingbasics.com** and click on the *PassKey* link. Customize instruction for your class using modules from Reading/Language Arts, Levels 3 & 4.

Intermediate 2 Student Edition

Introduce

READING SKILL

Use Reference Sources

Explain/Model: Explain to students that knowing about different kinds of reference sources can help them choose the one they need in order to find a certain kind of information. Then have them read the information about reference sources. Ask them to tell about some reference sources they have used and how they used them.

Guided Practice: Have students read the information on reference sources. Then work with them to complete the task given in the directions. Discuss why the responses given are correct. Ask students to share which reference sources they would choose to find information about mountain climbing.

Teach Lesson Skills

Practice: Have students read the list of reference sources. Tell them to think about how they would use each one. Discuss the answers to the questions and have students explain how they determined which reference source they would use.

Apply: After students answer the questions, have them read their responses aloud to the class. Encourage them to explain how they used the information in the glossary/index to answer each one.

Check Up: Have students work in small groups to read and answer the questions. Then check each group's responses with those of other groups in the class.

COMPREHENSION

Ask Questions: Encourage students to ask themselves questions as they read. Provide questioning models that progress from concrete to abstract. For example, *What does this mean? Is this a main idea? Do I remember the order of important events?* By asking themselves questions, students consciously monitor their own comprehension. They can also ask questions of peers or a teacher to clarify understanding.

Reading Extension

📖 Encourage students to read "Death on the Unsinkable *Titanic*" on page 59 of the *Intermediate 2 Reader*. Use this as an opportunity to teach reading strategies and the lesson reading skill.

ALPHABETICS

Explore Words

Spelling: Irregular Plurals: Model forming the irregular plurals of these words: *ox, woman, goose, fish, deer*. Then have students use the singular and plural form of each word in sentences.

Spelling: Homophones: Write the following pairs of homophones: *peace/piece, find/fined, pause/paws*. Discuss the meaning of each word. Then have volunteers use the words in sentences that show their meaning.

Suffixes *-ize, -ify*: Model adding these suffixes: *glory + -ify; item + -ize; civil + -ize*. Work with students to use each new word in a sentence.

VOCABULARY

Academic Vocabulary/Tier 2

source consult research general index

Before students complete the activity, write the academic vocabulary words and definitions on the board. Discuss each word's meaning with students. Then write the sentences below on the board. Read each sentence aloud and discuss it with students.

1. An encyclopedia is a good *source* of facts about different topics.
2. Gina likes to *consult* her mom before making a big decision.
3. I am doing *research* about bats for a report.
4. The poster gave *general* information about the event.
5. The *index* listed 10 pages about Alaska.

FLUENCY

Collaborative Reading: Gather in a group. Have each student read one or more lines of a passage and then pass the text to the next student. Supply pronunciation and phrasing corrections as needed.

Invite students to do a timed reading of "Death on the Unsinkable *Titanic*." Afterwards, have them enter their times on the Words-per-Minute table on page 129 and chart their reading speed on page 130 of the *Intermediate 2 Reader*.

📶 Encourage students to listen to "Death on the Unsinkable *Titanic*." Go to **www.mhereadingbasics.com** to play or download the recording. The recording provides modeled fluency and read-along support.

APPLICATION

Workplace Skill:

Use Reference Sources in an E-mail Attachment

Have students read the e-mail attachment. Tell them to think about the information in the attachment and what reference sources they would use to verify facts or find additional information. After students answer the questions, have them list reference sources they might use to find additional information about the area, location, and population of Brazil. This exercise will be helpful when they do the Write for Work activity.

Write for Work

Suggest that students revisit the list of reference sources in the Practice section if they need help choosing reference sources. After completing the activity, ask students to compare their answers and the reference sources they used with those of a classmate.

PASSKEY

📖 Go to **www.mhereadingbasics.com** and click on the *PassKey* link. Customize instruction for your class using modules from Reading/Language Arts, Levels 3 & 4.

Introduce

READING SKILL
Recognize Character Traits

Explain/Model: Explain that paying attention to things characters say or do or what the narrator says about them can help readers figure out what the characters are like. Then have students read aloud the passage about Mimi. Discuss what Mimi's actions show about her.

Guided Practice: Have students read the boxed passage. Then work with them to complete the task given in the directions. Discuss why the responses given after the passage are correct. Ask students to give some words based on the passage that describe the woman.

Teach Lesson Skills

Practice: Have students read the passage. Tell them to pay attention to the things Keisha does and says to help them determine what she is like. Discuss the methods the author used and have students give examples of things Keisha does that reveal her character traits.

Apply: After students answer the questions, have them read their responses aloud to the class. Ask them to point out specific examples of things the characters do, say, or think that help reveal their character traits.

Check Up: Have students work in small groups to read the passages and answer the questions. Then check each group's responses with those of other groups in the class.

COMPREHENSION

Make Connections: Encourage students to make connections as they read. Provide self-questioning models, such as *Have I learned something about this topic before? What was the context? Have I had any experiences in my own life that relate to this topic?* When students relate what they are reading to their own lives and educational experience, they consciously monitor their own comprehension.

Reading Extension

📖 Encourage students to read "Sarah's Ghost House: An Architectural Fun House" on page 68 of the *Intermediate 2 Reader*. Use this as an opportunity to teach reading strategies and the lesson reading skill.

ALPHABETICS
Explore Words

Syllables: List the following syllables in one column and help students identify the vowel sound in each as short or long: *ap, re, mi, sin*. Then list these syllables in a second column next to the other syllables: *ple, cess, grate, gle*. Help students read each pair of syllables and blend them together to form words. (*apple, recess, migrate, single*)

Prefixes *in-, dis-*: Model adding prefixes to these words: *dis- + organized, in- + secure, dis- + abled, in + capable*. Discuss the meaning of each word with students.

Multiple-meaning Words: Work with students to list as many meanings as possible for *rare, grave, vault,* and *present*. Have volunteers use the words in sentences that show their different meanings.

VOCABULARY
Academic Vocabulary/Tier 2

characters   traits   method   reveal   focus

Before students complete the activity, write the academic vocabulary words and definitions on the board. Discuss each word's meaning with students. Then write the sentences below on the board. Read each sentence aloud and discuss it with students.

1. I like to read about realistic *characters*.
2. Courage and determination are two *traits* many top athletes have.
3. Boiling is one *method* for cooking an egg.
4. The chef will not *reveal* his secret recipes.
5. Throughout the long rehearsal, the actors never lost their *focus*.

FLUENCY

Repeated Reading: Lead a group to read the same passage aloud together several times. As the leader, emphasize accuracy and phrasing until the group reading sounds smooth and consistent.

Invite students to do a timed reading of "Sarah's Ghost House: An Architectural Fun House." Afterwards, have them enter their times on the Words-per-Minute table on page 129 and chart their reading speed on page 130 of the *Intermediate 2 Reader*.

📶 Encourage students to listen to "Sarah's Ghost House: An Architectural Fun House." Go to **www.mhreadingbasics.com** to play or download the recording. The recording provides modeled fluency and read-along support.

APPLICATION
Workplace Skill:
Match Character Traits in a Job Description

Have students read the job description. Remind them that a job description gives the responsibilities of a job and what qualities a successful candidate will have. Tell them to pay close attention to the characteristics an employee needs and what he or she will be expected to do. After students answer the questions, have them start a list of traits a person would need in order to be successful in the position of Community Green Initiative Planner. This list will be helpful when they do the Write for Work activity.

Write for Work

Tell students to read the instructions for this task carefully to be sure they include all the requested information. Remind them to think about the character traits a person would need for this job. Have them share their work with a classmate and to cover all the character traits.

PASSKEY

💻 Go to **www.mhreadingbasics.com** and click on the *PassKey* link. Customize instruction for your class using modules from Reading/Language Arts, Levels 3 & 4.

Intermediate 2 Student Edition

Intermediate 2 Student Edition *(left margin vertical text)*

Introduce

READING SKILL
Use Supporting Evidence

Explain/Model: Explain that it is important to look for facts, statistics, examples, and reasons that support a statement or opinion. Have students read aloud the sentences about patterns in nature. Ask them to give you some additional examples.

Guided Practice: Have students read the boxed passage. Then work with them to complete the task given in the directions. Discuss why the responses given after the passage are correct. Ask students to explain how the details support the main idea.

Teach Lesson Skills

Practice: Have students read the passage about printing presses. Tell them to identify the main idea and supporting details as they read. Discuss the answers to the questions and have students explain how they determined which details did and did not support the main idea.

Apply: After students write their supporting details, have them read their sentences aloud to the class. Encourage them to explain how the details support the main idea.

Check Up: Have students work in small groups to read the passage and answer the questions. Then check each group's responses with those of other groups in the class.

COMPREHENSION
Look for Context Clues/Read On: Encourage students to look for context clues as they read. Investigating the context helps a reader to put words and paragraphs into a larger framework. Provide helpful self-questioning models, such as *What words surrounding this difficult word can help me understand it better? If I read a little farther, might I find additional clues that can help me understand?* When students proactively look for context clues, they consciously monitor their own comprehension.

Reading Extension
📖 Encourage students to read "Krakatoa: The Doomsday Crack Heard 'Round the World" on page 78 of the *Intermediate 2 Reader*. Use this as an opportunity to teach reading strategies and the lesson reading skill.

ALPHABETICS
Explore Words
Spelling: Possessives: Model forming possessives using these examples: *the saddles of the horses/the horses' saddles; the shoes belonging to the woman/the woman's shoes; the socks that my sister wore/my sister's socks.*

Spelling: Word Endings: Model adding the endings *-ed* and *-ing* to the following words: *hurry, imagine, worry,* and *vote.* Have students point out any spelling changes.

Latin Roots: Write these words with Latin roots, underlining the root as shown: *visible, export, inject, vocal.* Discuss the meaning of each word. Then have volunteers suggest additional words for each root.

VOCABULARY
Academic Vocabulary/Tier 2
evidence   support   statistics   example   eliminate

Before students complete the activity, write the academic vocabulary words and definitions on the board. Discuss each word's meaning with students. Then write the sentences below on the board. Read each sentence aloud and discuss it with students.

1. Fingerprints can be *evidence* in a crime.
2. Rosita gave facts to *support* her opinion.
3. *Statistics* show that it is unsafe to text while driving.
4. Look at this *example* of a business letter.
5. Try to *eliminate* sugar from your diet.

FLUENCY
Collaborative Reading: Gather in a group. Have each student read one or more lines of a passage and then pass the text to the next student. Supply pronunciation and phrasing corrections as needed.

Invite students to do a timed reading of "Krakatoa: The Doomsday Crack Heard 'Round the World." Then have them enter their times on the Words-per-Minute table on page 129 and chart their reading speed on page 130 of the *Intermediate 2 Reader*.

📶 Encourage students to listen to "Krakatoa: The Doomsday Crack Heard 'Round the World." Go to **www.mhereadingbasics.com** to play or download the recording. The recording provides modeled fluency and read-along support.

APPLICATION
Workplace Skill:
Find Supporting Evidence in a Leave-of-absence Policy

Have students read the policy. Remind them that a policy gives a company's rules and procedures. Identifying the main ideas and the details that support them will help employees make sure they understand the key points. After students answer the questions, have them make a web for their dream job. In the center oval, they should write a statement describing the job's key responsibility. In the surrounding ovals, they should write details that support the responsibility. This web will come in handy when they do the Write for Work activity.

Write for Work
Remind students that supporting evidence gives more information about a main idea. Tell them to make sure their details support the key job responsibility they wrote. Encourage them to share their job description with a classmate.

PASSKEY
📖 Go to **www.mhereadingbasics.com** and click on the *PassKey* link. Customize instruction for your class using modules from Reading/Language Arts, Levels 3 & 4.

Introduce

READING SKILL

Identify Author's Purpose

Explain/Model: Explain that authors may write to persuade, inform, explain, entertain, or describe. Determining the author's purpose helps readers interpret what they read. Then have students read the sentences about Easton. Ask them to state the author's purpose.

Guided Practice Have students read the boxed passage. Then work with them to complete the task given in the directions. Discuss why the response given after the passage is correct. Ask students to give specific details that show that the author's purpose is to explain.

Teach Lesson Skills

Practice: Have students match the type of writing with the purposes. Then have them give purposes for writing each passage. Discuss their responses and have students explain how they determined the purposes.

Apply: After students identify what the person in each scenario would write and what his or her purpose would be, have them read their responses aloud to the class. Encourage them to explain how they determined what each person would write and his or her primary purpose.

Check Up: Have students work in small groups to read the passages and decide the authors' purposes. Then check each group's responses with those of other groups in the class.

COMPREHENSION

Reread/Read More Slowly: Encourage students to become aware of the pace at which they read. Offer self-questioning models, such as *Did I read this passage too quickly? Does reading it again help me understand better? Does reading more slowly help me retain information?* When students actively consider the manner in which they are reading, they consciously monitor their own comprehension.

ALPHABETICS

Explore Words

Spelling: Words with *f, ph, gh*: Write these words and model correcting the spelling: *laph, phreeze, fone, rephinish.* Then have volunteers write additional words with *f, ph,* and *gh*.

Word Families: Write the following word families: *kindness/unkind/kindly, simply/simplify/simplistic, invitation/inviting/uninvited.* For each word family, have students say the base word that the words have in common.

Prefixes *inter-, semi-, multi-*: Model adding prefixes to the following words: *inter- + state, semi- + frozen,* and *multi- + faceted.* Discuss the meaning of each word.

VOCABULARY

Academic Vocabulary/Tier 2

author purpose persuade inform explain

Before students complete the activity, write the academic vocabulary words and definitions on the board. Discuss each word's meaning with students. Then write the sentences below on the board. Read each sentence aloud and discuss it with students.

1. The *author* has written five books.
2. Our *purpose* is to plan the fundraiser.
3. The candidate tried to *persuade* people to vote for her.
4. Please *inform* workers about schedule changes.
5. Jules had to *explain* why she was late for work.

FLUENCY

Marked Phrase Reading: Mark a passage with phrase boundaries, showing how words should be grouped for meaning and emphasis. Read the passage aloud, having students follow along, and then read aloud together with students.

APPLICATION

Workplace Skill:

Find Author's Purpose in a Business E-mail Memo

Have students read the memo. Remind them that a memo is a workplace document that sends a message to one or more persons. Point out that a memo's format can help make it easier to determine the author's purpose. For example, the subject line will often provide a clue to the purpose and intention of the memo. After students answer the questions, have them make a list of reasons why employees should drive slowly in the parking lot. This list will come in handy when they do the Write for Work activity.

Write for Work

Remind students to think about their purpose for writing the memo, which is to persuade employees to drive slowly. Tell them to make sure their word choice and details match their purpose. Encourage them to share their work with a classmate to make sure their e-mail conveys their intended purpose.

Workplace Extension

Have students review the passage about Rashid's body language. Discuss what Rashid is communicating to his boss through his actions and gestures and how he could behave in a more positive, respectful way. Have partners respond to the questions together and share their responses in a class discussion.

PASSKEY

Go to **www.mhereadingbasics.com** and click on the *Passkey* link. Customize instruction for your class using modules from Reading/Language Arts, Levels 3 & 4.

Intermediate 2 Student Edition *(sidebar)*

Introduce

READING SKILL

Make Generalizations

Explain/Model: Explain that a generalization uses text evidence to come to a conclusion that can apply to many people, facts, events, or situations. Have students read aloud the passage about wild animals. Model using text information to make a valid generalization about wild animals in urban environments.

Guided Practice: Have students read the boxed passage. Then work with them to complete the task given in the directions. Discuss why the response given after the passage is correct. Ask students to explain why the generalization is valid.

Teach Lesson Skills

Practice: Have students read the passages. Tell them to use information from the passage and their own knowledge to determine whether each generalization is valid. Discuss the answers and have students point out the information that supports the valid generalizations.

Apply: After students write their generalizations, have them read their generalizations aloud to the class. Then ask them to share the details that they used from each passage to make their generalization.

Check Up: Have students work in small groups to read the passages and answer the questions. Then check each group's responses with those of other groups in the class.

COMPREHENSION

Use Prior Knowledge: Encourage students to think about what they already know before they read. To get students started, provide self-questioning models, such as *Have I read about this topic before? Does this sound familiar?* When students can create a context or framework of known information in which to place new information, they consciously monitor their own comprehension.

Reading Extension

📖 Encourage students to read "The Mokele-Mbembe: Are All the Dinosaurs Gone?" on page 85 of the *Intermediate 2 Reader*. Use this as an opportunity to teach reading strategies and the lesson reading skill.

ALPHABETICS

Explore Words

Base Words and Roots: Write *import*, *invisible*, *uncertain*, and *pretest*, underlining as shown. Have students decide whether each underlined word part is a base word or a root. Then have them suggest additional words for each base word or root.

The Schwa Sound: Use the words *ran/dom*, *wag/on*, and *spi/der* to review the rules for syllable division. Point out that if a multisyllabic word has two consonants in the middle, as in *window*, you divide between them. If there is a single consonant in the middle, as in *wagon* and *spider*, you try dividing before and after the consonant. After dividing each word, read each part aloud, emphasizing the stressed syllable. Have volunteers circle the unstressed syllable with the schwa sound.

VOCABULARY

Academic Vocabulary/Tier 2

event typically introduce minor found

Before students complete the activity, write the academic vocabulary words and definitions on the board. Discuss each word's meaning with students. Then write the sentences below on the board. Read each sentence aloud and discuss it with students.

1. Moving to a new country was a major *event* in Manuel's life.
2. I *typically* drink water with my meals.
3. The first act of the play will *introduce* the characters.
4. The earthquake was *minor,* so there wasn't much damage.
5. Jan hopes to *found* a running club in her community.

FLUENCY

Echo Reading: Read a sentence from one of the passages aloud. Then have students echo you by reading the same sentence and trying to read with the same speed and expression as you do.

Invite students to do a timed reading of "The Mokele-Mbembe: Are All the Dinosaurs Gone?" Afterwards, have them enter their times on the Words-per-Minute table on page 129 and chart their reading speed on page 130 of the *Intermediate 2 Reader*.

🔊 Encourage students to listen to "The Mokele-Mbembe: Are All the Dinosaurs Gone?" Go to **www.mhereadingbasics.com** to play or download the recording. The recording provides modeled fluency and read-along support.

APPLICATION

Workplace Skill:

Make Generalizations in Fact-checking Guidelines

Have students look at the fact-checking guidelines. Point out that guidelines are usually broad and basic. It's up to readers to make generalizations about the information in order to apply it to specific situations or circumstances. After students answer the questions, have them brainstorm a list of general credible sources, such as encyclopedias or .gov or .edu websites. This list will come in handy when they do the Write for Work activity.

Write for Work

Have students review the fact-checking guidelines. Then have them list three credible sources. Invite students to discuss and compare their sources with a partner to make sure each source is credible.

PASSKEY

📖 Go to **www.mhereadingbasics.com** and click on the *PassKey* link. Customize instruction for your class using modules from Reading/Language Arts, Levels 3 & 4.

Introduce

READING SKILL

Recognize Author's Effect and Intention

Explain/Model: Explain that paying attention to word choice, language, and sentence structure can help readers determine an author's intention. Then have students read aloud the passage about the cruise. Discuss how the use of direct address and words such as "so-called delicacies" create an effect of scorn and humor that helps you determine the author's intention.

Guided Practice: Have students read the boxed passage. Then work with them to complete the task given in the directions. Discuss why the responses given after the passage are correct. Ask students to give examples of language that creates an effect of formality.

Teach Lesson Skills

Practice: Have students read the passages. Tell them to pay attention to the authors' style techniques and the effects they create. Discuss the answers to the questions and have students point out specific words and phrases that create a particular effect.

Apply: After students answer the questions, have them read their responses aloud to the class. Encourage them to point out examples of style techniques in each passage and discuss the effect they created.

Check Up: Have students work in small groups to read the passages and answer the questions. Then check each group's responses with those of other groups in the class.

COMPREHENSION

Ask Questions: Encourage students to ask themselves questions as they read. Provide questioning models that progress from concrete to abstract. For example, *What does this mean? Is this a main idea? Do I remember the order of important events?* By asking themselves questions, students consciously monitor their own comprehension. They can also ask questions of peers or a teacher to clarify understanding.

Reading Extension

📖 Encourage students to read "Spiritualism: Fact or Fraud" on page 93 of the *Intermediate 2 Reader*. Use this as an opportunity to teach reading strategies and the lesson reading skill.

ALPHABETICS

Explore Words

Prefixes: Model adding prefixes to these words: *in-* + *secure*, *im-* + *mature*, *il-* + *logical*, *ir-* + *regular*. Discuss the meaning of each word. Invite volunteers to suggest additional words for each prefix.

Suffixes -ion, -tion: Write these words: *decide/decision, revise/revision, infect/infection*. Underline the suffix in each word, as shown. Discuss the meaning of each word and point out any spelling changes.

Spelling: Plurals of Nouns Ending in -o: Model forming the plurals of these words: *ego/egos, torpedo/torpedoes, duo/duos, veto/vetoes*. Then have students form the plural of *logo, taco*, and *embargo*.

VOCABULARY

Academic Vocabulary/Tier 2

intention   approach   technique   assign   common

Before students complete the activity, write the academic vocabulary words and definitions on the board. Discuss each word's meaning with students. Then write the sentences below on the board. Read each sentence aloud and discuss it with students.

1. Her *intention* was to get to work early.
2. Keiko's attempts to train her dog weren't working, so she tried a new *approach*.
3. The dancer practiced her *technique*.
4. The group leader will *assign* the tasks.
5. It is *common* for children to cry when tired.

FLUENCY

Partner Reading: Have partners read aloud to one another and/or read aloud at the same time. Encourage them to offer support and correction to one another. Circulate to offer guidance as needed.

Invite students to do a timed reading of "Spiritualism: Fact or Fraud." Afterwards, have them enter their times on the Words-per-Minute table on page 129 and chart their reading speed on page 130 of the *Intermediate 2 Reader*.

📶 Encourage students to listen to "Spiritualism: Fact or Fraud." Go to **www.mhereadingbasics.com** to play or download the recording. The recording provides modeled fluency and read-along support.

APPLICATION

Workplace Skill:

Recognize Author's Effect and Intention in a Workplace Poster

Have students look at the poster. Explain that employers put posters in a central location in the workplace to communicate important information to all employees. Point out that headings, boldface type, and word choice can help them determine the intent of the poster and identify the most important ideas and information. After students answer the questions, have them brainstorm a list of reasons that an exercise program would be beneficial in the workplace. This list will come in handy when they do the Write for Work activity.

Write for Work

Tell students to think about why an exercise program would be beneficial and what effect they want their poster to create. For example, they might want their poster to generate enthusiasm for the program. Encourage them to share their work with a classmate to make sure their intention and effect are clear.

PASSKEY

🔑 Go to **www.mhereadingbasics.com** and click on the *PassKey* link. Customize instruction for your class using modules from Reading/Language Arts, Levels 3 & 4.

Intermediate 2 Student Edition

Introduce

READING SKILL

Compare and Contrast

Explain/Model: Explain that to compare and contrast, readers should think about how things are alike and different. Then have them read the passage about insects. Model using the signal word *similarly* to recognize a comparison.

Guided Practice: Have students read the boxed passage. Then work with them to complete the task given in the directions. Discuss why the responses given after the passage are correct. Ask students to compare and contrast the taste and color of Spanish onions and Bermuda onions.

Teach Lesson Skills

Practice: Have students read the passages. Tell them to look for clue words that signal comparisons and contrasts. Discuss the answers to the questions and have students point out the clue words they used to help them identify comparisons and contrasts.

Apply: After students complete their Venn diagrams, have them share their responses with the class. Then ask students to identify the clue words from the passage that helped them find comparisons and contrasts and list them on the page.

Check Up: Have students work in small groups to read the passages and answer the questions. Then check each group's responses with those of other groups in the class.

COMPREHENSION

Visualize: Encourage students to use sensory imaging as a mental tool when they read. Provide useful self-questioning models, such as *What do I see in this photo? Does this diagram help me understand the text? Can I form a mental image of what the author is describing?* When students visualize what they are reading, they consciously monitor their own comprehension.

Reading Extension

📖 Encourage students to read "Chupacabra: Bloodthirsty Beast" on page 103 of the *Intermediate 2 Reader*. Use this as an opportunity to teach reading strategies and the lesson reading skill.

ALPHABETICS

Explore Words

Latin Roots: Write on the board these words: *export, contain,* and *retract.* Underline the root as shown and model using it to define each word. *(carry out; hold within; pull back)*

Suffixes -ous, -ious: Write the following words on the board: *glamorous, dangerous,* and *anxious.* Model writing definitions for each word, using the phrase "having the quality of."

Prefixes uni-, bi-, tri-: Write on the board *uni-, bi-,* and *tri-.* Then write 2, 1, and 3. Have students match the prefixes and the numbers. Then ask volunteers to give examples of words with each prefix.

VOCABULARY

Academic Vocabulary/Tier 2

compare contrast relate distinct property

Before students complete the activity, write the academic vocabulary words and definitions on the board. Discuss each word's meaning with students. Then write the sentences below on the board. Read each sentence aloud and discuss it with students.

1. Van will *compare* several cars before buying one.
2. The *contrast* in temperature between yesterday and today took us by surprise.
3. Patrick finds it easy to *relate* to others.
4. The twins have *distinct* personalities.
5. Hardness is a *property* of diamonds.

FLUENCY

Collaborative Reading: Gather in a group. Have each student read one or more lines of a passage and then pass the text to the next student. Supply pronunciation and phrasing corrections as needed.

Invite students to do a timed reading of "Chupacabra: Bloodthirsty Beast." Afterwards, have them enter their times on the Words-per-Minute table on page 129 and chart their reading speed on page 130 of the *Intermediate 2 Reader*.

🔊 Encourage students to listen to "Chupacabra: Bloodthirsty Beast." Go to **www.mhereadingbasics.com** to play or download the recording. The recording provides modeled fluency and read-along support.

APPLICATION

Workplace Skill:

Compare and Contrast with a Graph

Have students look at the graph. Remind them that a graph is a visual way to compare and contrast data. Point out that reading the title, labels, and key will help them identify what kind of information is being compared and contrasted. After students answer the questions, have them write a sentence that summarizes how education affects the median weekly earnings of full-time workers. This exercise will be helpful when they do the Write for Work activity.

Write for Work

Tell students to use specific data from the graph to support their advice. Encourage them to share their advice with another student, delivering it as if they were the career counselor. Have them point to the data on the graph on which they based their advice.

PASSKEY

💻 Go to **www.mhereadingbasics.com** and click on the *PassKey* link. Customize instruction for your class using modules from Reading/Language Arts, Levels 3 & 4.

Intermediate 2 Student Edition

Introduce

READING SKILL

Predict Outcomes

Explain/Model: Explain that using text clues and prior knowledge can help readers make predictions about what will happen next in a passage. Then have students read aloud the example about a person getting ready to go swimming outside. Model using text information and your own prior knowledge to make a prediction about what will happen next.

Guided Practice: Have students read the boxed passage. Then work with them to complete the task given in the directions. Discuss why the response given after the passage is correct. Then ask students to make a prediction about what Winona will do when she gets to work the following day.

Practice: Have students read the passages. Tell them to use text information and their own knowledge and experience to make predictions. Have students share their predictions and explain how they made them.

Apply: After students respond to each situation, have them read their answers aloud to the class. Ask them to share the text information and personal knowledge they used to choose the most likely outcome.

Check Up: Have students work in small groups to read the situations and answer the questions. Then check each group's responses with those of other groups in the class.

Teach Lesson Skills

COMPREHENSION

Make Connections: Encourage students to make connections as they read. Provide self-questioning models, such as *Have I learned something about this topic before? What was the context? Have I had any experiences in my own life that relate to this topic?* When students relate what they are reading to their own lives and educational experience, they consciously monitor their own comprehension.

Reading Extension

📖 Encourage students to read "*Challenger: The Final Countdown*" on page 111 of the *Intermediate 2 Reader*. Use this as an opportunity to teach reading strategies and the lesson reading skill.

ALPHABETICS

Explore Words

Suffixes -ic, -al, -ly: Model adding suffixes to these words: *deny + al, artist + ic, gentle + ly*. Discuss the meaning of each word and point out any changes to the base word when the suffix was added.

Prefixes en-, em-: Write the following words on the board: *empower, encourage, embody*. Underline the prefix in each word and discuss each word's meaning.

Context Clues: Write the following sentence: *In autumn, some trees lose their foliage, and we must rake the leaves.* Have a volunteer define *foliage*. Discuss the words that give context for *foliage*.

VOCABULARY

Academic Vocabulary/Tier 2

predict   outcome   logical   prior   adjust

Before students complete the activity, write the academic vocabulary words and definitions on the board. Discuss each word's meaning with students. Then write the sentences below on the board. Read each sentence aloud and discuss it with students.

1. I *predict* that the teacher will give a quiz on Monday.
2. Yvette tried a new recipe and was pleased with the *outcome*.
3. It's *logical* to go to bed if you feel tired.
4. *Prior* to going to bed, Al brushes his teeth.
5. I frequently need to *adjust* the straps on my backpack.

FLUENCY

Repeated Reading: Lead a group to read the same passage aloud together several times. As the leader, emphasize accuracy and phrasing, until the group reading sounds smooth and consistent

Invite students to do a timed reading of "*Challenger: The Final Countdown.*" Afterwards, have them enter their times on the Words-per-Minute table on page 129 and chart their reading speed on page 130 of the *Intermediate 2 Reader*.

📶 Encourage students to listen to "*Challenger: The Final Countdown.*" Go to **www.mhereadingbasics.com** to play or download the recording. The recording provides modeled fluency and read-along support.

APPLICATION

Workplace Skill:

Predict Outcomes Using an Organizational Flowchart

Have students study the flowchart. Remind them that an organizational flowchart shows the overall reporting structure of a company. Model reading the flowchart, pointing out that each position directly reports to the position above it. After students answer the questions, have them make a two-column chart and list ways an employee would use a flowchart in one column and ways a job applicant would use it in the other. This chart will be helpful when they do the Write for Work activity.

Write for Work

Tell students to read the instructions for this task carefully to be sure they include all the requested information. Remind them to think about how both a job applicant and an employee might use a flowchart. Have them share their work with a classmate to be sure they correctly read the flowchart and described its uses.

PASSKEY

💻 Go to **www.mhereadingbasics.com** and click on the *PassKey* link. Customize instruction for your class using modules from Reading/Language Arts, Levels 3 & 4.

Introduce

READING SKILL
Identify Fact and Opinion

Explain/Model: Explain that it is important to be able to distinguish between facts and opinions in order to understand what you read. Have students read aloud the explanation about fact and opinion. Then discuss the fact and false fact about President Franklin Delano Roosevelt. Explain how students might prove or disprove a fact by checking a reliable source, such as an encyclopedia.

Guided Practice: Have students read the boxed passage. Then work with them to complete the task given in the directions. Discuss why the responses given after the passage are correct. Have students give an additional fact and opinion about destructive ocean waves.

Teach Lesson Skills

Practice: Have students read the statements. Tell them to look for statements that can be proved or words that signal opinions. Have students share their graphic organizers and ask them to explain how they distinguished between facts and opinions.

Apply: After students label each statement as a fact or an opinion, have them read their answers aloud to the class. Encourage them to explain how they determined whether each statement was a fact or an opinion.

Check Up: Have students work in small groups to answer the questions. Then check each group's responses with those of other groups.

COMPREHENSION
Understand Author's Purpose: Encourage students to consider the author's purpose as they read. Provide self-questioning models, such as *Why did the author decide to write this? What does the author want me to know?* By examining the author's purpose, students can better analyze their own reaction to the writing and consciously monitor their own comprehension.

Reading Extension
Encourage students to read "Oil, Oil Everywhere" on page 120 of the *Intermediate 2 Reader*. Use this as an opportunity to teach reading strategies and the lesson reading skill.

ALPHABETICS
Explore Words
Base Words and Roots: Write the following sets of words: *instruction, construction, destruction; creation, creative, creativity*. Discuss what base word or root each set has in common.

Synonyms: Write the following sentences, underlining the words as shown: *Jolene is known for being thrifty. Jolene is known for being cheap.* Discuss how the underlined words are alike and different. Have students suggest additional sentences for each word.

Greek Roots: Write these words with Greek roots, underlining as shown: *biopsy, psychology, automobile, telegraph.* Model how to use the root to help determine the meaning of each word. Then have volunteers suggest additional words for each underlined root.

VOCABULARY
Academic Vocabulary/Tier 2
fact opinion prove viewpoint reliable

Before students complete the activity, write the academic vocabulary words and definitions on the board. Discuss each word's meaning with students. Then write the sentences below on the board. Read each sentence aloud and discuss it with students.

1. The reporter checked the *fact* before putting it in his article.
2. In my *opinion*, cereal is the best breakfast.
3. My time card will *prove* that I was at work.
4. Your political *viewpoint* is completely different from mine.
5. The car is *reliable* for a long drive.

FLUENCY
Echo Reading: Read a sentence from one of the passages aloud. Then have students echo you by reading the same sentence and trying to read with the same speed and expression as you do.

Invite students to do a timed reading of "Oil, Oil Everywhere." Afterwards, have them enter their times on the Words-per-Minute table on page 129 and chart their reading speed on page 130 of the *Intermediate 2 Reader*.

Encourage students to listen to "Oil, Oil Everywhere." Go to **www.mhereadingbasics.com** to play or download the recording. The recording provides modeled fluency and read-along support.

APPLICATION
Workplace Skill:
Identify Fact and Opinion in a Press Release
Have students look at the press release. Remind them that the purpose of a press release is to publicize a company or product in a positive way. Therefore, it will contain a mix of facts and opinions. Distinguishing between facts and opinions will make readers better able to form their own opinions about the information. After students answer the questions, have them brainstorm a list of important details to include in a press release. This list will come in handy when they do the Write for Work activity.

Write for Work
Remind students to use their lists of important details to include in a press release. Tell them to use facts and opinions to describe the product. Encourage them to share their work with a classmate and discuss ways to make their facts and opinions more convincing.

PASSKEY
Go to **www.mhereadingbasics.com** and click on the *PassKey* link. Customize instruction for your class using modules from Reading/Language Arts, Levels 3 & 4.

Introduce

READING SKILL

Identify Genre

Explain/Model: Explain that identifying genres and recognizing their characteristics can help readers better understand and interpret what they read. Have students read aloud the information about genres and subgenres. Model giving examples for each genre or subgenre.

Guided Practice Have students read the boxed passage. Then work with them to complete the task given in the directions. Discuss why the response given after the passage is correct. Ask students to give examples that show the passage is historical fiction. For example, Franklin's working for the *New-England Courant* and his Dogood essays can be verified in an encyclopedia but his thoughts cannot be proven.

Practice: Have students read the passages and identify the genre or subgenre of each. Discuss their responses, and have students point out features or details in each passage that helped them identify its genre or subgenre.

Apply: After students answer the questions, have them read their responses aloud to the class. Encourage them to point out specific features or details in each passage that helped them determine its genre or subgenre.

Check Up: Have students work in small groups to read the passage and answer the questions. Then check each group's responses with those of other groups in the class.

COMPREHENSION

Reread/Read More Slowly: Encourage students to become aware of the pace at which they read. Offer self-questioning models, such as *Did I read this passage too quickly? Does reading it again help me understand better? Does reading more slowly help me retain information?* When students actively consider the manner in which they are reading, they consciously monitor their own comprehension.

Teach Lesson Skills

ALPHABETICS

Explore Words

Spelling: Homophones: Write the following homophones: *scent/cent, wait/weight, groan/grown.* Discuss the meaning of each word in the pair. Then invite volunteers to use each word in a sentence.

Word Families: Write the following word families: *transportation, portable, report; tasty, tasting, tasteless; biography, biology, bionic.* Identify the common base word or root for each word family.

Analogies: Write these analogies: *fast : slow* as *clumsy : graceful; smart : intelligent* as *generous : giving.* Model pointing out the relationship in each analogy.

VOCABULARY

Academic Vocabulary/Tier 2

genre prose emphasize drama comprise

Before students complete the activity, write the academic vocabulary words and definitions on the board. Discuss each word's meaning with students. Then write the sentences below on the board. Read each sentence aloud and discuss it with students.

1. The library is organized into sections by *genre.*
2. Armando would rather write *prose* than poetry.
3. Darlene put on red lipstick to *emphasize* her lips.
4. The actors performed the *drama* on stage.
5. Soap, shampoo, and toothpaste *comprise* John's travel kit.

FLUENCY

Marked Phrase Reading: Mark a passage with phrase boundaries, showing how words should be grouped for meaning and emphasis. Read the passage aloud, having students follow along, and then read aloud together with students.

APPLICATION

Workplace Skill:

Understand Genre in Training Materials

Remind students that company training materials are company and job specific. The information they give varies depending on where employees work and what positions they hold. Point out that headings and subheadings can help employees quickly identify important information in these documents. After students answer the questions, have them make an outline of what types of documents and materials help them in their jobs. This outline will come in handy when they do the Write for Work activity.

Write for Work

Tell students to make sure they include details about their job responsibilities and how these documents and materials helped them be successful in their jobs. Encourage students to share their work with a classmate to make sure their paragraph is written in the proper tone and includes the necessary details about their jobs.

Workplace Extension

Discuss the purpose of the supervisor's meeting with Adom. Ask students whether Adom's behavior helped or interfered with the problem-solving process. Have them brainstorm some ways that Adom could have responded more professionally. Then have partners respond to the questions together and share their responses.

PASSKEY

Go to **www.mhereadingbasics.com** and click on the *PassKey* link. Customize instruction for your class using modules from Reading/Language Arts, Levels 3 & 4.

Unit 1 Workplace Skill Activity
Role-play Resolving a Conflict with a Coworker

Employers expect their employees to have good communication and interpersonal skills. This means that employees know how to talk to one another clearly and treat each other with respect. Sometimes conflicts may arise between coworkers as a result of misunderstandings, miscommunication, or differing values. Knowing how to resolve a conflict with a coworker is an important skill. Employees who can peacefully find solutions to disagreements make the workplace more pleasant and productive. Here are some steps for resolving conflicts.

1. Distance yourself from the situation and think about it from the other person's perspective.
2. Ask for information to help you determine the other person's goals. Explore solutions to the problem.
3. Respect the other person's point of view and look for a solution that is agreeable to both parties.

Read the passage about a conflict between two coworkers. With a partner, answer the questions below. Then role-play the situation.

Carlos and Eli work together at an electronics store. Carlos notices that when Eli finishes his lunch break, he always leaves the break room messy, with dirty dishes and containers on the counter. The first few times this happened, Carlos cleaned up the mess, but now he wants Eli to clean up after himself. When Carlos mentions the mess to Eli, Eli responds that he tries to eat quickly so that he can get back to the sales floor as soon as possible. Eli worries that taking time to clean up after he eats will leave the floor shorthanded.

1. What is the cause of the conflict between Carlos and Eli?

    _____

    _____

2. What does Carlos hope to accomplish by confronting Eli?

    _____

3. What is each person's point of view in this situation?

    _____

    _____

4. What are some ways to resolve the conflict between Carlos and Eli?

    _____

    _____

Unit 2 Workplace Skill Activity
Coordinate a Volunteer Charitable Activity

As a member of a workplace, you may be asked to help coordinate and participate in a workplace volunteer activity. Volunteering helps employees develop valuable teamwork and leadership skills. Volunteering can also enhance the company's public image and community presence. Imagine that you and several coworkers are coordinating a food drive in your workplace. To plan the drive, you would need to divide up responsibilities so that each member of the volunteer group has a role that matches his or her talents.

> ### Food Drive, November 15–21
> Help us create a happy holiday for families in need. Bring in canned and boxed food by November 21. No glass jars or fresh produce, please! Place the items in the box marked Food Drive in the break room. Cash donations are also welcome.

Work with three other people to plan the food drive. Arrange the tasks in sequence: what needs to be done first, second, third, and fourth. Assign each member of the planning group to the task that best suits his or her skills. List the the task each person will perform and the key steps in the task. Then complete the chart with this information.

Tasks
- transport collected food to food bank
- send out memos to employees
- organize drop-off boxes
- accept cash donations and shop

Sample Steps in Task
- arrange a drop-off time with the food bank
- gather information for memo
- label the boxes clearly
- list food needed

Name	Task	Steps in Task

Intermediate 2 Student Edition

Unit 3 Workplace Skill Activity
Use a Problem-solving Model to Resolve a Workplace Problem

Problem solving and decision making are critical elements of most jobs, so it's important to know how to deal with problems effectively. Though most employees would prefer to avoid problems and conflicts, resolving them actually provides opportunities to improve interpersonal relationships and job processes. There are many ways to tackle workplace problems. Here is a model that can be used in a group, between two employees, or by one person who must make a decision:

Step 1: Clearly state the problem and identify the issues.
Step 2: Make a list of all the options or potential decisions.
Step 3: For each alternative, make a list of the pros and cons.
Step 4: Evaluate each option, based on the pros and cons you listed.
Step 5: Do not rely on memory or verbal agreements for important decisions. Document each decision in writing and keep this written record to hold everyone accountable.

Read the passage about a workplace problem. Then work with a small group to complete the problem-solving steps to resolve the conflict.

> You have been working on the day shift at a factory for six months. You are applying to night school to take classes in computer skills and finance to increase your workplace skills and get a better job. You plan to start your first semester in a few months. However, your manager just told you that a position on the night shift has opened up. Working the night shift would pay more than working the day shift, and it would also be easier to get raises and promotions. You wouldn't be able to attend classes if you were to change shifts, but you would be earning more money right away.

1. What is the problem?

   _____

2. Copy the chart below in a notebook, listing three ways to resolve the conflict and the pros and cons for each decision.

Possible Decision	Pros	Cons

3. How did you decide to resolve the conflict, based on the pros and cons you listed?

   _____

Intermediate 2 Student Edition

Answer Key Intermediate 2 Student Edition

Unit 1 Lesson 1.1

Practice, page 15
1. the 14th century
2. chin wigs
3. crimson, yellow, black
4. They wanted to match their clothes.
5. Beards disguised the criminals and caused confusion.
6. *Sample answers:* People wearing similar beards were mistaken for one another. Police arrested the wrong bearded men. Villains could escape trouble by changing their beards.

Apply, page 16
1. A
2. *Sample answers:* Leopards' spots disguise the outline of their bodies. Many arctic animals change from brown in summer to white in winter.
3. F
4. *Sample answers:* It removes waste from cells. It keeps the body at the right temperature.

Check Up, page 17
1. C   3. D   5. A   7. B
2. J   4. F   6. G   8. G

Workplace Skill, page 18
1. C   3. B
2. H   4. H

Sample answers:
5. The person should be licensed and have high standards and a sense of humor.
6. You should send your résumé to Dr. Achebe by mail or e-mail.

Write for Work, page 19
Check that the writing includes the following points: The writer identifies the main idea that Dr. Achebe wants to hire an assistant. The details relate to the main idea or topic: The position is full-time, Tuesday to Saturday, and includes medical, dental, and paid vacation.

Reading Extension, page 19
1. B   2. H   3. D   4. J
5. The joints allowed the models to be set in different positions.
6. *Sample answers: Son of Kong, Mighty Joe Young, King Kong versus Godzillas*

Explore Words, page 20
Vowel Combinations
2. goal   5. goes
3. due   6. pie
4. Monday

Compound Words
1. d   3. b
2. c   4. a

Synonyms
1. glad   4. silly
2. dull   5. end
3. tiny   6. sleepy

Page 21
Prefixes pre-, re-, sub-
1. replay   6. prerinse
2. predawn   7. subtropical
3. rediscover   8. rebuild
4. subbasement   9. presale
5. prepay

Academic Vocabulary
1. subject
2. clarify
3. passage
4. detail
5. recall

Unit 1 Lesson 1.2

Practice, page 23
1. false; Ocean thermal energy conversion is a way to change the ocean's heat into useable energy.
2. true
3. false; The first OTEC plant was built in 1930, so OTEC was first developed before 1960.
4. false; Georges Claude built it in Cuba.
5. false; The first plant was a failure.
6. true

Apply, page 24
Sample answers:
1. Maxwell Montes is one of the tallest mountain ranges in the solar system.
2. It is located on Venus.
3. It reaches more than 35,000 feet above the planet's plain level.
4. Tasmanian devils live on the island of Tasmania.
5. Tasmanian devils were named devils because of their wild temper tantrums.
6. Tasmanian devils bare their teeth, growl, and lunge when they are threatened.
7. Nor'easters are strong windstorms.
8. Nor'easters create heavy snow and rain.
9. Nor'easters have caused severe damage.

Check Up, page 25
1. C   3. B   5. D   7. A
2. F   4. H   6. G   8. H

Workplace Skill, page 26
1. C
2. F

Write for Work, page 27
Check that the writing includes the following points: The employee clearly expresses reasons why using the Internet for personal use is not a good idea. The tone should be friendly and respectful.

Reading Extension, page 27
1. B   2. G   3. D
4. *Sample answer:* They were afraid the children would have birth defects from their damaged chromosomes.
5. *Sample answer:* Her son already had problems, and he might get worse.

Explore Words, page 28
Consonant Blends
1. shr   3. nt   5. scr
2. nd   4. br   6. thr

Answer Key Intermediate 2 Student Edition

Spelling: Plurals
1. ladies
2. branches
3. hairbrushes
4. desks
5. buses
6. boxes

Antonyms
1. high
2. answer
3. fancy
4. false

Page 29

Context Clues
1. cry
2. brave
3. dangerous
4. celebrations
5. soaked
6. red

Academic Vocabulary
1. state
2. infer
3. distinguish
4. imply
5. directly

Unit 1 Lesson 1.3

Practice, page 31
Sample answers:
1. In areas where earthquakes happen, architects should design flexible buildings.
2. The more rigid a building is, the more damage an earthquake will do to it.
3. It is important to build on solid rock rather than on loose earth, especially where earthquakes are likely to occur.

Apply, page 32
Sample answers:
1. People make time capsules to share today's events with people in the future.
2. Time capsules are filled with memorabilia, buried in special places, and stay in the ground for many years.
3. My grandmother told me that she had buried a time capsule when she was young. She hopes it won't be found and opened for a long time.
4. different.

5. When people first began to measure things, they probably used their own feet. Everyone has different-sized feet, so measurements would not be the same.
6. I know that two people measuring a room using their feet will come up with different results.

Check Up, page 33
1. B
2. G
3. D

Workplace Skill, page 34
1. A   2. G

Write for Work, page 35
Check that the writing includes the following points: The form has been filled in correctly. The correct type of request has been checked. The information provided is reasonable.

Reading Extension, page 35
1. C
2. G
3. *Sample answer:* He thinks that there may have been other UFOs around.
4. *Sample answer:* Gill was interested in UFOs before the encounter in New Guinea.

Explore Words, page 36
Long e and Long i Spelled -y
1. I
2. E
3. E
4. I
5. E
6. I

Syllables
1. ro̲dent
2. wagon
3. pinecone
4. to̲ken

Suffixes -ness, -ment
1. ness; sweetness
2. ment; enjoyment
3. ment; payment
4. ness; darkness

Page 37

Spelling: Base Words and Endings
1. regretted
2. inventing
3. supplied
4. simplifying
5. cried
6. deciding
7. replaced
8. visiting

Academic Vocabulary
1. draw
2. valid
3. conclusion
4. appropriate
5. always

Unit 1 Lesson 1.4

Practice, page 39
1. A
2. G

Apply, page 40
Sample answers:
1. The Dead Sea is the lowest body of water on Earth's surface. It is unusual because of its high salt content, which allows people to float easily.
2. The Dead Sea is located between Israel and Jordan. It is the lowest body of water on Earth's surface at 1,312 feet below sea level. Its salt content is more than eight times higher than that of normal seawater.
3. Cells are organized differently depending on what their purpose is. The main purpose of every cell is to survive. If any part of the cell dies, the whole cell dies.

Check Up, page 41
1. B   2. F   3. A   4. G

Workplace Skill, page 42
1. D
2. F

Write for Work, page 43
Check that the writing includes the following points: The writer has written an accurate description of the steps of the internal transfer procedure. The writer should briefly summarize the most important ideas of each step.

Reading Extension, page 43

1. B
2. H
3. A
4. *Sample answer:* Mary's son Robert built the house that became known as the Ocean-born Mary House. Mary never lived there at all.

Explore Words, page 44

Hard and Soft c *and* g

1. hard
2. hard
3. soft
4. soft
5. soft
6. hard

Syllables

2. out / side
3. be / fore
4. con / sole
5. lo / cate
6. spi / nal

Suffixes -y, -en

1. en; soften
2. y; rubbery
3. y; summery
4. en; straighten
5. en; sharpen
6. y; moldy

Page 45

Multiple-meaning Words

1. b   2. a   3. a   4. b

Academic Vocabulary

1. paraphrase
2. brief
3. sustain
4. summary
5. include

Unit 1 Lesson 1.5

Practice, page 47

1. D   2. F   3. C   4. J

Apply, page 48

Sample answers:

1. Since Greenland is cold enough to be covered by permanent ice, icebergs may drift thousands of miles south before they melt.
2. Some people cannot take aspirin since they have a bad reaction to the medication.

3. Windshields are made of special safety glass so that they won't shatter when hit.
4. If scientists study clamshell fossils, then they can learn the secrets of the ancient seas.

Check Up, page 49

1. A
2. J
3. B
4. G
5. C

Workplace Skill, page 50

1. C
2. H

Write for Work, page 51

Sample answers: Overall Rating: Average. This employee's job performance is average and meets expectations and goals. His weak areas are that he gets behind in his assignments and does not initiate improvements to projects. He is exemplary in his ability to work as a good team member, and he has a good work attitude. Improvements in his weak areas could lead to a rating of Good on his next performance assessment.

Reading Extension, page 51

1. C
2. F
3. A

Explore Words, page 52

Base Words

2. mis read
3. afford able
4. re format
5. weak ness
6. short en

Spelling: Possessives

1. the students' classroom
2. my sisters' hats
3. Beto's CDs
4. the artists' paints

Syllables

2. remember
3. recombine
4. basketball

Page 53

Silent Consonants

1. s c ene
2. g nome
3. w rap
4. w rite
5. k nee
6. s c ent
7. k nock

Academic Vocabulary

1. effect
2. benefit
3. examine
4. cause
5. signal

Unit 1 Lesson 1.6

Practice, page 55

1. Writer C
2. Writer D
3. Writer A

Apply, page 56

1. descriptive details, long sentences; *Sample answer:* He'd ridden the train for days, crouched in a pile of hay that scratched his body and caused him to sneeze.
2. long sentences, descriptive details; *Sample answer:* Her closet, too, had clothes and shoes piled every which way, like she'd been looking for something in a hurry.
3. dialogue; *Sample answer:* "Not when my guild kicks me out," I said. They were going to be very angry.

Check Up, page 57

1. B
2. G
3. C
4. H

Workplace Skill, page 58

1. C
2. H

Write for Work, page 59

Check that the writing includes the following points: The style is appropriate for the purpose and audience chosen. The writer understands that e-mails to a hiring manager should be formal. Word choice should be appropriate and consistent.

Workplace Extension, page 59

1. formal language; Thank you for coming so promptly.
2. informal language; Wow, I'm really glad I got this interview.
3. *Sample answer:* No; her language is too informal for a job interview.

Explore Words, page 60

r-Controlled Vowels
2. curly
3. upstairs
4. shirt

Base Words and Roots
2. sweat(y)   5. (pre)dict
3. cruel(est)   6. (re)peat
4. (mis)take

Spelling: Contractions
1. f   3. e   5. a
2. d   4. b   6. c

Page 61

Syllables
2. title   7. (cir)cle
3. (cur)dle   8. maple
4. cradle   9. beagle
5. (gir)dle   10. (spar)kle
6. (hur)dle

Academic Vocabulary
1. communicate
2. individual
3. structure
4. highlight
5. style

Unit 1 Lesson 1.7

Practice, page 63

1. D   2. F   3. A   4. G

Apply, page 64

1. *Sample answer:* The banyan tree can grow many new trunks by touching its branches to the ground.
2. The platypus is an unusual creature unlike any other mammal.

3. *Sample answer:* People enjoy watching giant sea turtles lay their eggs.

Check Up, page 65

1. A   2. G   3. D   4. H

Workplace Skill, page 66

1. D
2. H

Write for Work, page 67

Check that the writing includes the following points: There is a clear main idea and supporting details or examples.

Workplace Extension, page 67

1. C
2. H
3. *Sample answer:* I would have tried to check in with my boss before the meeting. If that didn't work, I would also have stayed late to finish.
4. *Sample answer:* The boss would have been very appreciative. She would have complimented Maya on her strong work ethic.

Explore Words, page 68

Vowel Combinations
1. crook   4. stool
2. town   5. pause
3. joy

Spelling: Word Endings -er, -est
2. braver   5. smarter
3. fatter   6. lazier
4. saddest

Syllables
2. cra / ter
3. sam / ple
4. (mar)/ ble

Page 69

Context Clues
1. very cold   4. top
2. exactly the   5. not polite
   same   6. tired
3. carefree   7. meet

Academic Vocabulary
1. determine   4. overlap
2. topic   5. develop
3. main

Unit 1 Assessment

Pages 71–76

1. B   18. J
2. H   19. C
3. D   20. J
4. H   21. B
5. D   22. J
6. J   23. D
7. B   24. F
8. F   25. D
9. A   26. F
10. G   27. B
11. C   28. H
12. H   29. C
13. A   30. F
14. J   31. D
15. A   32. J
16. J   33. B
17. D   34. G

Unit 1 Workplace Skill Activity

Sample answers:
1. Carlos is upset that Eli leaves the break room messy after eating and that he has to clean up after Eli.
2. Carlos hopes that Eli will start cleaning up after himself.
3. Carlos thinks that the most responsible way to act is to clean up one's own mess after eating. Eli thinks he is being responsible by rushing back to the floor after lunch.
4. Carlos could cover the sales floor for Eli while Eli is eating. Eli could make sure to finish eating in time to clean up.

Intermediate 2 Student Edition

Unit 2 Lesson 2.1

Practice, page 79
1. Organize people into a group.
2. Leave a space for yourself.
3. Turn on the self-timer button.
4. Set the camera on a flat, even surface.
5. Push the shutter button halfway.
6. Check the screen.
7. Push the button the rest of the way.
8. Move into your spot.
9. first, next, now, then, as you push

Apply, page 80
1. f
2. h
3. a
4. b
5. e
6. g
7. d
8. c
9. one day in July 1938, before the flight, when, a day later, afterward, from then on

Check Up, page 81
1. C
2. F
3. C
4. H
5. D

Workplace Skill, page 82
1. D
2. G

Write for Work, page 83
Check that the writing includes the following points: The résumé is structured in the same sequence of steps as the instructions for writing a résumé on page 82. The objective statement is strong and focused. There are no errors or typographical mistakes.

Reading Extension, page 83
1. D
2. G
3. C
4. *Sample answer:* Kim and her cousins walked to a field to pick pussy willows.
5. *Sample answer:* Mrs. Baker called Allie King.

Explore Words, page 84
Prefixes mis-, un-
1. un
2. mis
3. mis
4. un
5. un
6. mis
7. un
8. un

Synonyms
1. distress
2. avoid
3. disappeared
4. plausible
5. announce
6. gratitude
7. commence
8. vacant

Page 85
Spelling: Word Endings
1. admitted
2. prepared
3. refusing
4. focused
5. disputing
6. labeled
7. seasoned
8. upsetting

Academic Vocabulary
1. subsequent
2. theme
3. concept
4. sequence
5. survey

Unit 2 Lesson 2.2

Practice, page 87
1. when the oil is below or at the ADD line

2. SAE 10W-30
3. This could cause engine damage.
4. The numbers are on the oil container.
5. the oil cap in the engine

Apply, page 88
1. You should do nothing; only toasters with red or white cases are affected by the recall.
2. You should stop using it and call Brierley to get a replacement. Even though it hasn't overheated yet, it still could.
3. You will have to pay nothing; replacements are free.
4. Call the company or go to its website to get more information.

Check Up, page 89
1. C
2. H
3. C
4. G
5. B
6. F

Workplace Skill, page 90
1. A   2. H

Write for Work, page 91
Check that the writing includes the following points: The writer understands the purpose of the consumer document he or she chose. The information is clear and corresponds to the chosen document.

Reading Extension, page 91
1. D
2. F
3. B
4. *Sample answer:* Someone broke open the Tylenol capsules and put cyanide inside them. Then, they put the bottles on store shelves. No one knew because there were no safety seals.

5. *Sample answer:* Safety packaging could have helped to prevent it.

Explore Words, page 92

Spelling: Contractions
1. don't
2. we're
3. shouldn't
4. wouldn't
5. aren't
6. he's

Suffixes -ive, -ish
1. yellowish
2. boyish
3. secretive
4. adoptive

Base Words and Roots
1. (previewed) revert(ed),
   (interviewing)
2. (disruptive) (interrupt), distract(ed)
3. (transport) (portable), depart

Page 93

Context Clues
Sample answers:
1. first
2. old-fashioned
3. go up and down
4. groupings of plants and animals

Academic Vocabulary
1. request
2. specific
3. excerpt
4. instructions
5. consume

Unit 2 Lesson 2.3

Practice, page 95
1. thesaurus
2. *Books in Print*
3. world almanac
4. world atlas
5. *Guinness World Records*
6. encyclopedia
7. *Bartlett's Familiar Quotations*

8. encyclopedia
9. world almanac
10. *Guinness World Records*
11. thesaurus

Apply, page 96
1. B
2. F
3. A
4. J
5. C
6. J

Check Up, page 97
1. B
2. G
3. D
4. F
5. C
6. F

Workplace Skill, page 98
1. B   2. G

Write for Work, page 99
Check that the writing includes the following points: The writer has used the appropriate reference sources to find the information on Brasilia.

Reading Extension, page 99
1. B   2. F
3. *Sample answers:* huge, massive, immense
4. *Guinness World Records*

Explore Words, page 100
Spelling: Irregular Plurals
1. series
2. salmon
3. mice
4. sheep
5. teeth

Spelling: Homophones
1. board
2. brakes
3. seem
4. allowed

Page 101
Suffixes -ize, -ify
Answers for words in box: false, immune, solid, visual, central, criminal
1. criminalize
2. immunize
3. falsify
4. centralize
5. visualize
6. solidify

Academic Vocabulary
1. consult
2. general
3. source
4. index
5. research

Unit 2 Lesson 2.4

Practice, page 103
Sample answers:
1. hardworking
2. calm
3. compassionate
4. selfless
5. & 6.
   Narrative: The author tells us that Keisha reassured the injured woman and remained composed while caring for her.
   Action: Keisha rushes over to help Mrs. De La Rosa.
   Dialogue: "Can I carry that for you?"

Apply, page 104
1. Calixto
2. *Sample answers:* messy, lazy, indecisive
3. action, narration
4. Miss MacGill and Steve
5. *Sample answers:* unpleasant, spiteful, stingy
6. narration, action, Steve's inner thoughts, what other characters think of Miss MacGill

Check Up, page 105
1. C   2. F   3. D   4. G

Answer Key Intermediate 2 Student Edition

Workplace Skill, page 106
1. A
2. G

Write for Work, page 107
Check that the writing includes the following points: The writer understands the kinds of character traits that would be most useful for this position: respect for people and groups, love of children, ability to listen to and work with others, passionate about the environment.

Reading Extension, page 107
1. C
2. F
3. A
4. *Sample answers:* She kept adding on to her house to have enough space for the ghosts. She served the ghosts dinner every night.
5. *Sample answer:* Sarah was superstitious.

Explore Words, page 108
Syllables
1. ro̱tate
2. ca̱bin
3. si̱mple
4. i̱nvite
5. bu̱gle
6. re̱sell
8. disconnect
9. prevented
10. fantastic

Prefixes in-, dis-
1. indirect
2. insane
3. disorder
4. dislike
5. disagreement
6. disobey

Page 109
Multiple-meaning Words
1. a
2. b
3. b
4. a
5. a

6. b
7. b
8. b

Academic Vocabulary
1. characters
2. focus
3. method
4. reveal
5. traits

Unit 2 Lesson 2.5

Practice, page 111
1. B
2. H
3. C
4. F

Apply, page 112
Sample answers:
1. Sometimes birds build nests under the eaves of houses.
2. Some birds make nests in planters near skyscrapers.
3. The Washington Monument offers a view of the city.
4. The White House tour is an interesting activity.
5. Tasty sauce from fresh tomatoes forms the base.
6. Freshly grated cheese is a must.
7. You can see every task you need to accomplish.
8. You will know if you start to run late and need to speed up somewhere else.

Check Up, page 113
1. A
2. G
3. B
4. H

Workplace Skill, page 114
1. D
2. H

Write for Work, page 115
Check that the writing includes the following points: The writer has written a clear and focused key job responsibility. The three details

support the key responsibility adequately.

Reading Extension, page 115
1. B
2. G
3. A
4. *Sample answer:* Yes; the author gives examples of many ways in which weather was affected all over the globe.

Explore Words, page 116
Spelling: Possessives
1. the dog's collar
2. your daughter's teacher
3. your sister's children
4. my cousins' party
5. Suchin's lunch

Spelling: Word Endings
1. supplied
2. relying
3. supposed
4. studying
5. donating
6. underlined
7. profiling
8. readying
9. reuniting
10. exploded

Page 117
Latin Roots
1. vis; d
2. port; f
3. ject; e
4. port; a
5. vis; g
6. voc; b
7. ject; c

Academic Vocabulary
1. statistics
2. evidence
3. example
4. eliminate
5. support

Answer Key Intermediate 2 Student Edition

Unit 2 Lesson 2.6

Practice, page 119
1. b
2. a
3. c
4. e
5. d
6. to inform
7. to entertain or to describe
8. to persuade

Apply, page 120
1. a recipe
2. to explain or instruct
3. a report
4. to inform
5. a letter to the editor
6. to persuade or express an opinion
7. a comedy routine
8. to entertain
9. an article
10. to describe
11. an essay
12. to describe or inform

Check Up, page 121
1. B
2. F
3. D
4. H

Workplace Skill, page 122
1. C
2. G

Write for Work, page 123
Check that the writing includes the following points: The writer recognizes that the purpose of the e-mail is to persuade workers to drive slowly in the parking lots; the word choice supports this purpose adequately.

Workplace Extension, page 123
1. B
2. H
3. *Sample answer:* Rashid should have avoided checking his watch often, tapping his fingers, looking down instead of making eye contact with his boss, slouching in his chair, and crossing his arms over his chest.

Explore Words, page 124
Spelling: Words with f, ph, gh
1. correct
2. fences
3. refrain
4. correct
5. enough
6. correct
7. alphabet
8. pharmacy

Word Families
1. decisive
2. uncreative
3. assistant

Antonyms
1. refuse
2. arrive
3. public

Page 125
Prefixes inter-, semi-, multi-
1. multicultural
2. interstate
3. semiconscious
4. international
5. semiprivate
6. multilevel

Academic Vocabulary
1. purpose
2. explain
3. inform
4. author
5. persuade

Unit 2 Assessment

Pages 127–132
1. A
2. H
3. D
4. J
5. C
6. F
7. B
8. H
9. D
10. F
11. B
12. F
13. B
14. J
15. C
16. H
17. D
18. J
19. A
20. G
21. B
22. F
23. B
24. J
25. D
26. H
27. A
28. G
29. A
30. J
31. D
32. J

Unit 2 Workplace Skill Activity

Sample answers:
Sara will send out a memo to the other employees. Steps in task: gather information, write memo, send e-mail to the rest of the company.
Lee will organize drop-off boxes. Steps in task: find clean, empty boxes; label the boxes clearly; let others know where the boxes are.
Desmond will accept money donations and shop for food. Steps in task: collect money, make a list of food needed, buy food.
Carla will transport collected food to the food bank. Steps in task: arrange a drop-off time with the food bank, gather all donations, bring food to food bank.

Unit 3 Lesson 3.1

Practice, page 135
1. valid
2. not valid
3. valid
4. valid
5. not valid

Apply, page 136
Sample answers:
1. Minor characters can be just as important to the plot as major characters.
2. Some things are good in small doses but deadly in large quantities.
3. Some American states were founded for religious reasons.
4. People are developing renewable energy technologies to limit the impact of global warming.

Check Up, page 137
1. A
2. H
3. D

Workplace Skill, page 138
1. A
2. H

Write for Work, page 139
Check that the writing includes the following points: The writer has selected three credible fact-checking sources to verify the information in the report.

Reading Extension, page 139
1. C
2. H
3. B
4. *Sample answer:* These areas have not changed much since before the Ice Age, when dinosaurs still existed.
5. *Sample answers:* sound recordings, casts of footprints, samples of droppings, and blurry pictures

Explore Words, page 140
Base Words and Roots
1. grateful, gratitude
2. create, recreation
3. employ, unemployed
4. portable, transportation
5. magnitude, magnificent
6. sanity, insane

The Schwa Sound
1. bro(ken)
2. lem(on)
3. i(dol)
4. vic(tim)
5. ba(con)
6. la(bel)
7. help(ful)
8. ras(cal)
9. sol(id)
10. hu(man)

Page 141
Multiple-meaning Words
1. b
2. b
3. b
4. a

Academic Vocabulary
1. found
2. minor
3. event
4. introduce
5. typically

Unit 3 Lesson 3.2

Practice, page 143
1. A
2. F
3. B
4. F
5. B
6. F

Apply, page 144
Sample answers:
1. formal language
2. authoritative
3. to provide a reference for facts about wasps
4. The first passage is formal and authoritative, while the second passage is informal and friendly.
5. friendliness
6. look like a pro in no time; frosting it will be a breeze; this is the best part
7. to provide instructions for cake decorating that seem easy to follow

Check Up, page 145
1. B
2. J
3. C
4. F

Workplace Skill, page 146
1. B
2. H

Write for Work, page 147
Check that the writing includes the following points: The writer has a clear idea of the intention of writing the poster, and the effect is reasonable and logical.

Reading Extension, page 147
1. D
2. H
3. *Sample answer:* The authors may have wanted to show that the sisters recanted their confession because they needed or wanted money, not because it was the truth.
4. *Sample answer:* a spooky feeling

Explore Words, page 148
Prefixes
1. improper
2. invisible
3. impatient
4. illegal
5. inconvenient
6. irrational
7. inaccurate
8. impolite
9. irresponsible

Suffixes -ion, -tion
1. celebration
2. collision
3. attention
4. illustrations
5. reflection
6. exceptions
7. destruction
8. explanation

Page 149

Spelling: Plurals of Nouns Ending in -o
1. patios
2. tomatoes
3. echoes *or* echos
4. memos
5. heroes
6. studios
7. rodeos
8. stereos

Academic Vocabulary
1. intention
2. assign
3. approach
4. technique
5. common

Unit 3 Lesson 3.3

Practice, page 151
1. killer bees and fire ants
2. *Sample answer:* They are both aggressive insects. Their stings can cause illness or death.
3. types of elements
4. *Sample answer:* Metals conduct heat and electricity well, while nonmetals are poor conductors. Metals are bendable, while nonmetals are brittle.
5. World War I and World War II
6. *Sample answers:* Alike: Both were international conflicts. Different: Their cost was different. World War II cost 10 times the amount of World War I.

Apply, page 152
International affairs: involve other countries; include foreign aid, wars, and trade relationships
Both: political, economic, social aspects; important in any presidential administration; subject of laws passed by Congress; dealt with at national level
Domestic affairs: involve only the United States; include health-care reform and tax cuts; affect national, state, and local levels of government
Clue words: both, but, on the other hand, while

Check Up, page 153
1. D
2. H
3. A
4. G

Workplace Skill, page 154
1. D
2. J

Write for Work, page 155
Check that the writing includes the following points: The writer understands that by attaining a bachelor's degree, the student would probably earn a higher weekly salary.

Reading Extension, page 155
1. D
2. G
3. C
4. *Sample answer:* outer space or an experiment gone wrong
5. *Sample answer:* a giant bat that looked like a witch

Explore Words, page 156
Latin Roots
Sample answers:
1. transportation; the act of carrying people and goods from one place to another
2. pertain; be appropriate, related, or applicable
3. distraction; something that interferes with concentration

Suffixes -ous, -ious
Sample answers:
1. adventurous; The early explorers were very adventurous.
2. cautious; You need to be cautious when crossing busy streets.
3. envious; Everyone is envious of my new car.

Page 157

Prefixes uni-, bi-, tri-
1. tri
2. tri
3. bi
4. bi
5. uni
6. bi
7. bi
8. uni
9. tri
10. bi
11. bi
12. tri

Academic Vocabulary
1. relate
2. compare
3. property
4. contrast
5. distinct

Unit 3 Lesson 3.4

Practice, page 159
Sample answers:
1. He will let go of the wool and then swim away.
2. She will choose different songs.
3. They knitted items for the Red Cross that used the patterns and colors provided.
4. She will apply for the job.

Apply, page 160
1. C
2. *Sample answer:* The climber is experienced. Because he's been planning the climb for so long, he'll know how dangerous it would be to climb in a storm.
3. G
4. *Sample answer:* The word *seemingly* is a clue that the weather would not be as pleasant as the family hoped. Another clue is that it had been a very wet month.
5. A
6. *Sample answer:* Irina has given dozens of presentations before. She will pull her act together and make her presentation a success.

Check Up, page 161
1. B
2. J
3. C

Workplace Skill, page 162
1. C
2. J

Write for Work, page 163
Check that the writing includes the following points: The writer understands how to read an organizational flowchart and explains how it can be useful to an employee or a job applicant.

Reading Extension, page 163
1. B
2. F
3. B
4. *Sample answer:* No; everything seemed to be going as planned.
5. *Sample answer:* NASA probably tried to work on ways to make the shuttles safer.

Explore Words, page 164
Suffixes -ic, -al, -ly
2. history; ic; al
3. biography; ic; al
4. quick; ly
5. economy; ic; al
6. rhythm; ic
7. smooth; ly

Prefixes en-, em-
1. e
2. c
3. a
4. b
5. d

Page 165
Context Clues
Sample answers:
1. useful
2. to make smaller
3. foolish
4. picture

Academic Vocabulary
1. predict
2. logical
3. adjust
4. outcome
5. prior

Unit 3 Lesson 3.5

Practice, page 167
Fact:
Marian Anderson was a famous African American singer.
Anderson was the first African American soloist to sing with the New York City Metropolitan Opera.
Arturo Toscanini was a conductor who said that a voice like Anderson's "comes once in 100 years."
In 1939 Anderson was barred from performing in Constitution Hall because she was African American. She gave a concert in front of the Lincoln Memorial in Washington, D.C., instead.
More than 75,000 people came out that day to see Anderson perform.
Opinion:
Marian Anderson was the best opera singer in America.
It is shameful that racism affected Anderson and her singing career.

Apply, page 168
1. F; encyclopedia
2. O
3. O
4. F; encyclopedia or atlas
5. O
6. F; newspaper
7. F; encyclopedia
8. F; newspaper
9. O

Check Up, page 169
1. D
2. F
3. A
4. G
5. A
6. J

Workplace Skill, page 170
1. B
2. J

Write for Work, page 171
Check that the writing includes the following points: The press

release uses the format of the press release on page 170, presents both facts and opinions to describe the new product, and uses appropriate word choice to convince customers.

Reading Extension, page 171
1. C
2. J
3. A
4. *Sample answer:* Ducks, sea lions, and other marine animals were drenched in oil.
5. *Sample answer:* It was Exxon's fault. If they knew about Hazelwood's drinking problem, they should not have allowed him to navigate the ship.

Explore Words, page 172
Base Words and Roots
1. inspection, perspective
2. misadventure, adventurous
3. appearance, disappeared
4. arrangement, prearranged
5. immortalize, mortician
6. structure, construct

Synonyms
1. fancy   5. save
2. colorful   6. cabin
3. surprise   7. trip
4. determined   8. snatched

Page 173
Greek Roots
Sample answers:
1. biohazard; a risk to human beings or their environment
2. geology; the study of the history of Earth, especially rocks
3. autopilot; a device that allows a vehicle to steer itself
4. autobiography; the written history of your own life

Academic Vocabulary
1. opinion   4. viewpoint
2. prove   5. fact
3. reliable

Answer Key Intermediate 2 Student Edition

Unit 3 Lesson 3.6

Practice, page 175

1. drama; *Sample answer:* It includes dialogue meant to be spoken by actors.
2. fiction; *Sample answer:* It is imaginary writing about an imaginary character.
3. myth; *Sample answer:* Atalanta is a character in Greek mythology.

Apply, page 176

1. C
2. J
3. A

Check Up, page 177

1. B   4. J
2. G   5. C
3. C   6. H

Workplace Skill, page 178

1. B   2. G

Write for Work, page 179

Check that the writing includes the following points: The paragraph includes information about the student's job responsibilities and the types of documents and materials the student has used in relation to his or her job.

Workplace Extension, page 179

1. A
2. H
3. C
4. G
5. *Sample answer:* He should have communicated respectfully and calmly with his supervisor. He should have shown respect for his coworkers. He should have realized that his supervisor's statements were not accusations but only an attempt at problem solving.

Explore Words, page 180

Suffixes -er, -or, -ist
1. visitor   3. gardener
2. pianist   4. actor

Spelling: Homophones
1. fined
2. through
3. patients
4. presence
5. hoarse
6. stationary

Word Families
1. inventor
2. unreliable
3. unemployed
4. portable

Page 181

Analogies
1. small
2. flower
3. seat
4. sick
5. airplane

Academic Vocabulary
1. prose
2. drama
3. genre
4. emphasize
5. comprise

Unit 3 Assessment

Pages 183–188

1. A   16. J
2. H   17. A
3. B   18. G
4. F   19. B
5. B   20. H
6. F   21. A
7. B   22. G
8. H   23. D
9. A   24. H
10. H   25. B
11. A   26. F
12. J   27. D
13. A   28. G
14. H   29. A
15. B   30. J

Unit 3 Workplace Skill Activity

Sample answers:
1. You want to go back to school, but you also want to take a job that pays more money. You cannot do both because they occur at the same time.
2. **Possible Decision:** agree to work the night shift and decide not to go to school at this time
   Pros: more money right away, greater possibility for promotion and raise
   Cons: delaying or indefinitely postponing your education and possible better job in the future
   Possible Decision: move to the night shift and look for daytime classes
   Pros: more money right away, greater possibility for promotion and raise
   Cons: may be hard to find classes with the right schedule, day classes may be more expensive, can be difficult to work and go to school at the same time
   Possible Decision: tell your supervisor that you will be unable to change your shift
   Pros: able to go to night school, already comfortable with job and coworkers, may eventually be able to make a career change using the skills learned in the classes
   Cons: no raise for changing shifts, promotions will not be as easy to get, can be difficult to work and go to school at the same time
3. The answer should explain why students chose the decision they did.

Lesson Plan Advanced Student Edition

Introduce

READING SKILL

Recognize and Recall Details

Explain/Model: Explain that it is important to read attentively to recognize and recall details. Have students read aloud the passage about gross domestic product. Model using details to determine China's gross domestic product.

Guided Practice: Have students read the boxed passage. Then work with them to complete the task given in the directions. Discuss why the response given after the passage is correct. Ask students to find two additional details that support the idea that space travel can be harmful to the body.

Teach Lesson Skills

Practice: Have students read the passages. Tell them to read the passages once all the way through and then scan them for specific details to answer the questions. Discuss the answers and have students point out the details in the passage that support their answers.

Apply: After students locate the main ideas and list the details, have them read the details aloud to the class. Ask students to explain how the details support the main ideas.

Check Up: Have students work in small groups to read the passage and answer the questions. Then check each group's responses with those of other groups in the class.

COMPREHENSION

Set a Purpose for Reading: Encourage students to set a purpose for reading. Provide self-questioning models, such as *What do I hope to learn? What do the directions tell me to look for? What will happen next?* By setting a purpose and then evaluating whether they achieved the purpose, students consciously monitor their own comprehension. They can also discuss the purpose they have determined with a peer or a teacher.

Reading Extension

📖 Encourage students to read "Secret Service Agents: Shield, Defend, Protect" on page 1 of the *Advanced Reader*. Use this as an opportunity to teach reading strategies and the lesson reading skill.

ALPHABETICS

Explore Words

Prefixes: Write *misunderstand, discontent, unwise,* and *nonfat.* Have volunteers underline the prefixes. Model using the prefixes to help determine the meanings of the words.

Spelling: Plurals: Model forming the plurals of these words: *ring, glass, puppy, cuff, calf, knife.* Have students point out any spelling changes.

Context Clues: Write the following sentence, underlining as shown: *I can think of several possible reasons why Carla invited me, but I don't know her real motive.* Model using context clues to determine the meaning of *motive.* Have a volunteer use a dictionary to confirm your definition.

VOCABULARY

Academic Vocabulary/Tier 2

recall detail economy standard output

Before students complete the activity, write the academic vocabulary words and definitions on the board. Discuss each word's meaning with students. Then write the sentences below on the board. Read each sentence aloud and discuss it with students.

1. Inez could not *recall* the name of her first grade teacher.
2. Jason planned every *detail* of the party.
3. Many people try to save money when the *economy* is poor.
4. The factory has a *standard* of quality for their products that must be met.
5. A positive work environment can increase employees' *output*.

FLUENCY

Echo Reading: Read a sentence from one of the passages aloud. Then have students echo you by reading the same sentence and trying to read with the same speed and expression as you do.

Invite students to do a timed reading of "Secret Service Agents: Shield, Defend, Protect." Afterwards, have them enter their times on the Words-per-Minute table on page 121 and chart their reading speed on page 122 of the *Advanced Reader*.

📶 Encourage students to listen to "Secret Service Agents: Shield, Defend, Protect." Go to **www.mhreadingbasics.com** to play or download the recording. The recording provides modeled fluency and read-along support.

APPLICATION

Workplace Skill:

Recognize Details in a Request for Proposal

Remind students that a request for proposal (RFP) is an invitation for suppliers to submit a bid for a client to use their services. Paying attention to the details as they read will help them understand what the proposal is for and what information must be included. After students answer the questions, have them imagine they are going to submit an RFP. Ask them to make a list of their food service qualifications and experience. This list will come in handy when they do the Write for Work activity.

Write for Work

Tell students to read the instructions for this task carefully to be sure they include all the requested information. Encourage them to share their work with a classmate to make sure they included sufficient details about their food service qualifications and experience.

PASSKEY

💻 Go to **www.mhreadingbasics.com** and click on the *PassKey* link. Customize instruction for your class using modules from Reading/Language Arts, Levels 4 & 5.

Advanced Student Edition

Lesson Plan Advanced Student Edition

Unit 1 Lesson 1.2 pages 22–29

<table>
<tr>
<td rowspan="2">Introduce</td>
<td colspan="3">

READING SKILL

Understand Stated and Implied Concepts

Explain/Model: Explain that it is important to distinguish between stated concepts and implied concepts. Then have students read aloud the passage about mold. Model distinguishing between the stated concepts (Sentences 2 and 3) and the implied one (Sentence 1).

Guided Practice: Have students read the boxed passage. Then work with them to complete the task given in the directions. Discuss why the response given after the passage is correct. Ask students to give another stated concept about the Pony Express and an implied one.

</td>
</tr>
</table>

<table>
<tr>
<td rowspan="8">Teach Lesson Skills</td>
<td colspan="3">

Practice: Have students read the passage about Pompeii. Tell them to look for concepts that are directly stated and concepts that are implied. Discuss the answers and have students point out stated concepts in the passage that support their answers.

Apply: After students read the passages and answer the questions, have them read their responses aloud to the class. Encourage students to show classmates where they found the stated and implied concepts.

Check Up: Have students work in small groups to read the passage and answer the questions. Then check each group's responses with those of other groups in the class.

</td>
</tr>
<tr>
<td colspan="2">

COMPREHENSION

Reread/Read More Slowly: Encourage students to become aware of the pace at which they read. Offer self-questioning models, such as *Did I read this passage too quickly? Does reading it again help me understand better? Does reading more slowly help me retain information?* When students actively consider the manner in which they are reading, they consciously monitor their own comprehension.

</td>
<td>

Reading Extension

 Encourage students to read "Humanitarian Aid Workers: Comfort Under Fire" on page 9 of the *Advanced Reader*. Use this as an opportunity to teach reading strategies and the lesson reading skill.

</td>
</tr>
<tr>
<td>

ALPHABETICS

Explore Words

Spelling: Word Endings: Model adding endings to these words: *pale + -er; brag + -ed; transmit + -ing; signal + -ing.* Ask for volunteers to point out any necessary spelling changes.

Spelling: Possessives: Provide these examples: *the teacher's book/the teachers' books; the student's desk/the students' desks.* Have students provide additional examples.

Suffixes -er, -or, -ist: Model adding suffixes to these words: *teach + -er; edit + -or; art + -ist.* Discuss the meanings. Then have volunteers suggest additional words with these suffixes.

</td>
<td>

VOCABULARY

Academic Vocabulary/Tier 2

distinguish   clarify   directly   state   infer

Before students complete the activity, write the academic vocabulary words and definitions on the board. Discuss each word's meaning with students. Then write the sentences below on the board. Read each sentence aloud and discuss it with students.

1. A color blind person can't always *distinguish* between red and green.
2. Ask your teacher to *clarify* any directions that you don't understand.
3. Byron plans to ask his boss *directly* for a big raise.
4. Please *state* your full name and address.
5. I can *infer* from Carly's frown that she is very unhappy.

</td>
<td>

FLUENCY

Partner Reading: Have partners read aloud to one another and/or read aloud at the same time. Encourage them to offer support and correction to one another. Circulate to offer guidance as needed.

Invite students to do a timed reading of "Humanitarian Aid Workers: Comfort Under Fire." Afterwards, have them enter their times on the Words-per-Minute table on page 121 and chart their reading speed on page 122 of the *Advanced Reader*.

Encourage students to listen to "Humanitarian Aid Workers: Comfort Under Fire." Go to **www.mhereadingbasics.com** to play or download the recording. The recording provides modeled fluency and read-along support.

</td>
</tr>
<tr>
<td colspan="2">

APPLICATION

Workplace Skill:

Locate Stated and Implied Concepts in a Letter of Appointment

Have students read the letter of appointment. Remind them that a letter of appointment confirms employment and gives details about the employee's position. Point out that the letter will directly state information about the position and clarify that information with details. After students answer the questions, have them start a list of additional questions they have about their position, such as whether they need a parking permit or what they need to bring with them on the first day. This list will come in handy when they do the Write for Work activity.

</td>
<td>

Write for Work

Remind students that when they write to a manager or supervisor, they should use a professional, respectful tone. Encourage them to share their work with a classmate to make sure their questions are clear and logical, and were not previously addressed in the letter of appointment.

</td>
</tr>
<tr>
<td colspan="3">

PASSKEY

Go to **www.mhereadingbasics.com** and click on the *PassKey* link. Customize instruction for your class using modules from Reading/Language Arts, Levels 4 & 5.

</td>
</tr>
</table>

Lesson Plan Advanced Student Edition

Introduce

READING SKILL

Draw Conclusions

Explain/Model: Explain to students that they should use facts and their own knowledge to draw valid conclusions. Then have them read the sentences about sleeping pills. Model making a valid conclusion about sleeping pill use.

Guided Practice: Have students read the boxed passage. Then work with them to complete the task given in the directions. Discuss why the responses given after the passage are correct. Ask students to share another conclusion they could draw about Aksum.

Teach Lesson Skills

Practice: Have students read the passages. Tell students to think about what each passage says and what they know as they read. Discuss whether each conclusion is valid, and have students share the facts and knowledge they used to evaluate each conclusion.

Apply: After students answer the questions, have them read their responses aloud to the class. Encourage students to explain how they drew each conclusion.

Check Up: Have students work in small groups to read the passages and answer the questions. Then check each group's responses with those of other groups in the class.

COMPREHENSION

Use Prior Knowledge: Encourage students to think about what they already know before they read. To get students started, provide self-questioning models, such as *Have I read about this topic before? Does this sound familiar?* When students can create a context or framework of known information in which to place new information, they consciously monitor their own comprehension.

Reading Extension

📖 Encourage students to read "Bomb Squad: No False Moves" on page 17 of the *Advanced Reader*. Use this as an opportunity to teach reading strategies and the lesson reading skill.

ALPHABETICS

Explore Words

Prefixes: Model adding prefixes to these words: *de-* + *hydrate*, *inter-* + *national*, *re-* + *visit*, *sub-* + *zero*. Discuss the meaning of each word. Then have volunteers use the words in sentences.

Latin Roots: Write the following words, underlining as shown: *dictate, inspect, reject*. Discuss the meaning of each word. Then have volunteers give examples of other words with these roots.

Synonyms: Write the following words: *endorse, mindful, eradicate, beckon*. Have students work in pairs to write a synonym or synonyms for each word. Allow them to use a thesaurus if necessary.

VOCABULARY

Academic Vocabulary/Tier 2

conclusion   draw   general   currency   grant

Before students complete the activity, write the academic vocabulary words and definitions on the board. Discuss each word's meaning with students. Then write the sentences below on the board. Read each sentence aloud and discuss it with students.

1. Rodrigo came to the *conclusion* that he needs to go to bed earlier.
2. Artists *draw* inspiration from the world around them.
3. The doctor asked *general* questions about my health.
4. Some Native Americans used shells and beads as *currency*.
5. Sasha hopes her boss will *grant* her request for a day off.

FLUENCY

Collaborative Reading: Gather in a group. Have each student read one or more lines of a passage and then pass the text to the next student. Supply pronunciation and phrasing corrections as needed.

Invite students to do a timed reading of "Bomb Squad: No False Moves." Afterwards, have them enter their times on the Words-per-Minute table on page 121 and chart their reading speed on page 122 of the *Advanced Reader*.

📶 Encourage students to listen to "Bomb Squad: No False Moves." Go to **www.mhreadingbasics.com** to play or download the recording. The recording provides modeled fluency and read-along support.

APPLICATION

Workplace Skill:

Draw Conclusions about a Table

Have students examine the table. Remind them that graphics, such as tables, charts, and diagrams, present information in a visual way. Tell students to use the data in the table and their own knowledge to draw conclusions about the information. After students answer the questions, have them choose an industry from the table and make a list of reasons why safety in this industry is important. This exercise will be helpful for the Write for Work activity.

Write for Work

Remind students to read the instructions carefully to be sure they include all the information in the memo. Encourage them to share their work with a classmate to make sure they supported their position with statistics from the table and at least three other reasons or examples.

PASSKEY

🔑 Go to **www.mhreadingbasics.com** and click on the *PassKey* link. Customize instruction for your class using modules from Reading/Language Arts, Levels 4 & 5.

Advanced Student Edition

Lesson Plan Advanced Student Edition

Introduce

READING SKILL

Summarize and Paraphrase

Explain/Model: Explain that it is important to read attentively to note main ideas and important details. Then have students read aloud the passage about Benjamin Franklin. Model summarizing and paraphrasing the passage.

Guided Practice: Have students read the boxed passage. Then work with them to complete the task given in the directions. Discuss the summary and paraphrase that follow. Ask students to explain which details weren't included in the summary and why.

Teach Lesson Skills

Practice: Have students read the passages. Tell them to think about what the passages are mostly about and how they could briefly state the most important ideas and details. Have students share their summaries, and ask students to explain how they decided which ideas and details to include.

Apply: After students write their paraphrases and summary, have them read their responses aloud to the class. Ask them to explain in what ways paraphrases are different from summaries.

Check Up: Have students work in small groups to read the passages and answer the questions. Then check each group's responses with those of other groups in the class.

COMPREHENSION

Ask Questions: Encourage students to ask themselves questions as they read. Provide questioning models that progress from concrete to abstract. For example, *What does this mean? Is this a main idea? Do I remember the order of important events?* By asking themselves questions, students consciously monitor their own comprehension. They can also ask questions of peers or a teacher to clarify understanding.

Reading Extension

📖 Encourage students to read "Tornado Chasers: Eyes of the Storm" on page 25 of the *Advanced Reader*. Use this as an opportunity to teach reading strategies and the lesson reading skill.

ALPHABETICS

Explore Words

Spelling: The Letters *f, ph, gh, ch*: Write the following words on the board, underlining as shown: *graph, tough, peach, charades, ache*. Read the words with students. Have them identify the sound the underlined letters stand for in each word.

Greek Roots: Write these words: *telegram, biodegradable, automobile,* and *autobiography*. Model using the root or roots to figure out the meanings of the words. Have students confirm the definitions in a dictionary.

Spelling: Word Endings: Model adding endings to these words: *tiny + -est, sturdy + -er, worry + -ing, cry + -ed, play + -ed*. Have students identify any spelling changes.

VOCABULARY

Academic Vocabulary/Tier 2

summarize   paraphrase   device   observe   conclude

Before students complete the activity, write the academic vocabulary words and definitions on the board. Discuss each word's meaning with students. Then write the sentences below on the board. Read each sentence aloud and discuss it with students.

1. Trista can *summarize* the story in three short sentences.
2. Tony likes to *paraphrase* fairy tales for his little sister.
3. Juanita has a special *device* for curling her eyelashes.
4. On his first day at work, Cruz will *observe* another employee.
5. The lights in the Parkers' house are off, so we can *conclude* they aren't home.

FLUENCY

Repeated Reading: Lead a group to read the same passage aloud together several times. As the leader, emphasize accuracy and phrasing until the group reading sounds smooth and consistent

Invite students to do a timed reading of "Tornado Chasers: Eyes of the Storm." Afterwards, have them enter their times on the Words-per-Minute table on page 121 and chart their reading speed on page 122 of the *Advanced Reader*.

📶 Encourage students to listen to "Tornado Chasers: Eyes of the Storm." Go to **www.mhereadingbasics.com** to play or download the recording. The recording provides modeled fluency and read-along support.

APPLICATION

Workplace Skill:

Summarize and Paraphrase a Purpose Statement

Remind students that a process-improvement plan sets goals for a company and outlines a plan for achieving them. As students read the purpose statement, have them look for main ideas and the details that support them to help summarize and paraphrase the document. After students answer the questions, have them start a list of the main goals of the process-improvement plan. This list will be helpful when they do the Write for Work activity.

Write for Work

Remind students that a summary includes just the most important information. Point out that an e-mail from a team leader should be written in a positive, professional tone. Encourage them to share their work with a classmate to make sure they included all the main points and no unnecessary details.

PASSKEY

💻 Go to **www.mhereadingbasics.com** and click on the *PassKey* link. Customize instruction for your class using modules from Reading/Language Arts, Levels 4 & 5.

Lesson Plan Advanced Student Edition

Introduce

READING SKILL

Identify Cause and Effect

Explain/Model: Explain that a cause is why something happens and an effect is what happens. Signal words can help readers identify causes and effects. Have students read aloud the sentence about the change of season. Model identifying the causes and effect.

Guided Practice: Have students read the boxed passage. Then work with them to complete the task given in the directions. Discuss the responses given after the passage. Ask students to explain how signal words and phrases can help them identify causes and effects.

Teach Lesson Skills

Practice: Have students read the passages. Tell them to think about *what happened* and *why* as they read about each topic. Discuss the answers to the questions, and have students point out signal words and phrases that helped them identify causes and effects.

Apply: After students complete their graphic organizers, have them share their responses with the class. Encourage students to point out signal words and phrases they used to help them determine the causes and effects.

Check Up: Have students work in small groups to read the passages and answer the questions. Then check each group's responses with those of other groups in the class.

COMPREHENSION

Look for Context Clues/Read On: Encourage students to look for context clues as they read. Investigating the context helps a reader to put words and paragraphs into a larger framework. Provide helpful self-questioning models, such as *What words surrounding this difficult word can help me understand better? If I read a little farther, might I find additional clues that can help me understand?* When students proactively look for context clues, they consciously monitor their own comprehension.

Reading Extension

📖 Encourage students to read "High-rise Window Washers: A Bird's-eye View" on page 33 of the *Advanced Reader*. Use this as an opportunity to teach reading strategies and the lesson reading skill.

ALPHABETICS

Explore Words

Suffixes -ive, -ic, -ish: Model adding suffixes to the following words: *assert* + -ive, *baby* + -ish, *acid* + -ic. Discuss the meaning of each word. Then have volunteers give additional examples for each suffix.

Spelling: Homophones: Write the following homophone pairs: *air/heir, cereal/serial, morning/mourning*. Discuss the meaning of each word. Then have students work in pairs to write a sentence that shows the meaning of each homophone.

Multiple-meaning Words: Write this sentence: *At the party you will present your friends with a present*. Model using context to determine the meaning of each word.

VOCABULARY

Academic Vocabulary/Tier 2

cause effect likewise identify obvious

Before students complete the activity, write the academic vocabulary words and definitions on the board. Discuss each word's meaning with students. Then write the sentences below on the board. Read each sentence aloud and discuss it with students.

1. A dead battery was the *cause* of my car not starting this morning.
2. Better health is an *effect* of exercise.
3. Rosita will order the fish and Sal thinks he will do *likewise*.
4. Josiah's suitcase had a ribbon on the handle so it was easy to *identify*.
5. It's *obvious* that Gina isn't feeling especially well today.

FLUENCY

Echo Reading: Read a sentence from one of the passages aloud. Then have students echo you by reading the same sentence and trying to read with the same speed and expression as you do.

Invite students to do a timed reading of "High-rise Window Washers: A Bird's-eye View." Afterwards, have them enter their times on the Words-per-Minute table on page 121 and chart their reading speed on page 122 of the *Advanced Reader*.

📶 Encourage students to listen to "High-rise Window Washers: A Bird's-eye View." Go to **www.mhereadingbasics.com** to play or download the recording. The recording provides modeled fluency and read-along support.

APPLICATION

Workplace Skill:

Identify Cause and Effect by Reading an Instrument Gauge

Have students read the instrument gauge. Remind them that graphics are a way of presenting information visually. To interpret the gauge, they should think about what will happen at certain speeds and why. After students answer the questions, have them explain to a partner how they would use the instrument gauge if they were a pilot. This activity will come in handy when they do the Write for Work activity.

Write for Work

Remind students that information in a training manual should be clear and concise. Tell them to make sure they explain what the instrument gauge does and give causes and effects that illustrate its importance. Encourage them to share their work with a classmate to make sure they have included all the important information.

PASSKEY

📘 Go to **www.mhereadingbasics.com** and click on the *PassKey* link. Customize instruction for your class using modules from Reading/Language Arts, Levels 4 & 5.

Introduce

READING SKILL

Understand Author's Purpose

Explain /Model: Tell students that determining the author's purpose, or reason for writing, can help them understand what they read. Then have students read aloud the passage about bedtime stories. Model determining the author's purpose.

Guided Practice: Have students read the boxed passage. Then work with them to complete the task given in the directions. Discuss why the responses given after the passage are correct. Ask students to give details that show that the author had a double purpose.

Teach Lesson Skills

Practice: Have students read the passages and identify the authors' purposes. Tell them to think about the authors' reasons for writing. Discuss the answers to the questions and have students point out details or information in each passage that supports their answers.

Apply: After students answer the questions, have them read their responses aloud to the class. Encourage students to point out details or information that support their answers.

Check Up: Have students work in small groups to read the passages and answer the questions. Then check each group's responses with those of other groups in the class.

COMPREHENSION

Visualize: Encourage students to use sensory imaging as a mental tool when they read. Provide useful self-questioning models, such as *What do I see in this photo? Does this diagram help me understand the text? Can I form a mental image of what the author is describing?* When students visualize what they are reading, they consciously monitor their own comprehension.

ALPHABETICS

Explore Words

Spelling: Contractions: Model forming contractions for *you have, she is, you are,* and *does not*. Have students identify the letter or letters the apostrophe replaces in each contraction.

Suffixes -ance, -ant, -ent: Write the following words: *assistant, hesitance, convenient*. Underline the suffix in each word. Have students use each word in a sentence.

Word Parts: Model breaking the following words into prefixes, suffixes, and roots or base words: *disagreeable, revision, unbelievable, microscopic*. Discuss the meaning of each word.

VOCABULARY

Academic Vocabulary/Tier 2

purpose inform persuade argument consequence

Before students complete the activity, write the academic vocabulary words and definitions on the board. Discuss each word's meaning with students. Then write the sentences below on the board. Read each sentence aloud and discuss it with students.

1. The *purpose* of the fund-raiser was to raise money for the animal shelter.

2. Irma sent an e-mail to *inform* her coworkers about the meeting.

3. Dominic tried to *persuade* Mia to go out to dinner with him.

4. Sonja gave examples to support her *argument*.

5. Rodolfo overslept. As a *consequence*, he was late for work.

FLUENCY

Marked Phrase Reading: Mark a passage with phrase boundaries, showing how words should be grouped for meaning and emphasis. Read the passage aloud, having students follow along, and then read aloud together with students.

APPLICATION

Workplace Skill:

Understand Author's Purpose in a Memo

Remind students that a memo is a workplace document that sends a message to one or more persons. Point out that the subject line and the information and details in the body of the memo can help them determine the author's purpose. After students answer the questions, have them summarize Odion Carter's main purpose for writing the memo. This activity will come in handy when they do the Write for Work activity.

Write for Work

Remind students which important details are needed in a good memo. Tell them to make sure their response shows that they understood the author's purpose for writing the first memo. Encourage them to share their work with a classmate and ask one another for suggestions about ways to make the memo clearer.

Workplace Extension

Have students review the passage about Kelly Smith. Discuss what she does that shows she is interested in nutrition. What do her actions show about her? What should she do next if she wants to advance her career? Have partners respond to the questions together and share their responses in a class discussion.

PASSKEY

Go to **www.mhereadingbasics.com** and click on the *PassKey* link. Customize instruction for your class using modules from Reading/Language Arts, Levels 4 & 5.

Advanced Student Edition

Lesson Plan Advanced Student Edition

Introduce

READING SKILL
Find the Main Idea

Explain/Model: Explain that main ideas can be stated directly or implied by the supporting details. Then have students read aloud the passage about the Mississippi River. Model identifying the stated main idea.

Guided Practice: Have students read the boxed passage. Then work with them to complete the task given in the directions. Discuss why the response given after the passage is correct. Ask students to read aloud the sentence that states the main idea.

Teach Lesson Skills

Practice: Have students read the passages. Tell students to look for the topic, a stated main idea, or details that can help them determine the main idea. Discuss the answers to the questions, and have students point out the main idea or details that support their answers.

Apply: After students write the main ideas, have them read their main idea statements aloud to the class. Encourage students to show classmates which details they used to determine the implied main idea in the fourth passage.

Check Up: Have students work in small groups to read the passages and answer the questions. Then check each group's responses with those of other groups in the class.

COMPREHENSION
Understand Author's Purpose: Encourage students to consider the author's purpose as they read. Provide self-questioning models, such as *Why did the author decide to write this? What does the author want me to know?* By examining the author's purpose, students can better analyze their own reaction to the writing and consciously monitor their own comprehension.

ALPHABETICS
Explore Words

Prefixes *uni-, bi-, tri-*: Have students match the prefixes *uni-*, *bi-*, and *tri-* with the numbers 1, 2, and 3. Then write *tricycle, biannual,* and *unite.* Discuss the meaning of each word.

Analogies: Write these analogies: *night : knight* as *sale : sail; calm : nervous* as *weak : strong.* Model pointing out the relationship in each analogy. Challenge students to write their own analogies and share them.

Context Clues: Write this sentence on the board: *Zavian is impetuous and rarely thinks before he acts.* Have students tell what words give a clue to the meaning of *impetuous. (rarely thinks before he acts)*

VOCABULARY
Academic Vocabulary/Tier 2

deduce imply examine link establish

Before students complete the activity, write the academic vocabulary words and definitions on the board. Discuss each word's meaning with students. Then write the sentences below on the board. Read each sentence aloud and discuss it with students.

1. From the smell in the kitchen, I can *deduce* that Eligh is baking brownies.
2. Sydni did not mean to *imply* that Marla wasn't telling the truth.
3. The dentist will *examine* your teeth and gums.
4. Scientific studies *link* smoking and lung cancer.
5. Caleb hopes to *establish* a community theater in his town.

FLUENCY
Partner Reading: Have partners read aloud to one another and/or read aloud at the same time. Encourage them to offer support and correction to one another. Circulate to offer guidance as needed.

APPLICATION
Workplace Skill:

Find the Main Idea in a Memo about the Office Recycling Program

Have students read the memo. Point out that there is always a section at the top of a memo that tells the date, the subject, and the name of the sender. The subject line and headings within the memo can help students determine the main ideas. After students answer the questions, have them tell a partner the main ideas of the memo. This activity will come in handy when they do the Write for Work activity.

Write for Work

Remind students that the main idea should sum up what the section is about. Encourage them to share their work with a classmate to make sure they clearly and accurately stated the main idea of each section.

Workplace Extension:

Tell students that employees often earn raises by exceeding company expectations and taking on additional responsibilities. Have them review the passage about Juan Ramirez. Discuss why Juan might be deserving of a raise. What might Juan say to Ms. Chan? How should he say it? Have partners respond to the questions and share their responses.

PASSKEY

Go to **www.mhereadingbasics.com** and click on the *PassKey* link. Customize instruction for your class using modules from Reading/Language Arts, Levels 4 & 5.

Introduce

READING SKILL

Identify Sequence

Explain/Model: Explain that in order to recognize the sequence of events, it is helpful to look for words that signal time order. Have students read aloud the passage about butterflies. Model using signal words to determine the order of events in a butterfly's life cycle.

Guided Practice: Have students read the boxed passage. Then work with them to complete the task given in the directions. Discuss why the responses given after the passage are correct. Ask students to tell what happened to the bridge in 1831.

Teach Lesson Skills

Practice: Have students read the passage. Tell them to look for dates and clue words such as *subsequent* and *after* as they read about this topic. Discuss the correct order, and have students explain how they determined the sequence.

Apply: After students put each set of events in order, have volunteers read their responses aloud to the class. Ask students to point out clue words or dates they used to put the events in order.

Check Up: Have students work in small groups to read the passage and answer the questions. Then check each group's responses with those of other groups in the class.

COMPREHENSION

Set a Purpose for Reading: Encourage students to set a purpose for reading. Provide self-questioning models, such as *What do I hope to learn? What do the directions tell me to look for? What will happen next?* By setting a purpose and then evaluating whether they achieved the purpose, students consciously monitor their own comprehension. They can also discuss the purpose they have determined with a peer or a teacher.

Reading Extension

📖 Encourage students to read "Tiger Trainers: Schooling the Big Cat" on page 41 of the *Advanced Reader*. Use this as an opportunity to teach reading strategies and the lesson reading skill.

ALPHABETICS

Explore Words

Prefixes *en-, em-:* Write *endanger*, *embitter*, and *ennoble* on the board. Have volunteers underline the prefixes. Model using the prefixes to determine the meanings of the words.

Suffixes *-ion, -tion:* Model adding *-ion* or *-tion* to these words: *revise + ion, restrict + -tion, correct + -ion*. Discuss the meaning of each word you form.

Multiple-meaning Words: Write the following sentence, underlining as shown: *My mother prefers for children to address her as Mrs. Kim.* Model using context to determine the meaning of *address*. Then have volunteers suggest other sentences for the additional meanings of *address*.

VOCABULARY

Academic Vocabulary/Tier 2

sequence   interpret   inevitable   subsequent
violate

Before students complete the activity, write the academic vocabulary words and definitions on the board. Discuss each word's meaning with students. Then write the sentences below on the board. Read each sentence aloud and discuss it with students.

1. If you want your cake to turn out well, follow the steps in the recipe in *sequence*.
2. People can *interpret* the same song in different ways.
3. I left my headlights on overnight, so it was *inevitable* that my car battery died.
4. The *subsequent* pain Denise felt after her fall led her to call a doctor.
5. If you *violate* the theater's rules, you may be asked to leave.

FLUENCY

Echo Reading: Read a sentence from one of the passages aloud. Then have students echo you by reading the same sentence and trying to read with the same speed and expression as you do.

Invite students to do a timed reading of "Tiger Trainers: Schooling the Big Cat." Afterwards, have them enter their times on the Words-per-Minute table on page 121 and chart their reading speed on page 122 of the *Advanced Reader*.

📶 Encourage students to listen to "Tiger Trainers: Schooling the Big Cat." Go to **www.mhreadingbasics.com** to play or download the recording. The recording provides modeled fluency and read-along support.

APPLICATION

Workplace Skill:

Identify Sequence in Instructions

Have students read the instructions. Remind them that instructions explain how to make or do something. Paying attention to the sequence, or order, of steps will help them ensure they complete the task correctly. After students answer the questions, have them make a list of numbered steps for backing up a file. This list will come in handy when they do the Write for Work activity.

Write for Work

Tell students to make sure their e-mail summarizes all the steps they might have used to back up a file and also uses sequence words to make the order clear to their coworker. Encourage them to read their e-mail aloud to a partner to make sure their summary is clear and complete.

PASSKEY

🔑 Go to **www.mhreadingbasics.com** and click on the *PassKey* link. Customize instruction for your class using modules from Reading/Language Arts, Levels 4 & 5.

Introduce

READING SKILL

Understand Consumer Materials

Explain/Model: Explain that it is important to carefully read consumer materials because they contain information consumers need to correctly use or maintain a product. Then have students read aloud the points about reading advertisements. Model how you would use these steps if you were reading an ad for a bike sale at your local cycle shop.

Guided Practice: Have students read the ads. Then work with them to complete the task given in the directions. Discuss why the responses given after the ads are correct. Have students tell which flat screen television they would buy and why.

Teach Lesson Skills

Practice: Have students review the form and answer the questions. Tell them to think about how they would complete each section of the form. Discuss the answers, and have students share their own experiences with returning items ordered online.

Apply: After students answer the questions, have them read their responses aloud to the class. Encourage them to point out information from the ratings chart that supports their answers.

Check Up: Have students work in small groups to read the prescription label and answer the questions. Then check each group's responses with those of other groups in the class.

COMPREHENSION

Clarify Meaning: Encourage students to actively clarify meaning as they read. Provide self-questioning models, such as *What clues can I find in other sentences to help me understand this word? Does this word resemble any other words I have learned? Can I find someone to ask about this?* When students proactively try to clarify meaning, they consciously monitor their own comprehension.

Reading Extension

📖 Encourage students to read "Bull Riders: Ride or Run!" on page 49 of the *Advanced Reader*. Use this as an opportunity to teach reading strategies and the lesson reading skill.

ALPHABETICS

Explore Words

Latin Roots: Write the words *transport* and *retain*. Underline the roots *port* and *tain* in each word. Discuss the meaning of each word. Then have volunteers suggest additional words for each root.

Accented and Unaccented Syllables: Tell students that in most two-syllable words, the accent is on the first syllable. The second syllable often has the schwa sound, which is similar to the short *i* or short *u* sound. In two-syllable words that have a prefix, however, the accent is usually on the second syllable. Write these words: *per/son, fi/nal, re/peat, un/kind.* Model dividing them into syllables. Then read them aloud with students, emphasizing the stressed syllables in each word. Have volunteers underline the stressed syllable.

VOCABULARY

Academic Vocabulary/Tier 2

consume instructions crucial maintain common

Before students complete the activity, write the academic vocabulary words and definitions on the board. Discuss each word's meaning with students. Then write the sentences below on the board. Read each sentence aloud and discuss it with students.

1. A smaller car may *consume* less gas than a minivan.
2. Mrs. Alban left *instructions* for the babysitter.
3. The team was excited when it won a *crucial* game.
4. Eligh and Angel *maintain* their fitness by running four times a week.
5. Stripes and plaids are *common* patterns for shirts.

FLUENCY

Partner Reading: Have partners read aloud to one another and/or read aloud at the same time. Encourage them to offer support and correction to one another. Circulate to offer guidance as needed.

Invite students to do a timed reading of "Bull Riders: Ride or Run!" Afterwards, have them enter their times on the Words-per-Minute table on page 121 and chart their reading speed on page 122 of the *Advanced Reader*.

🔊 Encourage students to listen to "Bull Riders: Ride or Run!" Go to **www.mhreadingbasics.com** to play or download the recording. The recording provides modeled fluency and read-along support.

APPLICATION

Workplace Skill:

Understand Consumer Materials by Interpreting a Warranty

Have students read the warranty. Remind them that a warranty guarantees a product or service and gives the conditions under which problems can be remedied. Point out that most warranties have very specific time lines and conditions that must be met for repairs, replacements, and refunds to be issued. Consumers and employees must read closely to fully understand all the details and restrictions. After students answer the questions, have them make a two-column chart that lists things the warranty does and does not cover. This chart will come in handy when they do the Write for Work activity.

Write for Work

Remind students that when they write to a customer, they should use a professional, respectful tone. Encourage them to share their work with a classmate to make sure they have accurately and adequately addressed the customer's concern, based on the warranty.

PASSKEY

💻 Go to **www.mhreadingbasics.com** and click on the *PassKey* link. Customize instruction for your class using modules from Reading/Language Arts, Levels 4 & 5.

Introduce

READING SKILL

Use Reference Sources

Explain/Model: Explain to students that knowing about the different kinds of reference sources can help them choose the best source for their research needs. Then have them read about the different kinds of reference sources. Model by giving examples of reference sources that you use regularly and explaining how and why you use them.

Guided Practice: Have students read the boxed items. Then work with them to complete the task given in the directions. Discuss why the response given is correct. Ask students to share another reference source that gives information about words.

Teach Lesson Skills

Practice: Have students read the catalog entries. Tell them to pay attention to what kind of information each section of the entries gives. Discuss their answers, and have students point out where they found the information in each entry.

Apply: After students complete and write their sentences, have them read their sentences aloud to the class. Encourage them to explain how they decided which synonym to choose for each sentence.

Check Up: Have students work in small groups to read and answer the questions. Then check each group's responses with those of other groups in the class.

COMPREHENSION

Ask Questions: Encourage students to ask themselves questions as they read. Provide questioning models that progress from concrete to abstract. For example, *What does this mean? Is this a main idea? Do I remember the order of important events?* By asking themselves questions, students consciously monitor their own comprehension. They can also ask questions of peers or a teacher to clarify understanding.

Reading Extension

📖 Encourage students to read "Sherpas: Helpers in High Altitudes" on page 57 of the *Advanced Reader*. Use this as an opportunity to teach reading strategies and the lesson reading skill.

ALPHABETICS

Explore Words

Prefixes: Write the following words on the board: *copay, collate, companion, connect*. Underline the prefix in each word and discuss its meaning. Then have volunteers use each word in a sentence that shows its meaning.

Latin Roots: Write the following words, underlining as shown: *dictionary, spectator, destruction, admission*. Discuss the meaning of each word. Then have volunteers give examples of other words with these roots.

Multiple-meaning Words: Write the following sentence: *I will be back in one second*. Model using context to determine the meaning of *second*. Then ask volunteers to suggest sentences for other meanings of *second*.

VOCABULARY

Academic Vocabulary/Tier 2

research   general   index   available   assist

Before students complete the activity, write the academic vocabulary words and definitions on the board. Discuss each word's meaning with students. Then write the sentences below on the board. Read each sentence aloud and discuss it with students.

1. Javian is doing *research* about rain forests before he goes to Costa Rica.
2. In *general*, people eat dessert after dinner.
3. Arden checked the *index* and then turned to page 150.
4. There are many seats still *available* for the concert.
5. Liana asked her dad to *assist* her in changing her tire.

FLUENCY

Collaborative Reading: Gather in a group. Have each student read one or more lines of a passage and then pass the text to the next student. Supply pronunciation and phrasing corrections as needed.

Invite students to do a timed reading of "Sherpas: Helpers in High Altitudes." Afterwards, have them enter their times on the Words-per-Minute table on page 121 and chart their reading speed on page 122 of the *Advanced Reader*.

📶 Encourage students to listen to "Sherpas: Helpers in High Altitudes." Go to **www.mhereadingbasics.com** to play or download the recording. The recording provides modeled fluency and read-along support.

APPLICATION

Workplace Skill:

Use Reference Sources to Locate Information

Have students read the food-handling guidelines. Explain that workplace documents that give information should be verified for accuracy before being distributed to employees or the public. Tell students to think about which reference sources would help them verify the facts in a set of food-handling guidelines. After students answer the questions, have them list the key points made in the guidelines. This exercise will be helpful when they do the Write for Work activity.

Write for Work

Remind students that a poster should give important information in a clear, easy-to-read format. The main points should be visible at a glance. Encourage them to share their poster with a classmate to make sure they covered the main points and have used correct facts and spelling.

PASSKEY

💻 Go to **www.mhereadingbasics.com** and click on the *PassKey* link. Customize instruction for your class using modules from Reading/Language Arts, Levels 4 & 5.

Lesson Plan Advanced Student Edition

Unit 2 Lesson 2.4 pages 102–109

READING SKILL

Use Supporting Evidence

Explain/Model: Explain that it is important to pay attention to supporting evidence in order to determine whether a generalization or opinion is valid. Then have students read aloud the passage about birds. Model evaluating the evidence to determine how it supports the main idea of the paragraph.

Guided Practice: Have students read the boxed passage. Then work with them to complete the task given in the directions. Discuss why the responses given after the passage are correct. Ask students to explain why the fourth sentence wasn't underlined.

Practice: Have students read the passages. Tell them to identify the main ideas and to think about which details support them. Have students share the main ideas and supporting evidence. Ask them to explain how the evidence supports the main ideas.

Apply: After students answer the questions, have them read their responses aloud to the class. Ask them to explain how the evidence supports the ideas.

Check Up: Have students work in small groups to read the passage and answer the questions. Then check each group's responses with those of other groups in the class.

COMPREHENSION

Make Connections: Encourage students to make connections as they read. Provide self-questioning models, such as *Have I learned something about this topic before? What was the context? Have I had any experiences in my own life that relate to this topic?* When students relate what they are reading to their own lives and educational experience, they consciously monitor their own comprehension.

Reading Extension

Encourage students to read "Astronaut Mechanics: Hanging in Space" on page 65 of the *Advanced Reader*. Use this as an opportunity to teach reading strategies and the lesson reading skill.

ALPHABETICS

Explore Words

Suffixes -ous, -ious: Write the following words on the board: *poisonous, harmonious, gracious,* and *dangerous.* Underline the suffix in each word and model determining its meaning. Then invite volunteers to use each word in a sentence.

Spelling: Homophones: Write the following pairs of homophones: *manner/ manor, groan/grown,* and *suite/sweet.* Discuss the meaning of each word. Then have volunteers use the words in sentences that show their meaning.

Greek Roots: Write the following words with Greek roots, underlining as shown: *microbe, geography, biology, telephone.* Model using the underlined roots to determine the meaning of each word. Then have volunteers suggest additional words for each root.

VOCABULARY

Academic Vocabulary/Tier 2

evidence   support   example   evaluate
irrelevant

Before students complete the activity, write the academic vocabulary words and definitions on the board. Discuss each word's meaning with students. Then write the sentences below on the board. Read each sentence aloud and discuss it with students.

1. The lawyer will present *evidence* about the case to the jury.
2. Some voters will not *support* the large sales tax increase.
3. A German Shepherd is an *example* of a guard dog.
4. The judges will *evaluate* each singer's solo performance.
5. Your hair color is *irrelevant* to how smart you are.

FLUENCY

Repeated Reading: Lead a group to read the same passage aloud together several times. As the leader, emphasize accuracy and phrasing, until the group reading sounds smooth and consistent

Invite students to do a timed reading of "Astronaut Mechanics: Hanging in Space." Afterwards, have them enter their times on the Words-per-Minute table on page 121 and chart their reading speed on page 122 of the *Advanced Reader.*

Encourage students to listen to "Astronaut Mechanics: Hanging in Space." Go to **www.mhereadingbasics.com** to play or download the recording. The recording provides modeled fluency and read-along support.

APPLICATION

Workplace Skill:

Use Supporting Evidence to Understand a Procedure

Have students read the procedure. Remind them that a procedure is a set of steps that should be followed to accomplish a task. Supporting evidence will often be given to explain why a particular step is important or what might happen if it is not followed. After students answer the questions, have them summarize the clocking in and out procedure for a partner. This activity will be helpful when they do the Write for Work activity.

Write for Work

Point out that an e-mail to a fellow employee should be written in a positive, professional tone. Encourage them to share their work with a classmate to make sure they included all the main points and supporting evidence.

PASSKEY

Go to **www.mhereadingbasics.com** and click on the *PassKey* link. Customize instruction for your class using modules from Reading/Language Arts, Levels 4 & 5.

Lesson Plan Advanced Student Edition

Introduce

READING SKILL
Recognize Character Traits

Explain/Model: Explain that paying attention to things characters say or do or what the narrator says about them can help readers figure out what the characters are like. Have students read aloud the passage about Jacqueline Kennedy. Model using the narration to make inferences about what Jacqueline Kennedy was like.

Guided Practice: Have students read the boxed passage. Then work with them to complete the task given in the directions. Discuss the responses given after the passage. Ask students to explain how Jose's actions and appearance help them understand what he is like.

Teach Lesson Skills

Practice: Have students read the passages. Tell them to pay attention to the things the characters think or do and what the narrator says about them. Discuss the answers, and have students point out words, action, or narration that helped them determine each character's trait.

Apply: After students complete the graphic organizer and answer the questions, have them read their responses aloud to the class. Ask students to explain how these words or actions helped them understand what Emmett is like.

Check Up: Have students work in small groups to read the passage and answer the questions. Then check each group's responses with those of other groups in the class.

COMPREHENSION
Look for Context Clues/Read On: Encourage students to look for context clues as they read. Investigating the context helps a reader to put words and paragraphs into a larger framework. Provide helpful self-questioning models, such as *What words surrounding this difficult word can help me understand it better? If I read a little farther, might I find additional clues that can help me understand?* When students proactively look for context clues, they consciously monitor their own comprehension.

Reading Extension
📖 Encourage students to read "James Herman Banning: Pioneer Pilot" on page 73 of the *Advanced Reader*. Use this as an opportunity to teach reading strategies and the lesson reading skill.

ALPHABETICS
Explore Words

Analogies: Write these analogies on the board: *hat : head* as *sock : foot; calf : cow* as *puppy : dog.* Discuss the relationships in each analogy. Then have students complete this analogy: *asleep : awake* as *stop : _____.* (*start; go*) Discuss their responses.

Word Families: Write the following word families: *inspector, spectator, spectacle; visit, visible, revise.* Discuss the root each word family shares. Then have students suggest an additional word for each family.

Context Clues: Write this sentence: *After a long run, Will drank a glass of water because he was dehydrated.* Model using context to determine the meaning of *dehydrated.* Then invite volunteers to use it in another sentence that shows its meaning.

VOCABULARY
Academic Vocabulary/Tier 2

characters traits encounter key technique

Before students complete the activity, write the academic vocabulary words and definitions on the board. Discuss each word's meaning with students. Then write the sentences below on the board. Read each sentence aloud and discuss it with students.

1. Animals are often *characters* in fables and fairy tales.
2. Kindness and honesty are always *traits* of good friends.
3. I hope never to *encounter* a shark while I'm swimming in the ocean.
4. Hot peppers are a *key* ingredient in my Uncle Sal's chili.
5. Maya has an unusual *technique* for tying her running shoes.

FLUENCY
Echo Reading: Read a sentence from one of the passages aloud. Then have students echo you by reading the same sentence and trying to read with the same speed and expression as you do.

Invite students to do a timed reading of "James Herman Banning: Pioneer Pilot." Afterwards, have them enter their times on the Words-per-Minute table on page 121 and chart their reading speed on page 122 of the *Advanced Reader*.

🔊 Encourage students to listen to "James Herman Banning: Pioneer Pilot." Go to **www.mhreadingbasics.com** to play or download the recording. The recording provides modeled fluency and read-along support.

APPLICATION
Workplace Skill:
Evaluate Character Traits in a Performance Assessment Review

Have students read the performance assessment review. Remind them that reviews are a way for employers to evaluate their employees' job performances. The things employees say and do on the job and in response to their reviews show employers what kind of employees they are. After students answer the questions, have them jot down in a notebook a few words describing what kinds of employees they think Amala Singh and Lien Nguyen are. This activity will come in handy when they do the Write for Work activity.

Write for Work
Remind students to look closely at the things Amala Singh says and does. Tell them to make sure they support their review with reasons and examples. Encourage them to share their work with a classmate to make sure their review is fair and accurate.

PASSKEY
💻 Go to **www.mhreadingbasics.com** and click on the *PassKey* link. Customize instruction for your class using modules from Reading/Language Arts, Levels 4 & 5.

Lesson Plan Advanced Student Edition

Unit 2 Lesson 2.6 pages 118–125

Introduce

READING SKILL

Identify Style Techniques

Explain /Model: Tell students that paying attention to the words and language an author uses can help them determine the author's style. Then have students read aloud the sentence about Carlotta. Model pointing out the imagery and the senses to which the images appeal. Then discuss the additional examples of figurative language.

Guided Practice: Have students read the boxed passage. Then work with them to complete the task given in the directions. Discuss why the response given after the passage is correct. Have students identify the senses to which the words and imagery appeal.

Teach Lesson Skills

Practice: Have students read the passages. Tell them to think about how the author's style is conveyed in each passage. Discuss the answers to the questions, and have students explain how they determined what style technique was used.

Apply: After students identify the senses, have them read their responses aloud to the class. Encourage them to point out specific words and phrases that support their choices.

Check Up: Have students work in small groups to read the passages and answer the questions. Then check each group's responses with those of other groups in the class.

COMPREHENSION

Visualize: Encourage students to visualize when they read. Provide useful self-questioning models, such as *What do I see in this photo? Does this diagram help me understand the text? Can I form a mental image of what the author is describing?* When students visualize what they are reading, they consciously monitor their own comprehension.

ALPHABETICS

Explore Words

Synonyms: Model choosing the correct synonym to complete these sentences: *My grandmother likes to (save, scrimp) on groceries. The child hid behind his mother because he felt (bashful, reserved).* Then have students suggest sentences for the other synonyms.

Prefixes *semi-*, *multi-*, *mid-*: Write the following words: *semipermanent, multimillionaire, midweek.* Underline the prefix in each word and discuss the word's meaning. Have students use each word in a sentence.

Latin Roots: Write the following words on the board, underlining as shown: *sentimental, disrupt, proclaim, prescribe.* Discuss the meaning of each word.

VOCABULARY

Academic Vocabulary/Tier 2

style   specific   communicate   element   figurative

Before students complete the activity, write the academic vocabulary words and definitions on the board. Discuss each word's meaning with students. Then write the sentences below on the board. Read each sentence aloud and discuss it with students.

1. The author's *style* was defined by his page-long sentences.
2. Ariel likes a *specific* brand of peanut butter.
3. Johann prefers to *communicate* by text messaging.
4. Liam's determination was a key *element* of his success.
5. The poet used *figurative* language to describe a winter day.

FLUENCY

Marked Phrase Reading: Mark a passage with phrase boundaries, showing how words should be grouped for meaning and emphasis. Read the passage aloud, having students follow along, and then read aloud together with students.

APPLICATION

Workplace Skill:

Understand Style Techniques in Business Ads

Have students read the ads. Remind them that the purpose of an ad is to sell a product or service. Point out that using an effective style is an important part of reaching a target audience. After students answer the questions, have them brainstorm words and phrases they would use to describe a computer game for 10- to 14-year-olds. This activity will come in handy when they do the Write for Work activity.

Write for Work

Remind students that an ad must persuade its target audience. Tell them to make sure their style and word choice are appropriate for 10- to 14-year-olds. Encourage them to read their ad to a partner and ask for suggestions about ways to make the style and word choice more appealing to their audience.

Workplace Extension

Have students review the passage about Raymond Chen. Discuss the problem he has and some possible solutions. Why can't he file his report? Would it be more effective for him to speak to his boss or to Rosalind about the problem? Why? Have partners respond to the questions together and share their responses in a class discussion.

PASSKEY

Go to **www.mhereadingbasics.com** and click on the *PassKey* link. Customize instruction for your class using modules from Reading/Language Arts, Levels 4 & 5.

Lesson Plan Advanced Student Edition

Introduce

READING SKILL

Make Generalizations

Explain/Model: Explain that a generalization uses text evidence to come to a conclusion that can apply to many people, facts, events, or situations. Have students read aloud the passage about seaweed. Model using text information to make a valid generalization about seaweed. Then model giving an invalid generalization.

Guided Practice: Have students read the boxed passage. Then work with them to complete the task given in the directions. Discuss why the responses given after the passage are correct. Ask students to explain why the generalizations are valid.

Teach Lesson Skills

Practice: Have students read the passages. Tell them to use information from the passages and their own knowledge to identify the most valid generalizations. Discuss the answers and have students point out the information that supports the valid generalizations.

Apply: After students write their generalizations, have them read the generalizations aloud to the class. Then ask students to share the details from each passage that they used to make their generalization.

Check Up: Have students work in small groups to read the passages and answer the questions. Then check each group's responses with those of other groups in the class.

COMPREHENSION

Use Prior Knowledge: Encourage students to think about what they already know before they read. To get students started, provide self-questioning models, such as *Have I read about this topic before? Does this sound familiar?* When students can create a context or framework of known information in which to place new information, they consciously monitor their own comprehension.

Reading Extension

📖 Encourage students to read "Embedded Journalists: Writing from the Front Lines" on page 81 of the *Advanced Reader*. Use this as an opportunity to teach reading strategies and the lesson reading skill.

ALPHABETICS

Explore Words

Synonyms and Antonyms Write *nervous* on the board, and model giving a synonym, such as *worried*, and an antonym, such as *calm*. Then have students work in pairs to give a synonym and antonym for the words *far* and *generous*.

Accented and Unaccented Syllables Use the words *can/o/py, re/vis/ion, fi/nal/ist* and *un/like/ly* to review the rules for syllable division. Point out that in most three-syllable words, such as *canopy*, the first syllable is accented and the second syllable has the schwa sound, which sounds similar to short *i* or short *u*. In three-syllable words with prefixes and suffixes, such as *revision*, and *unlikely*, the second syllable is usually accented. After dividing each word, read each part, stressing the accented syllable.

VOCABULARY

Academic Vocabulary/Tier 2

statement apply utilize valid essential

Before students complete the activity, write the academic vocabulary words and definitions on the board. Discuss each word's meaning with students. Then write the sentences below on the board. Read each sentence aloud and discuss it with students.

1. The manager made a *statement* about the store's new return policy.
2. The discount will *apply* only if you purchase two of the items.
3. The coach must find a way to *utilize* all of his players.
4. Leona made a *valid* argument, so Julio was forced to agree with her.
5. Fruits and vegetables are an *essential* part of a balanced diet.

FLUENCY

Echo Reading: Read a sentence from one of the passages aloud. Then have students echo you by reading the same sentence and trying to read with the same speed and expression as you do.

Invite students to do a timed reading of "Embedded Journalists: Writing from the Front Lines." Afterwards, have them enter their times on the Words-per-Minute table on page 121 and chart their reading speed on page 122 of the *Advanced Reader*.

🔊 Encourage students to listen to "Embedded Journalists: Writing from the Front Lines." Go to **www.mhreadingbasics.com** to play or download the recording. The recording provides modeled fluency and read-along support.

APPLICATION

Workplace Skill:

Make Generalizations about Sections of an Employee Handbook

Have students read the excerpts from the employee handbook. Point out that the rules and guidelines are usually broad and basic so that they can be applied to the company as a whole. It's up to readers to make generalizations about the information in order to apply it to specific situations or circumstances. After students answer the questions, have them briefly summarize the policies to a partner. These summaries will come in handy when they do the Write for Work activity.

Write for Work

Have students briefly summarize either the dress code policy or the computer usage policy in two to four sentences. Have them write generalizations that they made about the policy. Invite students to present their presentation to a partner as if they were delivering it at the company staff meeting.

PASSKEY

💻 Go to **www.mhreadingbasics.com** and click on the *PassKey* link. Customize instruction for your class using modules from Reading/Language Arts, Levels 4 & 5.

Introduce

READING SKILL

Recognize Author's Effect and Intention

Explain/Model: Explain that paying attention to word choice, language, and sentence structure can help readers determine an author's intention. Then have students read aloud the passage about Camilla. Model using the style techniques and word choice to determine the author's intention.

Guided Practice: Have students read the passage. Then work with them to complete the task given in the directions. Discuss why the responses given after the passage are correct. Ask students to give additional examples of language that creates an effect of wonder and excitement.

Teach Lesson Skills

Practice: Have students read the passages. Tell them to pay attention to the authors' style techniques and the effects they create. Discuss the answers to the questions, and have students point out specific words and phrases that create a particular effect.

Apply: After students answer the questions, have them read their responses aloud to the class. Encourage them to point out examples of style techniques in each passage.

Check Up: Have students work in small groups to read the passages and answer the questions. Then check each group's responses with those of other groups in the class.

COMPREHENSION

Ask Questions: Encourage students to ask themselves questions as they read. Provide questioning models that progress from concrete to abstract. For example, *What does this mean? Is this a main idea? Do I remember the order of important events?* By asking themselves questions, students consciously monitor their own comprehension. They can also ask questions of peers or a teacher to clarify understanding.

Reading Extension

Encourage students to read "Bush Pilots: Tough Takeoffs, Rough Landings" on page 89 of the *Advanced Reader*. Use this as an opportunity to teach reading strategies and the lesson reading skill.

ALPHABETICS

Explore Words

Greek Roots: Write these words, underlining as shown: chronicle; asteroid, thermal, and maneuver. Point out the Greek root in each word, and model using it to determine the word's meaning.

Synonyms: Write these sentences: *Susan is very (self-assured, smug) about her abilities as a dancer. She has long, (slender, scrawny) legs.* Model choosing the best word to complete each sentence.

Suffixes -al, -ial: Write these words on the board: *instrumental, bacterial, accidental.* Underline the suffix in each word and model using it to help determine word meaning.

VOCABULARY

Academic Vocabulary/Tier 2

approach   intention   convey   constant   unique

Before students complete the activity, write the academic vocabulary words and definitions on the board. Discuss each word's meaning with students. Then write the sentences below on the board. Read each sentence aloud and discuss it with students.

1. Dalton's *approach* to studying for the test was to review one chapter per night.

2. Natalie's *intention* is to get a summer job.

3. Grant sent a letter to the mayor to *convey* his disapproval of the mayor's actions.

4. The dog's *constant* barking kept Arden awake all night.

5. Brooke's grandmother made her dress so it was *unique*.

FLUENCY

Partner Reading: Have partners read aloud to one another and/or read aloud at the same time. Encourage them to offer support and correction to one another. Circulate to offer guidance as needed.

Invite students to do a timed reading of "Bush Pilots: Tough Takeoffs, Rough Landings." Afterwards, have them enter their times on the Words-per-Minute table on page 121 and chart their reading speed on page 122 of the *Advanced Reader*.

Encourage students to listen to "Bush Pilots: Tough Takeoffs, Rough Landings." Go to **www.mhereadingbasics.com** to play or download the recording. The recording provides modeled fluency and read-along support.

APPLICATION

Workplace Skill:

Understand Author's Effect and Intention in a Cover Letter

Have students read the cover letter. Explain that cover letters are a chance to make a good first impression and gain an interview, so job candidates should choose their words and language carefully in order to appear well-qualified and professional. After students answer the questions, have them brainstorm a list of Rima Freeman's qualifications for the job. This list will come in handy when they do the Write for Work activity.

Write for Work

Tell students that a thank you letter following an interview should be written in the same professional, formal tone as a cover letter. Remind them to include details, reasons, and examples. Ask them to share their work with a classmate to make sure their intention is clear and their letter achieves the desired effect.

PASSKEY

Go to **www.mhereadingbasics.com** and click on the *PassKey* link. Customize instruction for your class using modules from Reading/Language Arts, Levels 4 & 5.

Advanced Student Edition

Introduce

READING SKILL
Compare and Contrast

Explain/Model: Explain that to compare and contrast, readers should think about how things are alike and different. Then have students read the passage about mixtures. Model using the signal words *likewise*, *also*, and *in contrast* to recognize comparisons and contrasts.

Guided Practice: Have students read the boxed passage about Tokyo and Kyoto. Then work with them to complete the task given in the directions. Discuss why the responses given after the passage are correct. Ask students to identify another way that Tokyo and Kyoto are different.

Teach Lesson Skills

Practice: Have students read the passage. Tell them to look for clue words that signal comparisons and contrasts. Discuss the answers to the questions and have students point out the clue words they used to help them identify comparisons and contrasts.

Apply: After students complete their tables, have them share their responses with the class. Have them use their tables to tell some ways that European football and American football are alike and different.

Check Up: Have students work in small groups to read the editorials and answer the questions. Then check each group's responses with those of other groups in the class.

COMPREHENSION

Visualize: Encourage students to use sensory imaging as a mental tool when they read. Provide useful self-questioning models, such as *What do I see in this photo? Does this diagram help me understand the text? Can I form a mental image of what the author is describing?* When students visualize what they are reading, they consciously monitor their own comprehension.

Reading Extension

📖 Encourage students to read "Pirate Chasers: Crime Waves on the High Seas" on page 97 of the *Advanced Reader*. Use this as an opportunity to teach reading strategies and the lesson reading skill.

ALPHABETICS
Explore Words

Accented and Unaccented Syllables: Use the words in/**vin**/ci/ble, in/**san**/i/ty, and e/**lec**/tric to review the rules for syllable division. Point out that in four syllable words, such as *invincible*, the accent is usually on the second syllable. When a multisyllabic word ends in *-ic*, as in *electric*, the accent is usually on the syllable that comes right before the ending. When the multisyllabic word ends in *-ity*, the accent is on the syllable before the two-syllable ending. After dividing each word, read each part aloud, stressing the accented syllable.

Prefixes: Model adding prefixes to the following words: in- + sane; im- + mature; il- + legal; ir- + regular. Discuss the meaning of each word you form. Then invite students to suggest additional words with each prefix.

VOCABULARY
Academic Vocabulary/Tier 2

compare   contrast   similar   consider
frequently

Before students complete the activity, write the academic vocabulary words and definitions on the board. Discuss each word's meaning with students. Then write the sentences below on the board. Read each sentence aloud and discuss it with students.

1. Omar will *compare* several apartments before he rents one.

2. Let's *contrast* the temperments of the two breeds of dogs you're considering.

3. Paige and Stacia wore *similar* dresses to the party.

4. Before you buy a pet, you should *consider* whether you will be able to care for it.

5. Our family *frequently* eats pizza on Friday or Saturday nights.

FLUENCY

Collaborative Reading: Gather in a group. Have each student read one or more lines of a passage and then pass the text to the next student. Supply pronunciation and phrasing corrections as needed.

Invite students to do a timed reading of "Pirate Chasers: Crime Waves on the High Seas." Afterwards, have them enter their times on the Words-per-Minute table on page 121 and chart their reading speed on page 122 of the *Advanced Reader*.

📶 Encourage students to listen to "Pirate Chasers: Crime Waves on the High Seas." Go to **www.mhreadingbasics.com** to play or download the recording. The recording provides modeled fluency and read-along support.

APPLICATION
Workplace Skill:

Compare and Contrast a Double Bar Graph

Have students look at the Greeting Card Sales Comparison graph. Remind them that in the wokrplace they may need to compare and contrast sales figures from one year to the next. Point out what is being compared and contrasted in the graph. After students answer the questions, have them write down two more similarities and differences between 2009 and 2010. This exercise will be helpful when they do the Write for Work activity.

Write for Work

Tell students to use specific examples from the graph to write their descriptions. Remind them to use signal words to make comparisons and contrasts clear. Encourage them to share their work with another student to make sure they adequately explained the sales graph.

PASSKEY

🔑 Go to **www.mhreadingbasics.com** and click on the *PassKey* link. Customize instruction for your class using modules from Reading/Language Arts, Levels 4 & 5.

Advanced Student Edition

Lesson Plan Advanced Student Edition

Unit 3 Lesson 3.4 pages 158–165

Unit 3 Lesson 3.4 pages 158–165

Introduce

READING SKILL

Predict Outcomes

Explain/Model: Explain that using text clues and prior knowledge can help readers make predictions about what will happen next in a passage. Then have students read aloud the sentence about a person packing for a trip. Model using text information and your own prior knowledge to make a prediction about what will happen next.

Guided Practice: Have students read the boxed passage. Then work with them to complete the task given in the directions. Discuss why the response given after the passage is correct. Ask students to share how they used their own knowledge and experience to help them make a prediction.

Teach Lesson Skills

Practice: Have students read the passages. Tell them to use text information and their own knowledge and experience to make predictions. Have students share their answers and point out the text clues and prior knowledge they used to make predictions.

Apply: After students make their predictions, have them read their responses aloud to the class. Ask them to share the text information and personal knowledge they used to make their predictions.

Check Up: Have students work in small groups to read the passages and answer the questions. Then check each group's responses with those of other groups in the class.

COMPREHENSION

Make Connections: Encourage students to make connections as they read. Provide self-questioning models, such as *Have I learned something about this topic before? What was the context? Have I had any experiences in my own life that relate to this topic?* When students relate what they are reading to their own lives and educational experience, they consciously monitor their own comprehension.

Reading Extension

📖 Encourage students to read "Ranching: You've Got to Love It" on page 105 of the *Advanced Reader*. Use this as an opportunity to teach reading strategies and the lesson reading skill.

ALPHABETICS

Explore Words

Accented and Unaccented Syllables:
Use the words *ma/gi/cian, ded/i/ca/tion, con/fu/sion, ar/ti/fi/cial,* and *re/un/ion* to review the rules for syllable division. Point out that in multisyllabic words that end in *-tion, -sion, -cian,* or *-cial,* the accent is usually on the syllable that comes before the ending. In multisyllabic words that have an *i* that sounds like *y,* the accent is usually on the syllable right before the syllable with the *i*. After dividing each word, read each part, stressing the accented syllable.

Analogies: Write these analogies: *broken : fixed* as *sick : well; fox : den* as *bird : nest.* Model identifying the relationships between the pairs of words. Then have students complete this analogy: *breakfast : morning* as *dinner : _____.*

VOCABULARY

Academic Vocabulary/Tier 2

predict outcome logical prior adjust

Before students complete the activity, write the academic vocabulary words and definitions on the board. Discuss each word's meaning with students. Then write the sentences below on the board. Read each sentence aloud and discuss it with students.

1. My grandfather can *predict* rain by looking at the sky.
2. We are still waiting to hear the *outcome* of the election.
3. If there's a thunderstorm, it's *logical* to assume that soccer practice will be canceled.
4. Miah hopes to get the job, even though she has no *prior* experience.
5. Jaquavis had to *adjust* the rearview mirror before backing the car up.

FLUENCY

Repeated Reading: Lead a group to read the same passage aloud together several times. As the leader, emphasize accuracy and phrasing, until the group reading sounds smooth and consistent.

Invite students to do a timed reading of "Ranching: You've Got to Love It." Afterwards, have them enter their times on the Words-per-Minute table on page 121 and chart their reading speed on page 122 of the *Advanced Reader*.

📶 Encourage students to listen to "Ranching: You've Got to Love It." Go to **www.mhereadingbasics.com** to play or download the recording. The recording provides modeled fluency and read-along support.

APPLICATION

Workplace Skill:

Predict Outcomes with a Job Posting

Have students read the job posting. Remind them that job postings give descriptions of open jobs at a company or institution and list the qualifications applicants need to be considered. Point out that the headings and basic information in a posting can help them make some predictions about what the job might be like. After students answer the questions, have them write a list of reasons why this job is or is not right for Sonrisa. This list will be helpful when they do the Write for Work activity.

Write for Work

Tell students to match the description of the job with Sonrisa's job needs to determine whether it is a good match. Remind them to include reasons and details to support their conclusion. Have them share their work with a classmate to be sure they adequately supported their conclusion.

PASSKEY

💻 Go to **www.mhereadingbasics.com** and click on the *Passkey* link. Customize instruction for your class using modules from Reading/Language Arts, Levels 4 & 5.

Advanced Student Edition

Lesson Plan Advanced Student Edition

Introduce

READING SKILL

Identify Fact and Opinion

Explain/Model: Explain that it is important to be able to distinguish between facts and opinions. Have students read aloud the facts and the opinion. Model distinguishing between them. Explain how you might prove or disprove each fact. Point out words that signal opinions.

Guided Practice: Have students read the boxed passage. Then work with them to complete the task given in the directions. Discuss why the responses given after the passage are correct. Ask students to tell how they might prove the facts and to point out words that signaled the opinions.

Teach Lesson Skills

Practice: Have students read the statements. Tell them to look for statements that can be proved or words that signal opinions. Discuss their answers and ask them to explain how they distinguished between facts and opinions.

Apply: After students complete their graphic organizers, have them read their responses aloud to the class. Encourage them to explain how they determined whether each statement was a fact or an opinion.

Check Up: Have students work in small groups to read the passage and answer the questions. Then check each group's responses with those of other groups in the class.

COMPREHENSION

Understand Author's Purpose: Encourage students to consider the author's purpose as they read. Provide self-questioning models, such as *Why did the author decide to write this? What does the author want me to know?* By examining the author's purpose, students can better analyze their own reaction to the writing and consciously monitor their own comprehension.

Reading Extension

📖 Encourage students to read "Delta Force: Under Cover and Out of Sight" on page 113 of the *Advanced Reader*. Use this as an opportunity to teach reading strategies and the lesson reading skill.

ALPHABETICS

Explore Words

Prefixes *inter-*, *super-*: Model adding prefixes to these words: *inter-* + *national*, *inter-* + *twine*, *super-* + *conductor*, and *super-* + *fine*. Discuss how adding the prefix changes the meaning of each word.

Latin Roots: Write these words on the board, underlining as shown: *visual*, *liberation*, *audible*, and *vocal*. Give the meaning of each root, and then model using the roots to determine the meaning of each word.

Context Clues: Write this sentence: *I find onions repugnant, so I don't eat them or cook with them.* Model using context to determine the meaning of *repugnant*. Have students use a dictionary to confirm your definition.

VOCABULARY

Academic Vocabulary/Tier 2

fact opinion prove viewpoint decline

Before students complete the activity, write the academic vocabulary words and definitions on the board. Discuss each word's meaning with students. Then write the sentences below on the board. Read each sentence aloud and discuss it with students.

1. Aleksandra checked the *fact* before putting it in her report.
2. In Huong's *opinion*, it's fine to eat ice cream for dinner.
3. No one could *prove* that the man committed the crime.
4. Denali expressed her *viewpoint* in a letter to the editor.
5. After the movie got bad reviews, ticket sales started to *decline*.

FLUENCY

Echo Reading: Read a sentence from one of the passages aloud. Then have students echo you by reading the same sentence and trying to read with the same speed and expression as you do.

Invite students to do a timed reading of "Delta Force: Under Cover and Out of Sight." Afterwards, have them enter their times on the Words-per-Minute table on page 121 and chart their reading speed on page 122 of the *Advanced Reader*.

📶 Encourage students to listen to "Delta Force: Under Cover and Out of Sight." Go to **www.mhreadingbasics.com** to play or download the recording. The recording provides modeled fluency and read-along support.

APPLICATION

Workplace Skill:

Understand Fact and Opinion in a Letter to School Employees

Have students read the letter. Remind them that a letter to employees is a way for managers and supervisors to share their ideas with their staff. Point out that distinguishing between facts and opinions will help them determine the letter writer's point of view. After students answer the questions, have them start a list of things they would like about working at Fairfax Middle School. This list will come in handy when they do the Write for Work activity.

Write for Work

Remind students to include both facts and opinions. Tell them to use signal words to make their opinions clear. Encourage them to share their work with a classmate and to practice identifying facts and opinions in one another's letters.

PASSKEY

💻 Go to **www.mhreadingbasics.com** and click on the *PassKey* link. Customize instruction for your class using modules from Reading/Language Arts, Levels 4 & 5.

Lesson Plan Advanced Student Edition

<table>
<tr><td rowspan="1">Introduce</td><td colspan="3">

READING SKILL
Identify Genre

Explain /Model: Explain that identifying genres and recognizing their characteristics can help readers better understand and interpret what they read. Have students read aloud the information about genres and subgenres. Model giving examples for each genre or subgenre.

Guided Practice: Have students read the boxed passage. Then work with them to complete the task given in the directions. Discuss why the response given after the passage is correct. Ask students to give examples from the text that show that the passage is a mystery.

</td></tr>
</table>

Teach Lesson Skills

Practice: Have students read the passages and identify the genre or subgenre of each. Discuss their responses and have students point out features or details in each passage that helped them identify its genre or subgenre.

Apply: After students read the passages and identify the genres or subgenres, have them read their responses aloud to the class. Encourage them to point out specific features or details in each passage that helped them determine its genre or subgenre.

Check Up: Have students work in small groups to read the passages and answer the questions. Then check each group's responses with those of other groups in the class.

COMPREHENSION

Reread/Read More Slowly: Encourage students to become aware of the pace at which they read. Offer self-questioning models, such as *Did I read this passage too quickly? Does reading it again help me understand better? Does reading more slowly help me retain information?* When students actively consider the manner in which they are reading, they consciously monitor their own comprehension.

ALPHABETICS	VOCABULARY	FLUENCY
Explore Words	**Academic Vocabulary/Tier 2**	**Marked Phrase Reading:** Mark a
Analogies: Model determining the relationship between the word pairs in this analogy: *Painter : painting* as *sculptor : sculpture.* Then have students complete this analogy: *calm : relaxed* as *anxious : _____.*	genre drama prose audience list Before students complete the activity, write the academic vocabulary words and definitions on the board. Discuss each word's meaning with students. Then write the sentences below on the board. Read each sentence aloud and discuss it with students.	passage with phrase boundaries, showing how words should be grouped for meaning and emphasis. Read the passage aloud, having students follow along, and then read aloud together with students.
Multiple Suffixes: Write each word, drawing slashes to set off the suffixes from each other and from the rest of the word: *thought/less/ly, ar/tis/tic, care/ful/ness.* Model using the suffixes to determine meaning.	1. Most of the books I read are from the fiction *genre.*	
Spelling: Homophones: Write these word pairs: *heal/heel; vain/vein;* and *pedal/peddle.* Discuss the meaning of each word. Model using *heal* and *heel* in sentences. Then have students work in pairs to write sentences for *vain/vein* and *pedal/peddle.*	2. Shanti is writing a *drama* with roles for each of her friends. 3. Dan thinks *prose* is easier to read than poetry. 4. The *audience* fidgeted and whispered as they waited for the play to start. 5. The music magazine published a *list* of the most popular songs of the week.	

APPLICATION
Workplace Skill:

Identify Genre in Business Documents

Have students read the list. Explain that knowing the different forms of business writing will help them better understand what they read for work. It will also help them choose the correct format for their own business writing. After students answer the questions, have them talk with a partner about the different forms of business writing and how they are used. This exercise will come in handy when they do the Write for Work activity.

Write for Work

Remind students that choosing the correct form for their writing is an important part of business communication. Tell them to make sure they use the correct format and style for the form of business writing they choose. Encourage them to share their work with a classmate and discuss why they chose the format they did.

Workplace Extension

Have students review the passage about Mark Verga. Discuss how Mark's employer and coworkers might feel about Mark's inability to work overtime. How could Mark show that he wants to be a team player while still honoring his other commitments? Have partners answer the questions and share their responses.

PASSKEY

Go to **www.mhereadingbasics.com** and click on the *PassKey* link. Customize instruction for your class using modules from Reading/Language Arts, Levels 4 & 5.

Advanced Student Edition

Name_____ Date _____

Unit 1 Workplace Skill Activity
Identify Transferable Skills

Transferable skills are skills that can be used in many occupations and transferred from one job to the next. They are skills you have gained through everyday experience, education, and jobs. These skills are particularly valuable to first-time job seekers, people seeking a new career, or those who are re-entering the work force. There are four main types of transferable skills: self-management skills, people skills, physical skills, and learned skills.

When applying for a job that is not directly related to your prior work experience, include information on your application or résumé that relates your transferable skills to the job description. This will show an employer that your skill set is a good match for the opening.

Read the section of a résumé below. What skills might be transferable to another job?

> **Assistant Office Receptionist, Oakland High School**
> - Sorted mail and set up morning handouts before teaching staff arrived each day
> - Responded to all incoming calls
> - Filed paperwork and student forms
> - Greeted all parents and visitors
> - Assisted principal with projects, meetings, and schedules
> - Maintained professional, businesslike appearance
>
> **Skills & Abilities**
> - Working knowledge of Microsoft Office
> - Typing ability (40+ wpm)
> - Ability to establish priorities

The bulleted items in the résumé above show the applicant's punctuality and ability to interact with the public. These are self-management and people skills that would be useful at many jobs. Filing is a learned skill that would transfer to many different types of work.

Work with a partner to complete the chart with transferable skills shown in the résumé. An example for each category has been given to get you started. After completing the chart, choose two skills and tell your partner how they relate to a job you would like to have.

Self-management Skills	People Skills	Physical Skills	Learned Skills
punctual	good listener	energetic	typing

Unit 2 Workplace Skill Activity
Role-play Responding to Feedback

The success of any business depends upon how well the employees do their job. Your supervisor will probably offer you feedback periodically on how well you are performing your responsibilities. Sometimes the feedback will be positive, and other times your supervisor may offer you constructive criticism on how you can be more successful in your position. How you accept feedback will influence your supervisor's perception of you, so it is important to respond appropriately. When you receive feedback, you should do the following:

- Make eye contact, nod your head, and use comments, such as "I see," that acknowledge your understanding of the message.
- Repeat your supervisor's message in your own words to confirm your understanding and ask questions about anything you don't understand.
- Maintain a positive attitude and avoid pouting, complaining, blaming others, or being argumentative.

Imagine that you are the employee receiving the following feedback. Answer the questions below the box to plan your response. Then role-play the situation with a partner.

> I appreciate how efficiently you type and prepare letters, reports, and memos, and I've noticed how promptly you attend to an item when it is placed in your inbox. However, sometimes when you try to work so quickly, your attention to detail isn't as strong as it could be and errors, such as typos and missed lines, creep into your work.

1. What problem is your supervisor bringing to your attention?

   _____

2. What could you say to show that you understand what your supervisor is saying to you?

   _____

3. What questions do you have for your supervisor about the feedback he or she has given you?

   _____

4. What might you say to your supervisor in response to the feedback?

   _____

5. What could you do to improve your performance?

   _____

Unit 3 Workplace Skill Activity
Role-play Positive Body Language

Whether you are taking part in an interview, giving a presentation, or meeting with your supervisor to discuss your performance, your body language speaks volumes, even if you haven't said a word. The ways you move, gesture, sit, stand, and look at others are all forms of nonverbal communication, and they all affect how others perceive you. Appropriate body language, such as making eye contact, standing up straight, and using subtle hand gestures, can make you seem honest, open, and enthusiastic. Conversely, fidgeting, slouching, looking around, and checking your watch all send the message that you would rather be doing something else.

Read the passage below about a meeting between an employee and her supervisor. Then work with a partner to complete each activity.

> Nadia's supervisor, Sam Chen, requests a meeting to discuss training her to become a cash-handling lead in the electronics department at SaveMart. Nadia listens attentively, but yawns occasionally. She also stares down at the desk as she absentmindedly twists her hair. Nadia tells Sam that she would be interested in becoming a cash-handling lead and is surprised when Sam says nothing further about it and then chooses another employee instead.

1. Decide what each of Nadias gestures might convey to her supervisor and complete the chart.

Gesture	Nonverbal Message
yawning	
staring down at the desk	
twisting her hair	

2. Discuss with your partner what Nadia could have done differently. Take turns role-playing the meeting. Then complete the chart below with the gestures used in your role-play and the messages conveyed.

Gesture	Nonverbal Message

Advanced Student Edition

Answer Key Advanced Student Edition

Unit 1 Lesson 1.1

Practice, page 15
1. John Dalton, J. J. Thomson, Ernest Rutherford
2. He showed that atoms contained electrons.
3. 1803
4. trains, trolleys, automobiles
5. Trucking allowed industries to ship goods in a way other than on the railroads.
6. highways

Apply, page 16
In the first passage, second part of first sentence or the last sentence should be underlined.
In the second passage, the first sentence should be underlined.
Sample answers:
1. In 2002 more than 99 percent of U.S. businesses were small businesses.
2. In 2002 small businesses created over two-thirds of all new jobs.
3. In 2002 small businesses produced about half the country's output of goods and services.
4. Small businesses are an important part of the American economy.
5. Change the antifreeze to keep the water that cools your engine from freezing.
6. Check that your heater and defroster are in good working condition.
7. Check the treads on your tires.
8. Check that you have enough windshield-wiper fluid.
9. Clean the slush off your windshield.
10. Make sure you have a scraper, brush, and gloves in the car.

Check Up, page 17
1. B	3. C	5. B	7. C
2. F	4. J	6. F	8. H

Workplace Skill, page 18
1. C	2. G	3. B	4. H

Write for Work, page 19
Check that the writing includes the following points: The writer should include a description of his or her experience and qualifications. Details should be included that relate to examples specific to food service workers. The details should support the qualifications listed in the statement of experience.

Reading Extension, page 19
1. A	2. G	3. D	4. H
5. *Sample answer:* Presidents are no longer allowed to ride in open-topped cars.
6. *Sample answers:* quick reflexes, ability to withstand extreme stress, willingness to put oneself in danger to protect someone else

Explore Words, page 20
Prefixes
Sample answers:
1. misheard; I misheard the directions and got lost.
2. disabilities; The woman's disabilities make it hard for her to walk.
3. nontoxic; The man uses nontoxic cleaners so his dog won't get sick.
4. unbelievable; The man's story about being lost at sea was unbelievable.
5. misspelled; I misspelled the name of the restaurant.

Spelling: Plurals
1. countries	4. blemishes
2. scarves	5. lives
3. cockroaches	6. roofs

Page 21
Context Clues
Sample answers:
1. relating to ships or sailing
2. heading toward somewhere
3. disappeared
4. wreckage
5. reasonable

Academic Vocabulary
1. detail	4. recall
2. economy	5. standard
3. output	

Unit 1 Lesson 1.2

Practice, page 23
1. stated	6. not known
2. implied	7. not known
3. implied	8. implied
4. stated	9. stated
5. stated	

Apply, page 24
1. sentence 2	3. sentence 5
2. sentence 3	4. sentence 6
5. *Sample answer:* The carnivores, or meat-eaters, ate herbivore dinosaurs.
6. sentence 2	7. sentence 3
8. *Sample answer:* Hundreds of thousands of people were killed.

Check Up, page 25
1. A	3. C	5. C	7. D
2. G	4. J	6. J	8. J

Workplace Skill, page 26
1. D	2. F
3. *Sample answer:* Permanent employees receive paid time off and paid holidays; temporary employees do not.

Write for Work, page 27
Check that the letter clearly states the main reason for writing. The tone should be professional and respectful. The three questions should be sensible and request additional details.

Reading Extension, page 27
1. D	2. G
3. *Sample answer:* She thought the world needed food and medical care more than fast horses.
4. *Sample answer:* She wears a helmet and bulletproof jacket and she takes a security team with her.

Answer Key Advanced Student Edition

Explore Words, page 28
Spelling: Word Endings
1. stupidest
2. zigzagged
3. upsetting
4. finest
5. confusing
6. refused
7. disputing
8. repelled
9. wiser
10. focused

Spelling: Possessives
1. my parents' house
2. my neighbor's dogs
3. your brother's children
4. my friends' party
5. the dog's toy
6. the workers' lunches

Page 29
Suffixes -er, -or, -ist
Sample answers:
1. actor; The Oscar went to the best actor in a drama.
2. wrestlers; Wrestlers have strong upper bodies.
3. psychologist; A psychologist can help you understand your feelings.
4. cartoonists; Cartoonists have to be good at drawing.
5. conservationist; A conservationist probably recycles at home.
6. landscaper; A landscaper has to like working outdoors.

Academic Vocabulary
1. state
2. clarify
3. distinguish
4. infer
5. directly

Unit 1 Lesson 1.3

Practice, page 31
1. valid
2. *Sample answer:* Inventors made improvements on the early typewriters over time.
3. valid

Apply, page 32
Sample answers:
1. American colonists made most of their household supplies.
2. Susan B. Anthony's work was very important in getting women the right to vote.
3. Electric bills rise in the months when people use air conditioning.

Check Up, page 33
1. B   2. J   3. C

Workplace Skill, page 34
1. C   2. G

Write for Work, page 35
Check that the writing includes the following points: In writing the memorandum, the writer should think about his or her own prior knowledge about workplace safety and use the information in the table. The memo should be professional in tone.

Reading Extension, page 35
1. C   2. F
3. *Sample answer:* They might not have access to manufactured bombs. Since each IED is unique, there is no standard way to defuse IEDs, which makes them harder to disarm.
4. *Sample answer:* It is valid. There are many bombs, and they could go off at any time, injuring soldiers and civilians. The author also says that the IEDs have killed more American soldiers in Iraq and Afghanistan than any other weapon, so disarming them is especially important.

Explore Words, page 36
Prefixes
Sample answers:
1. remarry; She is going to remarry her first husband.
2. substandard; The plumber's work was substandard.
3. deactivate; Please deactivate the device before it goes off.
4. intermix; I intermixed the red flowers with the yellow flowers.

Latin Roots
Sample answers:
1. dictation
   Dictionary definition: the act of saying something so that it can be written down
2. spectacle
   Dictionary definition: an object or event that is seen or witnessed, especially one that is impressive or unusual
3. interject
   Dictionary definition: to throw in between or among other things

Page 37
Synonyms
1. d	5. g	9. d	13. g
2. c	6. e	10. f	14. b
3. a	7. h	11. h	15. c
4. b	8. f	12. a	16. e

Academic Vocabulary
1. conclusion
2. general
3. draw
4. grant
5. currency

Unit 1 Lesson 1.4

Practice, page 39
Sample answers:
1. Advertising comes in many forms. Sometimes it's difficult to separate radio and television programming from the commercials, even though rules regulate the separation of the two.
2. Movies were at their most popular after World War II. When the movie business suffered due to competition with television, producers began making fewer but more spectacular movies.
3. In the 1950s, Hollywood started filming epic movies, such as *Ben Hur*, in an effort to attract audiences. The films took years to film, involved movie stars, and were often shot on location in vivid color.

Answer Key Advanced Student Edition

Apply, page 40

Sample answers:
1. The largest inland body of water in the Western Hemisphere also has three to five times more salt content than the ocean. It is the Great Salt Lake in Utah.
2. Many people want to improve their memory. Thomas De Quincey said that a person's memory strengthens when he or she challenges it and trusts it.
3. In the United States, the first reported deaths from hailstones occurred in 1784 during a severe South Carolina storm.

Check Up, page 41
1. C   2. F   3. D

Workplace Skill, page 42
1. A   2. G
3. *Sample answer:* There will be quarterly updates of process-improvement goals, as well as milestones for achieving those goals. There will also be an outline of the process-improvement strategy.

Write for Work, page 43
Check that the writing includes the following points: The writer understands the concept of summarizing a text. The key idea is clearly stated. The writing is concise and to the point. The writing reflects a formal style appropriate to a workplace.

Reading Extension, page 43
1. D   2. F
3. *Sample answer:* Amateurs chase tornadoes for the thrill of it, but scientists chase tornadoes to learn more about them.
4. *Sample answer:* Faidley became the first full-time, professional storm chaser in the mid-1980s, taking pictures of severe weather. He went on to set up a news agency that covered severe weather events.

Explore Words, page 44

Spelling: The Letters f, ph, gh, ch
1. (f)antastic
2. tou(gh)er
3. stoma(ch)
4. trium(ph)
5. (ch)ocolate

Greek Roots
Sample answers:
1. something that is too small to see
2. written account of someone's life
3. the study of writing
4. pilot oneself
5. to work at home by means of an electronic linkup with the central office

Page 45

Spelling: Word Endings
1. sunnier   7. denying
2. surveyed   8. applied
3. studying   9. reviving
4. fanciest   10. enjoyed
5. envying   11. playing
6. beautified   12. worrier

Academic Vocabulary
1. device   4. paraphrase
2. summarize   5. conclude
3. observe

Unit 1 Lesson 1.5

Practice, page 47
Sample answers:
1. The walls did not have to bear the weight of the building.
2. Scientists think Venus may once have had oceans and an atmosphere.
3. Rising levels of carbon dioxide caused the greenhouse effect to increase.
4. People of the colonies all wanted the capital in their own state.

Apply, page 48
Sample answers:
1. A chemical bond breaks.
2. The "victim" changes into a free radical.
3. Cell and tissue damage occurs.
4. Antioxidants donate electrons.

Check Up, page 49
1. B   2. J   3. C   4. J

Workplace Skill, page 50
1. C   2. F   3. C   4. G

Write for Work, page 51
Check that the writing indicates knowledge of the graphic and what it shows. Cause-and-effect relationships should be included.

Reading Extension, page 51
1. C   2. H   3. A
Sample answers:
4. The fall may have resulted in better inspection procedures for windows and other repairs.
5. Working higher up the ladder results in higher salaries.

Explore Words, page 52
Suffixes -ive, -ic, -ish
1. foolish; The jester is supposed to act in a foolish manner.
2. heroic; The heroic lifeguard risked her life to save mine.
3. creative; I like your creative solution to the problem.

Spelling: Homophones
1. seller   6. boarder
2. isle   7. serial
3. carat   8. meddle
4. allowed   9. jeans
5. banned

Page 53
Multiple-meaning Words
1. a   3. b   5. a
2. a   4. a   6. b

Academic Vocabulary
1. effect   4. obvious
2. identify   5. likewise
3. cause

Answer Key Advanced Student Edition

Unit 1 Lesson 1.6

Practice, page 55
1. describe   3. inform
2. inform   4. explain

Apply, page 56
1. B   2. H   3. A   4. F

Check Up, page 57
1. A   2. G   3. B   4. J

Workplace Skill, page 58
1. C   2. H

Write for Work, page 59
Check that the writing includes the following points: The memo is formatted correctly and shows an understanding of the author's purpose in the first memo.

Workplace Extension, page 59
1. B   2. G
3. *Sample answer:* (1) Schedule a meeting with my supervisor. (2) Talk to a dietary technician and a nutritionist. (3) Arrange to meet a college counselor.

Explore Words, page 60
Spelling: Contractions
1. e   6. there's
2. a   7. can't
3. d   8. I'm
4. b   9. I've
5. c   10. didn't

Suffixes -ance, -ant, -ent
1. ant   4. ant   6. ance
2. ance   5. ent   7. ant
3. ant

Page 61
Word Parts
1. sub   ject   ed
2. in   struct   ing
3. non   believe   er
4. uni   cycle   ist
5. inter   nation   al
6. dis   appear   ance
7. re   format   ed
8. mis   identify   ed
9. trans   port   ing

Academic Vocabulary
1. purpose   4. inform
2. persuade   5. argument
3. consequence

Unit 1 Lesson 1.7

Practice, page 63
1. implied; *Sample answer:* The shape of a cell is often related to its function.
2. stated; A formidable group of people sparked America's industrialization.
3. implied; *Sample answer:* As a library volunteer, you can help the professional staff with many different tasks.

Apply, page 64
Sample answers:
1. U.S. Postal Service workers in remote areas deliver mail by unusual means.
2. Although kangaroos cannot run, their hind legs allow them to make fast, high leaps.
3. The *Mayflower* carrying the Pilgrims landed first at Provincetown, not Plymouth.
4. A book published in the early 1960s about the destruction of plants and animals by pesticides sparked the ecology movement in the United States.

Check Up, page 65
1. A   2. G   3. D

Workplace Skill, page 66
1. B   2. J

Write for Work, page 67
Check that the writing includes the following points: The writer clearly identifies the main idea of each of the four categories of recyclables.

Workplace Extension, page 67
1. C   2. F
3. *Sample answer:* Juan's friend Hoa gave him good advice. Juan had accomplished a lot in his job, and he was in a good position to ask for a raise. Sometimes you have to take the initiative to move head.

Explore Words, page 68
Prefixes uni-, bi-, tri-
1. B   3. D   5. D
2. G   4. G   6. G

Analogies
1. small   3. bear
2. horse   4. sick

Page 69
Context Clues
1. A   2. H   3. D   4. G

Academic Vocabulary
1. examine   4. deduce
2. imply   5. establish
3. link

Unit 1 Assessment

Pages 71–76

1. A	12. F	23. B
2. J	13. D	24. H
3. B	14. G	25. D
4. F	15. D	26. F
5. C	16. G	27. C
6. F	17. B	28. H
7. C	18. H	29. A
8. G	19. C	30. G
9. B	20. H	31. C
10. J	21. C	32. G
11. C	22. J	

Unit 1 Workplace Skill Activity

Sample answers:
Self-management Skills: motivated, responsible, organized
People Skills: team player, respectful of authority
Physical Skills: good eye-hand coordination
Learned Skills: computer, filing

Students should be able to explain why the skills they chose are appropriate to the job they desire.

Answer Key Advanced Student Edition

Unit 2 Lesson 2.1

Practice, page 79
1. Rosa Parks was asked to give up her seat on a bus to a white man.
2. Rosa Parks was arrested.
3. A 381-day bus boycott began.
4. Rosa Parks's case was appealed to the Supreme Court.
5. The Supreme Court ruled that discrimination on buses violated federal law.

Apply, page 80
1. A lake forms with clear water.
2. It begins filling with microscopic organisms, seeds, and decayed matter.
3. Animals such as insects, fish, and birds move in.
4. Debris collects at the bottom of the lake.
5. Plants take root in the sediments.
6. The lake becomes a wetland.
7. The lake fills completely with sediment.
8. Communist forces invaded South Korea.
9. President Truman did not ask Congress to declare war.
10. President Truman asked the United Nations to send troops to defend South Korea.
11. North Korean forces pushed the UN troops to the southern tip of South Korea.
12. The UN troops pushed back north.

Check Up, page 81
1. B
2. H
3. C
4. G
5. C
6. J
7. A

Workplace Skill, page 82
1. C
2. J

Write for Work, page 83
Check that the writing includes the following points: The instructions are clear and organized and include sequence words.

Reading Extension, page 83
1. C
2. H
3. B
4. *Sample answer:* They might become killers.
5. *Sample answer:* The tiger sank its teeth into his neck and dragged him off stage.

Explore Words, page 84
Prefixes en-, em-
1. c
2. g
3. f
4. h
5. a
6. b
7. d
8. e

Suffixes -ion, -tion
1. decoration
2. discussion
3. attraction
4. complication
5. adoption
6. inspection

Page 85
Multiple-meaning Words
1. a
2. a
3. b
4. a
5. b
6. a

Academic Vocabulary
1. interpret
2. sequence
3. violate
4. inevitable
5. subsequent

Unit 2 Lesson 2.2

Practice, page 87
1. quantity
2. check the box for "too small"
3. check the box for "doesn't look like picture" or check the box for "other" and write comment on lines
4. Check the box for "return?" or "exchange?"
Sample answers:
5. wide selection, don't have to leave home
6. can't try things on, items may not look the same as they did in the picture

Apply, page 88
1. poor, fair, good, very good, excellent
2. salt, fat content, size of shells
3. Momma's
4. Healthy Heart
5. Healthy Heart
6. Timesaver
7. Eddie's

Check Up, page 89
1. B
2. H
3. A
4. G
5. B
6. G
7. A
8. G

Workplace Skill, page 90
1. D
2. F

Write for Work, page 91
Check that the writing includes the following points: The letter or e-mail is an adequate response to the customer based on the contents of the warranty, including the specific part of the warranty that applies to this request.

Reading Extension, page 91
1. B
2. H
3. C

Answer Key Advanced Student Edition

4. *Sample answer:* A bull can step on them and seriously injure or kill them.
5. *Sample answer:* It is extremely dangerous.

Explore Words, page 92
Latin Roots
Sample answers:
1. deport: to banish someone from a country
2. transport: to carry people or goods from one place to another
3. detain: to hold back or delay somebody or something
4. obtain: to get possession of something

Word Families
1. direction, redirected, directory
2. disbelieve, unbelievable, believer
3. approval, unproved, disapproving

Page 93
Accented and Unaccented Syllables
2. en / joy
3. cot / tage
4. dis / rupt
5. slug / ger
6. trum / pet
7. re / sell
8. fab / ric

Academic Vocabulary
1. consume
2. maintain
3. instructions
4. crucial
5. common

Unit 2 Lesson 2.3

Practice, page 95
1. *The Grapes of Wrath*
2. 619
3. yes; Springfield Main branch
4. 340
5. 1989
6. Simon and Schuster

Apply, page 96
Sample answers:
1. shape
2. say
3. realm
4. condition
5. governmental
6. declare
7. kingdom
8. formal
9. The sick woman was in no condition to drive a car.
10. The official title of the head of school is headmaster.
11. He announced the winner of the contest.
12. Her country of origin is Nepal.

Check Up, page 97
1. D	6. H
2. F	7. C
3. D	8. G
4. H	9. D
5. B	10. H

Workplace Skill, page 98
1. C
2. H
3. B
4. H

Write for Work, page 99
Check that the writing includes the following points: The poster includes the key points of the food-handling guidelines; all words are spelled correctly.

Reading Extension, page 99
1. C
2. H
3. D
4. *Sample answer:* They spend their whole lives in high altitudes and are used to the atmosphere.
5. *Sample answers:* carrying food and equipment, clearing ice from paths, anchoring ropes, cooking

Explore Words, page 100
Prefixes
1. conference
2. collision
3. correlation
4. communicate
5. congratulate

Latin Roots
1. b	4. d
2. e	5. a
3. c	

Page 101
Multiple-meaning Words
1. a	3. a
2. b	4. a

Academic Vocabulary
1. available	4. general
2. assist	5. research
3. index	

Unit 2 Lesson 2.4

Practice, page 103
1. main idea: In the early days of movies, Mary Pickford was both a major Hollywood film star and a successful businesswoman.
   supporting evidence: *Sample answers:* She became known as America's sweetheart. She formed Mary Pickford Studios.
2. main idea: Social insurance programs give financial or other benefits to people who have made regular financial contributions to the program.
   supporting evidence: *Sample answer:* Upon retirement these retirees receive income and health benefits from the government.
3. main idea: Some hazardous wastes come from the products that we produce and use in our homes.
   supporting evidence: *Sample answer:* Leftover house paints are hazardous waste.

Answer Key Advanced Student Edition

Apply, page 104
1. Quito, Ecuador
2. *Sample answer:* They are examples of cities that support the generalization that cities near the equator have warm temperatures.
3. cholera, polio, smallpox
4. Smallpox nearly wiped out whole Native American nations in 1616 and killed more than a 100,000 people between 1775 and 1782.
5. Cholera first hit in 1832, killing many thousands of people.

Check Up, page 105
1. A
2. G
3. A
4. H
5. D

Workplace Skill, page 106
1. A
2. H

Write for Work, page 107
Check that the writing includes the following points: The written response is clear and based on the steps in the procedure for clocking in and out.

Reading Extension, page 107
1. B
2. H
3. *Sample answer:* Touching something that has been directly exposed to the sun's rays for a substantial period of time could burn an astronaut badly
4. *Sample answer:* Heidemarie Stefanyshyn-Piper's tool bag slipped out of her hands, and $100,000 worth of tools floated away.

Explore Words, page 108
Suffixes -ous, -ious
1. having the quality of disaster
2. having the quality of anxiety
3. characterized by caution
4. characterized by mystery
5. having the quality of ambition
6. characterized by glamour
7. having the quality of joy
8. having the quality of a melody

Spelling: Homophones
1. shown
2. presence
3. whether
4. overdue
5. pedal
6. patients
7. stationery
8. sundae
9. scent

Page 109
Greek Roots
1. c
2. e
3. f
4. h
5. b
6. g
7. a
8. d

Academic Vocabulary
1. irrelevant
2. support
3. evidence
4. evaluate
5. example

Unit 2 Lesson 2.5

Practice, page 111
1. ambition
2. obsession
3. anxiety

Apply, page 112
Sample answers:
1. smug
2. fast
3. oblivious to others
4. self-confident
5. narration: telling what Emmett thinks about himself and what others think about him.
6. the teacher's dialogue revealing his or her thoughts about Emmett

Check Up, page 113
1. B
2. H
3. C
4. J
5. C

Workplace Skill, page 114
1. B   2. H

Write for Work, page 115
Check that the writing includes the following points: The writing and the performance rating are rational, and the writer includes logical reasons for why Amala received this rating.

Reading Extension, page 115
1. A
2. G
3. what other characters say about the main characters
4. *Sample answer:* Determination; he never gave up on his dream of flying.

Explore Words, page 116
Analogies
1. waist
2. genes
3. loaf
4. preview
5. stable
6. children

Word Families
1. courted
2. sportsman
3. secular

Page 117
Context Clues
1. b
2. c
3. a
4. d

Academic Vocabulary
1. key
2. characters
3. encounter
4. traits
5. technique

Answer Key Advanced Student Edition

Unit 2 Lesson 2.6

Practice, page 119
1. B
2. F
3. A
4. G
5. A

Apply, page 120
1. sight
2. sound
3. smell
4. taste
5. sight
6. smell
7. smell
8. touch
9. taste
10. touch

Check Up, page 121
1. C
2. J
3. A
4. H
5. B
6. J

Workplace Skill, page 122
1. C
2. F

Write for Work, page 123
Check that the writing includes the following points: The advertisement uses a correct style of writing to appeal to the company's targeted audience of 10- to 14-year-olds; word choices are appropriate for this audience.

Workplace Extension, page 123
1. B
2. J
3. *Sample answer:* Since Rosalind does not report to Raymond, he should not confront her directly. Doing so could cause bad feelings between the coworkers. I think it is the responsibility of Raymond's boss to improve the situation. Therefore, I would speak with the district account director to resolve the problem.

Explore Words, page 124
Synonyms
1. proud
2. frenzied
3. surprise
4. clean
5. selective

Prefixes semi-, multi-, mid-
Sample sentences:
1. partly retired; My brother is only 50 years old, but he is semiretired.
2. in the middle of town; That tunnel will take you to midtown.
3. having many levels; A multilevel house has too many steps for me.

Page 125
Latin Roots
1. exc<u>lam</u>ation
2. re<u>sent</u>ment
3. inter<u>rupt</u>
4. <u>scrib</u>ble
5. <u>scrib</u>e
6. <u>sens</u>itive

Academic Vocabulary
1. figurative
2. style
3. communicate
4. specific
5. element

Unit 2 Assessment

Pages 127–132
1. B
2. G
3. D
4. J
5. B
6. H
7. A
8. G
9. C
10. H
11. D
12. F
13. B
14. F
15. C
16. H
17. B
18. G
19. C
20. G
21. D
22. H
23. D
24. G
25. A
26. F
27. C
28. J
29. B

Unit 2 Workplace Skill Activity

Sample answers:
1. The supervisor is asking me to pay closer attention to detail in order to avoid errors.
2. I'm glad you appreciate my promptness. I hadn't realized that I was making mistakes.
3. Would you like me to take back the work I just submitted so that I can recheck it?
4. Thanks for bringing this to my attention.
5. Before submitting my work, I could carefully proofread it and correct any errors.

Answer Key Advanced Student Edition

Unit 3 Lesson 3.1

Practice, page 135
1. C
2. J
3. B

Apply, page 136
Sample answers:
1. Anise is a versatile plant.
2. Some American legends are exaggerated versions of real people.
3. Disease made building transportation systems across Panama difficult and dangerous in the 19th century.

Check Up, page 137
1. C
2. F
3. C
4. G

Workplace Skill, page 138
1. D
2. H

Write for Work, page 139
Check that the writing includes some or all of the points in the one of the employee handbook sections. Make sure students have included one of these generalizations: The dress code is business casual Monday through Thursday and casual attire on Friday. *or* The company computer is to be used for work purposes only.

Reading Extension, page 139
1. C
2. H
3. A
4. *Sample answer:* They don't always get to write important stories.

Explore Words, page 140
Synonyms and Antonyms
Sample answers:
1. lucky; unlucky
2. break; fix
3. strong; weak
4. construct; destroy
5. smart; stupid
6. trustworthy; irresponsible
7. daring; cowardice
8. careful; careless

Accented and Unaccented Syllables
2. (cin)/na/mon
3. dis/(gust)/ing
4. un/(stea)/dy
5. (sat)/is/fied
6. mis/(tak)/en
7. (care)/ful/ly
8. (o)/ver/ly
9. un/(yield)/ing
10. (sim)/u/late
11. re/(sist)/ing
12. (dan)/ger/ous

Page 141
Suffixes -ness, -ship
1. alertness
2. championship
3. bitterness
4. boastfulness
5. carelessness
6. citizenship
7. healthiness
8. partnership
9. politeness

Academic Vocabulary
1. utilize
2. statement
3. apply
4. essential
5. valid

Unit 3 Lesson 3.2

Practice, page 143
1. A   3. B
2. G   4. F

Apply, page 144
1. lighthearted
2. *Sample answer:* to caution other travelers to make sure they are boarding the correct train when they travel
3. humorous
4. *Sample answer:* to point out the different national stereotypes of the hostel owner
5. inspiration
6. *Sample answer:* to inspire others to go mountain climbing

Check Up, page 145
1. A
2. J
3. C
4. F

Workplace Skill, page 146
1. C
2. G

Write for Work, page 147
Check that the writing includes the following points: The writer uses the appropriate word choice and language style to create an effect of professionalism and enthusiasm.

Reading Extension, page 147
1. B
2. H
3. A
4. H
5. *Sample answers:* toughness, hero, tenacious, immeasurable help
6. *Sample answer:* to show that some bush pilots can play serious and important roles

Explore Words, page 148
Greek Roots
1. e
2. a
3. d
4. g
5. f
6. c
7. h
8. b

Synonyms
1. encouraged
2. chatty
3. mistaken
4. strong-willed
5. responsibilities

Answer Key Advanced Student Edition

Page 149

Suffixes -al, -ial
1. architectural
2. political
3. educational
4. commercial
5. musical
6. bacterial
7. ceremonial
8. familial
9. proverbial

Academic Vocabulary
1. approach
2. constant
3. intention
4. convey
5. unique

Unit 3 Lesson 3.3

Practice, page 151
1. the Tower of Pisa and the Washington Monument
Sample answers:
2. The Tower of Pisa is over 400 years older than the Washington Monument. The Tower of Pisa is in Italy, and the Washington Monument is in the United States.
3. They were both built on unstable soil. They are both famous buildings.
4. Both buildings had major construction done after they were completed. The work was done to stop the buildings from sinking or collapsing.
5. in common, both, in comparison
6. on the other hand

Apply, page 152
1. mostly round
2. pointed oval
3. kick the ball into the net for one point
4. carry the ball across the goal line for six points, additional scoring methods
5. shin guards
6. heavy padding and helmets
7. 90 minutes

8. 60 minutes
9. rare
10. frequent

Check Up, page 153
1. C
2. G

Workplace Skill, page 154
1. A
2. H
3. D
4. G

Write for Work, page 155
Check that the writing includes the following points: The writer understands how to compare the data in the graphs. The writer includes signal words to show comparison and contrast.

Reading Extension, page 155
1. B
2. H
3. A
4. *Sample answer:* Modern ships have smaller crews than old-fashioned ships. The smaller crews make them an easier target.
5. *Sample answer:* Modern pirates have cell phones and machine guns.

Explore Words, page 156
Accented and Unaccented Syllables
2. ge/o/graph/ic
3. com/mu/ni/cate
4. en/vi/ron/ment
5. ne/ces/si/ty
6. math/e/mat/ics
7. pho/tog/ra/phy
8. char/ac/ter/is/tic
9. im/mu/ni/ty
10. e/lab/o/rate
11. an/ti/sep/tic
12. sim/pli/ci/ty

Prefixes
1. illogical
2. inappropriate

3. infrequently
4. inexperienced
5. impersonal
6. incompetent
7. irrational
8. inaccurate
9. inexcusable
10. impolitely

Page 157

Spelling: Homophones
1. chews
2. sense
3. great
4. heard
5. coral
6. symbol
7. prince
8. rows
9. flu
10. right

Academic Vocabulary
1. compare
2. frequently
3. contrast
4. similar
5. consider

Unit 3 Lesson 3.4

Practice, page 159
1. A
2. H
3. B

Apply, page 160
Sample answers:
1. A fierce storm would descend upon Galveston and cause great loss of life and property.
2. The ship would hit an iceberg and sink, causing many people onboard to die.
3. Liddell would win medals in both the 200- and 400-meter races.
4. Lashonda will get a good grade on her history paper.

Check Up, page 161
1. C
2. F
3. D

Workplace Skill, page 162
1. C
2. J

Write for Work, page 163
Check that the writing includes the following points: The writing includes logical reasons based on the job qualifications and Sonrisa's current job needs as to why this is not a good match for Sonrisa. The writing cites the required hours, the low pay, and the fact that the job is only part time as reasons.

Reading Extension, page 163
1. C
2. F
3. A
4. *Sample answer:* There will always be dangers associated with ranching because animals and the weather can be unpredictable.

Explore Words, page 164
Word Families
1. projected, conjecturing, dejectedly
2. accompany, companion, accompanist
3. infrastructure, constructively, instructor
4. inability, disabled, unable

Accented and Unaccented Syllables
1. fa/mil/iar
2. dis/ci/pli/nar/i/an
3. o/pin/ion
4. sub/scrip/tion
5. cer/e/mo/ni/al
6. ter/ri/tor/i/al
7. de/com/pres/sion
8. bo/he/mi/an
9. in/ter/mis/sion
10. op/er/a/tion

Page 165
Analogies
1. night
2. eat

3. box
4. start
5. draw *or* color

Academic Vocabulary
1. adjust
2. prior
3. predict
4. logical
5. outcome

Unit 3 Lesson 3.5

Practice, page 167
1. opinion
2. fact
3. opinion
4. opinion
5. fact
6. opinion
7. fact
8. fact
9. fact
10. fact
11. opinion
12. opinion
13. opinion
14. fact
15. fact
16. opinion
17. fact
18. opinion
19. opinion
20. opinion
21. fact
22. fact

Apply, page 168
Facts: Polio is a contagious disease caused by a virus that may attack nerve cells of the brain and spinal cord.
In the years following the development of the polio vaccine, the reported cases of polio in the United States were cut by more than 80 percent.
Franklin Delano Roosevelt contracted polio when he was 39 years old.
Roosevelt hoped that the mineral-rich waters of Warm Springs, Georgia, would cure him.

Opinions: The polio vaccine is one of the most thrilling stories in the history of medicine.
All children should be vaccinated early in life.
It's amazing that one of the most dreaded of diseases was brought under control by a simple vaccination.
Despite his disease, he was the greatest president in U.S. history.
FDR was a more impressive president than his cousin Teddy Roosevelt.

Check Up, page 169
1. B   3. D
2. F   4. G

Workplace Skill, page 170
1. C
2. G

Write for Work, page 171
Check that the writing includes the following points: The writer understands the difference between facts and opinions, and the writing includes both facts and opinions in the note.

Reading Extension, page 171
1. B   2. H   3. D
4. *Sample answer:* Delta Force members are selected by invitation only.

Explore Words, page 172
Prefixes inter-, super-
1. interchangeable
2. supernatural
3. interstate
4. superimposed
5. intervention
6. superintendent

Latin Roots ;
1. d; advocate
2. b; invisible
3. a; audition
4. c; liberated
5. e; vocation

Answer Key Advanced Student Edition

Page 173

Context Clues
1. d
2. a
3. b
4. c

Academic Vocabulary
1. prove
2. fact
3. viewpoint
4. opinion
5. decline

Unit 3 Lesson 3.6

Practice, page 175
1. nonfiction
2. nonfiction
3. drama
4. poetry

Apply, page 176
1. mystery
2. romance
3. autobiography
4. historical fiction

Check Up, page 177
1. C
2. F
3. D

Workplace Skill, page 178
1. A
2. J
3. *Sample answer:* If you are launching a new project and need to train project members, you would write project start-up procedures.

Write for Work, page 179
Item 1: internal e-mail
Item 2: letter on company letterhead
Item 3: procedural document
Check that the writing includes the following points: The writer makes a logical conclusion about the form of business writing that would be appropriate. The item selected is written in an acceptable format for the type of document selected.

Workplace Extension, page 179
1. B
2. G
3. *Sample answer:* Dear Ms. Martinez: I am sorry I will not be able to work extra hours this season as I usually do. I am taking two evening courses toward my associate's degree and have important tests coming up. Once these commitments are finished, I will be able to work extra hours as needed.

Explore Words, page 180
Analogies
1. milk
2. dirt *or* dust
3. ears
4. least
5. sailing
6. distrust
7. teeth
8. real

Multiple Suffixes
1. educat / ion / al
2. beauti / ful / ly
3. help / ful / ness
4. fear / less / ly
5. effort / less / ly

Page 181
Spelling: Homophones
1. peace
2. waste
3. paced
4. quarts
5. fourth
6. rung
7. cite
8. straight

Academic Vocabulary
1. audience
2. genre
3. drama
4. prose
5. list

Unit 3 Assessment

Pages 183–188
1. D	17. A
2. J	18. G
3. A	19. C
4. H	20. G
5. A	21. A
6. H	22. H
7. B	23. C
8. H	24. J
9. D	25. B
10. J	26. F
11. A	27. C
12. G	28. H
13. A	29. D
14. J	30. G
15. B	31. B
16. F	32. H

Unit 3 Workplace Skill Activity

Sample answers:
1. yawning: bored, tired
   staring down at the desk: lack of confidence
   twisting her hair: bored, distracted
2. sitting up straight: attentive
   making eye contact: respectful, confident
   nodding head: involved, engaged
   leaning forward slightly: enthusiastic

reading

basics

PART 3: READERS

Lesson Plan Introductory Reader

Unit 1 Lesson 1.1 🔊 "A Young Man Speaks Out," pages 1–8

Introduce

Summary Nkosi Johnson and his mother both suffered from AIDS. They left their small South African town in order to escape possible persecution and to get medical help. Gail Johnson, a health worker in Johannesburg, raised Nkosi when his mother became too sick to care for him. Nkosi and his foster mother had to fight the local school system to let Nkosi attend school. Although he was sick and young, Nkosi became a well-known AIDS activist. He died in 2001 at the age of 12.

Teach Lesson Skills

BEFORE READING

Build Vocabulary List the vocabulary words and their definitions on the board. Discuss each word's meaning with students. Then write the sentences that contain the words on the board. Read the sentences aloud and discuss them with students.

disease: sickness

shunned: left alone

normal: like others in his group

frail: weak

coma: a state much like deep sleep

bold: brave

1. The doctors are trying to find a cure for the *disease*.
2. The poor man was *shunned* by the neighbors.
3. His dog eats less than a *normal* dog.

4. Her *frail* grandmother could not climb the stairs.
5. The woman in the hospital finally came out of her *coma*.
6. The *bold* hero saved the children from the fire.

Activate Prior Knowledge
1. Ask students what they know about AIDS.
2. Help students find South Africa on a map.

Preview and Predict Ask students what clues the title of the article, the photograph, and the photo caption provide. What predictions about the article might students make? *(Possible answer: Nkosi Johnson was a boy who spoke out about AIDS.)*

Build Background Acquired immunodeficiency syndrome (AIDS) is the disease caused by the human immunodeficiency virus (HIV). HIV is passed between people through bodily fluids. This means that HIV can be passed from a mother to her child during pregnancy or delivery or through breast feeding. In 2008 around 430,000 children around the world were born with HIV, and about 90 percent of them live in Africa, where AIDS is a medical crisis. In Africa, there were about 2.5 million new HIV infections in 2007, and more than 14 million children have been orphaned. Increased awareness of AIDS worldwide, education about the disease, and increased access to quality medical treatment are needed to combat this epidemic.

DURING READING

Cause and Effect A cause is an event or action that makes something else happen. An effect is the result or the outcome of that action. Writers use clue words such as *because, so, since, if,* and *therefore* to signal cause and effect. Have students look for cause and effect relationships by asking *What happened? Why?*

AFTER READING

Respond to the Article Have students write a journal or blog entry about the courage that Nkosi Johnson showed. Ask students: Why do you think it was so important to Nkosi to go to school? Would you fight to go to school? What parts of the article surprised you, and what parts met your expectations?

Support Individual Learners

DIFFERENTIATED INSTRUCTION

Kinesthetic learners may benefit from using physical movements to understand cause-and-effect relationships. Have students perform actions that illustrate cause and effect: for example, clapping their hands to cause a sound. Also have them brainstorm actions in a sport that demonstrate cause-and-effect relationships, such as plays in a soccer match that result in a score.

ENGLISH LANGUAGE LEARNERS

Have students fold pieces of paper in half lengthwise and label the left side *Cause* and the right side *Effect*. They should draw sketches or cut pictures from magazines that show cause-and-effect relationships. For example, they may place a picture of a speeding car on the left and draw a traffic ticket on the right.

GRAPHIC ORGANIZERS

💻 Go to **www.mhereadingbasics.com.** Use Graphic Organizer 5 as a Sequence-of-Events Chart. Make copies for each student. Ask students to write the following events in order in the boxes of the chart according to what they learned about Nkosi Johnson in the article. Discuss their responses.

Nkosi went into a coma.

Nkosi spoke to a crowd of 10,000 people.

Nkosi and his mother left their village.

Nkosi fought to be allowed to go to school.

Lesson Plan Introductory Reader

Unit 1 Lesson 1.2 🔊 "Alone across the Atlantic," pages 9–16

Introduce

Summary Debra and Andrew Veal decided to row across the Atlantic Ocean in the Ward Evans Atlantic Rowing Challenge that began in October 2001. During the race Andrew developed a fear of the open sea and was taken away on a rescue boat. Debra continued the remaining 2,650 miles of the race by herself. Although she feared sharks and huge ships, which might have smashed into her small boat, she managed to finish the race 70 days after the winning crew.

Teach Lesson Skills

BEFORE READING

Build Vocabulary List the vocabulary words and their definitions on the board. Discuss each word's meaning with students. Then write the following sentence stems on the board. Read the sentence stems aloud and ask students to complete them.

challenge: something that is hard to do

consists: is made or formed from

overcome: win out over

consumed: eaten up or ruined

threats: things that cause danger

boost: raise

1. The hike was a *challenge* because . . .
2. A meal that is good for you *consists* of . . .
3. To *overcome* her fear of flying, the woman . . .

4. The man was *consumed* by love because . . .
5. Some of the *threats* that animals face are . . .
6. They wanted to *boost* her spirits because . . .

Activate Prior Knowledge

1. Ask students to talk about a fear they have overcome or would like to overcome. If students are reluctant to talk about their fears, ask them to discuss situations where they have seen other people who were afraid.
2. Help students locate the Canary Islands and Barbados on a map.

Preview and Predict Ask students what clues the title of the article, the photograph, and the photo caption provide. What predictions about the article might students make? *(Possible answer: Debra Veal will complete a rowing challenge across the Atlantic Ocean. She will make this journey alone.)*

Build Background The Atlantic Ocean is a vast body of water that separates North and South America from Europe and Africa. The Atlantic can be very rough in stormy weather, with waves up to 40 or 50 feet high. The Ward Evans Atlantic Rowing Challenge is considered to be one of the toughest races in the world. The small boats used to row across the Atlantic must be able to withstand the waves and right themselves if they capsize. They must also be equipped with the supplies the rowers need to stay alive for up to three months at sea. These include a device to convert the ocean's salt water into drinking water, solar panels to produce electricity, food and a cooker, a navigation system, and a radio for communication with those on land.

DURING READING

Predict Predicting is thinking ahead to guess how events might become resolved. Predicting helps readers become involved in the text. Readers base predictions on details in the text and their own knowledge. Tell students that their predictions may change as details change or are added.

AFTER READING

Respond to the Article Have students write a journal or blog entry about their responses to Debra's decision to continue the race alone. Ask students: What do you think were Debra's reasons for completing the race alone? How do you think Debra felt when she finished the race? How do you think her husband Andrew felt?

Support Individual Learners

DIFFERENTIATED INSTRUCTION

Give students a comic strip with the final frame missing. Ask them to draw their prediction of what happens at the end. Remind them to use clues the cartoonist has provided. When they finish, give them the final frame of the comic and have them compare their predictions to the ending.

ENGLISH LANGUAGE LEARNERS

Have students pair up to practice predicting the outcomes of stories. Students may choose a real story or tell the plot of a book or film. The stories should present a problem that is solved. Have the storyteller stop before the end of the story and ask, "What do you think happened next?" The partner should make a prediction. Then students should switch roles. Have students tell each other if their predictions were correct.

GRAPHIC ORGANIZERS

💻 Go to **www.mhreadingbasics.com.** Use Graphic Organizer 2 as a Fact-and-Opinion Chart. Make copies for each student. Ask students to write *Fact* at the top of the left column and *Opinion* at the top of the right column. Then have students organize the following sentences about the article according to whether each sentence is a fact or opinion. Discuss their responses.

It was a mistake for the Veals to enter the race.

Andrew should have tried harder to keep rowing.

Debra rowed 2,650 miles by herself.

Debra had more courage than her husband.

Debra faced the dangers of sharks and huge ships.

Debra's courage made her the biggest winner in the race.

Introductory Reader (side tab)

Introduce

Summary Fidel Castro's daughter, Alina Fernandez, wanted to leave Cuba with her daughter. Fearing how it would look to the outside world if Castro's own daughter left the country, the government refused her permission to leave. Eventually, Fernandez got a fake passport. She had to gain weight and make other changes to match the picture on the passport. Posing as a Spanish tourist, Fernandez finally left the country in 1993. A few days later, Castro allowed Fernandez's daughter to join her in the United States.

Teach Lesson Skills

BEFORE READING

Build Vocabulary List the vocabulary words and their definitions on the board. Discuss each word's meaning with students. Then write the following questions on the board. Read the questions aloud and discuss the answers with students.

scarce: not enough to fill needs
severely: in a way that causes pain
legally: in a way allowed by law

tourist: a person who travels for fun
suspicious: like a person who has done wrong
reveal: make known

1. If food is *scarce*, will people be hungry? Why?
2. If someone is treated *severely*, will that person be happy or unhappy? Why?
3. If you do something *legally*, will you get in trouble with the police? Why?

4. What kinds of things might a *tourist* do while traveling?
5. What are some things people might do that would make them look *suspicious*?
6. Is it better to keep or to *reveal* a friend's secret? Why?

Activate Prior Knowledge

1. Help students locate Cuba and Florida on a map.
2. Prompt a discussion about family. How do students define family? Ask students: Is it more important to be loyal to yourself or to your family?
3. Ask students to think about what freedom means. What is necessary for a person to consider himself or herself free?

Preview and Predict Ask students what clues the title of the article, the photograph, and the photo caption provide. What predictions about the article might students make? *(Possible answer: Fidel Castro's daughter and granddaughter will escape to the United States.)*

Build Background In Cuba, the Communist Party is the only legal political party. Fidel Castro took power in Cuba in 1959. That year he became the prime minister after leading a rebellion against the corrupt Cuban government. Although Castro made health care and education available to more people, he also jailed many of the people who opposed him. Fidel Castro ruled Cuba as a dictator, controlling the movements of the people. Castro broke relations between Cuba and the United States in 1961. Thousands of Cubans left the country. Castro's brother Raul became president of Cuba in 2008. Today there is still tension between the United States and Cuba.

DURING READING

Infer An inference is a logical guess about information that the writer suggests but doesn't directly state. Making inferences helps readers find deeper meaning in what they read. Ask students to look for details that aren't fully explained. Have them combine clues from the text with their personal knowledge to identify what the author suggests.

AFTER READING

Respond to the Article Have students write a journal or blog entry about why they think Fernandez wanted to leave Cuba and why Castro wanted her to stay. Ask students to discuss what it would feel like to leave their country for a new one. What difficulties would they face?

Support Individual Learners

DIFFERENTIATED INSTRUCTION

Collect articles, newspaper headlines, jokes, or cartoons that require students to make inferences in order to understand the text fully. Place students in groups and have them work together to make inferences based on the texts. The dialogue among students builds background knowledge, and those who have difficulty with this skill can learn from those who are more adept at it. Have groups share their inferences with the class.

ENGLISH LANGUAGE LEARNERS

Picture books for older readers can be useful for helping students understand the concept of making inferences. Have students read the books in small groups and make three inferences about what happened in each book. For example, *You Can't Take a Balloon into the Museum of Fine Arts*, by Jacqueline Preiss Weitzman and Robin Preiss Glasser, shows what happens when a child's balloon is set free.

GRAPHIC ORGANIZERS

💻 Go to **www.mhereadingbasics.com.** Use Graphic Organizer 5 as a Sequence-of-Events Chart. Make copies for each student. Ask students to write the following events in order in the boxes of the chart according to what they learned from the article. Discuss their responses.

Fernandez built up her weight.

Fernandez told her daughter about her plan.

Fernandez got a fake passport.

Fernandez tried to go to Mexico.

Lesson Plan Introductory Reader

Unit 1 Lesson 1.4 🔊 **"The Heroes of Flight 93," pages 25–32**

Introduce

Summary On September 11, 2001, the passengers and crew of Flight 93 from New Jersey to California discovered that the plane they were on was taken over by terrorists. Through cell phone conversations with friends and family, they learned that terrorists had already crashed planes into important U.S. buildings. The passengers and crew decided to fight against the terrorists on the plane to keep them from flying it into another building. No one survived the crash, but the heroes of Flight 93 saved the lives of many others.

Teach Lesson Skills

BEFORE READING

Build Vocabulary List the vocabulary words and their definitions on the board. Discuss each word's meaning with students. Then write the following questions on the board. Read the questions aloud and discuss the answers with students.

terrorists: people who scare others

cockpit: the part of the plane where the pilot sits

terrified: scared

vowed: promised

survived: lived through

enormous: huge

1. What word goes with "very great or large"? *(enormous)*
2. What word goes with "airplane"? *(cockpit)*
3. What word goes with "causing people pain and fear"? *(terrorists)*

4. What word goes with "doing what you say you'll do"? *(vowed)*
5. What word goes with "scream and shake"? *(terrified)*
6. What word goes with "being alive after going through something difficult"? *(survived)*

Activate Prior Knowledge

1. Ask students what they know about the terrorist attacks of September 11, 2001.
2. Discuss with students what it means to be a hero. Have students share a few stories of heroism.

Preview and Predict Ask students what clues the title of the article, the photograph, and the photo caption provide. What predictions about the article might students make? *(Possible answer: This article will tell about the brave people who died in the crash of Flight 93 on September 11, 2001.)*

Build Background In February 1998 Osama bin Laden and four Islamic groups signed a statement encouraging the killing of Americans. According to bin Laden, Americans were not living by certain religious beliefs. This was the latest of many declarations bin Laden had been making against Americans since 1992. These declarations led to the World Trade Center bombing in 1993, the bombings of the U.S. embassies in Kenya and Tanzania in East Africa in 1998, and the attacks on the World Trade Center and the Pentagon on September 11, 2001.

DURING READING

Identify Sequence Sequence is the order in which events, ideas, or things are arranged. Time order refers to the order in which events occur. Following the sequence of events helps you see how the text is organized and how events relate to each other. As students read, ask them to look for key words such as *now, then, during, soon,* and *next.*

AFTER READING

Respond to the Article Have students write a journal or blog entry about the situation in which the passengers and crew of Flight 93 found themselves. Ask students: What do you think these people were feeling when they decided to attack the terrorists? What parts of the article surprised you, and what parts met your expectations?

Support Individual Learners

DIFFERENTIATED INSTRUCTION

Explain that common types of sequence are time order, spatial order, order of importance, and steps-in-a-process order. Time order refers to the order in which events occur. Spatial order refers to where things are in relation to one another. Order of importance refers to events or ideas arranged from most to least important. Steps-in-a-process order refers to the order in which something is done: for example, a recipe.

ENGLISH LANGUAGE LEARNERS

Have students describe an event from their past in time order or explain something they can do using steps-in-a-process order. Prompt them to use signal words in their descriptions. Have students create a time line of the events they are describing as a visual aid.

GRAPHIC ORGANIZERS

📖 Go to **www.mhereadingbasics.com.** Use Graphic Organizer 1 as a Characteristics Map. Make copies for each student. Ask students to write *The Heroes of Flight 93* in the center bubble of the graphic organizer. Have students write a characteristic of one of the Flight 93 passengers or a characteristic of the passengers as a whole in each of the outer bubbles. Students should also write the evidence for each characteristic. Discuss their responses.

Introductory Reader

Lesson Plan Introductory Reader

Unit 1 Lesson 1.5 🔊 "Seeing for the First Time," pages 33–40

Introduce

Summary Harun-ur-Rashid was born blind with cataracts. In his country of Bangladesh, there was little help available for him. When he was a young boy, a stranger took him to an eye hospital, where his cataracts were removed. Harun grew up, married, and had children. All five of his children were born with cataracts. The Childhood Blindness Project was able to find doctors who helped all five of his children see for the first time.

Teach Lesson Skills

BEFORE READING

Build Vocabulary List the vocabulary words and their definitions on the board. Discuss each word's meaning with students. Then write the following questions on the board. Read the questions aloud and discuss the answers with students.

blind: not able to see

miracles: wonderful things

million: 1,000,000

cataracts: cloudy eyes

lenses: the clear parts of eyes

operation: set of actions done to fix a problem with the body

1. If a man is *blind*, which of his senses does he not have?
2. Tell about some things that you think are *miracles*.
3. Many big cities have *millions* of people living in them. What other things might number in the millions?
4. What would be something that would be difficult to do if you had *cataracts*?
5. Which part of your body has *lenses*?
6. Why might you need an *operation*?

Activate Prior Knowledge

1. Explain to students that they will read about a family from Bangladesh. Help them find Bangladesh on a map.
2. Name the five senses. Ask students to discuss what it would be like to live without one of these senses. Have students imagine what it might be like to be blind and then be able to see. For more information about blindness, see http://www.nfb.org.
3. Prompt students to discuss charity organizations. Ask students to name various charity organizations they have heard of, such as UNICEF or the World Wildlife Fund. What kind of work do these charities do? Have students done any charitable or volunteer work of their own? How do they feel when they help others?

Preview and Predict Ask students what clues the title of the article, the photograph, and the photo caption provide. What predictions about the article might students make? *(Possible answer: The article will tell how eye doctors can help some people who are blind to see.)*

Build Background The lens of the eye lies behind the pupil and iris. It focuses light onto the retina at the back of the eye. A lens is made up mostly of water and protein. Sometimes the protein in a lens can start to build up into clumps. This usually happens as people get older, but diseases like diabetes can cause the protein to build up in younger people. When the proteins clump together, they cloud up the lens, making it very hard to see. Doctors can perform cataract surgery to allow people to see again. During cataract surgery, doctors make a small cut in the eye and take out the cloudy lens. Then they put in a new clean plastic lens that will not cloud up. In North America alone, more than three million cataract surgeries are performed every year.

DURING READING

Ask Questions Asking themselves questions helps students monitor their understanding of the text. Have students ask *who, what, when, where, why,* and *how* questions and look for the answers. Questions may include: What is the conflict? How was the conflict resolved? Why did the subject of the article do/believe something and not something else?

AFTER READING

Respond to the Article Have students write a journal or blog entry about what Harun and his family might have felt when they finally got the help they needed to be able to see. Ask students: How do you think Harun felt when the doctors removed the cataracts from his eyes? How do you think Harun felt when his children were born blind? What do you think it was like for the children when they were finally able to see?

Support Individual Learners

DIFFERENTIATED INSTRUCTION

Help students become better interactive and independent readers by having them use a variety of comprehension strategies as they read. For example, have students adjust their reading speed, restate a difficult sentence, skip ahead to the next sentence, reread the paragraph, and look for context clues around difficult phrases or words.

ENGLISH LANGUAGE LEARNERS

It is especially important for English language learners to ask questions as they monitor comprehension. Assign proficient English-speaking partners to ELLs and ask the partners to help them form questions. Having ELLs actively question what they don't understand will help them as they encounter difficult passages in a new language.

GRAPHIC ORGANIZER

💻 Go to **www.mhereadingbasics.com.** Use Graphic Organizer 5 as a Sequence-of-Events Chart. Make copies for each student. Ask students to write the following events in order in the boxes of the chart according to the order in the article. Discuss their responses.

A doctor helped Harun see.

Harun's children saw their mother.

A stranger took Harun to an eye hospital.

Harun asked for help from people in his village.

Lesson Plan Introductory Reader

Unit 2 Lesson 2.1 🔊 "Pigs to the Rescue," pages 41–48

Introduce

Summary People don't normally think of pigs when they think of pets, but pigs can be loyal pets. This article tells three stories of pigs saving their owners' lives. Because of zoning laws, Cathy Carder had to move to keep her pet pig Iggy. Later, Iggy saved Carder from a fire by waking her from a nap. Honeymoon was another pig who saved her owners from a fire. Still another pig, LuLu, stopped traffic to get help for her owner, who was having a heart attack.

Teach Lesson Skills

BEFORE READING

Build Vocabulary List the vocabulary words and their definitions on the board. Discuss each word's meaning with students. Then write the following questions on the board. Read the questions aloud and discuss the answers with students.

grunted: made a deep sound in the throat

screeching: making a sharp, high sound

plopped: fell heavily

ambulance: a car or truck that carries sick people

reward: something given for a good act

national: of a country

1. Which word goes with "flag" and "anthem"? *(national)*
2. Which word goes with "tires going too fast around a corner" *(screeching)*
3. Which word goes with "stone falling into water"? *(plopped)*
4. Which word goes with "pigs in mud"? *(grunted)*
5. Which word goes with "finding a lost dog"? *(reward)*
6. Which word goes with "accident"? *(ambulance)*

Activate Prior Knowledge

1. Ask students if they could imagine having a pig for a pet. What do they think that would be like? How would having a pig be different from having another pet, such as a dog?
2. Ask students to make a list of adjectives about pigs. Students may work on the list individually or as a class.

Preview and Predict Ask students what clues the title of the article, the photograph, and the photo caption provide. What predictions about the article might students make? *(Possible answer: I will learn about Spot, a potbellied pig, and other pigs that have protected or rescued their families in some way.)*

Build Background There are many different kinds of pigs. Some, like the potbellied pig, are kept as pets. Other pigs are raised on farms for their meat and other parts, which are turned into products such as makeup, insulin, glue, and antifreeze. Still others live in the wild. All pigs have several things in common. They all have four toes on each hoof but walk on only two of the toes. They have poor eyesight. A mother pig can give birth to 8–12 piglets in one litter and can have up to two litters per year. Pigs do not sweat and are very clean animals. Pigs are also considered to be among the smartest animals in the world, comparable to dogs.

DURING READING

Find Vocabulary in Context As students read the article, have them note the new vocabulary words. Ask them to think about each word's meaning as they read.

AFTER READING

Respond to the Article Have students write a journal or blog entry about their responses to the pigs in the article. Have students refer to their list of adjectives and discuss if the article changed their opinion about pigs. Ask students if they think laws preventing people from having pigs in their houses are fair.

Support Individual Learners

DIFFERENTIATED INSTRUCTION

Help students look for ideas in common across various texts. Have students read or recall pig characters from literature, such as *Charlotte's Web* by E. B. White or *Animal Farm* by George Orwell. Once students understand how to connect across texts, have them expand the skill into other media, such as film or TV. Ask students to look for other cultural connections to pigs as well.

ENGLISH LANGUAGE LEARNERS

Read aloud a short article or a letter that would appeal to students so that they can make connections to themselves and to the world. Have students use their prior knowledge and experiences to tell or write about something related to the article or letter. For example, if you read about a certain animal's relationship to its owner, students could describe a personal experience or tell what they know about humans' relationships with animals. Point out that in this discussion, they are making a connection with the text.

GRAPHIC ORGANIZERS

📖 Go to **www.mhereadingbasics.com.** Use Graphic Organizer 3 as a Categories Chart. Make copies for each student. Have students label the first column *Iggy*, the second column *Honeymoon*, and the last column *LuLu*. Have students write facts from the article about each animal in the appropriate column. Point out that students are classifying information about the pigs in the article.

Lesson Plan Introductory Reader

Unit 2 Lesson 2.2 🔊 "In the Line of Fire," pages 49–56

Introduce

Summary Alfred Rascon was born in Mexico, but his family moved to the United States when he was a young boy. Although Rascon was not a U.S. citizen, he joined the U.S. Army as a medic during the Vietnam War. Rascon risked his life several times to save his fellow soldiers, and he suffered terrible injuries as a result. Although the men in Rascon's unit recommended that he receive the Medal of Honor after the battle, he did not receive the medal until many years later.

Teach Lesson Skills

BEFORE READING

Build Vocabulary List the vocabulary words and their definitions on the board. Discuss each word's meaning with students. Then write the following questions on the board. Read the questions aloud and discuss the answers with students.

parachute: equipment that is carried on the back of people who jump from airplanes, which opens up to slow their fall

citizen: a member of a nation who has full rights, such as the right to vote

unit: a group who trains and works together

grenade: a small bomb thrown by hand or fired from a gun

chaplain: a minister

outraged: angered

1. What word goes with "belonging to a country"? *(citizen)*
2. What word goes with "jumping from a plane"? *(parachute)*
3. What word goes with "church"? *(chaplain)*

4. What word goes with "very angry"? *(outraged)*
5. What word goes with "weapon"? *(grenade)*
6. What word goes with "staying together"? *(unit)*

Activate Prior Knowledge

1. Help students locate Vietnam on a map.
2. Ask students if they know anyone who is or was a soldier. What qualities do they think a good soldier should have?
3. Ask students what they think makes someone a good citizen of a country.

Preview and Predict Ask students what clues the title of the article, the photograph, and the photo caption provide. What predictions about the article might students make? *(Possible answer: Alfred Rascon was a soldier who received an award for something he did that was dangerous.)*

Build Background American involvement in the Vietnam War lasted from 1965 to 1975. It was a difficult and dangerous war, particularly because the Vietnamese fighters used a strategy called guerilla warfare. They carried out surprise attacks against small platoons of U.S. troops, often in the jungle. During the Vietnam War, more than 58,000 American soldiers died, and almost 200,000 were wounded. Only 246 Medal of Honor citations were issued to U.S. soldiers for extraordinary courage and heroism during the Vietnam War. The Vietnam War was very controversial with the American public, and for many years many Vietnam War veterans were not treated fairly.

DURING READING

Determine Word Meanings from Context Think of context as the words or sentences that surround a word you don't know. This information can help you make a good guess about what the word means. Have students look for clues such as descriptions, synonyms, or examples to help them figure out the meaning of an unfamiliar word.

AFTER READING

Respond to the Article Have students write a journal or blog entry about the courage that Alfred Rascon showed. Ask students: What do you think Alfred Rascon was feeling when he risked his life to save his friends? What parts of the article surprised you, and what parts met your expectations?

Support Individual Learners

DIFFERENTIATED INSTRUCTION

Ask students to bring in some song lyrics or poems that contain words that may be unfamiliar to other students. Have students take turns explaining to the class how they determined the meaning of an unfamiliar word using context clues.

ENGLISH LANGUAGE LEARNERS

Tell students that they sometimes can find out the meaning of a word by seeing how the word relates to other words around it. Use the following sentence as an example. "Lazlo could not see the bottom of the murky pond." Descriptive sentences like this one often help students visualize the event and help their comprehension.

GRAPHIC ORGANIZERS

💻 Go to **www.mhereadingbasics.com.** Use Graphic Organizer 4 as a Cause-and-Effect Chart. Make copies for each student. Ask students to label the columns *Causes* and *Effects*. Have students write each one of the sentences below in the boxes of the *Causes* column. Then ask students to write one effect in the boxes of the *Effects* column for each cause. Discuss their responses.

Rascon had no money for college.

Rascon dragged a machine gun back to his unit.

Rascon threw himself between a man and an exploding grenade.

Rascon's friends got the army to hear Rascon's case again.

Lesson Plan Introductory Reader

Unit 2 Lesson 2.3 🔊 **"How Fast Is Too Fast?," pages 57–64**

Introduce

Summary Going on a roller coaster, with its high inclines and fast speeds, can feel exhilarating to riders. But some say that modern roller coasters, which are faster and have more twists and turns than ever, are dangerous. Some coasters have left the tracks, causing injuries and deaths. Other coasters are blamed for causing blood clots in the brains of several riders.

Teach Lesson Skills

BEFORE READING

Build Vocabulary List the vocabulary words and their definitions on the board. Discuss each word's meaning with students. Then write the sentences that contain the words on the board. Read the sentences aloud and discuss them with students.

roller coaster: a ride on which cars on tracks go up and down suddenly

health: the state of feeling well

clots: lumps in a liquid

1. The road had so many hills, I felt like I was on a *roller coaster*.
2. A doctor's job is to check people's *health*.
3. I knew the milk was bad because of the *clots* in it.

blood vessels: tubes that carry blood through the body

hazardous: dangerous

risk: chance of failing or getting hurt

4. *Blood vessels* take blood from your heart to other parts of your body
5. It is *hazardous* not to wear a seat belt.
6. If you do something dangerous, you take a *risk* of getting hurt.

Activate Prior Knowledge

1. Prompt students to discuss their experiences riding roller coasters or other thrill rides. Ask students: What does your body feel like on these rides?
2. Ask students: Do you feel these rides could be dangerous? Why or why not? What devices are used to keep riders safe?

Preview and Predict Ask students what clues the title of the article, the photograph, and the photo caption provide. What predictions about the article might students make? *(Possible answer: The roller coaster in the photograph looks like it would be fun to ride. However, from the title and caption, it looks like this article will explain how roller coasters could be dangerous for riders.)*

Build Background Roller coasters do not have any engines of their own. A roller coaster ride starts when the coaster is lifted up a big incline by an external engine. The coaster gains energy for the rest of the ride by going up this first incline. The higher the coaster climbs, the greater the distance that gravity has to pull it back down and the faster the speed of the ride. The track makes sure the cars all stay in line with each other and go the right way. At the end of a roller coaster ride, the energy that was built up in the first big incline is almost gone, and the roller coaster comes to a stop.

DURING READING

Predict Predicting is thinking ahead to guess how events might become resolved. Predicting helps readers become involved in the text. Readers base predictions on details in the text and on their own knowledge. Tell students that their predictions may change as details change or are added.

AFTER READING

Respond to the Article Have students write a journal or blog entry based on the evidence presented the article. Ask students: Which evidence makes roller coasters seem dangerous? Which evidence makes roller coasters seem safe? Do you think that roller coasters should have a limit on the g-force? Why or why not?

Support Individual Learners

DIFFERENTIATED INSTRUCTION

Give students a comic strip with the final frame missing. Ask them to draw their prediction of what happens at the end. Remind them to use clues the cartoonist has provided. When they finish, give them the final frame of the comic and have them compare their predictions to the ending.

ENGLISH LANGUAGE LEARNERS

Have students pair up to practice predicting the outcomes of stories. Students may choose a real story or tell the plot of a book or film. The stories should present a problem that is solved. Have the storyteller stop before the end of the story and ask, "What do you think happened next?" The partner should make a prediction. Then students should switch roles. Have students tell each other if their predictions were correct.

GRAPHIC ORGANIZER

📖 Go to **www.mhereadingbasics.com.** Use Graphic Organizer 2 as a Fact-and-Opinion Chart. Make copies for each student. Ask students to write *Fact* at the top of the first column and *Opinion* at the top of the second column. Then have students organize the following sentences about the article according to whether they are facts or opinions. Discuss their responses.

Roller coasters can go from zero to 80 miles an hour in less than three seconds.

The woman who lived after she had blood clots in her brain was lucky.

Roller coasters are fun.

Experts studied roller coasters and their g-forces.

Lesson Plan Introductory Reader

Unit 2 Lesson 2.4 🔊 "The Mysteries of the Maya," pages 65–72

Introduce

Summary The Maya lived more than 1,000 years ago in parts of Mexico and Central America. The Maya were great artists and writers, they were talented in math and science, they made calendars, and they built large, beautiful cities. In A.D. 800 the Maya appeared to be at the top of their power, but by A.D. 900 the Maya civilization had ended. No one is sure what happened. Wars, fighting among the people, crowded conditions, and lack of rain could all have contributed to the end of this great civilization.

Teach Lesson Skills

BEFORE READING

Build Vocabulary List the vocabulary words and their definitions on the board. Discuss each word's meaning with students. Then write the following sentence stems on the board. Read the sentence stems aloud and ask students to complete them.

temples: holy places where people pray

heavenly: having to do with the sky

calendars: charts that show the days, weeks, and months of the year

1. People go to *temples* so that they can . . .
2. Stars and planets are called *heavenly* bodies because . . .
3. *Calendars* are a good place to write things down because . . .

outstanding: wonderful

society: a way of life for people

weapons: things used for fighting

4. You would be happy with an *outstanding* report card because . . .
5. One *society* in the world today is . . .
6. *Weapons* can hurt people because . . .

Activate Prior Knowledge

1. Write *computers* and *motor engines* on the board. Ask students to name common activities that would be impossible without these modern tools. *(Possible answers: farming with tractors, buying things without going to a store)*
2. Help students locate Mexico and Central America on a map.
3. Explain the concept of a time capsule to students. Ask students to list things they would put in a time capsule for future historians to learn about our culture.

Preview and Predict Ask students what clues the title of the article, the photograph, and the photo caption provide. What predictions about the article might students make? *(Possible answers: The Maya built pyramids, some of which were abandoned. I will learn about the mysteries surrounding the Maya and their pyramids.)*

Build Background Mesoamerica is the region extending from Central America through central Mexico. The area produced several culturally related societies before the 15th century. The most well-known cultures are the Olmec, Maya, Teotihuacan, and Aztec. All of these groups grew corn (maize), worshiped many different gods, used numbering systems and calendars, and studied the stars. They also built pyramids that still survive. Some people believe that the Maya had very advanced knowledge of acoustics, or the science of sound. It is said that if you stand at the base of the Mayan Temple of Kukulcan and clap your hands, the echo sounds like the call of the quetzal bird. The quetzal bird was sacred in Mayan culture. How the Maya achieved this effect, and whether they did so on purpose, is one of the many mysteries surrounding this culture.

DURING READING

Visualize Visualizing is picturing in your mind the details of the setting, events, and characters in the text. Encourage students to draw pictures or diagrams of these images as they read.

AFTER READING

Respond to the Article Have students write a journal or blog entry about the Mayan people. Ask students: What accomplishments of the Maya surprised you the most? How do you think the Maya were able to do such great things without modern technology? What theories about the disappearance of the Maya do you think are true? Why do you think so?

Support Individual Learners

DIFFERENTIATED INSTRUCTION

Poetry is a good resource for helping students visualize something. Choose a poem that describes a place or a behavior to which students could make connections. Read the stanzas to the students. Have them act out what they see in their mind's eye. Then have them sketch or write a description of their visualizations.

ENGLISH LANGUAGE LEARNERS

Have students take turns describing one of their favorite places to other students. As they describe it, ask the other students to visualize what the place is like and then draw pictures or write descriptions of the place. Have students ask questions if they need additional information to clarify their visualizations.

GRAPHIC ORGANIZERS

📖 Go to **www.mhereadingbasics.com.** Use Graphic Organizer 2 to classify information from the article. Make copies for each student. Have students label the top of the left column *What the Maya Did* and the top of the right column *Why the Maya Disappeared*. Students can work with you to add information from the selection to the appropriate column on their charts. Remind students that no one knows for sure why the Maya disappeared—the article explains some theories.

Lesson Plan Introductory Reader

Unit 2 Lesson 2.5 🔊 "Journey to Saturn," pages 73–80

Introduce

Summary In 2004 the spacecraft *Cassini* went into orbit around Saturn. Other spacecraft have flown by Saturn, but *Cassini* is the first spacecraft to orbit the planet. *Cassini* contained a probe named Huygens that was dropped onto Titan, Saturn's largest moon, in early 2005. More than 8,000 scientists and workers from 18 countries have worked on the *Cassini* mission. It took *Cassini* almost seven years to reach Saturn. The pictures sent back by *Cassini* since it reached Saturn have helped scientists learn new things about the planet.

Teach Lesson Skills

BEFORE READING

Build Vocabulary List the vocabulary words and their definitions on the board. Discuss each word's meaning with students. Then write the sentences that contain the words on the board. Read the sentences aloud and discuss them with students.

spacecraft: a ship that flies through space

orbit: the path a spacecraft flies on around a planet

mammoth: huge

launch: the act of sending off

destination: the place someone or something is going toward

astounding: very surprising

1. Sputnik I became the first *spacecraft* to enter outer space in October 1947.
2. Sputnik I's *orbit* of the Earth took only 98 minutes.
3. She had to study for a *mammoth* test.

4. The *launch* of a rocket is an amazing thing to watch.
5. On one flight, the final *destination* was the moon.
6. The first landing of men on the moon was *astounding* for people who thought it couldn't happen.

Activate Prior Knowledge

1. Invite students to share information they know about Saturn. *(Possible answers: The planet has rings. It has numerous moons. It is made up of gasses. It is the sixth planet from the sun.)*
2. Use Graphic Organizer 3 as a KWL Chart. Have students label the first column *Know* and write what they already know about Saturn or about space exploration. Have students label the middle column *Want to Know* and write what they would like to learn about these topics. For more information, see http://saturn.jpl.nasa.gov/home/index.cfm.

Preview and Predict Ask students what clues the title of the article, the photograph, and the photo caption provide. What predictions about the article might students make? *(Possible answer: This spacecraft was sent to Saturn to explore the planet. I think I will read about what was learned during the journey.)*

Build Background Saturn is the sixth planet from the sun and the second largest planet in our solar system. It takes 29.5 Earth years for Saturn to make one complete trip around the sun. Saturn has been known for many centuries because it is so bright in the night sky. Before the *Cassini* mission, most of what we knew about the planet came from *Voyager*, the first spacecraft to go near Saturn in 1980. Saturn's moon Titan is very interesting to scientists because it is the only body in the solar system other than Earth known to have a significant amount of nitrogen in its atmosphere. Nitrogen is one of the basic building blocks for life on Earth. Scientists think that by finding out more about Titan, they can understand more about how Earth and its life forms developed. The Cassini mission was extended through September 2010.

DURING READING

Infer An inference is a logical guess about what the writer suggests but doesn't directly state. Making inferences helps readers find deeper meaning in what they read. Ask students to look for details that aren't fully explained. Have them combine clues from the text with their personal knowledge to identify what the writer suggests.

AFTER READING

Respond to the Article Have students write a journal or blog entry about their reaction to the goals the scientists set out to accomplish with the *Cassini-Huygens* mission. Ask students to predict what *Cassini-Huygens* may find as it explores Saturn and its moons. Have students predict what the future holds for space exploration and travel.

Support Individual Learners

DIFFERENTIATED INSTRUCTION
Collect articles, headlines, jokes, or cartoons that require students to make inferences to fully understand the texts. Have students work together in groups to make inferences based on the texts. The dialogue among students builds background knowledge, and those who have difficulty with this skill can learn from those who are more adept at it. Have groups share their inferences with the class.

ENGLISH LANGUAGE LEARNERS
Picture books for older readers can be useful for helping students understand the concept of making inferences. Have students read the books in small groups and make three inferences about what happened in each book. For example, *Smoky Night*, by Eve Bunting and David Diaz, addresses the issue of the Los Angeles riots.

GRAPHIC ORGANIZER
📖 Go to **www.mhereadingbasics.com.** Use Graphic Organizer 3 as a KWL Chart. Make copies for each student. Have students use the charts they started before reading the article. If students did not do this exercise before reading, they can start it now. Students should label the third column *Learned* and add in any information they learned from the article about Saturn or about space exploration. Students may wish to add more questions to the *Want to Know* column. Have students discuss their charts. Encourage students to find answers to their questions online or at the library.

Lesson Plan Introductory Reader

Unit 3 Lesson 3.1 🔊 "Separate Lives," pages 81–88

Introduce

Summary Two conjoined twin girls born in Uganda were joined from the chests to the hips. Conjoined twins are very rare—only about 200 sets of them are born every year, and sadly many of them die. Dr. Cindy Howard of the University of Maryland Medical Center happened to be at a Ugandan hospital when the newborn conjoined twin girls were brought in. She arranged for the girls and their parents to go to Maryland for an operation. A volunteer medical team of 35 people conducted a 12-hour surgery that successfully separated the two girls.

Teach Lesson Skills

BEFORE READING

Build Vocabulary List the vocabulary words and their definitions on the board. Discuss each word's meaning with students. Then write the following questions on the board. Read the questions aloud and discuss the answers with students.

newborn: just born

pregnancy: the state of having a baby growing inside the body

identical: exactly the same

incomplete: not finished

vein: a blood vessel

inherent: built in

1. Which word goes with "two days old"? *(newborn)*
2. Which word goes with "natural"? *(inherent)*
3. Which word goes with "part" or "half-done"? *(incomplete)*
4. Which word goes with "baby"? *(pregnancy or newborn)*
5. Which word goes with "two of a kind"? *(identical)*
6. Which word goes with "flow" and "body?" *(vein)*

Activate Prior Knowledge

1. Ask students what they know about twins. *(Students may know that twins can come from one egg or from two separate eggs.)* Invite them to share what they know about conjoined twins.

2. Ask students: Have you ever heard or read about doctors and other professionals who help people for free? Why do you think doctors might help people without charging them for their services? What do you think motivates people to help others?

Build Background
Conjoined twins used to be known as Siamese twins because the most famous pair of conjoined twins came from Siam, which is now called Thailand. In the past, conjoined twins were often put in circus shows or locked away, or scientists performed experiments on them. Today conjoined twins are more accepted and can live relatively normal lives. Conjoined twins also have a much greater chance of surviving surgery to separate them than in the past. This is because doctors have many more modern tools to work with as well as greater knowledge of the human body than before.

Preview and Predict Ask students what clues the title of the article, the photograph, and the photo caption provide. What predictions about the article might students make? *(Possible answer: This article tells about twins who were conjoined and are now separated. The twins look like they are doing fine.)*

DURING READING

Determine Word Meanings from Context Think of context as the words or sentences that surround a word you don't know. This information can help you make a good guess about what the word means. Have students look for clues such as descriptions, synonyms, or examples to help them figure out the meaning of an unfamiliar word.

AFTER READING

Respond to the Article Have students write a journal or blog entry about the doctor's actions. Ask: Why do you think Dr. Howard decided to help the Ugandan family? What do you think would have happened to the girls if they had not gotten Dr. Howard's help? How do you think the parents felt before, during, and after the surgery?

Support Individual Learners

DIFFERENTIATED INSTRUCTION

Ask students to bring in some song lyrics or poems that contain words that may be unfamiliar to other students. Have students take turns explaining to the class how they determined the meaning of an unfamiliar word using context clues.

ENGLISH LANGUAGE LEARNERS

Show students how to use appositives to define a word within a sentence. Point out that when commas surround a phrase, the writer might be using the phrase to describe or define the word that comes before it. Provide an example, such as "Chet claims his inherent, natural, speed will be enough to win any race."

GRAPHIC ORGANIZER

🔵 Go to **www.mhreadingbasics.com.** Use Graphic Organizer 5 as a Sequence-of-Events Chart. Make copies for each student. Ask students to write the following events in order in the boxes of the chart according to what they learned in the article. Discuss their responses.

The girls returned to Uganda.

The doctors finished the surgery.

The doctors practiced the surgery with dolls.

The girls' rib cages had to be divided.

Lesson Plan Introductory Reader

Unit 3 Lesson 3.2 🔊 "Together Again after 50 Years," pages 89–96

Introduce

Summary In 1950 war broke out between North and South Korea, trapping many South Koreans in North Korea. Ryang Han-sang was one of these people. It was not until 50 years later that the North and South Korean governments, technically still at war, allowed Ryang and others to visit their families for three days in South Korea. Ryang's mother was ill and not able to get to the official meeting site. Afraid he would not get to see his mother, Ryang and his family finally found a way.

Teach Lesson Skills

BEFORE READING

Build Vocabulary List the vocabulary words and their definitions on the board. Discuss each word's meaning with students. Then write the following questions on the board. Read the questions aloud and discuss the answers with students.

contact: a bringing together

reunions: get-togethers for people who are separated

siblings: brothers and sisters

technically: officially

bitterly: angrily

regards: messages of love and respect

1. What word goes with "telling someone you care"? *(regards)*
2. What word goes with "together"? *(reunions)*
3. What word goes with "family"? *(siblings)*
4. What word goes with "the way things really are"? *(technically)*
5. What word goes with "upset"? *(bitterly)*
6. What word goes with "telephone call"? *(contact)*

Activate Prior Knowledge

1. Ask students what families who are separated by divorce or other circumstances can do to remain close.
2. Help students locate North and South Korea on a map.

Preview and Predict Ask students what clues the title of the article, the photograph, and the caption provide. What predictions about the article might students make? *(Possible answer: Siblings are briefly reunited after being separated for 50 years.)*

Build Background Korea was divided into two countries after World War II. North Korea, a communist country, was led by Kim Il-sung. South Korea, a democracy, was led by Syngman Rhee. The North Koreans wanted to unify the country, and they were willing to use force to do so. On June 25, 1950, North Korea launched an attack on South Korea, starting the Korean War. The war lasted until 1953. Millions of people were separated from their families during the war. North and South Korea remain officially at war today. In recent years, the two governments have talked about peace. Many people in North and South Korea hope for a reunited country.

DURING READING

Ask Questions Questioning helps you to monitor your understanding of the text. Have students ask *who, what, where, when, why,* and *how* questions and look for the answers. Questions may include: Whom is the article mainly about? What problem did that person face? How was the problem resolved? Where did the events take place?

AFTER READING

Respond to the Article Have students write a journal or blog entry about their responses to the situation Ryang Han-sang and his family faced. Ask students: Why do you think the government did not let Ryang Han-sang visit his mother? How do you think Ryang felt when he saw his mother?

Support Individual Learners

DIFFERENTIATED INSTRUCTION

Have students choose a newspaper article that interests them. Then have them pretend that they are the editor of the paper, who wants more information about the article. Have them write at least five questions the editor can ask the writer to gain the additional information.

ENGLISH LANGUAGE LEARNERS

Have students scan an article from a magazine that includes pictures. Ask them to come up with three questions about the pictures accompanying the article. Then have students read the article with a partner to find out if their questions about the pictures are answered in the text.

GRAPHIC ORGANIZERS

📖 Go to **www.mhereadingbasics.com.** Use Graphic Organizer 2 as a Fact-and-Opinion Chart. Make copies for each student. Ask students to write *Fact* at the top of the left column and *Opinion* at the top of the right column. Then have students organize the following sentences about the article according to whether each sentence is a fact or opinion. Discuss their responses.

Ryang Han-sang grew up in southern Korea.

Ryang's mother should not have worried about her son.

Three days were not enough for the families to be together.

Ryang could see his mother at a hospital.

It was wrong for Ryang to be angry when he thought he could not see his mother.

Ryang spoke to his mother on the phone.

Introductory Reader

Introduce

Summary Caton Parelli was born with a virus that affected his brain. His parents were told he would probably never walk or talk. His father was a horse trainer and liked to take Caton for rides on a horse. Riding helped Caton learn to sit up, and eventually he learned to speak and walk. His parents believe it was because of the horseback rides. Other special-needs children have been helped by riding horses. Horses walk in a similar fashion to humans, so riding horses helps people gain a sense of balance. This article tells the stories of several children helped in this way.

Teach Lesson Skills

BEFORE READING

Build Vocabulary List the vocabulary words and their definitions on the board. Discuss each word's meaning with students. Then write the following questions on the board. Read the questions aloud and discuss the answers with students.

infant: a young baby

excellent: very good

responsible: deserving of thanks or blame

stirrups: flat-bottomed rings that hang from a saddle and are used to hold a rider's feet

bonding: process of connecting

countless: too many to be counted

1. If someone was just born, would that person be an *infant* or an adult? Why?
2. Which do you think is *excellent*—having a sunny day or getting soaked in the rain? Why?
3. What would make you feel *responsible*—something you did or something someone else did? Why?

4. Would you use *stirrups* to ride a horse or a bicycle? Why?
5. Which is a better example of *bonding*—a dog feeding her puppies or a fish in a fish bowl? Why?
6. Which would be *countless*—the stars in the sky or the steps on a ladder? Why?

Activate Prior Knowledge

1. Ask students to share what they know about horses. Have them make a list of adjectives describing horses.
2. Have students discuss how they think a horse might help people. Ask them to share any stories they may have heard about how horses have helped people.

Preview and Predict Ask students what clues the title of the article, the photograph, and the photo caption provide. What predictions about the article might students make? *(Possible answer: Riding horses has helped special-needs children both physically and emotionally.)*

Build Background Children often get sick with colds or the flu, but they almost always get better. Some children, however, are born with disabilities and conditions they will have for the rest of their lives. One of these is cerebral palsy. Cerebral palsy makes it difficult or impossible to move certain parts of the body. People with cerebral palsy sometimes cannot walk and have trouble with other physical activities such as feeding themselves. Cerebral palsy has no cure, but different kinds of therapy can help people with this condition to move, talk, and feel better about themselves.

DURING READING

Find Vocabulary in Context As students read the article, have them note the new vocabulary words. Ask them to think about each word's meaning as they read.

AFTER READING

Respond to the Article Have students write a journal or blog entry about their responses to the way horses help people in the article. Ask students: Why do you think the children responded well to the horses?

Support Individual Learners

DIFFERENTIATED INSTRUCTION

Have students work in pairs to examine a newspaper and find an article that presents at least one problem and one solution. Tell students to search for an article they can act out. Have one student identify the problem and the other student find the solution. The pair of students could then find a way to act out the problem and solution to the class. Allow students to use only one approved prop. Have the rest of the class guess what the problem and solution are.

ENGLISH LANGUAGE LEARNERS

Explain to students that a problem is a difficulty or conflict and a solution is a way to solve the problem. Multiple problems may be solved by one solution, or there may be multiple solutions for one problem. Have students think about a movie or television show they saw recently. Ask them to describe one problem a character experienced and how he or she solved that problem.

GRAPHIC ORGANIZERS

💻 Go to **www.mhereadingbasics.com.**
Use Graphic Organizer 4 as a Cause-and-Effect Chart. Make copies for each student. Ask students to label the left column *Causes* and the right column *Effects*. Have students write each of the sentences below in separate boxes of the *Causes* column. Then ask students to write an effect in separate boxes of the *Effects* column for each *Cause*. Discuss their responses.

Caton had a virus in his brain.

Horses walk a bit like humans and give children a sense of balance.

Horses accept children for who they are.

Vojta is too weak to sit on his horse.

Introduce

Summary Kristina Strode-Penny, an adventure racer, competed in one of the toughest races of all, the Eco-Challenge. In 2002 the Eco-Challenge was held in Fiji. The race covered 300 miles of rough terrain, including mountains, jungles, and swift rivers. Strode-Penny became ill during the race, forcing her four-person team to rest 10 hours in the first three days. This break turned out to be a blessing in disguise, as Strode-Penny's well-rested team passed the other teams and finished first.

Teach Lesson Skills

BEFORE READING

Build Vocabulary List the vocabulary words and their definitions on the board. Discuss each word's meaning with students. Then write the following questions on the board. Read the questions aloud and discuss the answers with students.

rugged: difficult

ultimate: greatest

trudge: walk slowly, in a tired way

constantly: without stopping

disguise: clothes or ways of acting that hide who you are

sprinted: ran fast

1. What might a *rugged* path look like?
2. What would be the *ultimate* reward for passing a tough test in school?
3. What would you think if you saw a runner *trudge* through a race?

4. Does it rain *constantly* in the desert? Why or why not?
5. What would you do if you wanted to *disguise* how you look?
6. Which animal could best be described as having *sprinted* across a field—a horse, a bird, or a turtle?

Activate Prior Knowledge

1. Prompt discussion on physical challenges. Ask students to describe difficult physical activities they have participated in.
2. Invite students to visualize themselves running a race 300 miles long through hot jungles, over high mountains, and across rivers. Ask them what they think some of the challenges of such a race might be.
3. Tell students that they will read about a competition that takes place in Fiji. Help students locate Fiji on a map. Prompt discussion on the likely weather conditions on this island.

Build Background The first Eco-Challenge was held in Utah in 1995, with 50 four-person teams from six countries competing 24 hours a day over a 300-mile course. Eco-Challenge races include mountain climbing, canoeing, horseback riding, kayaking, scuba diving, mountain biking, and running. According to the rules of Eco-Challenge, teams must make as little impact on the land as possible and leave the environment as they found it. If one person on a team quits because of injury or any other reason, the whole team is disqualified from the race. Eco-Challenge races have been held in the United States, Canada, Australia, Argentina, Morocco, Malaysia, and New Zealand.

Preview and Predict Ask students what clues the title of the article, the photograph, and the photo caption provide. What predictions about the article might students make? *(Possible answer: Adventure races are very challenging and require team members to continue even if they are in pain.)*

DURING READING

Visualize Visualizing is picturing in your mind the details of the setting, events, and characters in the text. Encourage students to draw pictures or diagrams of these images as they read.

AFTER READING

Respond to the Article Have students write a journal or blog entry about what motivates people to participate in the Eco-Challenge. Ask students why they think people participate in a race that has these risks. What do they think motivated Kristina Strode-Penny to compete in the Eco-Challenge?

Support Individual Learners

DIFFERENTIATED INSTRUCTION

Poetry is a good resource for helping students visualize something. Choose a poem that describes a place or a behavior to which students could make connections. Read the stanzas to the students. Have them act out what they see in their mind's eye. Then have them sketch or write a description of their visualizations.

ENGLISH LANGUAGE LEARNERS

Have students take turns describing one of their favorite places to other students. As they describe it, ask the other students to visualize what the place is like and then draw pictures or write descriptions of the place. Have students ask questions if they need additional information to clarify their visualizations.

GRAPHIC ORGANIZERS

📖 Go to **www.mhreadingbasics.com.** Use Graphic Organizer 2 as a Fact-and-Opinion Chart. Make copies for each student. Ask students to write *Fact* at the top of the left column and *Opinion* at the top of the right column. Then have students organize the sentences about the article according to whether each sentence is a statement of fact or opinion.

The Seagate team began the race in Fiji.

The Seagate team won the race.

Strode-Penny should have quit when she got sick.

Eco-Challenges are fun.

The race was 300 miles long.

Strode-Penny was very brave.

Lesson Plan Introductory Reader

Summary On June 22, 1996, the Ku Klux Klan held a rally in Ann Arbor, Michigan. Only 15 Klan members showed up, but many protesters came to keep the Klan's voices from being heard. As heated words turned to physical violence, Keshia Thomas risked injury to protect a man with a Confederate flag T-shirt from the protesters. Although Thomas did not agree with this man's views, she believed he should not be attacked for holding these views.

Teach Lesson Skills

BEFORE READING

Build Vocabulary List the vocabulary words and their definitions on the board. Discuss each word's meaning with students. Then write the sentences that contain the words on the board. Read the sentences aloud and discuss them with students.

reject: do not accept

tolerated: put up with

rally: a get-together to support a cause

riot: a scene of wild confusion

shielded: protected

cycle: a set of events done over and over

1. She will *reject* any ideas that she does not think will work.
2. He *tolerated* the shoes even though they hurt his feet.
3. The group planned a *rally* to get more support from the people.

4. There was a *riot* in the streets after the basketball game.
5. The baseball player *shielded* her eyes from the sun.
6. The people wanted to stop the *cycle* of hatred.

Activate Prior Knowledge

1. Ask students why they think people might hold a rally. *(Possible answers: to support a political candidate, to speak out about their beliefs, to gather people together for a common goal)*

2. Discuss with students the meaning of *freedom of speech*. Mention that this right is guaranteed to all U.S. citizens by the Constitution.

   See http://www.house.gov/Constitution/Amend.html, and http://www.usconstitution.com for more information on freedom of speech.

Build Background The Ku Klux Klan, or KKK, was formed in 1866, just after the Civil War. The KKK believes that white people are superior and that they should live separately from other races. It was established to keep power in the hands of southern whites and to stop African Americans from voting or practicing other civil rights. In the early 1900s the KKK added a new message of hate against Jews, Catholics, and immigrants, as well as African Americans. During the Civil Rights Movement of the 1960s, the KKK spoke out again through violence and hate crimes. The Klan still exists today but keeps a low profile and claims to disavow violence.

Preview and Predict Ask students what clues the title of the article, the photograph, and the photo caption provide. What predictions about the article might students make? *(Possible answer: Keshia Thomas risked her life to protect a stranger.)*

DURING READING

Identify Sequence Sequence is the order in which events, ideas, or things are arranged. Time order refers to the order in which events occur. Following the sequence of events helps you see how the text is organized and how events relate to each other. As students read, ask them to look for key words and phrases such as *before, then, later, during,* and *next.*

AFTER READING

Respond to the Article Have students write a journal or blog entry about how Keshia Thomas defended Albert McKeel's right to free speech, even though she did not agree with his views. Ask students: Do you think that freedom of speech is a good thing? Why or why not? What do you think life would be like in the United States without freedom of speech? What parts of the article surprised you, and what parts met your expectations?

Support Individual Learners

DIFFERENTIATED INSTRUCTION

Have students place photographs or magazine pictures in sequence and explain why they chose to order the pictures in time order, in spatial order, in order of importance, or as steps in a process. They could also use objects to create special-order sequences, such as arranging pens, paper clips, and books on a desk. Help them to find signal words to describe the order they chose.

ENGLISH LANGUAGE LEARNERS

Have students describe an event from their past in time order or explain something they can do using steps in a process. Prompt them to use signal words in their description. Have students create a time line of the events they are describing as a visual aid.

GRAPHIC ORGANIZERS

💻 Go to **www.mhreadingbasics.com.** Use Graphic Organizer 5 as a Sequence-of-Events Chart. Make copies for each student. Ask students to write the following events in order in the boxes of the chart according to what they learned about the KKK rally and Keshia Thomas in the article. Discuss their responses.

Keshia Thomas risked her safety to protect a man.

Someone in the crowd threw a stick.

Hundreds of protesters showed up at the Ku Klux Klan rally.

The police fired tear gas into the crowd.

Name_____ Date _____

Unit 1 Assessment Article

Directions: Read this story. Then answer each question that follows. Circle the letter of your answer.

Not Just Clowning Around

Creed Law knew a lot about driving in mountains. In fact, what he knew and did saved two lives. His actions left him looking like a clown, however.

² It was December 1983. Law was driving his mother-in-law home. The two lived in Jackson Hole, Wyoming. They had been in Idaho. Their route went through the Teton Pass in the Teton Mountains. This pass crosses between Idaho and Wyoming. Part of the road is over 8,400 feet above sea level. That's more than a mile and a half up! In the pass, Law drove into a winter storm. The car spun off the road and into a drift. They were stuck. It could be hours before anyone found them.

³ Usually Law would have been ready. In his car he had a shovel, a signal flag, and a sleeping bag. Unfortunately, he and his mother-in-law were in her car. It held a shovel. It also held carpet samples and a Halloween clown suit.

⁴ Law ran the engine for 10 or 15 minutes each hour. That gave the car heat. He and his mother-in-law put the carpet samples around themselves. That kept the wind out and the heat in. After a few hours, Law had to clean snow out of the tailpipe. Outside, his clothes were soaked by the snow. Back in the car, he changed to the clown suit. He laid his clothes out in the warmed area to dry. Every few hours he repeated this. He changed from clown suit to clothes and back, over and over.

⁵ Before dark, an Idaho road crew drove nearby for a look. The car stuck in the snow was white, so the crew saw nothing and left.

⁶ The next morning Law's wife hired a helicopter. She sent the crew to look for the missing car. The helicopter flew over the car, but once again no one could see it. One more time the helicopter flew over. This time Law heard the engine, jumped out, and waved. Finally, 15 hours after being trapped, Law was seen. This time, he was hard to miss. He was dressed like Bozo the Clown.

⁷ Soon Law and his mother-in-law were aboard the helicopter. Law returned home safely and still in the clown suit. The car could not be dug out for several more days.

⁸ Experts agree that Law and his mother-in-law did just what they had to do. They did not wander away from the car. They did not use up their gas too quickly. They kept the tailpipe clear. They cracked a window to keep the air inside fresh. Having a signal flag might have brought help more quickly. In this case, however, the clown suit did the trick.

INTRODUCTORY READER
Unit 1 Assessment Questions

1. Which sentence best states the main idea of the article?
   a. Creed Law carried a shovel, signal flag, and sleeping bag in his own car, but he ran into trouble in his mother-in-law's car.
   b. When two people were trapped in a car in a winter storm, good thinking and a clown suit saved them.
   c. Drivers who travel in mountains during the winter should be prepared for all kinds of problems with snow.

2. The Teton Pass crosses between
   a. Idaho and Canada.
   b. Wyoming and Canada.
   c. Idaho and Wyoming.

3. Which answer is probably true?
   a. Law's mother-in-law was thankful that he was traveling with her.
   b. Law's mother-in-law always carried at least one clown suit in her car.
   c. Many drivers who hear about this trip will decide to carry clown suits with them.

4. What is the meaning of the underlined word? This road to the cabin is paved, but the dirt path through the woods is a more direct route.
   a. one who gives directions
   b. an object on wheels that can carry people or things from place to place
   c. a way or road for travel

5. What is the author's purpose in writing this article?
   a. to give the reader ideas about how to reuse old Halloween costumes
   b. to tell about a man who used things at hand to save his own life and another's
   c. to explain how to get from Idaho to Jackson Hole, Wyoming

6. Which answer correctly restates this sentence from the story?
   Having a signal flag might have brought help more quickly, but in this case, the clown suit did the trick.
   a. A signal flag can bring help, but a clown suit can help you do tricks.
   b. The trick in using a signal flag correctly is to wear a clown suit at the same time.
   c. In this story, the clown suit did what a signal flag usually does—bring help.

7. Which statement below states an opinion?
   a. Law and his mother-in-law were lucky she hadn't cleaned out her car since Halloween.
   b. Every few hours Law got out of the car to clean snow out of the tailpipe.
   c. The road that goes through the Teton Pass is used by people traveling between Idaho and Wyoming.

8. Law and his mother-in-law are alike because
   a. they both put on clown suits when their clothes got soaked by snow.
   b. they both put carpet samples around themselves to keep warm.
   c. Law kept a sleeping bag and signal flag in his car, and his mother-in-law kept carpet samples and a clown suit in hers.

9. Which paragraph provides information that supports your answer to question 8?
   a. paragraph 4
   b. paragraph 3
   c. paragraph 2

10. What caused the helicopter to fly over the trapped car?
    a. Law's wife hired the helicopter to search for the car.
    b. Law was dressed like a clown.
    c. The car could not be dug out of the snow.

INTRODUCTORY READER

Unit 2 Assessment Article

Directions: Read this story. Then answer each question that follows. Circle the letter of your answer.

The Nicholas Effect

The Greens were on their way from California to Italy. As their trip began, the family made up a game. In the game, Nicholas, seven years old, was a soldier going back to his home in ancient Rome. The soldier was a hero. The people of Rome would name streets after him. They would give him a gold medal. The family could not have guessed how much of the game would come true.

² In Italy the Greens rented a car. A few days later, they were driving on a main road. In a nearby car were two young men. The young men were looking for another car that looked like the Greens' car. The other car was carrying precious jewels to stores. The men wanted to steal the jewels. When they saw the Greens' car, they thought it was the one with the jewels. One of the men shot at the Greens' car. He shot Nick in the head.

³ Nick was rushed to a hospital. The doctors did all they could. Nick's parents waited in the hospital for news, worrying about Nick. They also thought of other sick or hurt people in the hospital. Some of those patients needed new hearts. Others needed lungs, eyes, or other organs. The organs they needed would have to come from people who died. Families of the dead people would have to decide whether to donate, or give, the organs.

⁴ Two days later, Nick died. When they heard the sad news, Nick's parents sat for a while in silence. Then one said, "Now that he's gone, shouldn't we donate the organs?" "Yes," the other said.

⁵ Within a few days, seven people in Italy received organs from Nick. Four of the people were teenagers. Without these organs, five of the seven would have died within weeks. Instead, their lives were saved.

⁶ The news of what had happened spread through Italy. Italians were surprised. Few people there thought of donating organs. They wasted the chance to save others' lives. Now this American couple and their son had saved seven Italians. Soon streets, parks, and schools were named after Nicholas Green. A gold medal was made to honor him.

⁷ One more good thing happened. More Italians thought of donating organs. Soon three times as many Italians said their organs should be donated. This change was called "the Nicholas effect."

⁸ One Italian girl named Pia was dying when she received Nick's liver. With the new liver, she soon got well. In a few years, she married and had a baby. She named her boy Nicholas.

INTRODUCTORY READER

Unit 2 Assessment Questions

1. Which sentence best states the main idea of the article?
   a. When their son was killed in Italy, an American couple donated his organs to save lives, and others chose to donate organs too.
   b. Seven-year-old Nicholas Green was killed when robbers thought the car he was in was carrying jewels.
   c. Not enough people leave orders that their organs should be donated to sick people who need them.

2. The organs that Nicholas Green's parents donated went to
   a. seven teenagers.
   b. five people.
   c. seven people.

3. Which answer is probably true?
   a. Many travelers in Italy are killed by jewel robbers.
   b. Organs may not be taken from the body of a dead child unless the child's parents allow it.
   c. Because of the Nicholas effect, everyone in Italy who needs a new organ gets it easily.

4. What is the meaning of the underlined word? When you smoke, your heart is not the only organ that you hurt.
   a. a part of the body, such as the lungs, with a particular job
   b. a game of cards that you play by yourself
   c. the smell of something burning

5. The main purpose of the first paragraph is to
   a. explain why ancient Rome was important.
   b. make the reader wonder what would happen to Nicholas.
   c. tell how the Greens traveled from California to Italy.

6. Which statement below is the weakest argument for choosing to have your organs donated?
   a. You may have a park named for you.
   b. Your organs may save other people's lives.
   c. Knowing that your organs are helping other people may make your family feel less sad about your death.

7. Which answer correctly restates this passage from the story?
   The family could not have guessed how much of the game would come true.
   a. The family was playing a guessing game but not making good guesses.
   b. The family did not know that some of what they were pretending would come true.
   c. In their game, family members guessed the answers to true-or-false questions.

8. From information in the article, you can predict that
   a. Nick's parents will leave orders that their organs should be donated, if possible.
   b. Americans traveling in Italy will never again rent cars there.
   c. everyone whose organs are donated will have streets named after him or her.

9. Which answer states an effect of Nicholas Green's death?
   a. Two young robbers shot at the car that the Green family was using.
   b. The doctors did all they could, but it was not enough.
   c. An Italian girl named Pia received one of his organs and got well.

10. Nick's parents and Pia are alike because
    a. they both named their sons Nicholas.
    b. they were all Italian.
    c. they each received one of Nicholas's organs.

Name_____ Date _____

INTRODUCTORY READER

Unit 3 Assessment Article

Directions: Read this story. Then answer each question that follows. Circle the letter of your answer.

Walking the Walk

Granny D started her walk with pain in her joints. Then problems with heat, cold, and wind came up. The 89-year-old just moved on. She was walking across the United States to send a message to Congress.

2 Granny D's real name was Doris Haddock. In 1998 she had something to say to lawmakers. She decided to do something unusual. That would make her news. Then, perhaps, people would listen to her. So on the first day of 1999, Haddock started from California for Washington, D.C. Soon people from coast to coast knew her as Granny D.

3 Each day, Granny D walked about 10 miles. She stopped along the way to give speeches. In each speech she explained why she was walking.

4 She thought that the way money was raised for election campaigns was wrong. Rich people and companies gave large amounts of money to campaigns. Their money helped elect certain lawmakers. Then those lawmakers helped the people and companies that had given money. They voted for laws that favored those people and companies. That was not fair to everyone else.

5 Some U.S. senators wanted to change this system. They wanted to limit how much money a person or company could give to a campaign. They asked Congress to vote for a law that would set limits. Granny D wanted to show her support for this law and to get other people to support it too. She carried a flag stating her feelings. All along the way she urged people to sign a letter. It asked members of Congress to vote for the law.

6 In Arizona, Granny D went into a hospital for a while. Lack of water had made her sick. Then in Texas she was almost swept off the road by a tornado. Months later she climbed the Appalachian Range. The snow and wind of a blizzard made the climb very hard.

7 She had hoped to reach Washington, D.C., by her 90th birthday, January 24. She had to spend that day on the road. In February deep snow lay between her and Washington, D.C. So she skied 100 miles. By the end of her trip, Granny D had traveled 3,200 miles on foot.

8 Finally, on February 29, 2000, she reached Washington, D.C. Several dozen members of Congress joined her for the last few miles. Granny D had made her point. People across the country wanted changes in how campaigns received money. Congress had to pay attention.

9 In March 2002 Congress passed the law that was the reason for Granny D's long walk.

Name_____ Date _____

INTRODUCTORY READER
Unit 3 Assessment Questions

1. Which sentence best states the main idea of the article?
   a. Every person in the United States should tell Congress what he or she thinks about laws.
   b. On February 29, 2000, Granny D reached Washington, D.C., after walking 3,200 miles.
   c. By walking across the United States, an 89-year-old woman helped get a law passed.

2. Granny D turned 90 years old
   a. before she started her walk across the United States.
   b. about a month before she ended her walk.
   c. the day she arrived in Washington, D.C.

3. Which answer is probably true?
   a. Although Granny D asked them, few people signed the letter in support of the law.
   b. Because of her age, Granny D walked only when the weather was good.
   c. Getting a law passed may take months or even years.

4. What is the meaning of the underlined word? It's hard for Dad to hold a hammer because of pain in the joints of his fingers.
   a. the ends of long bones
   b. the part where two bones meet that lets them move separately
   c. the act of moving one's hand back and forth to greet another person

5. Choose the statement below that you believe the author would agree with.
   a. Granny D is a good example of a concerned citizen.
   b. Everyone with something to say about our laws must walk across the country to say it.
   c. People over 65 should not put their health at risk by going outside in bad weather.

6. The author uses the first sentence of the article to
   a. let the reader know where and when the story takes place.
   b. tell the reader a little about Granny D.
   c. compare Granny D with a younger person.

7. Which answer correctly restates this passage? She was walking across the United States to send a message to Congress.
   a. She didn't trust the mail, so she was carrying a letter to Congress by herself.
   b. The message that she had for Congress was that she was walking across the country.
   c. The reason for her walk was to get Congress members to pay attention to what she said.

8. Which statement below states a fact?
   a. Lawmakers should not make laws to help their friends.
   b. In 2002 Congress passed a law concerning how election campaigns can receive money.
   c. Doris Haddock is a brave woman who doesn't let anything stop her.

9. Which lesson about life does this story teach?
   a. You're never too old to take a stand.
   b. There's some good in every person.
   c. When you get angry, count to 10 before you say anything.

10. If you wanted a law to be passed, how could you use the information in this article?
    a. I'd ask everyone I know to send letters to Congress asking members to vote for the law.
    b. I'd ski to Washington to get the attention of members of Congress.
    c. I'd wait till I was 89 years old and then walk across the country, making speeches in favor of the law.

Introductory Reader

Unit 1 Language Development Activity: *Suffixes*

ESL/DI Skill	*The Suffix* -er: rower, winner

Activity Highlights

1. Suffix diagram: whole class, small group, and individual
2. Analyzing word construction: whole class and small group
3. Sharing personal experiences/opinions: small group
4. Creating sentences orally: individual
5. Creating suffix diagram: individual, small group
6. Note Taker: individual role

Teacher Preparation

1. Review the article "Alone across the Atlantic" (Unit 1, Lesson 1.2, page 9).
2. 🖥 Go to **www.mhereadingbasics.com**. Print a copy of Unit 1 Activity Sheet: *Suffix Diagram* for each student and a copy of Unit 1 Activity Sheet Answers: *Suffix Diagram* for yourself.
3. Write the following sentences on the board: *Andrew was a famous <u>rower</u>. Debra knew that she, too, was a <u>winner</u>.*
4. Draw the blank diagram from Activity Sheet: *Suffix Diagram* (from step 2) on the board.

Activity Steps

1. Review the article "Alone across the Atlantic" (Unit 1, Lesson 1.2, p. 9) with the class.

2. Give one copy of the Unit 1 Activity Sheet: *Suffix Diagram* to each student.

3. Point out the sentences on the board and ask students what word part is in both underlined words (the suffix *-er*). Write *-er* on the board in the middle box of your drawing on the board. Students do the same on their activity sheets.

4. Ask volunteers what a *winner* is and what a *rower* does. Volunteers guess or tell what the suffix *-er* means at the end of a word. *(Possible response: someone who, a person that)*

5. Write *(someone who)* under *-er* in the middle box of your drawing. Students fill in their activity sheets.

6. Write *row* and *win* inside the left-hand boxes of your diagram. Students fill in their own diagrams.

7. Volunteers act out what it means to row. Others tell what winning a game means.

8. Model filling in the second item in the box on the right: "winner (someone who wins)." Note that an extra *n* is added to *winner* to keep the short *i* sound.

9. Students form small groups.

10. Group members help each other complete their activity sheets *(rower [someone who rows])*.

11. Refer to the article theme of being a *winner*. Why was Debra a winner? Students share opinions on what makes a winner, using the model "A winner is someone who ___." *(Possible responses: is good at sports, doesn't give up, is good to other people)* Circulate among the groups to support the conversations.

12. Refer to the article and have students discuss times when they have felt like a winner. Students use the model "I felt like a winner when ___." *(Possible responses: I helped my son understand his homework, my soccer team won a game)* Volunteers share their responses with the class.

13. Each group brainstorms a list of other *-er* words. *(Possible words: teacher, runner, farmer, trumpeter, baker, swimmer)* The group chooses a Note Taker to write down the list. Students take turns forming sentences using the words. Each student picks two words and draws a five-box diagram on his or her sheet, filling it in to show the formation and definition of the chosen words. Group members assist each other as needed.

Unit 2 Language Development Activity: *Syntax*

ESL/DI Skill | *Syntax:* Adjective Placement

Activity Highlights

1. Constructing correct syntax with paper word squares: small group, individual kinesthetic role
2. Discussion/analysis of syntax: small group
3. Sharing prior knowledge of parts of speech: individual

Teacher Preparation

1. Review the article "The Mysteries of the Maya" (Unit 2, Lesson 2.4, page 65).
2. 💻 Go to **www.mhereadingbasics.com**. Print one copy of Unit 2 Activity Sheet: *Word Squares* for each group of 3–5 students.
3. Cut each activity sheet to make a set of 22 paper word squares (one set for each group). Shuffle the squares within each set of 22.

Activity Steps:

1. Review the article "The Mysteries of the Maya" (Unit 2, Lesson 2.4, page 65) with the class.

2. Students form groups of 3–5. Distribute a set of 22 paper word squares from Unit 2 Activity Sheet: *Word Squares* to each group.

3. Each group chooses a student, the Mover, to move the squares around as the group dictates.

4. Write on the board: *The Maya built parks.*

5. Each group finds the paper squares for these words. The Mover puts the squares in the correct order to form the sentence.

6. Tell students that *syntax* means "word order." With help from volunteers, label each word on the board by its part of speech and use those labels to describe the syntax: article, noun, verb, noun. You may want to provide additional instruction in parts of speech.

7. Write the following sentence on the board under the first one: *The parks were big.*

8. The group leaves the first sentence intact and gives the Mover new squares with which to create the second sentence below the first one.

9. Volunteers help you identify the sentence order: article, noun, verb, adjective. Write the parts of speech under the words on the board, stressing that *big* is an adjective and is at the end of the sentence.

10. Leaving the first two sentences intact, groups collaborate to create a third sentence that expresses the combined meaning of the first two, using five of the eight squares. Circulate to check progress. The result should be: *The Maya built big parks.*

11. As you write each word of the third sentence on the board, ask the class to name the part of speech chorally: article, noun, verb, adjective, noun. Point out that the adjective *big* is immediately before the noun. Note the placement of the adjective in this sentence versus its placement in the second sentence.

12. Repeat the process with the following sentences, using the same set of word squares: *The Maya built cities./The cities were great. (The Maya built great cities.); The Maya built fields./The fields were raised. (The Maya build raised fields.); The Maya drank water./The water was fresh. (The Maya drank fresh water.); The Maya made calendars./The calendars were outstanding. (The Maya made outstanding calendars.)* If time permits, give additional practice with sentences created by you and/or the students.

Introductory Reader

Unit 3 Language Development Activity: *Vocabulary Review*

ESL/DI Skill	*Vocabulary Review:* infant, excellent, responsible, countless

Activity Highlights

1. Reading sentences aloud: individual
2. Constructing word meanings from context: whole class
3. Note taking: individual
4. Sharing/summarizing partner's responses: individual
5. Game: whole class

Teacher Preparation

1. Review the article "A Special Kind of Horse Power" (Unit 3, Lesson 3.3, page 97).
2. Write on the board or otherwise present the Lesson 3.3 vocabulary words: *infant* (a young baby), *excellent* (very good), *responsible* (deserving of thanks or blame), *countless* (too many to be counted)
3. Review the interview questions below and have a copy on hand.

Interview Questions

1. Where did you live when you were an **infant**?
2. Who was **responsible** for taking care of you?
3. Name something you did **countless** times in your childhood.
4. Give an example of your idea of an **excellent** place to live.

Activity Steps

1. Review the article "A Special Kind of Horse Power" (Unit 3, Lesson 3.3, page 97) with the class.

2. Review the definitions of the Lesson 3.3 vocabulary with the class.

3. The class discusses how the vocabulary was used in the article. Tell students that they will be interviewing each other using the Lesson 3.3 vocabulary words in a new context.

4. Dictate the first interview question to the class. Each student writes the sentence in his or her notebook.

5. Volunteers read the sentence aloud, first as is and then substituting the definitions on the board for the underlined words. For example: *Where did you live when you were an infant?/Where did you live when you were a young baby?*

6. Students pair off.

7. Partners ask each other the interview question. As one partner answers the question, the other partner takes notes on the answer.

8. Repeat steps 4 to 7 with the number of interview questions desired.

9. When partners have finished asking each other all the questions, the first partner summarizes the second partner's answers to him or her. The second partner suggests any corrections that may be necessary. Partners then reverse the process so that each has acted as interviewer once. Each student summarizes the other's answers to the class.

10. You may extend the activity into a game of "Who Am I?" in which volunteers give you selected interview answers to read aloud and the class tries to guess who was being interviewed in each case.

Introductory Reader

Introductory Reader, Unit 1

Lesson 1.1: A Young Man Speaks Out
A. Recognize and Recall Details
   1. a   2. c   3. a   4. b
B. Find the Main Idea
   1. B   2. N   3. M
C. Summarize and Paraphrase
   1. c   2. b
D. Make Inferences
   1. F   2. C   3. F   4. F   5. F   6. C
E. Recognize Author's Effect and Intentions
   1. b   2. a   3. b
F. Evaluate and Create
   1. c   2. b   3. a

Lesson 1.2: Alone across the Atlantic
A. Recognize and Recall Details
   1. c   2. b   3. a   4. b
B. Find the Main Idea
   1. B   2. N   3. M
C. Summarize and Paraphrase
   1. a   2. b
D. Make Inferences
   1. b   2. c
E. Recognize Author's Effect and Intentions
   1. b   2. c   3. a
F. Evaluate and Create
   1. c   2. a   3. a

Lesson 1.3: Flight to Freedom
A. Recognize and Recall Details
   1. b   2. c   3. a   4. c
B. Find the Main Idea
   1. B   2. M   3. N
C. Summarize and Paraphrase
   1. a   2. c
D. Make Inferences
   1. b   2. a
E. Recognize Author's Effect and Intentions
   1. c   2. b   3. a
F. Evaluate and Create
   1. b   2. a   3. c

Lesson 1.4: The Heroes of Flight 93
A. Recognize and Recall Details
   1. b   2. c   3. a   4. b
B. Find the Main Idea
   1. M   2. B   3. N
C. Summarize and Paraphrase
   1. c   2. a
D. Make Inferences
   1. c   2. b
E. Recognize Author's Effect and Intentions
   1. b   2. c   3. a
F. Evaluate and Create
   1. a   2. c   3. b

Lesson 1.5: Seeing for the First Time
A. Recognize and Recall Details
   1. b   2. a   3. c   4. b
B. Find the Main Idea
   1. B   2. M   3. N
C. Summarize and Paraphrase
   1. c   2. b
D. Make Inferences
   1. a   2. b
E. Recognize Author's Effect and Intentions
   1. b   2. c   3. a
F. Evaluate and Create
   1. a   2. b   3. c

Unit 1 Assessment
Not Just Clowning Around
1. b   2. c   3. a   4. c   5. b
6. c   7. a   8. b   9. a   10. a

Introductory Reader, Unit 2

Lesson 2.1: Pigs to the Rescue
A. Recognize and Recall Details
   1. a   2. b   3. b
B. Find the Main Idea
   1. B   2. M   3. N
C. Summarize and Paraphrase
   1. c   2. a
D. Make Inferences
   1. a   2. c
E. Recognize Author's Effect and Intentions
   1. b   2. c   3. b
F. Evaluate and Create
   1. c   2. c   3. b

Lesson 2.2: In the Line of Fire
A. Recognize and Recall Details
   1. c   2. a   3. c
B. Find the Main Idea
   1. M   2. B   3. N
C. Summarize and Paraphrase
   1. b   2. c
D. Make Inferences
   1. c   2. a
E. Recognize Author's Effect and Intentions
   1. a   2. b   3. b
F. Evaluate and Create
   1. c   2. a   3. b

Lesson 2.3: How Fast Is Too Fast?
A. Recognize and Recall Details
   1. b   2. a   3. c   4. b
B. Find the Main Idea
   1. M   2. N   3. B
C. Summarize and Paraphrase
   1. c   2. a
D. Make Inferences
   1. b   2. a
E. Recognize Author's Effect and Intentions
   1. b   2. a
F. Evaluate and Create
   1. b   2. a   3. c   4. c

Lesson 2.4: The Mysteries of the Maya
A. Recognize and Recall Details
   1. a   2. c   3. a   4. b
B. Find the Main Idea
   1. N   2. M   3. B
C. Summarize and Paraphrase
   1. a   2. b
D. Make Inferences
   1. a   2. b
E. Recognize Author's Effect and Intentions
   1. b   2. c   3. b
F. Evaluate and Create
   1. b   2. a   3. c

Lesson 2.5: Journey to Saturn
A. Recognize and Recall Details
   1. a   2. b   3. c   4. c
B. Find the Main Idea
   1. N   2. B   3. M
C. Summarize and Paraphrase
   1. a   2. c
D. Make Inferences
   1. b   2. c
E. Recognize Author's Effect and Intentions
   1. a   2. b   3. c
F. Evaluate and Create
   1. c   2. c   3. a

Unit 2 Assessment
The Nicholas Effect
1. a   2. c   3. b   4. a   5. b
6. a   7. b   8. a   9. c   10. a

Introductory Reader, Unit 3

Lessson 3.1: Separate Lives

A. Recognize and Recall Details
  1. c   2. b   3. a
B. Find the Main Idea
  1. M   2. N   3. B
C. Summarize and Paraphrase
  1. c   2. a
D. Make Inferences
  1. c   2. a
E. Recognize Author's Effect and Intentions
  1. a   2. b   3. c
F. Evaluate and Create
  1. b   2. a

Lesson 3.2: Together Again after 50 Years

A. Recognize and Recall Details
  1. a   2. c   3. a   4. b
B. Find the Main Idea
  1. B   2. M   3. N
C. Summarize and Paraphrase
  1. c   2. a
D. Make Inferences
  1. b   2. c
E. Recognize Author's Effect and Intentions
  1. a   2. b   3. a
F. Evaluate and Create
  1. b   2. c   3. a

Lesson 3.3: A Special Kind of Horse Power

A. Recognize and Recall Details
  1. a   2. c   3. b   4. b
B. Find the Main Idea
  1. B   2. M   3. N
C. Summarize and Paraphrase
  1. c   2. b
D. Make Inferences
  1. b   2. a
E. Recognize Author's Effect and Intentions
  1. a   2. b   3. c
F. Evaluate and Create
  1. b   2. b   3. c

Lesson 3.4: Racing through the Pain

A. Recognize and Recall Details
  1. b   2. a   3. c
B. Find the Main Idea
  1. N   2. M   3. B
C. Summarize and Paraphrase
  1. a   2. b
D. Make Inferences
  1. c   2. a
E. Recognize Author's Effect and Intentions
  1. b   2. c
F. Evaluate and Create
  1. b   2. a   3. c   4. a

Lesson 3.5: In the Face of Danger

A. Recognize and Recall Details
  1. b   2. a   3. b   4. c
B. Find the Main Idea
  1. M   2. B   3. N
C. Summarize and Paraphrase
  1. a   2. b
D. Make Inferences
  1. a   2. a
E. Recognize Author's Effect and Intentions
  1. b   2. b   3. c
F. Evaluate and Create
  1. b   2. a   3. a

Unit 3 Assessment

Walking the Walk
1. c   2. b   3. c   4. b   5. a
6. b   7. c   8. b   9. a   10. a

Introductory Reader
Units 1–3

Lesson 1.1: A Young Man Speaks Out
Graphic Organizer 5: Sequence-of-Events Chart
Nkosi and his mother left their village.
Nkosi fought to be allowed to go to school.
Nkosi spoke to a crowd of 10,000 people.
Nkosi went into a coma.

Lesson 1.2: Alone across the Atlantic
Graphic Organizer 2: Fact-and-Opinion Chart
It was a mistake for the Veals to enter the race.
Opinion
Andrew should have tried harder to keep rowing.
Opinion
Debra rowed 2,650 miles by herself. *Fact*
Debra had more courage than her husband.
Opinion
Debra faced the dangers of sharks and huge ships.
Fact
Debra's courage made her the biggest winner in the race. *Opinion*

Lesson 1.3: Flight to Freedom
Graphic Organizer 5: Sequence-of-Events Chart
Fernandez tried to go to Mexico.
Fernandez got a fake passport.
Fernandez built up her weight.
Fernandez told her daughter about her plan.

Lesson 1.4: The Heroes of Flight 93
Graphic Organizer 1: Characteristics Map
Possible answers:
brave: The passengers were brave because they stormed the cockpit.
loving: Todd Beamer was loving because he tried to call his family.
scared: The passengers were scared because the article says they were terrified.
smart: Sandy Bradshaw was smart because she figured out how to use a coffeepot as a weapon.
heroic: The passengers were heroic because they saved the lives of many people.

Lesson 1.5: Seeing for the First Time
Graphic Organizer 5: Sequence-of-Events Chart
A stranger took Harun to an eye hospital.
A doctor helped Harun see.
Harun asked for help from people in his village.
Harun's children saw their mother.

Lesson 2.1: Pigs to the Rescue
Graphic Organizer 3: Categories Chart
Possible answers:
Iggy:
Belonged to Cathy Carder
Lived in West Virginia
Woke her owner up from a nap by grunting and barking
Warned her owner of a fire
Saved her owner and her two sons
Honeymoon:
Belonged to the Abmas
Threw himself against the door to wake his owners
Warned his owners of a fire
Saved his owners and their home
LuLu:
Belonged to the Altsmans
Squeezed through a doggy door
Stopped traffic
Saved her owner who was having a heart attack
Was on TV and in the newspaper

Lesson 2.2: In the Line of Fire
Graphic Organizer 4: Cause-and-Effect Chart
Possible answers:
Effects:
Rascon joined the Army.
Rascon was injured by an exploding grenade; pieces of metal flew into his stomach and face; saving the gun saved Americans' lives.
Rascon saved the man's life; he suffered more wounds; he bled from the ears and nose; he lost his hearing.
President Clinton awarded Rascon a Medal of Honor in 2000.

Lesson 2.3: How Fast Is Too Fast?

Graphic Organizer 2: Fact-and-Opinion Chart

Roller coasters can go from zero to 80 miles an hour in less than three seconds. *Fact*

The woman who lived after she had blood clots in her brain was lucky. *Opinion*

Roller coasters are fun. *Opinion*

Experts studied roller coasters and their g-forces. *Fact*

Lesson 2.4: The Mysteries of the Maya

Graphic Organizer 2: Classification Chart

Possible answers:

What the Maya Did:

They built cities with wide streets and big parks.

They made huge temples.

They were good farmers.

They were great artists.

They wrote books.

They were talented in math and science.

They made calendars and used a number system.

They built a huge room in such a way that a whisper at one end could be heard at the opposite end.

Why the Maya Disappeared:

There were fights between the rich and the poor.

There were wars between cities.

There was a lack of rain.

There was no fresh water.

The cities were too crowded.

Lesson 2.5: Journey to Saturn

Graphic Organizer 3: KWL Chart

Possible answers:

Learned:

Cassini was launched on October 15, 1997.

The purpose of the mission was to increase scientists' knowledge about Saturn.

Saturn is made of mostly gas and is large enough for 750 Earths to fit inside.

Cassini took 300,000 pictures during the four years it orbited Saturn.

Lesson 3.1: Separate Lives

Graphic Organizer 5: Sequence-of-Events Chart

The doctors practiced the surgery with dolls.

The girls' rib cages had to be divided.

The doctors finished the surgery.

The girls returned to Uganda.

Lesson 3.2: Together Again after 50 Years

Graphic Organizer 2: Fact-and-Opinion Chart

Ryang Han-sang grew up in southern Korea. *Fact*

Ryang's mother should not have worried about her son. *Opinion*

Three days were not enough for the families to be together. *Opinion*

Ryang could see his mother at a hospital. *Fact*

It was wrong for Ryang to be angry when he thought he could not see his mother. *Opinion*

Ryang spoke to his mother on the phone. *Fact*

Lesson 3.3: A Special Kind of Horse Power

Graphic Organizer 4: Cause-and-Effect Chart

Possible answers:

Effects:

Caton had trouble walking and talking.

Horses help children with special needs to walk.

Riding a horse lifts a child's spirit.

Vojta lies on the horse when he rides.

Lesson 3.4: Racing through the Pain

Graphic Organizer 2: Fact-and-Opinion Chart

The Seagate team began the race in Fiji. *Fact*

The Seagate team won the race. *Fact*

Strode-Penny should have quit when she got sick. *Opinion*

Eco-Challenges are fun. *Opinion*

The race was 300 miles long. *Fact*

Strode-Penny was very brave. *Opinion*

Lesson 3.5: In the Face of Danger

Graphic Organizer 5: Sequence-of-Events Chart

Hundreds of protesters showed up at the Ku Klux Klan rally.

Someone in the crowd threw a stick.

The police fired tear gas into the crowd.

Keshia Thomas risked her safety to protect a man.

Lesson Plan Intermediate 1 Reader

Introduce

Summary Building a railroad across east Africa in 1898 was a difficult job for the British. When workers reached the Tsavo River, things turned from difficult to deadly. Two large lions began attacking the workers while they slept. The railroad project stopped because many workers, fearing for their lives, ran away or refused to work. Colonel John Henry Patterson, the man in charge of the railroad project, took on the dangerous task of killing the lions. It took several weeks, skillful hunting, and many shots to finally kill both lions. Before Patterson successfully ended the lions' reign of terror, they had taken the lives of 120 railroad workers.

Teach Lesson Skills

BEFORE READING

Build Vocabulary List the vocabulary words and their definitions on the board. Discuss each word's meaning with students. Then write the sentences that contain the words on the board. Read the sentences aloud and discuss them with students.

dragged: pulled

entice: attract

ceased: stopped

crouched: lying close to the ground

shattered: broken

1. The cat *dragged* its toy mouse by the tail.
2. The smell from the bakery will *entice* people to go in.
3. After an hour, the rain *ceased* and we could go outside again.

4. The child *crouched* under the table to hide from her brother.
5. When I dropped the vase, it *shattered* into small pieces.

Activate Prior Knowledge

1. Ask students to name some places where they have seen lions. *(Possible answers: zoos, circuses, nature programs on television)* Explain that African lions used to live in the wild throughout Africa. Today they live mostly in the south Sahara desert and in portions of southern and eastern Africa.

2. Help students locate the Tsavo River in Kenya on a map. Tell students that this is the setting for the article they are about to read.

Build Background Lions are hunters, but they don't typically eat people. They work together to kill large prey, such as zebras, rhinos, hippos, and giraffes. They may also eat leftover food killed by animals such as hyenas. Scientists aren't sure why the Tsavo lions were man-eaters. Some think that disease killed much of the lions' usual prey, so the lions began attacking humans as another source of food. Another theory is that the lions had an infection or other sickness that made it hard for them to hunt and kill large animals. The railroad workers were smaller and slower-moving than other animals, so they would have been easier prey.

Preview and Predict Ask students what clues the title of the article, the photograph, and the photo caption provide. What predictions about the article might students make? *(Possible answer: This article will tell about a period of time when lions were attacking people in Tsavo.)*

DURING READING

Identify Sequence Sequence is the order in which events, ideas, or things are arranged. Time order refers to the order in which events occur. Following the sequence of events helps readers see how the text is organized and how events relate to each other. As students read, ask them to look for key words and phrases such as *meanwhile, soon, then, the next day, when, later, just before, at last,* and *finally*.

AFTER READING

Respond to the Article Have students write a journal or blog entry about Colonel John Henry Patterson's actions. Ask students: Why do you think Colonel Patterson decided to hunt the lions? What might have happened if he had not been successful? How do you think the railway workers felt after Patterson killed the lions?

Support Individual Learners

DIFFERENTIATED INSTRUCTION

Explain that the most common types of sequence are time order, spatial order, order of importance, and steps in a process. Time order refers to the order in which events occur. Spatial order refers to where things are in relation to one another. Order of importance refers to events or ideas arranged from most to least important. Steps in a process refers to the order in which something is done: for example, a recipe.

ENGLISH LANGUAGE LEARNERS

Have students describe an event from their past in time order or explain something they can do using steps in a process. Prompt them to use signal words in their description. Have students create a time line of the events they are describing as a visual aid.

GRAPHIC ORGANIZERS

💻 Go to **www.mhreadingbasics.com.** Use Graphic Organizer 5 as a Sequence-of-Events Chart. Make copies for each student. Have students put the steps below in the correct sequence. Discuss their responses.

Colonel Patterson decided to hunt the lions.

Lions started attacking railroad workers.

The workers returned to work.

Colonel Patterson was in charge of the railroad project in east Africa.

Introduce

Summary In the 1970s French doctors began Doctors Without Borders. The doctors who started the program wanted to make sure that people who needed medical attention were getting it, no matter where they lived or how dangerous or difficult it was to get there. By the 1990s Doctors Without Borders had grown to include thousands of volunteers from around the world. Mary Lightfine, a former emergency room nurse, was one such volunteer. For eight years she traveled around the world treating and comforting people. Though the conditions were difficult, the hours were long, and the pay nonexistent, the gratitude of those she helped was all the payment Lightfine needed.

Teach Lesson Skills

BEFORE READING

Build Vocabulary List the vocabulary words and their definitions on the board. Discuss each word's meaning with students. Then write the following questions on the board. Read the questions aloud and discuss the answers with students.

grim: awful

remote: far away

risky: dangerous

plush: fancy

hardships: difficulties

1. What word goes with "jumping out of an airplane"? *(risky)*
2. What word goes with "challenges"? *(hardships)*
3. What word goes with "a very nice hotel room"? *(plush)*

4. What word goes with "distant"? *(remote)*
5. What word goes with "depressing"? *(grim)*

Activate Prior Knowledge

1. Ask students to give reasons people go to the doctor. *(Possible answers: sore throat, bad cough, injuries, the flu)* Discuss what can happen if people don't get medical care when they are hurt or sick.
2. Help students locate Macedonia, the Sudan, and Nicaragua on a map.

Preview and Predict Ask students what clues the title of the article, the photograph, and the photo caption provide. What predictions about the article might students make? *(Possible answer: A special group of doctors and nurses provide medical aid to people in need around the world.)*

Build Background Around the world, millions of people have left their homes to escape war. They live in camps or shelters. Some are refugees, crossing the border into a nearby country to get away from violence or persecution. Those who aren't able to leave their countries and who try to find shelter in camps or other towns or communities are called internally displaced persons (IDPs). Both of these groups need the basic things required for survival—food, water, shelter, and medical care. Palestine, Afghanistan, Iraq, Colombia, Sudan, Somalia, Myanmar, Haiti, and the Democratic Republic of Congo are just a few of the countries worldwide with people who need aid. Doctors Without Borders works to provide basic and emergency medical care to refugees and IDPs in these countries and regions.

DURING READING

Determine Word Meanings from Context Think of context as the words or sentences that surround a word you don't know. This information can help you make a good guess about what the word means. Have students look for clues such as descriptions, synonyms, or examples to help them figure out what an unfamiliar word means.

AFTER READING

Respond to the Article Have students write a journal or blog entry about the work that Doctors Without Borders does. Ask students: What do you think about the volunteer work Mary Lightfine did? Would you want to volunteer for Doctors Without Borders? Why or why not?

Support Individual Learners

DIFFERENTIATED INSTRUCTION

Ask students to bring in song lyrics or poems that contain words that may be unfamiliar to other students. Have students take turns explaining to the class how they determined the meaning of unfamiliar words using context clues.

ENGLISH LANGUAGE LEARNERS

Tell students that they can sometimes figure out the meaning of an unfamiliar word by seeing how the word relates to other words around it. Use the word *volunteers* in paragraph 4 in the article as an example: "These workers came from 45 different nations. They weren't paid for their services. They were volunteers." Have students use the words *workers* and *weren't paid for their services* in the first two sentences to figure out the meaning of *volunteers*.

GRAPHIC ORGANIZERS

💻 Go to **www.mhereadingbasics.com.**
Use Graphic Organizer 1 as a Concept Map. Make copies for each student. Ask students to write *Mary Lightfine* in the center bubble and one of the phrases below in each other bubble. Have them write sentences by each bubble telling what they learned about Mary Lightfine. Discuss their responses.

Why she joined Doctors Without Borders

Ways she helped

What was difficult

What she enjoyed

Lesson Plan Intermediate 1 Reader

Introduce

Summary In 1971 experts were amazed to discover a Stone Age tribe called the Tasaday, who lived in caves in the rain forests of the Philippines. The tribe members wore clothes made from tree leaves, used stone tools, and gathered food rather than growing it. At first, scientists were excited by the discovery, but the tribe was later revealed to be a hoax. It turned out that the Tasaday were really members of two modern-day tribes who pretended to be cave people to make money. A Philippine official named Manuel Elizalde, who was in charge of protecting all the tribes in the Philippines, was believed to be behind the scam.

Teach Lesson Skills

BEFORE READING

Build Vocabulary List the vocabulary words and their definitions on the board. Discuss each word's meaning with students. Then write the following questions on the board. Read the questions aloud and discuss the answers with students.

innocent: natural; simple

domestic: tame

ancestors: those from whom one is descended

sustain: maintain; keep going

established: modern; up-to-date

1. Who is more likely to be *innocent*, a baby or a teenager? Why?
2. Which is an example of a *domestic* animal, a dog or a wolf?
3. Who are some of your *ancestors*?

4. Would you need to *sustain* your energy for a short walk or a long run? Why?
5. If a city is *established*, what are some things you would expect to see there?

Activate Prior Knowledge

1. Ask students what they know about Stone Age people. Go to http://humanorigins.si.edu/, enter "early stone age tools" in the search box, and click on the second result.
2. Point to the Philippines on a map and, if possible, show photographs of a rain forest. Discuss how the thick rain forests are difficult to explore.

Preview and Predict Ask students what clues the title of the article, the photograph, and the photo caption provide. What predictions about the article might students make? *(Possible answer: The Tasaday were not a real tribe. I will find out why people pretended to be members of the Tasaday.)*

Build Background The Stone Age is a period in human history when people made tools from stone. The earliest such tools that have been discovered are about 2.5 million years old. These tools helped early humans hunt and fish as well as dig roots and cut plants to eat. Stone tools could even be used to chop down trees. At that time, many humans lived in caves or rock shelters. Archeologists have discovered engravings on the walls of ancient caves, proving that Stone Age people also used their tools to make art.

DURING READING

Infer An inference is a logical guess about information that the author suggests but doesn't state directly. Making inferences helps readers find deeper meaning in what they read. Ask students to look for details that aren't fully explained. Have them combine clues from the text with their personal knowledge to identify what the author suggests.

AFTER READING

Respond to the Article Have students write a journal or blog entry about finding out that the Tasaday people were a hoax. Ask students: Why do you think people were fooled by the Tasaday? What parts of the article surprised you, and what parts met your expectations?

Support Individual Learners

DIFFERENTIATED INSTRUCTION

Give students a comic strip or political cartoon that requires them to make inferences in order to understand the text fully. Place students in groups and have them work together to make inferences about the comic strip. The dialogue among students builds background knowledge, and those who have difficulty with this skill can learn from those who are stronger at it. Allow groups to share their inferences with the class.

ENGLISH LANGUAGE LEARNERS

Picture books for older readers can be useful for helping students understand the concept of making inferences. Have students read books in small groups and make three inferences about what happens in each book. For example, *Smoky Night*, by Eve Bunting and David Diaz, addresses the Los Angeles riots. *The Stranger*, by Chris Van Allsburg, tells about a mysterious stranger. The reader must use clues to figure out who he is.

GRAPHIC ORGANIZERS

📖 Go to **www.mhereadingbasics.com**. Use Graphic Organizer 3 as an Inference Chart. Make copies for each student. Ask students to label the columns *What the Text Says, What I Know,* and *My Inference*. Then have students write the information below in the first column. Ask students to complete their charts by filling in the second and third columns. Discuss their responses.

What the Text Says

Elizalde kept people away from the tribe.

The experts faced tough questions.

Before the new government took over, Elizalde disappeared with $35 million.

Intermediate 1 Reader

Lesson Plan Intermediate 1 Reader

Unit 1 Lesson 1.4 🔊 "Near Death on the Football Field," pages 26–33

Summary On December 21, 1997, the New York Jets and the Detroit Lions met to play the game that would decide which team would play in the National Football League playoffs. When Reggie Brown, a linebacker for the Lions, tackled one of the Jets, he injured his spine. The Lions' trainer, Kent Falb, and team doctor, Terry Lock, quickly rushed to Brown's aid. Many people with spinal cord injuries never walk again, but Brown beat the odds. Though he would never be able to play football again, Brown considered himself a lucky man.

Intermediate 1 Reader

Introduce

Teach Lesson Skills

BEFORE READING

Build Vocabulary List the vocabulary words and their definitions on the board. Discuss each word's meaning with students. Then write the following sentence stems on the board. Read the sentence stems aloud and ask students to complete them.

immobile: still

support: hold up

drive: desire

recovered: got better

blacked out: passed out

1. The car is *immobile* because . . .
2. I need crutches to *support* me because . . .
3. The athlete had a strong *drive* to . . .

4. The mother knew her child had *recovered* from her illness because . . .
5. The man who *blacked out* was taken to the hospital because . . .

Activate Prior Knowledge

1. Ask students what they know about football. Have them describe the basic rules of the game and the different positions.
2. Point to a volunteer's spinal cord, showing students how it runs from the base of the brain and down the back.

Preview and Predict Ask students what clues the title of the article, the photograph, and the photo caption provide. What predictions about the article might students make? *(Possible answer: We will find out how Reggie Brown was seriously injured playing football and if he got better.)*

Build Background The spinal cord is a group of nerves that connect the brain to the nerves in the rest of the body. It's the way the brain gets messages to the arms, legs, and other body parts to move or do their jobs. Bony pieces called vertebrae cover and protect the spinal cord. A blow to one of the vertebrae can cause it to fracture or dislocate, pressing down onto the nerve bundle. In this case, the brain can no longer get signals to parts of the body that are below the point of the injury. People with spinal cord injuries may have trouble breathing, have low blood pressure, or be unable to move their arms, legs, or torso.

DURING READING

Cause and Effect A cause is an event or action that makes something else happen. An effect is the result or the outcome of that event or action. Writers use clue words such as *because, so,* and *therefore* to signal cause and effect. Have students look for cause-and-effect relationships by asking: What happened? Why?

AFTER READING

Respond to the Article Have students write a journal or blog entry about Reggie Brown's experience. Ask students: What do you think about the way Reggie Brown recovered from his injury? What part did other people play in helping him to get well? What role did Reggie Brown's own attitude play?

Support Individual Learners

DIFFERENTIATED INSTRUCTION

Kinesthetic learners may benefit from using physical movements to understand cause-and-effect relationships. Have them brainstorm actions in a sport that demonstrate cause-and-effect relationships, such as plays in a soccer match or football game that result in a score. Then have them act out or demonstrate these actions.

ENGLISH LANGUAGE LEARNERS

Have students fold a piece of paper in half lengthwise and label the left side *Cause* and the right side *Effect*. Have them draw or cut out pictures that show cause-and-effect relationships. For example, on the left side, they might draw a person kicking a soccer ball toward a goal, and on the right side, they might show the ball in the goal.

GRAPHIC ORGANIZERS

📖 Go to **www.mhreadingbasics.com.** Use Graphic Organizer 4 as a Cause-and-Effect Chart. Make copies for each student. Have students label the left column *Causes* and the right column *Effects*. Ask students to write each sentence below in a separate box under *Effects*. Then, in the *Causes* column, students should write one cause for each effect. Discuss their responses.

Effects

Reggie Brown could not get up.

Reggie Brown was able to walk again.

Reggie Brown considered himself a lucky man.

Reggie Brown is exploring lots of different paths in life.

Lesson Plan Intermediate 1 Reader

Summary People used to think that identical twins were alike because they grew up in the same environment at the same time. Therefore, it made sense that they learned to like the same things. However, a scientist named Dr. Bouchard decided to take a closer look at the science behind being a twin. He studied pairs of identical twins who had been separated at birth. He found that most had the same hobbies, interests, and habits. They even made identical life choices, including choosing the same career paths and marrying spouses with the same name. We still don't know for sure what this information means. It could be that twins are able to communicate in a way that other siblings are not, or it could simply be that genes are more powerful than we thought.

Introduce

BEFORE READING

Build Vocabulary List the vocabulary words and their definitions on the board. Discuss each word's meaning with students. Then write the sentences that contain the words on the board. Read the sentences aloud and discuss them with students.

coincidence: chance event

weird: odd

communicate: make things known

bond: link

amazing: incredible

1. It was a _coincidence_ that Maya and Susan decided to call each other at the same time.

2. It would be _weird_ to see a two-headed frog.

3. The teacher sent out an e-mail to _communicate_ with his students about a schedule change.

4. The dog had a special _bond_ with its owner.

5. The magician performed _amazing_ tricks for the audience.

Activate Prior Knowledge

1. Ask students what they know about twins. Have them tell about twins they know or have read about. Explain that identical twins have the same genes and look exactly or almost exactly alike.

2. Have students discuss ways they are similar to and different from their brothers, sisters, or other family members. Invite them to share why they think they are alike or different in these ways.

Preview and Predict Ask students what clues the title of the article, the photograph, and the photo caption provide. What predictions about the article might students make? _(Possible answer: The article is about twins and some surprising things about their unique relationships.)_

Build Background Genes are like a pattern, or blueprint, for the body. They carry the information that decides your traits, or hereditary characteristics. Children inherit one copy of each parent's genes. The combination of these genes determines the children's physical features, such as hair color and height, but can also influence behavior and personality. Genes are also responsible for hereditary diseases, such as sickle-cell anemia and cystic fibrosis. Identical twins are identical because they have exactly the same genes.

Teach Lesson Skills

DURING READING

Find Vocabulary in Context As students read the article, have them note the new vocabulary words. Ask them to think about each word's meaning as they read.

AFTER READING

Respond to the Article Have students write a journal or blog entry about the information in the article. Ask students: Why do you think the twins are so much alike? Do you think having the same genes would explain all the ways they are alike? Why or why not?

DIFFERENTIATED INSTRUCTION

Explain that the author's purpose is the reason that an author has written something. Generally, an author will write to persuade, describe, explain, inform, or entertain. An author can have more than one purpose. Then provide students with comics or graphic novels. Have them discuss the cartoonists' or authors' purposes.

ENGLISH LANGUAGE LEARNERS

Have students share words or phrases from their first languages that writers might use for different purposes. For example, English words that may be used to persuade include _fantastic_ or _incredible_. Spanish words may include _muy bueno_ and _excelente_. Descriptive words may include colors. Explanations often include words or phrases such as _because_ or _the reason is_. Informative words could be statements of fact like "It snowed five inches yesterday." Stories that entertain may begin with "It was a dark, stormy night."

GRAPHIC ORGANIZERS

📖 Go to **www.mhereadingbasics.com.**
Use Graphic Organizer 2 as a Fact-and-Opinion Chart. Make copies for each student. Ask students to label the columns _Fact_ and _Opinion_. Have students write the following sentences about identical twins in the correct column. Discuss their responses.

Identical twins have the same genes.

It would be fun to be a twin.

Many twins like the same things and have the same habits.

Some scientists believe genes explain all the similarities between twins.

The special connection between twins is just a coincidence.

Support Individual Learners

Unit 2 Lesson 2.1 🔊 "Mummies," pages 41–48

Introduce

Summary A mummy is more than a bundle of bandages. It is actually a preserved body with skin, bones, and sometimes even muscles, hair, and fingernails. The ancient Egyptians were experts at the complicated process of mummy making. They made mummies because they believed that spirits needed their bodies after death so they could rest. Mummies were also made by people in other parts of the world, such as South America and Italy. While some people think mummies are a good way to honor the dead, others find them horrifying.

Intermediate 1 Reader

Teach Lesson Skills

BEFORE READING

Build Vocabulary List the vocabulary words and their definitions on the board. Discuss each word's meaning with students. Then write the following questions on the board. Read the questions aloud and discuss the answers with students.

decay: rot

thoroughly: completely

shriveled: shrunken and wrinkled

afterlife: life after death

preserve: keep safe from decay

1. Which would *decay*, a seed that has sprouted or a dead tree?
2. If you cleaned your room *thoroughly*, did you clean all of it or part of it?
3. Which is *shriveled*, a raisin or a grape?

4. If a person believes in the *afterlife*, does he or she think life continues after death or ends with death?
5. If you *preserve* something, are you saving it or throwing it away?

Activate Prior Knowledge

1. Ask students what they know about mummies from movies, museums, or books.
2. Point to Egypt on a map and ask students to share what they know about Egyptian culture. They may be familiar with pyramids, pharaohs, or King Tut. For more information go to http://www.ancientegypt.co.uk.

Preview and Predict Ask students what clues the title of the article, the photograph, and the photo caption provide. What predictions about the article might students make? *(Possible answer: The article is about mummies and why ancient Egyptians believed that preserving bodies was important.)*

Build Background Mummies were made as recently as 1920 when Rosali Lombardo was preserved after death. In 2007 scientist Dario Piombino-Mascali discovered the secret formula used to preserve the body of Rosali Lombardo. This recipe had been considered lost to the world when its inventor, Alfredo Salafia, died in 1933. When Piombino-Mascali found out that it was Salafia who embalmed little Rosali, he got in touch with some of Salafia's living relatives and was able to look at the embalmer's papers. Among the notes, Piombino-Mascali found a manuscript that detailed Salafia's special formula for embalming a human body. The secret ingredients, it turned out, were zinc salts. These chemicals allowed the body of Rosali Lombardo to be kept perfectly preserved.

DURING READING

Identify Sequence Sequence is the order in which events, ideas, or things are arranged. Time order refers to the order in which events occur. Following the sequence of events helps you see how the text is organized and how events relate to each other. As students read, ask them to look for key words and phrases such as *first, second, once, then, during, next,* and *finally*.

AFTER READING

Respond to the Article Have students write a journal or blog entry about their feelings regarding mummies. Ask students: How do you feel about the concept of mummy making? Do you think mummies are a good way of honoring the dead? Why or why not?

Support Individual Learners

DIFFERENTIATED INSTRUCTION

Have students place cut-apart comic strips, instructions, or simple steps in a process in sequence and explain what clues they used to determine how the strips, instructions, or steps should be arranged. They could also place magazine pictures or objects around the room and use signal words to describe their locations.

ENGLISH LANGUAGE LEARNERS

Have students describe how to make or do something by using steps in a process. Prompt them to use signal words in their description. Have students pantomime or demonstrate following the steps in the process.

GRAPHIC ORGANIZERS

💻 Go to **www.mhreadingbasics.com**. Use Graphic Organizer 5 as a Sequence-of-Events Chart. Make copies for each student. Have students put the steps below about mummification in the correct sequence. Discuss their responses.

Stuff the body with cloth or sand.

Coat the body with glue.

Dry the body.

Wrap the body in bandages.

Lesson Plan Intermediate 1 Reader

Introduce

Summary On November 4, 1979, a mob of Iranians attacked the U.S. Embassy in Tehran. Fifty-two Americans were captured and held hostage, but six managed to escape the mob. They went to the Canadian Embassy and asked the Canadians to hide them. Even though it was dangerous, Canada's Ambassador, Ken Taylor, agreed. The Canadians hid the Americans and then worked with the CIA to help the Americans get back home by posing as members of a phony Irish film crew. The plan worked, and the Americans made it home safely.

Teach Lesson Skills

BEFORE READING

Build Vocabulary List the vocabulary words and their definitions on the board. Discuss each word's meaning with students. Then write the following questions on the board. Read the questions aloud and discuss the answers with students.

taken hostage: taken prisoner

phony: fake

tense: stressful

flashy: shiny

outrage: anger

1. What word goes with "a red sports car"? *(flashy)*
2. What word goes with "not real"? *(phony)*
3. What word goes with "bad temper"? *(outrage)*

4. What word goes with "held against your will"? *(taken hostage)*
5. What word goes with "anxious"? *(tense)*

Activate Prior Knowledge
1. Ask students what they know about spies and secret agents from reading books or watching movies. Discuss how secret agents might be able to help people in dangerous situations.
2. Point to Iran and Canada on a map. Ask students to share what they know about Canada or the Canadian people. Point out that Canada is sometimes called "our neighbor to the north" and tell students that, like neighbors, Canada and the United States are allies, meaning they help each other.

Build Background The Iran hostage crisis occurred during the presidency of Jimmy Carter. President Carter tried to free the hostages, but his negotiations failed. On January 20, 1981, the hostages were freed after Ronald Reagan was sworn in as president. In 2001 the building of the former U.S. Embassy in Tehran became a museum to the Iranian Revolution. On opposite sides of the entrance to the museum stand two statues: one is a bronze model of the Statue of Liberty; the other is a statue of one of the hostages.

Preview and Predict Ask students what clues the title of the article, the photograph, and the photo caption provide. What predictions about the article might students make? *(Possible answer: The article is about how Canada helped get trapped Americans out of Iran.)*

DURING READING

Ask Questions Questioning helps you to monitor your understanding of the text. Have students ask *who, what, where, when, why,* and *how* questions and look for the answers. Questions may include: What event is this article about? When did the event take place? Who was Antonio Mendez? How did he help the Americans? Why were the Canadians heroes?

AFTER READING

Respond to the Article Have students write a journal or blog entry about the Canadians' actions. Ask students: Why do you think the Canadians decided to help the Americans even though it was risky? What might have happened to the Americans if the Canadians had not decided to help them?

Support Individual Learners

DIFFERENTIATED INSTRUCTION
Have students choose a newspaper article that interests them. Then have them pretend that they are the editor of the paper and want more information about the article. Have them write at least five questions the editor can ask the writer to gain additional information.

ENGLISH LANGUAGE LEARNERS
Have students locate an article in a news magazine. Help students read the headline and picture captions if necessary. Ask them to think of three questions about the pictures accompanying the article. Then have students read the article with a partner to find out if their questions about the pictures are answered in the text.

GRAPHIC ORGANIZERS
💻 Go to **www.mhreadingbasics.com**. Use Graphic Organizer 5 as a Problem-and-Solution Chart. Make copies for each student. Have students write the following problem above the top box. Then have them write the steps leading to the resolution in the other boxes. Finally, have them write the solution below the last box. Discuss their responses.

Problem
Six Americans needed help after escaping an attack on the U.S. Embassy.

Intermediate 1 Reader

Lesson Plan Intermediate 1 Reader

Unit 2 Lesson 2.3 🔊 "Alone at Sea," pages 57–64

Summary Sailors have long believed that if they are ever lost or stranded at sea, they should never drink the salt water. Doing so would surely bring about a painful death. French doctor Alain Bombard did not agree with this theory. He knew people could survive for only 10 days without water, but he believed stranded sailors would live longer than that if they drank salt water. Bombard set out to cross the Atlantic, drinking salt water along the way, to prove his theory. He successfully completed the trip and survived without touching his emergency supplies. The trip lasted 65 days, 55 days longer than he would have been able to survive without drinking the salt water.

Introduce

Intermediate 1 Reader

Teach Lesson Skills

BEFORE READING

Build Vocabulary List the vocabulary words and their definitions on the board. Discuss each word's meaning with students. Then write the following sentence stems on the board. Read the sentence stems aloud and ask students to complete them.

hasten: speed up

dehydrated: dry

raw: uncooked

hollow: hole

meager: small

1. If you want to *hasten* the process of cooking something, you should . . .
2. After exercising for a long time, you might feel *dehydrated* because . . .
3. You should not eat *raw* meat because . . .

4. A squirrel might live in a *hollow* because . . .
5. I took a *meager* portion for lunch because . . .

Activate Prior Knowledge

1. Ask students to share their experiences with tasting ocean water. Why would they not want to drink it? Then discuss how they feel after eating salty foods.
2. Ask students what things all people need to survive. *(Possible answers: food, water, shelter)* Discuss why being able to find these things might save their lives if they were lost at sea.

Preview and Predict Ask students what clues the title of the article, the photograph, and the photo caption provide. What predictions about the article might students make? *(Possible answer: The article is about Alain Bombard, a doctor who sailed alone across the Atlantic Ocean to prove that a person can survive by drinking seawater.)*

Build Background More than half of your body weight is made up of water. All of the body's systems need water to work correctly. Water helps your body get rid of waste, brings nutrition to your cells, and keeps your body tissues moist. When you don't drink enough water, you get dehydrated, and you may feel tired. This means you don't have enough water in your body for it to function correctly. How much water you need will depend on your health, diet, and other factors. Although drinking eight cups of water per day is recommended, a simpler rule is just to drink enough to avoid feeling thirsty.

DURING READING

Infer An inference is a logical guess about information that the writer suggests but doesn't state directly. Making inferences helps readers find deeper meaning in what they read. Ask students to look for details that aren't fully explained. Have them combine clues from the text with their personal knowledge to identify what the writer suggests.

AFTER READING

Respond to the Article Have students write a journal or blog entry based on the evidence presented in the article. Ask students: What evidence does the article give to prove that people can survive by drinking salt water? Do you think it would be possible to survive this way? Why or why not?

Support Individual Learners

DIFFERENTIATED INSTRUCTION

Ask students to write riddles about animals, sports, classroom objects, or other subjects of interest. Have partners take turns reading and guessing the answers to their riddles. Encourage them to discuss how clues in the riddles and their previous knowledge helped them make inferences and solve the riddles.

ENGLISH LANGUAGE LEARNERS

Picture books for older readers can be useful for helping students understand the concept of making inferences. Have students read the books in small groups and make three inferences about what happens in each book. *Hey, Al*, by Arthur Yorinks, is the story of a man named Al who works as a janitor. One morning a bird calls to Al and tells him he has a solution to all of his problems.

GRAPHIC ORGANIZERS

💻 Go to **www.mhereadingbasics.com.**
Use Graphic Organizer 1 as a Characteristics Map. Make copies for each student. Ask students to write *Dr. Alain Bombard* in the center bubble and one of the adjectives below that describe Bombard in each other bubble. Have them add a fact they learned from the article to support each adjective. Discuss their responses.

Brave

Determined

Curious

Resourceful

Introduce

Summary Although they are not much bigger than your thumb, vampire bats are capable of killing a large cow. Contrary to what you might think, vampire bats do not kill by drinking a victim's blood but by spreading deadly diseases, such as rabies. Vampire bats usually drink the blood of large birds, cows, horses, and pigs, but they have been known to drink human blood when these other options are unavailable. When this happens, bat killers are often employed to keep vampire bat numbers down and prevent them from harming people and livestock.

Teach Lesson Skills

BEFORE READING

Build Vocabulary List the vocabulary words and their definitions on the board. Discuss each word's meaning with students. Then write the sentences that contain the words on the board. Read the sentences aloud and discuss them with students.

gory: bloody and horrible

trigger: set off

permanent: lasting

slaying: killing

in big demand: wanted badly

1. The horror movie had many *gory* scenes.
2. If someone breaks into the car, it will *trigger* the alarm.
3. The big oak tree is a *permanent* part of our yard.

4. Storybook knights always seem to be *slaying* dragons.
5. That toy is *in big demand* during the holiday season.

Activate Prior Knowledge
1. Ask students to share what they know about vampires. Discuss what features vampire bats might have in common with vampires.
2. Have students share what they know about rabies. Explain that rabies is a disease that people or animals may get after being bitten by an animal that has the disease. People can get a vaccine that protects them against rabies if they have been bitten by an infected animal.

Build Background Vampire bats can walk, run, and jump, unlike some of their other bat cousins. They have strong back legs and a unique kind of long thumb, which helps them push off after feeding. Vampire bats are the only known mammals that rely on blood from other animals for survival. If they go two nights without blood, they will die. Unlike other bats, vampires will sometimes feed other bats in the group which are hungry. Bats are very clean animals, grooming themselves and each other frequently. Unfortunately, this does not prevent them from carrying and transmitting the rabies virus, which affects the victim's nervous system and leads to brain disease and death.

Preview and Predict Ask students what clues the title of the article, the photograph, and the photo caption provide. What predictions about the article might students make? *(Possible answer: The article is about vampire bats and their victims.)*

DURING READING

Find Vocabulary in Context As students read the article, have them note the new vocabulary words. Ask them to think about each word's meaning as they read.

AFTER READING

Respond to the Article Have students write a journal or blog entry about bat killers. Ask students: Do you think that killing vampire bats is cruel or necessary? Explain.

Support Individual Learners

DIFFERENTIATED INSTRUCTION

Explain that a fact is a statement that can be proved to be true. An opinion is a statement that reflects someone's beliefs or feelings and cannot be proved. Then read aloud letters to the editor from a newspaper or magazine. Ask students to decide if each letter includes facts, opinions, or both.

ENGLISH LANGUAGE LEARNERS

Students may need to see pictures to help them understand the differences between fact and opinion. Have them look at a picture from a book, newspaper, or magazine. Ask them to identify and record as many facts as they can about what they see in the picture. Then have them record their opinions.

GRAPHIC ORGANIZERS

💻 Go to **www.mhereadingbasics.com**. Use Graphic Organizer 1 as a Concept Map. Make copies for each student. Ask students to write *Vampire Bats* in the center bubble and one of the clauses below in each of the other bubbles. Then have students write sentences in the appropriate bubble according to what they learned about vampire bats in the article. Discuss their responses.

What vampire bats look like

What they eat

Problems they cause

How people kill them

Unit 2 Lesson 2.5 🔊 "Escape to Freedom," pages 73–80

Intermediate 1 Reader

Introduce

Summary Frederick Douglass was a slave in Baltimore, Maryland, but he longed for freedom. He decided to try to escape to a northern state where slavery was illegal. He borrowed papers and a uniform from an African American sailor. Although it was extremely dangerous, Douglass used the papers to board a train to Pennsylvania, the nearest free state. There were a few close calls, but Douglass made it to freedom. He went on to New York City and eventually became a famous writer and journalist. He worked tirelessly to fight slavery during his lifetime and lived to see its end in 1863.

Teach Lesson Skills

BEFORE READING

Build Vocabulary List the vocabulary words and their definitions on the board. Discuss each word's meaning with students. Then write the following questions on the board. Read the questions aloud and discuss the answers with students.

fending for: caring for
incentive: reason
bold: brave

1. Would you be *fending for* yourself if you made dinner or if someone made it for you?
2. What would be an *incentive* for studying hard in school?
3. Which would show that you are *bold*—jumping off the high dive or sitting by the pool?

brightened: cheered up
foiled: ruined

4. Would your day be *brightened* if someone smiled at you? Why or why not?
5. If your plan was *foiled*, was it a success or a failure?

Activate Prior Knowledge

1. Ask students to name some freedoms they enjoy. Have them discuss why freedom is something people value.
2. Have students share what they know about the history of slavery in the United States.

Preview and Predict Ask students what clues the title of the article, the photograph, and the photo caption provide. What predictions about the article might students make? *(Possible answer: The article is about a slave named Frederick Douglass who escaped to freedom.)*

Build Background Europeans began using Africans as slaves in the 1400s. The practice continued when Europeans came to America. Most slaves in America worked on plantations, or large farms, in the South. They were considered the property of their owners and had no legal rights. The practice of using slaves grew so widespread that by 1860 there were almost 4 million slaves in America. The Civil War helped to bring an end to slavery. During the war, President Abraham Lincoln signed the Emancipation Proclamation in 1863, which declared that slaves in rebel states were free. When the North won the war in 1865, slavery officially came to an end.

DURING READING

Visualize Visualizing is picturing in your mind the details of the setting, events, and characters in the text. Encourage students to draw pictures or diagrams of these images as they read.

AFTER READING

Respond to the Article Have students write a journal or blog entry about Frederick Douglass's actions. Ask students: How do you know that Frederick Douglass valued freedom more than anything else? How might his life have been different if he had not risked escape?

Support Individual Learners

DIFFERENTIATED INSTRUCTION

Choose a descriptive poem and read it aloud to students. Have them visualize the poem as they listen. Then reread the poem and have students act out what they see in their mind's eye. Finally, ask students to make a sketch or write a description of their visualizations.

ENGLISH LANGUAGE LEARNERS

Have students take turns describing what a friend or family member looks like. As they describe the person, ask the other students to visualize the person and then draw a picture or write a description of him or her.

GRAPHIC ORGANIZERS

💻 Go to **www.mhreadingbasics.com.**
Use Graphic Organizer 1 as a Characteristics Map. Make copies for each student. Ask students to write *Frederick Douglass* in the center bubble and one of the adjectives about Douglass below in each of the other bubbles. Then have students add a fact that they learned from the article that supports each adjective. Discuss their responses.

Intelligent   Thoughtful

Brave   Determined

Lesson Plan Intermediate 1 Reader

Unit 3 Lesson 3.1 📶 "A Horrible Way to Die," pages 81–88

Summary In April 1995 a man felt ill and went to the hospital in Kikwit, Zaire. A few days later his condition took a horrible turn, and blood began to pour from his eyes, ears, and nose. He had the deadly Ebola virus. The virus quickly spread through Zaire, and doctors feared it would turn into a worldwide plague. Luckily, by August, the epidemic was over. Doctors aren't sure where the Ebola virus comes from, but many think it may live in a rodent or insect deep in Africa's rain forests. As people cut down rain forests, they may come in contact with the virus. Though the fear has passed for now, we don't know when or if the Ebola virus may return.

Introduce

BEFORE READING

Build Vocabulary List the vocabulary words and their definitions on the board. Discuss each word's meaning with students. Then write the sentences that contain the words on the board. Read the sentences aloud and discuss them with students.

horrifying: frightening

hideous: ugly

horrendous: terrible; nasty

fanned out: spread out

refrain from: skip

1. The child was frightened because she dreamed about a *horrifying* monster.
2. The actor wore a *hideous* mask to make himself look ugly.
3. The storm caused *horrendous* damage to the house.

4. The librarian *fanned out* the magazines on the table.
5. She was asked to *refrain from* talking on her cell phone.

Activate Prior Knowledge

1. Ask students to describe a time when they were sick. How did they feel, and what did they have to do to get better?
2. Have students describe things they can do to avoid spreading germs, such as washing their hands, not coming to school or work when sick, and coughing into their elbows.

Preview and Predict Ask students what clues the title of the article, the photograph, and the photo caption provide. What predictions about the article might students make? *(Possible answer: The article is about the Ebola virus and the horrible way it kills people.)*

Build Background Viruses and bacteria are two agents that cause sickness. However, while a bacterium is a tiny organism that lives on its own, a virus is just a packet of genetic material. It needs a host in order to survive and reproduce. Once a virus gets inside a person, animal, or plant, it invades the living cells, which are forced to make more of the virus. Viruses cause many of the illnesses known to man, from the common cold and flu to the deadly Ebola. Unlike bacteria, viruses are not killed by antibiotics, so the best defense against them is prevention. Widespread vaccination has already reduced the occurrence of some viruses. Sanitary habits, such as covering your mouth when you cough and washing your hands regularly, can also help prevent the spread of a virus.

Teach Lesson Skills

DURING READING

Cause and Effect A cause is an event or action that makes something else happen. An effect is the result or the outcome of that event or action. Writers use clue words such as *because, so, since, if,* and *therefore* to signal cause and effect. Have students look for cause-and-effect relationships by asking *What happened? Why?*

AFTER READING

Respond to the Article Have students write a journal or blog entry about the evidence presented in the article. Ask students: What evidence makes it seem like the spread of the Ebola virus is related to cutting down the rain forest? Do you think knowing about the Ebola virus would prevent people from cutting down rain forests? Why or why not?

DIFFERENTIATED INSTRUCTION

Have students write three cause-and-effect statements that include the word *because* on sentence strips, for example, *I fell asleep because I was tired.* Have them cut the strips apart before the word *because.* Have them exchange the cut-apart strips with a partner and work to reassemble the sentence strips they receive. Have partners check each other's work.

ENGLISH LANGUAGE LEARNERS

Have students work with partners to name causes and effects. Model by saying a cause, such as "It snowed all day yesterday." Ask a volunteer to give an effect for that cause: "We had to shovel snow from the driveway." Then have partners take turns naming causes and possible effects of those causes.

GRAPHIC ORGANIZERS

💻 Go to **www.mhereadingbasics.com.** Use Graphic Organizer 2 as an Author's Purpose Chart. Make copies for each student. Ask students to write *Inform* at the top of the first column and *Persuade* at the top of the second column. Then have students list two facts from the article that support each purpose. Discuss their responses.

Support Individual Learners

Intermediate 1 Reader

Introduce

Summary It is rare for a person to be struck by lightning, but it can happen nearly anywhere. Although it's uncommon, lightning kills more Americans every year than almost any other kind of dangerous weather. For those who survive a strike, their lives are usually changed forever, and not for the better. A person's memory, eyesight, and hearing can all be affected. A lightning storm can be thrilling, but you need to take seriously the deadly threat that it poses.

Teach Lesson Skills

BEFORE READING

Build Vocabulary List the vocabulary words and their definitions on the board. Discuss each word's meaning with students. Then write the following questions on the board. Read the questions aloud and discuss the answers with students.

breed: create

gets bombarded with: gets hit heavily by

grueling: difficult

remarkable: amazing

picks off: kills

1. What word or phrase goes with "extraordinary"? *(remarkable)*
2. What word or phrase goes with "running a marathon"? *(grueling)*
3. What word or phrase goes with "to grow"? *(breed)*
4. What word or phrase goes with "get lots of homework"? *(gets bombarded with)*
5. What word or phrase goes with "gets rid of"? *(picks off)*

Activate Prior Knowledge

1. Ask students to share what they know about lightning.
2. Discuss when lightning happens and why it is dangerous. *(Possible answers: Lightning usually occurs during thunderstorms; it can strike people or cause fires.)*
3. Have students share safety tips regarding lightning. *(Possible answers: Don't stand under a tree; stay inside.)*

Preview and Predict Ask students what clues the title of the article, the photograph, and the photo caption provide. What predictions about the article might students make? *(Possible answer: The article is about being struck by lightning.)*

Build Background
Lightning is caused by an electrical imbalance in a storm cloud. When negative particles from the cloud flow down and meet positive charges from objects or people on the ground, lightning is created. Even though 9 out of 10 people survive a lightning strike, it is still very dangerous. When a lightning storm begins, try to stay in a building or a car with the windows rolled up. Don't use water or electrical appliances. If you're stranded outdoors, stay away from bodies of water and tall trees. Don't lie down, but rather crouch low to the ground and keep your feet together. This will minimize the area of your body that touches the ground and lower your risk of being hit by a current of lightning traveling along the ground's surface.

DURING READING

Ask Questions Questioning helps you to monitor your understanding of the text. Have students ask *who, what, where, when, why,* and *how* questions and look for the answers. Questions may include: Who is Roy Sullivan? Why is he unlucky? How do people get hit by lightning? What is it like to get hit by lightning?

AFTER READING

Respond to the Article Have students write a journal or blog entry about the way lightning affected the life of one person they read about. Ask students: How did lightning change the life of one person you read about? Was the change positive or negative? Explain.

Support Individual Learners

DIFFERENTIATED INSTRUCTION

Students may find it helpful to preview the article and generate questions before they start reading. Have them use Graphic Organizer 3 to create a KWL Chart about lightning. Before reading, have them fill in the first two columns with what they know about lightning and what they want to learn. After reading, have them complete the third column with what they learned.

ENGLISH LANGUAGE LEARNERS

Review the question words *who, what, where, when, why,* and *how* and, if necessary, model asking a question with each one. Then have students read the article with a partner. After each paragraph, have partners take turns asking and answering one question each about what they just read. Encourage them to use different types of question words to get a more complete understanding of the whole article.

GRAPHIC ORGANIZERS

💻 Go to **www.mhereadingbasics.com.** Use Graphic Organizer 2 as a Fact-and-Opinion Chart. Make copies for each student. Ask students to label the columns *Facts* and *Opinions.* Then have students organize the following sentences from the article according to whether each is a fact or an opinion. Discuss their responses.

Florida lies between two warm bodies of water.

You'd have to call any lightning victim unlucky.

Only one person in about 600,000 ever gets struck by lightning.

Sullivan worked as a park ranger in Virginia.

Being struck by lightning can be a blessing.

Lightning kills more Americans than almost any other weather hazard.

Lesson Plan Intermediate 1 Reader

Introduce

Summary Acupuncture is an ancient Chinese practice that uses strategically placed needles to cure a variety of aches, pains, and other medical problems. The Chinese people began using acupuncture more than 4,000 years ago. They believe that people have a flow of energy, or qi, inside them. When the flow gets blocked, pain or illness results. The needles are used to unblock the flow of energy. Western scientists are doing research to learn how acupuncture works. Some think that acupuncture causes the nervous system to release pain-relieving chemicals into the body. When more traditional methods fail, more and more patients are choosing acupuncture to help them heal.

Teach Lesson Skills

BEFORE READING

Build Vocabulary List the vocabulary words and their definitions on the board. Discuss each word's meaning with students. Then write the following sentence stems on the board. Read the sentence stems aloud and ask students to complete them.

banish: drive away

stimulate: excite to activity

disrupted: disturbed or upset

clogged: blocked

misery: suffering

1. If the dog chews the sofa, Jenna will *banish* him to the backyard because . . .
2. Smelling food can *stimulate* your appetite if . . .
3. The teacher does not like the class to be *disrupted* because . . .

4. We knew the bathtub drain was *clogged* because . . .
5. People may feel *misery* because . . .

Activate Prior Knowledge
1. Ask students to share experiences with injuries, aches, and pains.
2. Discuss some kinds of pains people have and what causes them.
3. Discuss things people do to treat pain or an injury. *(Possible answers: put heat on the sore area; ice the area; take aspirin)*
4. Discuss what it feels like to get stuck with a needle and whether students think acupuncture would be painful.

Preview and Predict Ask students what clues the title of the article, the photograph, and the photo caption provide. What predictions about the article might students make? *(Possible answer: The article is about acupuncture, the use of needles to cure pain.)*

Build Background Alternative or complementary medicine differs from conventional medicine in that its treatments, practices, and products are not generally used by MDs (medical doctors) or DOs (doctors of osteopathy). It is practiced in place of, or to complement, traditional medicine, often for pain relief. Using herbs and natural products, such as probiotic supplements instead of medicine prescribed by a doctor, is one kind of alternative medicine. Mind-body practice is another form of alternative medicine. It includes treatments such as yoga, meditation, and acupuncture. These practices encourage people to use their mind to make their physical health better. Spinal manipulation and massage therapy are alternative treatments that focus on moving or positioning parts of the body such as bones, joints, and tissues to promote healing, pain relief, and relaxation.

DURING READING

Find Vocabulary in Context As students read the article, have them note the new vocabulary words. Ask them to think about each word's meaning as they read.

AFTER READING

Respond to the Article Have students write a journal or blog entry about the evidence presented in the article. Ask students: What evidence makes acupuncture seem effective? Did the author convince you that acupuncture works? Why or why not?

Support Individual Learners

DIFFERENTIATED INSTRUCTION

Explain that when students summarize a text, they determine the most important ideas and give only the most important details. Tell students that thinking about who, what, where, when, why, and how will help them summarize. Then ask students to summarize a movie or television show that they have seen or an experience they have had.

ENGLISH LANGUAGE LEARNERS

Have students choose a short magazine or newspaper article. Help them write the main idea of each paragraph. Then ask students to use the main ideas to summarize the article.

GRAPHIC ORGANIZERS

💻 Go to **www.mhereadingbasics.com**. Use Graphic Organizer 1 as a Concept Map. Make copies for each student. Ask students to write *Acupuncture* in the center bubble and one of the clauses below in each of the other bubbles. Then have students write sentences in the appropriate bubbles according to what they learned from the article about acupuncture. Discuss their responses.

What it is

How it works

How it feels

Does it work?

Lesson Plan Intermediate 1 Reader

Unit 3 Lesson 3.4 🔊 "Hanging from a Cliff," pages 105–112

Summary When S. Hall Young set out to climb an 8,000-foot peak in southern Alaska with naturalist John Muir, he had no idea of the danger he'd face. While trying to keep up with Muir, Young lost his footing and slid toward a 1,000-foot crevasse. He dislocated his shoulders and was in danger of falling into the crevasse. Miraculously, Muir was able to rescue Young and carry him down the mountain to safety.

Introduce

Intermediate 1 Reader

Teach Lesson Skills

BEFORE READING

Build Vocabulary List the vocabulary words and their definitions on the board. Discuss each word's meaning with students. Then write the sentences that contain the words on the board. Read the sentences aloud and discuss them with students.

exerting: pushing
undeterred: not afraid
cautiously: carefully

sloped: slanted
ponder: think about

1. During the race, the swimmers were *exerting* themselves to swim faster.
2. The hikers were *undeterred* by the darkness and kept walking.
3. The waiter picked up the broken glass *cautiously*.

4. You need a *sloped* surface to go sledding.
5. A good mystery novel provides a lot of clues to *ponder*.

Activate Prior Knowledge

1. Ask students to share their experiences with hiking or mountain climbing.
2. Discuss the dangers of mountain climbing or hiking and why you should have someone with you. *(Possible answers: getting lost, falling, getting hurt; someone can go for help)*
3. Have students describe a time they helped someone or someone helped them. Discuss the characteristics of people who help or rescue others. *(Possible answers: brave, selfless, caring, clever)*

Preview and Predict Ask students what clues the title of the article, the photograph, and the photo caption provide. What predictions about the article might students make? *(Possible answer: The article is about someone, maybe John Muir, who had a close call while climbing a mountain.)*

Build Background John Muir was one of the most famous and important naturalists in America's history. He is sometimes referred to as "the father of our national parks." He is well known for his adventures in Alaska's glaciers and California's Sierra Nevadas. Muir's writings and actions were influential in convincing President Theodore Roosevelt to establish Yosemite National Park and the first national monuments. In 1892 Muir organized the Sierra Club and became its first president. The Sierra Club has worked to create new national parks and preserve wilderness areas.

DURING READING

Visualize Visualizing is picturing in your mind the details of the setting, events, and characters in the passage. Encourage students to draw pictures or diagrams of these images as they read.

AFTER READING

Respond to the Article Have students write a journal or blog entry about Young's experience. Ask students: How do you think Young felt as he was dangling from the cliff? How would the outcome have been different if Young had been alone or with a less experienced partner?

Support Individual Learners

DIFFERENTIATED INSTRUCTION

Read highly visual sentences or paragraphs to students. Ask students to close their eyes and visualize as you read to them. Then have them choose one sentence or paragraph to illustrate, based on their visualization.

ENGLISH LANGUAGE LEARNERS

Have students take turns describing one of their favorite places to other students. As they describe it, ask the other students to visualize what the place is like and then draw pictures or write descriptions of the place. Allow students to ask questions if they need additional information to clarify their visualizations.

GRAPHIC ORGANIZERS

💻 Go to **www.mhereadingbasics.com.** Use Graphic Organizer 5 as a Sequence-of-Events Chart. Make copies for each student. Have students put the steps below in the correct sequence. Discuss their responses.

Men helped Young put his shoulder back in place.

Muir climbed down to reach Young and carried him out of the crevasse.

Young stumbled and fell toward a deep crevasse and dislocated both shoulders.

Muir carried Young down the mountain.

Lesson Plan Intermediate 1 Reader

Introduce

Summary In the 1950s scientists had a plan to crossbreed European bees and African bees in an attempt to create a honeybee that liked hot weather and could thrive in Latin America. Unfortunately, a group of African bees escaped from the lab and began invading local hives. These very aggressive bees, which became known as killer bees, spread north to Texas, New Mexico, California, and Arizona. When disturbed, killer bees attack in large swarms, sometimes with deadly results.

Teach Lesson Skills

BEFORE READING

Build Vocabulary List the vocabulary words and their definitions on the board. Discuss each word's meaning with students. Then write the following questions on the board. Read the questions aloud and discuss the answers with students.

countless: so many that the number cannot be easily counted

adapted: became used to

humid: damp or muggy

mellow: easygoing

estimated: guessed

1. What word goes with "calm"? *(mellow)*
2. What word goes with "adjusted"? *(adapted)*
3. What word goes with "billions"? *(countless)*

4. What word goes with "sticky weather"? *(humid)*
5. What word goes with "made a guess at"? *(estimated)*

Activate Prior Knowledge

1. Have students share their experiences with bees and bee stings. Point out that bee stings can be deadly for people who are allergic or who are attacked by many bees.

2. Show students a map that shows where African killer bees can be found. Go to http://www.nationalatlas.gov/, enter "honey bees" in the search box, and click on the first result.

Preview and Predict Ask students what clues the title of the article, the photograph, and the photo caption provide. What predictions about the article might students make? *(Possible answer: The article is about killer bees and the way they attack their victims.)*

Build Background Most people can safely handle 10 bee stings per pound of body weight, but if they have been stung extensively, are feeling sick, or think they may be allergic to bee stings, they should seek medical attention as soon as possible. Advise students that if they see a beehive of any kind to try to stay away. If they inadvertently disturb a swarm of killer bees, they should start running immediately. They shouldn't swat at the bees—bees are drawn to movement, and the smell of a smashed bee will attract more angry bees. They should find shelter, such as a car or a building (but they shouldn't jump into water, because Africanized bees will wait for them to come up for air). Once they are safe, they should remove any stingers by scraping them out with a fingernail, credit card, or similar hard-edged object.

DURING READING

Identify Sequence Explain that sequence is the order in which events, ideas, or things are arranged. Time order refers to the order in which events occur. Following the sequence of events helps readers see how the text is organized and how events relate to each other. As students read, ask them to look for key words and phrases such as *long ago, soon, then, later,* and *today.*

AFTER READING

Respond to the Article Have students write a journal or blog entry about the information in the article. Ask students: Do you think it was a good idea for scientists to bring African bees to Brazil? Why or why not? What is another way that scientists could have created honeybees that like hot weather?

Support Individual Learners

DIFFERENTIATED INSTRUCTION

Have students write a paragraph about a change that happened in their life. Ask them to write about the events in time order. Then have students share their paragraphs. Ask other students to identify words that signal the sequence of events.

ENGLISH LANGUAGE LEARNERS

Working in pairs, have students find an article from a local or school newspaper. While reading the article, they should underline words that indicate the sequence of events. Then have students draw a visual representation of the article, clearly illustrating each event or step.

GRAPHIC ORGANIZERS

📖 Go to **www.mhereadingbasics.com.** Use Graphic Organizer 8 as a Compare-and-Contrast Venn Diagram. Make copies for each student. Tell students to label the left circle *African bees,* the middle area *Both,* and the right circle *European bees.* Ask students to write characteristics of African bees in the left circle, characteristics of European bees in the right circle, and characteristics shared by both kinds of bees in the middle section. Discuss their responses.

Intermediate 1 Reader

INTERMEDIATE 1 READER
Unit 1 Assessment Article

Directions: Read this story. Then answer each question that follows. Circle the letter of your answer.

The Sweepers of the Sea

In 2010 the remains of Navy Ensign Robert Langwell finally came home to the United States. The events that ended with Langwell's burial at Arlington National Cemetery had begun 60 years before, in the early months of the Korean War, aboard the minesweeper USS *Magpie*.

² The fighting in Korea began in June 1950, when the newly formed state of North Korea, backed by the Soviet Union, attacked South Korea. Fearing the spread of Soviet power, the United Nations Security Council voted to push the North Korean troops back. The United States would lead the military action.

³ As it prepared to bring troops to Korean ports, U.S. Naval command knew that North Korea would lace the waters around the Korean peninsula with naval mines. These mines explode when ships touch or approach them. The U.S. Navy scrambled to bring minesweepers to the area.

⁴ The minesweepers' job was to neutralize enemy mines. Some mines floated just below the surface. They were anchored to the ocean floor. If watchmen on the ship's bow spotted a mine, the ship towed a steel cable through the water. The cable detached the mine from its anchor. The sailors then exploded the mine from a distance.

⁵ Being a minesweeper required great nerve. A hidden mine could detonate at any moment. Enemy fire from the nearby shore was also a big risk. Minesweepers knew their job was critical. As Howard Kastens, who served on the USS *Magpie*, said, "The boys doing the fighting needed supplies that could only be brought in by ship."

⁶ On October 1, 1950, the *Magpie* struck a mine during a sweep off Korea's east coast. The mine detonated the ship's ammunition and created a huge blast. One of the survivors found two others clinging to debris. They had been on the ship's bow. The explosion was so close that it blew the entire bow, with them on it, over the ship and into the water. They were among the lucky ones. Only 12 of the 33-man crew survived. The others were lost at sea.

⁷ The North Koreans had deployed thousands of mines. However, by the end of the war, the U.S. Navy had lost only five ships. Four were minesweepers.

⁸ Flash forward 60 years. A South Korean man tells officials about an American sailor buried in his village in 1950. The sailor's body had turned up in a net a few days after the *Magpie* sank. The grave is found. The remains are identified as Robert Langwell's.

⁹ South Korea's ambassador spoke at Langwell's funeral. On behalf of his country, he wanted to thank all Americans who fought there 60 years ago for their sacrifice. Veteran minesweepers would appreciate that one of their own inspired that gratitude.

INTERMEDIATE 1 READER
Unit 1 Assessment Questions

1. Which sentence states the main idea best?
   a. South Korean fishermen helped U.S. minesweepers by locating bodies.
   b. U.S. Navy Ensign Robert Langwell never got the praise he deserved.
   c. In the Korean War, naval minesweeping was a risky but necessary job.

2. The Korean War started when
   a. North Korea entered South Korea.
   b. the U.S. Navy began looking for mines.
   c. the Soviet Union walked out on the United Nations Security Council.

3. Which answer is probably true?
   a. Minesweepers kept the U.S. Navy from losing numerous ships.
   b. Robert Langwell was killed by fishermen.
   c. Minesweepers were not aware of the risks.

4. What is the meaning of the underlined word? The minesweepers' job was to neutralize enemy mines.
   a. locate
   b. make harmless
   c. turn toward enemy ships

5. The purpose of the first paragraph is to
   a. persuade readers that Langwell should be given a medal.
   b. let readers know that a biography of Langwell will follow.
   c. make readers curious about Langwell and the Magpie.

6. Which of the following is an opinion?
   a. However, by the end of the war, the U.S. Navy had lost only five ships.
   b. Veteran minesweepers would appreciate that one of their own inspired that gratitude.
   c. Some mines floated just below the surface.

7. Which answer correctly restates this sentence from the article?
   Fearing the spread of Soviet power, the United Nations Security Council voted to push the North Korean troops back.
   a. To keep the Soviet Union from spreading its power, the United Nations decided to push the North Korean troops out of South Korea.
   b. The United Nations Security Council voted to push the North Korean troops back into the Soviet Union.
   c. The United Nations Security Council voted for the North Koreans to fight against the Soviet Union to keep it from spreading its power.

8. What made the mine that the Magpie struck more deadly than it might have been?
   a. The mine exploded at the bow of the ship, sinking the ship in one blast.
   b. There were more sailors on board the Magpie than usual that day.
   c. The mine blast set off the Magpie's own weapons, increasing the size of the blast.

9. Why was it important to rush minesweeping boats to Korea early in the war?
   a. If the waters around Korea weren't cleared of mines, navy vessels couldn't safely bring in supplies and soldiers.
   b. The United States wanted to stop North Korean ships from heading south.
   c. The navy minesweepers carried the equipment needed to clear land mines throughout Korea.

10. Why did the South Korean ambassador speak at Langwell's funeral?
    a. because Langwell had shown bravery during the blast and sinking of the Magpie
    b. because of the unusual circumstances of Langwell's funeral 60 years after his death
    c. because he wanted to improve relations between the United States and South Korea

Intermediate 1 Reader

INTERMEDIATE 1 READER

Unit 2 Assessment Article

Directions: Read this story. Then answer each question that follows. Circle the letter of your answer.

The Rabies Survivor

Fifteen-year-old Jeanna Giese loved animals. On September 12, 2004, she was attending church near her Wisconsin home. A bat had flown into the church, and Jeanna decided to rescue the little animal, which was lying on the floor. She picked it up by its wings and brought it outside. One of its sharp teeth sank painfully into her finger. She shook the bat loose by a tree.

2 The bat's bite had left a tiny wound on Jeanna's finger. She cleaned it with antiseptic and thought no more about it. Schoolwork, sports, and other activities kept her busy.

3 About a month later, Jeanna was feeling tired. Her arm tingled. She was seeing double and blacked out several times. When Jeanna arrived at Children's Hospital of Milwaukee on October 16, she was vomiting, could not stand or talk, and was having trouble breathing. Tests showed that she had rabies, a disease transmitted by infected animals. Dr. Rodney Willoughby thought that Jeanna would be dead within hours.

4 Dr. Willoughby, like most American doctors, had never seen a full-blown case of rabies. In developed countries, people are given a vaccine after they are bitten by an animal that might have rabies. The vaccine helps the body make antibodies to fight the rabies virus.

5 The vaccine works, but it must be given within several days of the bite. If symptoms develop, it is too late to give the vaccine. It is also too late to save the victim—rabies is fatal.

6 Although Dr. Willoughby thought there was little hope of saving Jeanna, he knew he had to try. He had an idea for a treatment that had never been tried before; Jeanna's parents gave their consent. Using drugs, the medical team put Jeanna into a coma, a dangerous state of slowed brain activity. Dr. Willoughby reasoned that rabies kills because the brain loses its ability to control breathing, heartbeat, swallowing, and other basic functions. By keeping brain activity low and controlling basic functions medically, he hoped to give Jeanna's body time to build up antibodies to fight rabies. Jeanna also received antivirus medicines.

7 Amazingly, after one week, Jeanna's rabies infection was gone! She was brought out of the coma. Nobody knew whether her brain would be permanently damaged. Her recovery took many months.

8 Jeanna later said, "I had to relearn how to speak, walk, stand, pick things up, point, eat, drink." Except for having to give up most sports because of reduced muscle control, Jeanna was able to lead a normal life and attend college. She pursued her dream of a career working with animals. "I'm more passionate about animals than I was before," she said.

9 Jeanna Giese was the first person in history to survive rabies without vaccination. What did Dr. Willoughby think about his patient's remarkable recovery? "In all honesty, we were probably just pretty lucky."

Intermediate 1 Reader

INTERMEDIATE 1 READER
Unit 2 Assessment Questions

1. Which sentence states the main idea best?
   a. Jeanna Giese recovered from a deadly disease.
   b. Jeanna Giese was the first person to survive rabies without getting the usual shots for it.
   c. Jeanna Giese was a 15-year-old girl who was bitten by a bat with rabies and survived.

2. What causes rabies?
   a. a cut that is not cleaned properly
   b. a disease that is not treated
   c. the bite of an animal that has the disease

3. Which answer is probably true?
   a. Very few people in the United States die of rabies.
   b. Almost no rabies cases are reported throughout the world.
   c. Most wild animals have rabies.

4. What is the meaning of the underlined word?
   It is also too late to save the victim—rabies is <u>fatal</u>.
   a. deadly
   b. harmful
   c. an illness

5. The main purpose of paragraph 6 is to
   a. describe the effects of rabies.
   b. tell a true story.
   c. explain what the doctors did and why.

6. Which answer correctly restates this sentence from the article?
   [Dr. Willoughby] had an idea for a treatment that had never been tried before; Jeanna's parents gave their consent.
   a. Dr. Willoughby and Jeanna's parents thought of a treatment that nobody had tried.
   b. Dr. Willoughby thought of a new treatment, and Jeanna's parents agreed to let him try it.
   c. Dr. Willoughby wanted to treat Jeanna with a new idea, and her parents wanted to help.

7. Jeanna did not seek treatment soon after she was bitten by the bat because she probably
   a. did not want to find out if she had rabies.
   b. did not think the bat had rabies.
   c. did not realize she had been bitten.

8. After other doctors learned of this treatment, they may have
   a. used it instead of the series of shots.
   b. tried it on other patients who were about to die of rabies.
   c. decided that it would not work again.

9. What might be the title of a book that includes this article?
   a. *True Stories of Animals*
   b. *Natural Disasters*
   c. *Medical Miracles*

10. What can Jeanna's story teach others?
    a. If you are bitten by a wild animal, go to a doctor right away.
    b. If you catch rabies, make sure your doctors know about this new treatment.
    c. If you are tired and seeing double, you might have rabies.

Intermediate 1 Reader

INTERMEDIATE 1 READER

Unit 3 Assessment Article

Directions: Read this story. Then answer each question that follows. Circle the letter of your answer.

The Truth about Lying

Why is someone suspected of lying told to look directly at the questioner's eyes? The reason is the belief that people shift their eyes when they are lying. There are other common ideas about lying behavior. It's said that a person who is lying speaks in a shaky or high voice, for example, or fidgets, or blinks a lot, or scratches his or her nose. Are any of these common ideas valid?

[2] In truth, these signs are not useful for lie detection. Human guesswork is simply not a reliable method for determining whether someone is lying.

[3] When a person is accused of a crime, finding the truth is essential. People may not be accurate detectors, but what about machines? How well do technologies for lie detection work?

[4] The best-known of these technologies is the polygraph, or "lie detector." A polygraph examiner asks questions of a person who is hooked up to several medical devices. The devices measure blood pressure, heart rate, breathing rate, and sweat activity. The theory behind the polygraph is that lying creates stress responses—physical changes beyond a person's control.

[5] Polygraphs have been around since the 1920s, and they have long caused debate. Opponents argue that measuring stress responses is not the same as measuring lying. Some people who lie don't experience stress; some people who tell the truth show signs of stress. Furthermore, a person who prepares for the polygraph exam can learn countermeasures that affect the results. Because polygraphs are not foolproof, the results of an exam are rarely admitted as evidence in courts of law.

[6] Other technologies go past the body's responses right to the source—the brain. Some scientists have measured the brain's electrical activity while the person makes truthful and dishonest statements. Other scientists have measured differences in blood flow to areas of the brain thought to be involved in lying. The scientists claim an accuracy rate for lie detection that is much better than chance guessing. There are, however, problems with using brain scans to detect lies. For one thing, no two brains work in exactly the same way.

[7] Police departments have spent thousands of dollars for "voice stress analyzers." The theory behind these machines is that a speaker's voice changes when lying. However, scientific studies of these machines do not support manufacturers' claims. Like the polygraph, these devices detect signs of stress, which may not be due to lying. Researchers say that these machines do not just fail to identify lies but also label too many truths as lies.

[8] It turns out that the familiar "look-me-in-the-eye" test is not the only one that is unreliable.

INTERMEDIATE 1 READER

Unit 3 Assessment Questions

1. Which sentence states the main idea best?
   a. It is very difficult to detect lies.
   b. Liars are good at fooling people and machines.
   c. Lie-detecting technology is better than human guessing.

2. What do lie-detecting machines measure?
   a. changes in thinking patterns
   b. false statements
   c. signs of stress

3. Which answer is probably true?
   a. It is almost impossible to look into someone's eyes and tell a lie.
   b. It is almost impossible to identify lies correctly all the time.
   c. It is almost impossible to fool a lie-detecting machine.

4. What is the meaning of the underlined word?
   Furthermore, a person who prepares for a polygraph exam can learn countermeasures that affect the results.
   a. methods for studying for a test
   b. opposite actions
   c. ways to add

5. The author wrote this article mainly to
   a. show that lying is sometimes necessary.
   b. explain how technology works.
   c. present some ideas about detecting lies.

6. Which answer correctly restates this sentence from the story?
   When a person is accused of a crime, finding the truth is essential.
   a. One basic truth is that anyone can be charged with a crime.
   b. It is very important to figure out what is true when a person is charged with a crime.
   c. Finding out what is true is very hard to do when a person is charged with a crime.

7. If a method for detecting lies is not reliable, then
   a. it is accurate about half the time.
   b. it may call a lie the truth and the truth a lie.
   c. scientists refuse to study the method.

8. What does the author seem to think of machines that measure voice changes?
   a. They work better than other machines at detecting stress.
   b. They are not perfect but are still useful.
   c. They are probably not useful.

9. Which of these ideas is suggested by the article?
   a. Some people are especially skilled at detecting lies.
   b. Everyone tells a lie now and then.
   c. It is important to be able to tell when someone is lying.

10. Which of these predictions seems likely?
    a. New technologies will be created to detect lying behaviors.
    b. Scientists of the future will be able to read the minds of lying people.
    c. People will no longer be able to lie without being caught.

Intermediate 1 Reader

Intermediate 1 Reader

Unit 1 Language Development Activity: *Parts of Speech*

| **ESL/DI Skill** | *Parts of speech:* nouns, verbs, adjectives |

Activity Highlights

1. Activity Sheet: individual, partners
2. Discussion/analysis: partners
3. Sharing prior knowledge: individual
4. Writing original sentences: individual
5. Reading sentences aloud: individual

Teacher Preparation

1. Review the article "Doctors (and Nurses) Without Borders" (Unit 1, Lesson 1.2, p. 10) on which the activity is based.
2. 💻 Go to **www.mhereadingbasics.com** and click Language Development Activity Sheets. Print one copy of Unit 1 Activity Sheet: *Sentence Models* for each student.

Activity Steps:

1. Review the article "Doctors (and Nurses) Without Borders" (Unit 1, Lesson 1.2, p. 10) with the class.

2. Review the following definitions: *noun* (a word that names a person, place, thing, or idea); *verb* (a word that expresses action or a state of being); *adjective* (a word that describes a noun).

3. Students pair off. Give a copy of Unit 1 Activity Sheet: *Sentence Models* to each student.

4. Partners choose one sentence model (that is, one row on the chart). Tell students that they will make sentences about the article using the row they chose.

5. Partners scan the article to search for words they can use to fill in the blanks in the row they chose, according to the parts-of-speech labels at the top of each box. They collaboratively create an original sentence. Either partner may share prior knowledge of parts of speech. Circulate to assist students as necessary.

6. Each student writes the original sentence in his or her chart.

7. Remind students that the sentences must be true with respect to the article. Circulate to assess students' sentences.

8. One partner reads the approved sentence to the class.

9. Partners choose a second sentence model and repeat steps 5–8, each creating an original sentence without using one that other pairs have read to the class.

10. Partners repeat steps 5–8 with the third sentence model (the only one they have not yet used), each creating an original sentence without using one that other pairs have read to the class.

(Possible responses:
#1 Doctors Without Borders/ is/ a/ group.
#3 The/ people/ were/ grateful.
#2 Many/ doctors/ are/ volunteers.)

Intermediate 1 Reader

Unit 2 Language Development Activity: *Idioms and Common Phrases*

ESL/DI Skill | *Idiom:* keep in touch

Activity Highlights

1. Flashcards: individual, partners
2. Substituting definitions for vocabulary words: individual
3. Reading sentences to the class: individual
4. Writing original sentences: partners
3. Sharing aspects of personal experience and culture: individual

Teacher Preparation

1. Review the article "Mummies" (Unit 2, Lesson 2.1, p. 41) on which the activity is based.
2. Provide three blank index cards per student.
3. Write on the board or otherwise present the following sentences: *About 400 years ago, some people in Italy started making mummies. They felt it would help them <u>keep in touch</u> with the spirits of those who had died.*

Activity Steps:

1. Review the article "Mummies" (Unit 2, Lesson 2.1, p. 41) with the class.

2. Read the sentences from step 3 of the Teacher Preparation aloud to the class. Volunteers describe the context of the sentences. What is a mummy? *(Possible response: a dead body that has been prepared to last a long time)*

3. Volunteers discuss what *keep in touch* probably means in the context of the sentences on the board. *(Possible responses: stay connected, stay in communication.)*

4. Write a concise definition of *keep in touch* on the board: *continue to communicate (even though you may not be near each other).* Students write the idiom on one side of an index card and its definition on the other.

5. A volunteer reads the sentence on the board, substituting the definition on the index card for the underlined words in the second sentence on the board: *They felt it would help them <u>continue to communicate</u> with the spirits of those who had died [even though they were not near each other].*

6. Write additional idioms and their definitions on the board, for example: *keep your fingers crossed* ("hope for a positive result"); *keep your chin up* ("keep cheerful during a difficult time").

7. Students pair off.

8. Partners talk about 1) the people they keep in touch with and 2) times they have had to keep their chin up.

9. Each partner writes each additional idiom on one side of an index card and the definition on the other side. Students practice silently with their own cards for several minutes. Then they quiz each other.

10. Partners collaborate to write a pair of sentences using one of the idioms, for example: *My cousin is applying for a job, so I will <u>keep my fingers crossed</u>. / My cousin is applying for a job, so I will <u>hope for a positive result</u>.*

11. If students know an idiom used in their home language or in their neighborhood, they write it on the board and share the meaning with the class. If the idiom is connected to a national or neighborhood culture, students explain why.

12. Time permitting: students collaborate on an original dialogue, poem, or paragraph, using the "Mummies" theme, that employs all of the idioms. Circulate among the groups to support the conversations. Individuals read the completed work to the class.

Unit 3 Language Development Activity: *Suffixes*

| **ESL/DI Skill** | *Suffix:* -ly *(freely, correctly)* |

Activity Highlights

1. Graphic organizer: whole class, small group, individual
2. Discussion: whole class, small group
3. Sharing of personal connections to the topic: small group
4. Reading sentences to the class: individual

Teacher Preparation

1. Review the article "Needles That Cure" (Unit 3, Lesson 3.3, p. 97).
2. 💻 Go to **www.mhereadingbasics.com** and click Language Development Activity Sheets. Print one copy of Unit 3 Activity Sheet: *Suffix Diagram* for each student and one copy of Unit 3 Activity Sheet Answers: *Suffix Diagram* for yourself.
3. Write on the board or otherwise present the following words: *flow <u>freely</u>, get your qi flowing <u>correctly</u> again.*
4. Draw the blank diagram from Unit 3 Activity Sheet: *Suffix Diagram* on the board.

Activity Steps:

1. Distribute Unit 3 Activity Sheet: *Suffix Diagram* (from step 2 of Teacher Preparation).

2. Review "Needles That Cure" (Unit 3, Lesson 3.3, p. 97) with the class and ask how the words on the board are used in the selection.

3. Volunteers tell what word part is in both underlined words [the suffix *-ly*]. Write *-ly* in the middle box. Students do the same on their activity sheets.

4. Ask volunteers what the meanings of *flowing freely* and *flowing correctly* are. *(Possible responses: Flowing freely means flowing in a free way. Flowing correctly means flowing in a correct way.)*

5. Assist volunteers in deducing a concise definition of the suffix *-ly*. *(Answer: in a way that is)* Write the definition under *-ly* in the middle box.

6. With participation from volunteers, fill in the left-hand boxes of the diagram with the following words and their definitions: *free* ("not blocked or trapped"), *correct* ("right or proper"), and *bad* ("causing great harm"). Students fill in their own diagrams. Tell students that all of these words are adjectives and that *-ly* is usually used with an adjective.

7. Model filling in the first item in the box on the right: *freely* ("in a way that is not blocked or trapped"). Volunteers describe how the two parts of the word make the new meaning.

8. Students form small groups.

9. Group members help each other complete their diagrams. Circulate to check definitions (of *freely* and *correctly*).

10. Each group member shares how to do something *correctly*. They use the model "To _____ correctly, you have to _____." *(Possible topics for the first blank: lift weights, make tamales, give a shot to a patient)* Circulate among the groups to assist the students with their conversations.

11. Students share how they know when their own "qi" is flowing correctly. *(Possible responses: I have more energy, I can read faster, I don't get frustrated by little things)*

12. Students make a list of other *-ly* words and say sentences using those words. *(Possible words: quickly, happily, extremely, quietly, loudly)* Circulate to assess the groups' sentences.

13. Volunteers read selected sentences to the class.

Intermediate 1 Reader, Unit 1

Lesson 1.1: The Man-Eaters of Tsavo

A. Recognize and Recall Details
   1. b   2. a   3. c   4. a

B. Find the Main Idea   1. M   2. N   3. B

C. Summarize and Paraphrase
   1. Summaries should include these points:
   When the lions grew quiet, it meant they were stalking their prey; Patterson set traps for the lions; the lions always struck somewhere else.
   2. Summaries should include these points:
   Patterson built a platform near a half-eaten donkey to lure the lions; the lion went after Patterson instead of the donkey; when the lion was near enough to see, Patterson shot and killed it.
   3. a

D. Make Inferences
   1. C   2. F   3. F   4. C   5. C

E. Recognize Author's Effect and Intentions
   1. a   2. b   3. c

F. Evaluate and Create   1. a   2. c   3. b

Lesson 1.2: Doctors (and Nurses) Without Borders

A. Recognize and Recall Details
   1. b   2. c   3. c   4. b

B. Find the Main Idea   1. B   2. M   3. N

C. Summarize and Paraphrase
   1. Summaries should include these points:
   Sometimes Mary Lightfine had a hard time believing people could treat each other the way they did. One person she treated had terrible bruises.
   2. c

D. Make Inferences   1. C   2. F   3. F   4. C

E. Recognize Author's Effect and Intentions
   1. b   2. c   3. b

F. Evaluate and Create   1. b   2. a

Lesson 1.3: The Truth about the Tasaday

A. Recognize and Recall Details
   1. c   2. a   3. b   4. a

B. Find the Main Idea
   1. B   2. M   3. N

C. Summarize and Paraphrase
   1. Summaries should include these ideas:
   the discovery of the Tasaday; studies by experts; the coverage of the Tasaday in various media.
   2. b

Lesson 1.3: The Truth about the Tasaday cont.

D. Make Inferences
   1. C   2. C   3. F   4. F   5. C

E. Recognize Author's Effect and Intentions
   1. a   2. b   3. c

F. Evaluate and Create   1. c   2. c   3. b

Lesson 1.4: Near Death on the Football Field

A. Recognize and Recall Details
   1. b   2. b   3. a   4. b

B. Find the Main Idea   1. M   2. N   3. B

C. Summarize and Paraphrase
   1. Summaries should include these points:
   Normally you should not move the neck of someone with a spinal injury; the trainer and the doctor had to remove Brown's helmet to revive him; when they got the helmet off, they were able to get him breathing again.
   2. b   3. c

D. Make Inferences
   1. F   2. C   3. C   4. F   5. C

E. Recognize Author's Effect and Intentions
   1. a   2. b   3. b

F. Evaluate and Create   1. c   2. a   3. c

Lesson 1.5: The Mysterious Life of Twins

A. Recognize and Recall Details
   1. a   2. b   3. c   4. c

B. Find the Main Idea   1. M   2. N   3. B

C. Summarize and Paraphrase
   1. c   2. a

D. Make Inferences
   1. F   2. C   3. F   4. F   5. C

E. Recognize Author's Effect and Intentions
   1. b   2. a

F. Evaluate and Create   1. c   2. b   3. a

Unit 1 Assessment

The Sweepers of the Sea
1. c   2. a   3. a   4. b   5. c
6. b   7. a   8. c   9. a   10. b

Intermediate 1 Reader, Unit 2

Lesson 2.1: Mummies
A. Recognize and Recall Details
    1. b   2. c   3. b   4. a
B. Find the Main Idea   1. B   2. M   3. N
C. Summarize and Paraphrase
    1. b   2. a   3. a
D. Make Inferences 1. C   2. C   3. F   4. C
E. Recognize Author's Effect and Intentions
    1. a   2. a
F. Evaluate and Create   1. c   2. b

Lesson 2.2: Escape from Iran
A. Recognize and Recall Details
    1. c   2. b   3. c
B. Find the Main Idea   1. N   2. B   3. M
C. Summarize and Paraphrase
    1. Summaries should include these points:
       Iranians took control of the American Embassy and
       captured 52 Americans; six Americans escaped, went
       to the Canadian Embassy, and asked the Canadians to
       hide them; helping the Americans was going to be risky
       for the Canadians.
    2. c
D. Make Inferences
    1. C   2. C   3. F   4. F   5. C
E. Recognize Author's Effect and Intentions
    1. b   2. a
F. Evaluate and Create   1. a   2. a   3. c

Lesson 2.3: Alone at Sea
A. Recognize and Recall Details
    1. b   2. c   3. a   4. a
B. Find the Main Idea   1. M   2. B   3. N
C. Summarize and Paraphrase
    1. a   2. a   3.c
D. Make Inferences
    1. F   2. C   3. F   4. C   5. F
E. Recognize Author's Effect and Intentions
    1. a   2. b   3. b

Lesson 2.3: Alone at Sea cont.
F. Evaluate and Create
    1. **Similarities**: rubber boats were used; Bombard ate what
       he found in the sea; Bombard drank salt water; Bombard
       didn't enjoy the experience
       Differences: One trip was in the Mediterranean Sea
       and the other across the Atlantic Ocean; on one trip
       Bombard went with a friend, but on the other he went
       alone; one trip lasted two weeks and the other 65 days
    2. c

Lesson 2.4: Night Killers
A. Recognize and Recall Details
    1. b   2. a   3. b   4. c
B. Find the Main Idea   1. M   2. B   3. N
C. Summarize and Paraphrase
    1. Summaries should include these points:
       Vampire bats can pass on diseases such as rabies;
       Murillo's cows got rabies from bats.
    2. a
D. Make Inferences
    1. F   2. C   3. F   4. C   5. F
E. Recognize Author's Effect and Intentions
    1. a   2. c
F. Evaluate and Create   1. b   2. a   3. c

Lesson 2.5: Escape to Freedom
A. Recognize and Recall Details
    1. b   2. a   3. b   4. a
B. Find the Main Idea   1. B   2. N   3. M
C. Summarize and Paraphrase   1. b   2. b
D. Make Inferences
    1. C   2. C   3. C   4. F   5. C
E. Recognize Author's Effect and Intentions
    1. b   2. c   3. b
F. Evaluate and Create   1. a   2. c   3. c

Unit 2 Assessment

The Rabies Survivor
1. c   2. c   3. a   4. a   5. c
6. b   7. b   8. b   9. c   10. a

Intermediate 1 Reader, Unit 3

Lesson 3.1: A Horrible Way to Die
A. Recognize and Recall Details
1.a 2.c 3. b 4.a 5. c
B. Find the Main Idea 1. B 2. N 3. M
C. Summarize and Paraphrase
1. Summaries should include these points:
Doctors who rushed to the hospital in Kikwit were shocked at the conditions. It was easy to see how the virus had spread.
2. b
D. Make Inferences
1. C 2. C 3. F 4. F 5. F
E. Recognize Author's Effect and Intentions
1. b 2. c 3. c
F. Evaluate and Create 1. a 2. a 3. b

Lesson 3.2: A Shocking Experience
A. Recognize and Recall Details
1. b 2. a 3. c 4.c
B. Find the Main Idea 1. B 2. N 3. M
C. Summarize and Paraphrase
1. Summaries should include these points:
Getting struck by lightning does strange things to people. George McBay's life changed for the worse after he was struck by lightning.
2. a 3. a
D. Make Inferences
1. C 2. F 3. C 4. C 5. F
E. Recognize Author's Effect and Intentions
1. b 2. c 3. b
F. Evaluate and Create
1. c
2. **Similarities:** Both were knocked unconscious. **Differences:** Changes in Spain's life were negative, but those in Robinson's were positive.

Lesson 3.3: Needles That Cure
A. Recognize and Recall Details
1. b 2. c 3. a 4. c
B. Find the Main Idea 1. N 2. M 3. B
C. Summarize and Paraphrase
1. Summaries should include these points:
When skeptical western doctors finally began to study acupuncture in the 1970s, they found that it actually gave relief to some patients.
2. b

Lesson 3.3: Needles That Cure cont.
D. Make Inferences
1. F 2. C 3. C 4. F 5. F
E. Recognize Author's Effect and Intentions
1. a 2. a
F. Evaluate and Create 1. a 2. b

Lesson 3.4: Hanging from a Cliff
A. Recognize and Recall Details
1. b 2. b 3. a 4. c
B. Find the Main Idea
1. M 2. N 3. B
C. Summarize and Paraphrase
1. Summaries should include these points:
Young's feet hung over the crevasse; his arms were useless; he was hanging on only by his chin; he thought there was no hope of surviving.
2. b
D. Make Inferences
1. C 2. C 3. C 4. F 5. F
E. Recognize Author's Effect and Intentions
1. a 2. b 3. a
F. Evaluate and Create
1. a 2. a 3. b

Lesson 3.5: Killer Bees
A. Recognize and Recall Details
1. b 2. a 3. b 4. c
B. Find the Main Idea 1. B 2. M 3. N
C. Summarize and Paraphrase
1. Summaries should include these points:
One killer bee can change a colony of honeybees into killer bees in 45 days.
2. c
D. Make Inferences
1. F 2. F 3. C 4. C 5. F
E. Recognize Author's Effect and Intentions
1. c 2. b 3. a
F. Evaluate and Create 1. c 2. c

Unit 3 Assessment
The Truth about Lying
1. a 2. c 3. b 4. b 5. c
6. b 7. b 8. c 9. c 10. a

Intermediate 1 Reader

Intermediate 1 Reader
Units 1–3

Intermediate 1 Reader

Lesson 1.1: The Man-Eaters of Tsavo
Graphic Organizer 5: Sequence-of-Events Chart
Colonel Patterson was in charge of the railroad project in east Africa.
Lions started attacking railroad workers.
Colonel Patterson decided to hunt the lions.
The workers returned to work.

Lesson 1.2: Doctors (and Nurses) Without Borders
Graphic Organizer 1: Concept Map
Possible answers:
Why she joined Doctors Without Borders: *She joined to help people and learn about other countries and ways of life.*
Ways she helped: *She bathed people; she bandaged people; she held their hands.*
What was difficult: *Many things were difficult, such as the heat, seeing suffering, and poor living conditions.*
What she enjoyed: *She enjoyed helping people and getting the gift of a thank you.*

Lesson 1.3: The Truth about the Tasaday
Graphic Organizer 3: Inference Chart
Possible answers:
What I Know:
People sometimes keep others away when they are hiding something.
People sometimes look past obvious signs that something isn't what it seems when they want to believe it.
If someone takes a lot of money and disappears suddenly, they are usually running away from something.
My Inference:
Elizalde isn't being honest about the Tasaday.
Experts wanted to believe that the Tasaday were a real tribe, so they didn't look too closely at the signs that proved it was a scam.
Elizalde knew that people were close to learning that the Tasaday were a scam and that he was behind it, so he fled.

Lesson 1.4: Near Death on the Football Field
Graphic Organizer 4: Cause-and-Effect Chart
Possible answers:
Causes:
Reggie Brown injured his spinal cord.
Reggie Brown had a powerful drive to get well.
Reggie Brown recovered fairly quickly.
Reggie Brown couldn't play football anymore.

Lesson 1.5: The Mysterious Life of Twins
Graphic Organizer 2: Fact-and-Opinion Chart
Identical twins have the same genes. *Fact*
It would be fun to be a twin. *Opinion*
Many twins like the same things and have the same habits. *Fact*
Some scientists believe genes explain all the similarities between twins. *Fact*
The special connection between twins is just a coincidence. *Opinion*

Lesson 2.1: Mummies
Graphic Organizer 5: Sequence-of-Events Chart
Dry the body.
Stuff the body with cloth or sand.
Coat the body with glue.
Wrap the body in bandages.

Lesson 2.2: Escape from Iran
Graphic Organizer 5: Problem-and-Solution Chart
Possible answers:
Box 1: *They went to the Canadian embassy for help.*
Box 2: *The Canadians hid the Americans in their homes.*
Box 3: *Antonio Mendez, a CIA agent, posed as an Irish filmmaker in Tehran to shoot a movie.*
Box 4: *The hostages pretended to be film crew members to get out of Iran.*
Solution: *The six Americans made it home safely.*

Answer Key Graphic Organizers

Lesson 2.3: Alone at Sea
Graphic Organizer 1: Characteristics Map
Possible answers:

Brave: *He sailed across the Atlantic Ocean alone in a raft.*

Determined: *After his first attempt in the Mediterranean Sea failed, he set out a second time in the Atlantic Ocean.*

Curious: *He was interested in testing his theory about drinking salt water.*

Resourceful: *He figured out a way to collect plankton so he could eat more than just fish.*

Lesson 2.4: Night Killers
Graphic Organizer 1: Concept Map
Possible answers:

What vampire bats look like: *They are small with wings and sharp teeth.*

What they eat: *They eat blood from animals.*

Problems they cause: *They can spread diseases, such as rabies, and kill livestock.*

How people kill them: *People kill them with nets and poison.*

Lesson 2.5: Escape to Freedom
Graphic Organizer 1: Characteristics Map
Possible answers:

Intelligent: *Douglass found ways to improve his reading skills.*

Brave: *He was willing to risk death for the chance to be free.*

Thoughtful: *Douglass didn't want to cause trouble for anyone who had helped him.*

Determined: *He spent years fighting to end slavery.*

Lesson 3.1: A Horrible Way to Die
Graphic Organizer 2: Author's Purpose Chart
Possible answers:

Inform:
Ebola was first identified in 1976.
By August 24, the epidemic was over.

Persuade:
The threat of Ebola is a real one.
It is one more reason why we should think twice before cutting down the world's remaining rain forests.

Lesson 3.2: A Shocking Experience
Graphic Organizer 2: Fact-and-Opinion Chart
Florida lies between two warm bodies of water. *Fact*
You'd have to call any lightning victim unlucky. *Opinion*
Only one person in about 600,000 ever gets struck by lightning. *Fact*
Sullivan worked as a park ranger in Virginia. *Fact*
Being struck by lightning can be a blessing. *Opinion*
Lightning kills more Americans than almost any other weather hazard. *Fact*

Lesson 3.3: Needles That Cure
Graphic Organizer 1: Concept Map
Possible answers:

What it is: *Acupuncture is a Chinese healing art that uses needles to cure pain.*

How it works: *Needles are used to unblock the qi, or energy flow.*

How it feels: *You may feel a little pain.*

Does it work? *Some believe it has helped them get rid of their pain.*

Lesson 3.4: Hanging from a Cliff
Graphic Organizer 5: Sequence-of-Events Chart
Young stumbled and fell toward a deep crevasse and dislocated both shoulders. Muir climbed down to reach Young and carried him out of the crevasse.
Muir carried Young down the mountain.
Men helped Young put his shoulder back in place.

Lesson 3.5: Killer Bees
Graphic Organizer 8: Compare-and-Contrast Venn Diagram
Possible answers:

African bees:
Like the heat
Very aggressive
Will chase people for a metric mile
Attack in huge numbers

Both:
Look similar
Produce honey
Live in hives

European bees:
Prefer cooler climates
Not very aggressive
Will chase people for only a short distance

Lesson Plan Intermediate 2 Reader

Unit 1 Lesson 1.1 📶 "King Kong," pages 1–9

Summary In 1933 people flocked to theaters to see a movie about a giant ape on the loose in New York City. Merian C. Cooper created the original *King Kong* film. The movie was shot in a studio using models of gorillas. Doll-sized figures for people were used in some of the scenes. The filming process was slow and took one year to complete, but the result was worth the hard work. *King Kong* was a huge success and prompted others to make additional King Kong movies through the years.

BEFORE READING

Build Vocabulary List the vocabulary words and their definitions on the board. Discuss each word's meaning with students. Then write the following questions on the board. Read the questions aloud and discuss the answers with students.

pierced: penetrated

withstand: resist

initially: at first

ventures: dares to go

ultimately: finally

1. Which word goes with "enduring something unpleasant"? *(withstand)*
2. Which word goes with "explores the unknown"? *(ventures)*
3. Which word goes with "a knife or a needle"? *(pierced)*

4. Which word goes with "the plan that you have to begin with"? *(initially)*
5. Which word goes with "arriving at your destination"? *(ultimately)*

Activate Prior Knowledge
1. Ask students to discuss what they know about King Kong. Invite them to tell about King Kong movies they have seen.
2. Have students discuss jobs associated with movies. *(Possible answers: actors, make-up artists, directors, stunt people)* For ideas, go to http://movies.about.com, enter "crew" into the search box, and click on "Movie Crew Glossary - Hollywood Movies."

Build Background There are different kinds of apes, including gibbons, gorillas, chimpanzees, and orangutans. King Kong was modeled after a gorilla, the largest of the apes. Gorillas can grow to more than five feet tall and weigh 400 pounds. Unlike King Kong, gorillas are gentle, quiet, peaceful creatures that are vegetarians. Male gorillas can eat up to 50 pounds of food a day! Like people, gorillas have opposable thumbs. *Opposable* means the thumb can be moved to face the other fingers on the hand. This provides the ability to grab hold of things. Unlike people, gorillas also have opposable big toes! Gorillas are currently an endangered species.

Preview and Predict Ask students what clues the title of the article, the illustration, and the caption provide. What predictions about the article might students make? *(Possible answer:* King Kong *is a movie about a giant ape. I think I will learn why the movie was so successful.)*

DURING READING

Cause and Effect A cause is an event or action that makes something else happen. An effect is the result or the outcome of that action. Writers sometimes use clue words such as *because, so, since, if,* and *therefore* to signal cause and effect. Have students look for cause-and-effect relationships by asking *What happened? Why?*

AFTER READING

Respond to the Article Have students write a journal or blog entry about why *King Kong* was such a successful movie. Ask students: How do you feel about how the story of King Kong changed? What were these changes and why were they made? Would you have gone to see *King Kong*? Why or why not?

DIFFERENTIATED INSTRUCTION

Kinesthetic learners may benefit from using physical movements to understand cause-and-effect relationships. Have students perform actions that illustrate cause and effect: for example, turning off the light to cause the room to get darker. Also have them brainstorm actions in a sport that demonstrates cause-and-effect relationships, such as plays in a soccer match or a football game that result in a score.

ENGLISH LANGUAGE LEARNERS

Have students fold pieces of paper in half lengthwise and label the left side *Cause* and the right side *Effect*. They should draw sketches or cut pictures from magazines that show cause-and-effect relationships. For example, they may place a picture of a racing car on the left and draw a finish line on the right.

GRAPHIC ORGANIZERS

💻 Go to **www.mhreadingbasics.com.** Use Graphic Organizer 2 as a Fact-and-Opinion Chart. Make copies for each student. Ask students to write *Fact* at the top of the left column and *Opinion* at the top of the right column. Then have students organize the following sentences about the article according to whether each sentence is a fact or an opinion. Discuss their responses.

It took one year to complete the filming of the original *King Kong* movie.

It was heartbreaking when King Kong was killed.

The 1976 version of *King Kong* is better than the original.

Other producers made movies about giant apes.

In the 1976 movie, King Kong climbs one of the World Trade Center Towers.

Intermediate 2 Reader

Unit 1 Lesson 1.2 🔊 "Nightmare on Chemical Street: The Love Canal Story," pages 10–18

Introduce

Summary In the late 1970s people noticed problems in Love Canal, a section of Niagara Falls, New York. Trees died, rusted metal barrels surfaced, and many residents were sick. Lois Gibbs, one of the residents, learned that Love Canal had been built on a toxic waste site. She and her neighbors founded the Love Canal Homeowners Association to ask the state to clean up the area. When that did not work, they asked the federal governments to buy the homes and help residents relocate. In 1980 the association won the battle. Many people were relocated, and Love Canal was covered with a thick layer of clay. Since then, however, people have moved back. But is the area safe?

Teach Lesson Skills

BEFORE READING

Build Vocabulary List the vocabulary words and their definitions on the board. Discuss each word's meaning with students. Then write the sentences that contain the words on the board. Read the sentences aloud and discuss them with students.

toxic: poisonous

severe: serious

residents: inhabitants

1. *Toxic* chemicals can kill trees, plants, people, and wildlife.
2. The wind knocked over trees and caused *severe* problems in our neighborhood.
3. Many of the *residents* in my town commute to the city for work.

publicity: attracting public interest

defects: flaws

4. The school play got so much *publicity* that we had a full house every night!
5. Toxic waste can cause birth *defects* in babies.

Activate Prior Knowledge

1. Ask students if they have seen the movies *A Civil Action* or *Erin Brockovich*. Discuss what they learned about the importance of speaking out for the good of an individual or a community, even when it means taking on a powerful company.
2. Ask students to discuss ways in which the EPA can help people and their neighborhoods. See http://www.epa.gov.
3. Ask students to discuss effects of illegal chemical dumping.

Preview and Predict Ask students what clues the title of the article, the photograph, and the photo caption provide. What predictions about the article might students make? *(Possible answer: Houses in Love Canal were built on a toxic waste site. That was a nightmare, or horrible experience, for the people who lived there.)*

Build Background Love Canal is part of the city of Niagara Falls, New York, home to the famous Niagara Falls waterfalls. Students might question how a community could be built atop a chemical dump site. At the time, the Hooker Chemical Company disposed of its toxic waste in the canal; however, the U.S. Environmental Protection Agency (EPA) did not exist. The agency was established in 1970. Therefore, certain regulations, such as the Clean Air Act (1970), the Clean Water Act (amended in 1977), and the Toxic Substances Control Act (1976), were not yet in place.

DURING READING

Predict Predicting is thinking ahead to guess the outcome of events. Predicting helps readers become involved in the text. Readers base predictions on details in the text and their own knowledge. Tell students that their predictions may change as details change or are added.

AFTER READING

Respond to the Article Have students write a journal or blog entry to give their opinions about people moving back to Love Canal. Ask students: Do you think the tragedy at Love Canal will happen all over again? Would you move there? Why or why not?

Support Individual Learners

DIFFERENTIATED INSTRUCTION

Give students a comic strip with the final frame missing. Ask them to draw their prediction of what happens at the end. Remind them to use clues the cartoonist has provided. When they finish, give them the final frame of the comic and have them compare their predictions to the ending.

ENGLISH LANGUAGE LEARNERS

Have students pair up to practice predicting the outcomes of stories. Students may read the book *Bea and Mr. Jones*, by Amy Schwartz, or tell the plot of a familiar book or film. Have the storyteller stop periodically and ask, "What do you think happens next?" Ask the partner to make a prediction. Have students discuss if their predictions were correct or if they had to revise them. Then ask students to switch roles.

GRAPHIC ORGANIZERS

📖 Go to **www.mhreadingbasics.com.** Use Graphic Organizer 2 as a Fact-and-Opinion Chart. Make copies for each student. Ask students to write *Fact* at the top of the left column and *Opinion* at the top of the right column. Then have students organize the following sentences according to whether each sentence is a fact or opinion. Discuss their responses.

Love Canal seemed like a great place to raise children.

Rusted metal barrels began to rise to the surface.

Many residents were suffering from severe health problems.

The federal government helped New York buy the homes closest to the dump site.

Love Canal must be one of the safest places to live in Niagara Falls by now.

Intermediate 2 Reader

Introduce

Summary In 1959 in New Guinea, Reverend William Booth Gill saw a strange object in the night sky. As the object descended toward Earth, Gill and other witnesses saw that it was a huge disk and that there were glowing humanlike figures inside. Four hours later, the UFO zoomed away, only to return the next evening. This time, Gill and the others waved to the figures inside and they waved back! Then Gill unexpectedly went inside and the UFO left. Did Gill really see a UFO? Some people believed he did, but others thought it was a story he made up.

Teach Lesson Skills

BEFORE READING

Build Vocabulary List the vocabulary words and their definitions on the board. Discuss each word's meaning with students. Then write the following sentence stems on the board. Read the sentence stems aloud and ask students to complete them.

remote: out-of-the-way

transfixed: motionless

impulse: a whim

theories: guesses

traumatic: stressful

1. A *remote* island is an island that is . . .
2. The people in the audience were *transfixed* for hours because . . .
3. When you act on *impulse*, you . . .
4. Scientists have different *theories* because . . .
5. The boy thought the experience was *traumatic* because . . .

Activate Prior Knowledge

1. Have students brainstorm words they think of when they hear the term *UFO*.
2. Ask students to discuss movies they have seen about aliens, flying saucers, or spaceships. Do students think events from these kinds of movies could happen in real life?
3. Have students find New Guinea on a world map. Is New Guinea a remote place? Explain your answer.

Preview and Predict Ask students what clues the title of the article, the photograph, and the photo caption provide. What predictions about the article might students make? *(Possible answer: Reverend Gill had an encounter with a UFO in New Guinea.)*

Build Background Over time, people around the world have reported seeing UFOs. There is even a museum in Roswell, New Mexico, that is devoted to UFOs! The International UFO Museum and Research Center studies reports of UFO sightings. One famous sighting, known as the Roswell incident, occurred in Roswell in July 1947. Some people believe a flying saucer crashed there. Soldiers collected what they reported was spaceship debris. Soon afterward, the report was retracted. The Roswell incident is still a mystery today.

In July 2010 two UFO sightings were reported in China. Twinkling lights above Hangzhou's Xiaoshan Airport caused flights to be delayed or rerouted. Other people saw a diamond-shaped object hovering in the sky above the city of Chongqing, China.

DURING READING

Visualize Visualizing is picturing in your mind the details of the setting, events, and characters in the text. Encourage students to draw pictures or diagrams of these images as they read.

AFTER READING

Respond to the Article Have students write a journal or blog entry about Reverend Gill's encounter. Ask students: Do you believe that Reverend Gill saw a UFO? What facts from the article support your opinion? What would you have done if you were Reverend Gill?

Support Individual Learners

DIFFERENTIATED INSTRUCTION

Poetry is a good resource for helping students visualize. Choose a descriptive poem and read it aloud to students. Ask them to visualize the poem as they listen. Then, reread the poem and have students act out what they see in their mind's eye. Finally, ask students to sketch or write a description of their visualizations.

ENGLISH LANGUAGE LEARNERS

Have students take turns describing one of their favorite places to other students. As each student describes a place, ask others to visualize it and then draw pictures or write descriptions of the place. Encourage students to ask questions as needed to help them clarify their visualizations.

GRAPHIC ORGANIZERS

💻 Go to **www.mhereadingbasics.com.** Use Graphic Organizer 5 as a Sequence-of-Events Chart. Make copies for each student. Have students write in the boxes of the chart the following main events of the article in the order in which they happened. Discuss their responses.

Events

The UFO hovered above the ground for about four hours and then flew away.

Gill went inside, and the UFO disappeared.

When the UFO returned, Gill waved to the aliens, and they waved back.

A sparkling object descended toward Reverend Gill.

Introduce

Summary On July 28, 1720, Elizabeth Wilson gave birth to a baby girl on board a ship. Shortly afterward, pirates boarded the ship with plans to kill all aboard and steal their treasures. The passengers were spared when the head pirate, Pedro, asked Elizabeth to name her daughter after his mother, Mary. From this true story, a legend was born. Louis Roy bought the house in Henniker, NH, that had been owned by one of Mary's sons. Roy started rumors about Mary and Pedro, a ghost, and a buried treasure. He charged people a fee to visit the house and dig for treasure. While the story has long been proven false, people still come to the house to look for the ghost of Ocean-born Mary!

Teach Lesson Skills

BEFORE READING

Build Vocabulary List the vocabulary words and their definitions on the board. Discuss each word's meaning with students. Then write the following questions on the board. Read the questions aloud and discuss the answers with students.

brandishing: waving

hesitant: uncertain

lack: do without

1. If you were making a salad, would you be *brandishing* a knife or chopping with a knife? Why?

2. If you feel *hesitant* about doing something, are you sure or unsure about doing it? Why?

3. If you *lack* an umbrella in a rain storm, would you stay dry or get wet? Why?

distressed: upset

plagued: tormented

4. Which would have *distressed* you—losing your wallet or winning a game? Why?

5. Would you be *plagued* by getting good grades on tests or by having nightmares? Why?

Activate Prior Knowledge

1. Ask students to discuss how urban legends, or untrue stories, might get started. Invite them to share ones they have heard.

2. Help students find Londonderry, Ireland, and Londonderry, New Hampshire, on a map. Ask how they would have gotten from one place to the other in the 1700s.

Preview and Predict Ask students what clues the title of the article, the photograph, and the photo caption provide. What predictions about the article might students make? *(Possible answer: I think the article will be about a woman named Mary who was born at sea. I think some strange things will happen in the house, and these happenings may involve ghosts.)*

Build Background Pirates are robbers who attack boats that carry valuable goods. Pirates have been around since ancient times. The years 1650–1720 were known as the Golden Age of Piracy. This was a good period for pirates because many ships traveling between Europe and the Americas were carrying silver, gold, and jewels. Pirates were known for their brutality, and they terrified the voyagers. Ships often surrendered quickly, and sometimes without a fight, when they spotted a pirate ship approaching with its dreaded skull-and-crossbones flag waving in the wind.

DURING READING

Infer An inference is a logical guess about information that the writer suggests but doesn't directly state. Making inferences helps readers find deeper meaning in what they read. Ask students to look for details that aren't fully explained. Have them combine clues from the text with their personal knowledge to identify what the writer suggests.

AFTER READING

Respond to the Article Have students write a journal or blog entry about Mary, Pedro, and the ghost story. Ask students: How would Mary feel about the ghost story? How would she feel about Pedro? Why?

Support Individual Learners

DIFFERENTIATED INSTRUCTION

Collect articles, newspaper headlines, jokes, or cartoons that require students to make inferences in order to fully understand the text. Have students form groups and work together to make inferences based on the text. The dialogue among students builds background knowledge, and those who have difficulty with this skill can learn from those who are more adept at it. Have groups share their inferences with the class.

ENGLISH LANGUAGE LEARNERS

Picture books for older readers can be useful for helping students understand the concept of making inferences. Have students read the books in small groups and make three inferences about what happened in each book. *Why?*, by Nikolai Popov, shows how disagreements can escalate into war. *The Stranger*, by Chris Van Allsburg, tells about a mysterious stranger. The reader must use clues to figure out who he is.

GRAPHIC ORGANIZERS

💻 Go to **www.mhereadingbasics.com.** Use Graphic Organizer 2 as a Classifying Chart. Make copies for each student. Ask students to write *Fact* at the top of the left column and *Legend* at the top of the right column. Then have students organize the following sentences according to whether each sentence is a fact or part of the legend. Discuss their responses.

Ocean-born Mary was born on a ship in 1720.

Pedro buried a treasure in Henniker, NH.

Mary wore a wedding dress made of green silk with embroidered flowers on it.

Mary lived in the Ocean-born Mary house.

Pedro gave Mary a coach-and-four to drive and took care of her children.

Mary is buried in a cemetery in Henniker, NH.

Lesson Plan Intermediate 2 Reader

Unit 1 Lesson 1.5 🔊 "Custer's Last Stand: Battle of Little Bighorn," pages 34–41

Introduce

Summary On June 25, 1876, General George Custer fought and lost the Battle of Little Bighorn. Custer had been a general in the Civil War. In 1874 he was with the Seventh Calvary when gold was discovered in the Black Hills. The government wanted the land, but it belonged to the Sioux, who refused to sell. In 1876 Custer disobeyed orders and led the Seventh Calvary in an attack against the Sioux-Cheyenne camp. Custer's men were surrounded and outnumbered by the Sioux and Cheyenne warriors. Custer and all 225 of his men were killed.

Teach Lesson Skills

BEFORE READING

Build Vocabulary List the vocabulary words and their definitions on the board. Discuss each word's meaning with students. Then write the following questions on the board. Read the questions aloud and discuss the answers with students.

resented: were offended by

overbearing: bossy

exploratory: fact-finding

restore: rebuild

devastating: disastrous

1. What word goes with "someone who always tells others what to do"? *(overbearing)*
2. What word goes with "an unexpected tragedy"? *(devastating)*
3. What word goes with "disliked what was said or done"? *(resented)*

4. What word goes with "make like new"? *(restore)*
5. What word goes with "an adventure to a new place"? *(exploratory)*

Activate Prior Knowledge

1. Show a map of the site of the Battle of Little Bighorn. Invite discussion of what students already know about Custer and the battle. See http://www.nps.gov/libi.
2. Ask students to discuss the army's chain of command. Invite discussion about what might happen if it is not followed.

Preview and Predict Ask students what clues the title of the article, the painting, and the caption provide. What predictions about the article might students make? *(Possible answer: Custer fought the Battle of Little Bighorn in 1876. Since the title says it was Custer's "last stand," Custer must have lost.)*

Build Background Crazy Horse was a warrior and leader of the Lakota Indians. His exact birth date is unknown, but most people think it was in the early 1840s. He died in 1877. He was known for preserving the Lakota way of life. He fought against settlers in Wyoming from 1865–1868. Later, he fought to prevent gold seekers from encroaching on land given to the Lakota by the Fort Laramie Treaty of 1868. In 1876 Crazy Horse joined forces with Sitting Bull to protect the Lakota land when the War Department ordered the Lakota onto reservations. Crazy Horse and his warriors defeated Custer at the Battle of Little Bighorn. The was a major victory for the Indians during the Great Sioux War. After this battle, the army reinforced its efforts to overpower Crazy Horse. He fought bravely but was eventually forced to give up. He surrendered on May 6, 1877.

DURING READING

Ask Questions Asking questions helps you to monitor your understanding of the text. Have students ask *who, what, when, where, why,* and *how* questions and look for the answers. Questions may include: Who was General Custer? What is he best known for? When and where does the battle take place? Why did Custer disobey orders? How did the battle end?

AFTER READING

Respond to the Article Have students write a journal or blog entry about Custer's last stand. Ask students: Do you think Custer was a good soldier? Why or why not? What are some of Custer's characteristics that support your opinion?

Support Individual Learners

DIFFERENTIATED INSTRUCTION

Have students choose a newspaper article that interests them. Then have them pretend they are the editor of the paper who wants more information about the article. Have students write at least five questions they can ask the writer to gain the additional information.

ENGLISH LANGUAGE LEARNERS

Have students scan an article in a magazine that includes pictures. Help students read the headline and picture captions. Ask them to come up with three questions about the pictures accompanying the article. Then have students read the article with a partner to find out if their questions about the pictures are answered in the text.

GRAPHIC ORGANIZERS

💻 Go to **www.mhereadingbasics.com.** Use Graphic Organizer 5 as a Sequence-of-vents Chart. Make copies for each student. Ask students to write in the boxes of the chart the following events in the order in which they happened. Discuss their responses.

Terry told Custer to take the Seventh to the Little Bighorn Valley and wait there.

Custer went to the Black Hills on an exploratory trip.

Custer was a general in the Civil War.

The Sioux and Cheyenne banded together near Little Bighorn River.

Lesson Plan Intermediate 2 Reader

Introduce

Summary In 1966 in Bingham, Maine, six-year-old Kimberly Baker claimed she saw a "big ball" or "bubble" land in a field. In her account of the experience, she described what she witnessed: a large, shiny object with a door, a window, red lights, and a flashing green light. Kim also claimed that she saw a man dressed in shiny white who winked at her before the object took off. Richard Bonenfant, a UFO investigator, interviewed Kim himself. He believed that Kim was a reliable witness and that the "bubble" was not a conventional aircraft.

Teach Lesson Skills

BEFORE READING

Build Vocabulary List the vocabulary words and their definitions on the board. Discuss each word's meaning with students. Then write the following questions on the board. Read the questions aloud and discuss the answers with students.

figment of her imagination: something she invented

readily: willingly; without effort

wavered: shifted away

din: loud noise

incessant: nonstop

1. If a girl thought the spaceship was a *figment of her imagination,* did she think it was real or make-believe? Why?
2. If you love to play soccer but do not like to play basketball, which game would you play *readily*? Why?
3. If a boy *wavered* from his original story, do you think he was telling the truth or lying? Why?

4. Would a group of people create a *din* at a party or at the library? Why?
5. Where would you probably see *incessant* traffic—on a city street or a country road? Why?

Activate Prior Knowledge

1. Ask students to discuss images they've seen of UFOs or how they imagine one might look. What shape is it? What features does it have?
2. Ask students what they would do if they thought they saw a UFO. Who would they call? What would they say? See http://www.cufos.org for more information about UFOs.
3. Have students find Bingham, Maine, on a map.

Build Background Ufologists are people who study UFOs. J. Allen Hynek (1910–1986) was an influential ufologist. He was a professor of astronomy who also worked for the air force on Project Blue Book. At first, he was skeptical about the possibility of UFOs. Over time, however, his opinion began to change. He thought the subject was worth researching, so he opened the Center for UFO Studies. The center gathers and publishes information about the UFO phenomenon. Other people also actively search for signs of extraterrestrial life. SETI, or the Search for Extraterrestrial Intelligence, is an exploratory science. Scientists use radio telescopes to search for signs of intelligent life in the universe.

Preview and Predict Ask students what clues the title of the article, the illustration, and the caption provide. What predictions about the article might students make? *(Possible answer: A girl named Kim claimed she saw a UFO. She described it as looking like a shiny bubble.)*

DURING READING

Determine Word Meanings from Context Think of context as the words or sentences that surround a word you don't know. This information can help you make a good guess about what the word means. Have students look for clues such as descriptions, synonyms, or examples to help them figure out the meaning of an unfamiliar word.

AFTER READING

Respond to the Article Have students write a journal or blog entry about Kim's story. Ask students: What are your thoughts about Kim's story? What do you think was the main reason Bonenfant found Kim to be a reliable witness? What actions would you take if you were in Kim's situation?

Support Individual Learners

DIFFERENTIATED INSTRUCTION

Ask students to bring in song lyrics or poems that contain words that may be unfamiliar to other students. Have students take turns explaining to the class how they determined the meaning of unfamiliar words using context clues.

ENGLISH LANGUAGE LEARNERS

Tell students that they can sometimes figure out the meaning of an unfamiliar word or phrase by seeing how it relates to the other words around it. Use the first sentence of paragraph 10 in the article as an example: "Kimberly . . . went on to describe the size and color of the 'bubble.'" Explain that *went on* means "continued." Have students read the text before and after the sentence to help figure out the meaning of *went on.*

GRAPHIC ORGANIZERS

📖 Go to **www.mhereadingbasics.com.** Use Graphic Organizer 1 as a Concept Map. Make copies for each student. Ask students to write *Kim's Bubble* in the center bubble of the graphic organizer. Then have students write a word or phrase in each of the outer bubbles to describe the UFO and alien that Kim saw. Discuss their responses.

Lesson Plan Intermediate 2 Reader

Unit 2 Lesson 2.2 🔊 "Poison on the Drugstore Shelf," pages 50–58

Introduce

Summary In 1982 in the Chicago area, seven people died after taking Tylenol capsules. Someone had filled the capsules with cyanide, a very dangerous poison. People around the country panicked. Johnson & Johnson, the company that makes Tylenol, temporarily stopped production and took Tylenol off store shelves. As a result of the poisonings, companies started using safer, tamper-proof packaging for products. The Tylenol killer was never found. Police suspected James Lewis, however, who was arrested for trying to extort money from Johnson & Johnson.

Teach Lesson Skills

BEFORE READING

Build Vocabulary List the vocabulary words and their definitions on the board. Discuss each word's meaning with students. Then write the following sentence stems on the board. Read the sentence stems aloud and ask students to complete them.

contaminated: poisoned

malicious: spiteful

alias: a fake name

extort: blackmail

convicted: found guilty

1. Food becomes *contaminated* when . . .
2. A *malicious* person might . . .
3. A person might use an *alias* because . . .

4. When people *extort* money, they . . .
5. After the woman was *convicted* of the crime, she . . .

Activate Prior Knowledge

1. Ask students to describe the containers and caps of medicines they buy. Ask why products are packaged that way.
2. Ask students if they are familiar with recent government recalls of products. Why are products recalled? What are products that have been recalled? What was the impact on the public and on the company whose product was recalled?

Build Background Cyanide is a chemical that can be fast acting and deadly. It can be in a gas or crystal form. Cyanide is used in controlled environments to make paper, textiles, and plastics. It is found in the materials used to develop photographs. It is also used to exterminate pests from ships and buildings. People can be exposed to cyanide by coming in contact with air, water, food, or soil that has cyanide in it. Cyanide prevents the cells in our bodies from using oxygen. It is most harmful to the heart and brain because they use so much oxygen.

Preview and Predict Ask students what clues the title of the article, the photograph, and the photo captions provide. What predictions about the article might students make? *(Possible answer: People died after taking poisoned Tylenol they bought at the drugstore. The article might tell how this happened and if the person or people responsible were caught.)*

DURING READING

Identify Sequence Sequence is the order in which events, ideas, or things are arranged. Time order refers to the order in which events occur. Following the sequence of events helps you see how the text is organized and how events relate to each other. As students read, ask them to look for key words and phrases, such as *an hour later, that evening, finally, then, next,* and *soon.*

AFTER READING

Respond to the Article Have students write a journal or blog entry about Johnson & Johnson's response to the Tylenol poisonings. Ask students: Do you agree with Johnson & Johnson's response? How might you have responded? Do you think tamper-proof packaging helps make products safer? Why or why not?

Support Individual Learners

DIFFERENTIATED INSTRUCTION

Explain that the most common types of sequence are time order, spatial order, order of importance, and steps in a process. Time order is the order in which events occur. Spatial order refers to where things are in relation to one another. Order of importance refers to events or ideas arranged from most to least important. Steps-in-a-process order refers to the order in which something is done, such as a time line.

ENGLISH LANGUAGE LEARNERS

Have students describe an event from their past in time order or explain something they can do using steps-in-a-process order. Prompt them to use signal words in their description. Have students create a time line of the events they are describing as a visual aid.

GRAPHIC ORGANIZERS

📖 Go to **www.mhereadingbasics.com.** Use Graphic Organizer 1 as a Cause-and-Effect Map. Make copies for each student. Ask students to write the cause below in the center bubble of the graphic organizer. Explain that this cause had multiple effects. Have students write an effect in each of the outer bubbles. Discuss their responses.

Seven people died from taking Tylenol filled with cyanide.

Lesson Plan Intermediate 2 Reader

Introduce

Summary In 1912 the *Titanic* set sail from England for New York City. It was the largest ship ever built at that time, and it was believed to be unsinkable. Then, during its first voyage, the *Titanic* hit an iceberg. The collision left a 300-foot gash in the *Titanic's* side. Water entered the ship at a pace so fast that it could not be pumped out, and the ship started to sink. In the confusion, only 711 of the more than 2,200 passengers and crew escaped in lifeboats. It was 1986 before *Alvin*, a small sub made for underwater exploration, found the remains of the *Titanic*. It lay on the ocean floor in two pieces more than 2.5 miles beneath the surface of the water.

Teach Lesson Skills

BEFORE READING

Build Vocabulary List the vocabulary words and their definitions on the board. Discuss each word's meaning with students. Then write the sentences that contain the words on the board. Read the sentences aloud and discuss them with students.

luxurious: rich and splendid

abandon: leave

fascination: strong attraction

assessed: took stock of

secured: obtained

1. The fancy hotel was the most *luxurious* hotel in the city.
2. People should find new homes for their pets and not *abandon* them.
3. Anthony wants to be an astronomer because he has always had a *fascination* with stars and planets.

4. We *assessed* our situation and decided it would not be wise to hike in the rain.
5. Portia climbed onto the train and *secured* her seat for the trip home.

Activate Prior Knowledge

1. Invite students who have seen the movie *Titanic* to share what they learned about the ship and the disaster.
2. Use Graphic Organizer 3 as a KWL Chart. Have students label the first column *Know* and write what they know about the *Titanic*. Have students label the second column *Want to Know* and write what they want to know. Explain that this exercise will be continued after reading. See http://www.encyclopedia-titanica.org for more information.

Preview and Predict Ask students what clues the title of the article, the painting, and the caption provide. What predictions about the article might students make? *(Possible answer: The title and image tell me that people died in a disaster. I think the article will tell why the ship sank.)*

Build Background Icebergs are pieces of ice that have formed on land and then float in water. They can break off from glaciers, ice shelves, or bigger icebergs. They can range in size from very small to very large. Some icebergs are as big as a small country! Small icebergs are more dangerous to ships because they are harder to see than large icebergs. In addition, nine-tenths of the iceberg is underwater, and it can be hard to tell the shape of the underwater portion. Most icebergs are found in the North Atlantic and in the waters around Antarctica. After the *Titanic* sank in the North Atlantic, the United States and other countries formed the International Ice Patrol. This patrol uses airplanes and radar to warn ships in the North Atlantic of icebergs.

DURING READING

Find Vocabulary in Context As students read the article, have them note new vocabulary words. Ask them to think about each word's meaning as they read.

AFTER READING

Respond to the Article Have students write a journal or blog entry about the sinking of the *Titanic* from a survivor's point of view. Ask students: If you were a survivor of the *Titanic*, what would you have told people about your experience? Do you think this disaster could have been avoided? If so, how?

Support Individual Learners

DIFFERENTIATED INSTRUCTION

Explain that the author's purpose is the reason an author has for writing something. Generally, an author will write to persuade, describe, explain, or entertain. An author can have more than one purpose, however. Provide students with some short articles or graphic novels. Have them discuss each author's purpose.

ENGLISH LANGUAGE LEARNERS

Have students share words or phrases from their first languages that writers might use for different purposes. For example, English words that may be used to persuade include *fantastic* or *incredible*. Spanish words may include *muy bueno* and *excelente*. Descriptive words may include colors. Explanations often include words or phrases such as *because* or *the reason is*. Stories that entertain may begin with "It was a dark, stormy night."

GRAPHIC ORGANIZERS

📖 Go to **www.mhereadingbasics.com.** Use Graphic Organizer 3 as a KWL Chart. Make copies for each student. Have students use the charts they started before reading the article. If students did not do this exercise before reading, they can start it now. Students should label the third column *Learned* and add information about the *Titanic that* they learned from the article. Students may wish to add more questions to the *Want to Know* column. Have students discuss their charts, and encourage them to find answers to their questions online or at the library.

Lesson Plan Intermediate 2 Reader

Unit 2 Lesson 2.4 🔊 "Sarah's Ghost House: An Architectural Fun House," pages 68–77

Summary In 1862 Sarah Pardee married William Winchester, heir to the Winchester rifle fortune. They had a baby girl who died when she was one month old. Soon after, William also died. Heartbroken, Sarah went to mediums to contact her baby and husband. One medium, Adam Coons, told Sarah to move to the West, buy a house, and keep adding rooms to it. If she housed the spirits of all the people killed by Winchester rifles, she would remain alive. Sarah bought a house in San Jose, California, and continued to build onto it until her death.

BEFORE READING

Build Vocabulary List the vocabulary words and their definitions on the board. Discuss each word's meaning with students. Then write the following questions on the board. Read the questions aloud and discuss the answers with students.

obsessed: totally absorbed

depicted: pictured

spewed: shot forth

1. What word or phrase goes with "a photograph or painting"? *(depicted)*

2. What word or phrase goes with "a person who works all the time"? *(obsessed)*

3. What word or phrase goes with "being sorry about something"? *(making amends)*

making amends: apologizing

despite: regardless of

4. What word or phrase goes with "water in a fountain"? *(spewed)*

5. What word or phrase goes with "you had an accident even though you were careful"? *(despite)*

Activate Prior Knowledge

1. Ask students if they have seen movies in which someone goes to a séance or otherwise communicates with spirits and have them describe what happens.

2. Have students find New Haven, Connecticut, and San Jose, California, on a map of the United States.

Preview and Predict Ask students what clues the title of the article, the photograph, and the photo caption provide. What predictions about the article might students make? *(Possible answer: Sarah Winchester lived in a huge and unusual house. The title says it is a ghost house. This article might explain why.)*

Build Background Oliver Winchester entered the gun business in 1855, when he bought stock in a gun company. In 1866 he bought out the New Haven Arms Company of Connecticut and renamed it the Winchester Repeating Arms Company. Winchester had patented the first reliable repeating rifle, Model 1866. Now people could fire a number of shots before they had to reload. This gun and the models that followed were popular in the American frontier. They were called "the gun that won the West."

DURING READING

Cause and Effect A cause is an event or action that makes something else happen. An effect is the result or the outcome of that action. Writers use clue words such as *because, so, since, if,* and *therefore* to signal cause and effect. Have students look for cause-and-effect relationships by asking: *What happened? Why?*

AFTER READING

Respond to the Article Have students write a journal or blog entry about Sarah's ghost house. Ask students: How would you describe Sarah? What other character that you have read about had a similar problem?

DIFFERENTIATED INSTRUCTION

Ask students to watch a news report about a cause-and-effect event, such as a fire caused by a space heater or a soccer victory as a result of a last-second goal. Ask students to rewrite the report using words such as *because, as a result, since, therefore,* and *so* to help show cause-and-effect relationships.

ENGLISH LANGUAGE LEARNERS

Ask students to tell a partner a common folktale or legend that has one or more cause-and-effect events. You may model by telling them about Rip van Winkle or the Headless Horseman. Point out how you use a cause-and-effect structure when retelling the story.

GRAPHIC ORGANIZERS

🖥 Go to **www.mhreadingbasics.com.** Use Graphic Organizer 4 as a Cause-and-Effect Chart. Make copies for each student. Have students write *Cause* at the top of the left column and *Effect* at the top of the right column. Then have students write each sentence below in a box under the *Cause* column. In each box in the *Effect* column, ask students to write one effect for each cause. Discuss their responses.

The Winchester rifle was responsible for the deaths of many people.

Sarah wanted to make contact with her daughter and husband after they died.

Coons said that the spirits of dead people would haunt Sarah unless she did as he said.

Either the ghosts did not like Sarah's plans, or they changed their minds.

Intermediate 2 Reader

Introduce

Teach Lesson Skills

Support Individual Learners

Introduce

Summary In August 1883 people around the world heard a loud noise. Krakatoa, an island between Java and Sumatra, erupted in a volcanic explosion. The eruption caused a cloud of ash to rise more than seven miles up into the air. The ash fell as far as 1,600 miles away. The eruption affected Earth's weather for months and the sunsets for two years. An earthquake jolted the area around the island, and a giant tsunami formed. The giant wave wiped out more than 300 villages in Southeast Asia. Krakatoa was torn to pieces.

Teach Lesson Skills

BEFORE READING

Build Vocabulary List the vocabulary words and their definitions on the board. Discuss each word's meaning with students. Then write the following sentence stems on the board. Read the sentence stems aloud and ask students to complete them.

buoyancy: tendency to float
generated: produced
attained: reached

1. A boat must have *buoyancy* because . . .
2. Smoke can be *generated* by . . .
3. The race car *attained* a high speed when . . .

casualties: deaths
emerge from: rise out of

4. The earthquake resulted in *casualties* because . . .
5. The whales *emerge from* the ocean because . . .

Activate Prior Knowledge

1. Ask students to discuss what they know about volcanic eruptions.
2. Ask students to discuss the difference among a volcanic eruption, an earthquake, and a tsunami.
3. Have students find Krakatoa on a map.

Preview and Predict Ask students what clues the title of the article, the photograph, and the photo caption provide. What predictions about the article might students make? *(Possible answer: The article will be about a volcanic eruption on Krakatoa.)*

Build Background Why do volcanoes erupt? Pressure from deep inside Earth releases to make a volcanic eruption. First, magma collects deep underground. The magma is less dense than the rock around it, so the magma pushes up. When enough pressure builds up, the magma rises inside the volcano and erupts from the crater.

DURING READING

Visualize Visualizing is picturing in your mind the details of the setting, events, and characters in the text. Encourage students to draw pictures or diagrams of these images as they read.

AFTER READING

Respond to the Article Have students write a journal or blog entry about what they think will happen to Anak Krakatoa. Ask students: Will it grow into a full-size island? Will it have a gigantic volcano eruption? What facts support your opinion?

Support Individual Learners

DIFFERENTIATED INSTRUCTION

Have students choose descriptive paragraphs from stories they have read. Have partners work together to practice visualizing the paragraphs. Partners take turns reading their paragraphs and visualizing the details. Ask students to draw pictures to show their visualizations.

ENGLISH LANGUAGE LEARNERS

Have students choose pictures from books or magazines. As each student describes a picture (without showing it), have others visualize it and then draw pictures or write about the description they heard. When students have finished drawing or writing, invite them to compare their pictures to the original.

GRAPHIC ORGANIZERS

📷 Go to **www.mhreadingbasics.com.** Use Graphic Organizer 4 as a Visualizing Chart. Make copies for each student. Have students write *Description* at the top of the left column and *Visualize* at the top of the right column. Then, have students write each sentence below in a box in the *Description* column. Ask students to draw in the right column what they visualize when they read each description. Discuss their visualizations. Finally, have students write another description from the article in the bottom box and draw what they visualize.

Description

The people of Texas heard a sound they thought was cannon fire.

A ship more than 15 miles from Krakatoa was covered with volcanic ash 15 feet deep.

It was this great hill of moving water that caused most of the 36,000 deaths associated with Krakatoa.

Introduce

Summary Some people believe they have seen a dinosaur-like monster living in remote regions of Africa. European reports go back at least 200 years. In 1913 an explorer was told about a monster call Mokele-Mbembe that had a long neck and one very long tooth. In 1979 villagers described a monster, similar to Mokele-Mbembe, called N'yamala living in Gabon. In 1981 and 1983, people claimed to have seen the monster in Lake Tele in the Congo. Many people do not believe the monster exists and that the "sightings" are really elephants or pythons.

Teach Lesson Skills

BEFORE READING

Build Vocabulary List the vocabulary words and their definitions on the board. Discuss each word's meaning with students. Then write the following questions on the board. Read the questions aloud and discuss the answers with students.

cataclysmic: disastrous

adapt to: adjust to

wrought: brought about

flexible: elastic

mutilated: disfigured

1. Which would be a *cataclysmic* event—a tornado or a sunset? Why?
2. If animals *adapt to* a new environment, can they survive there, or do they die? Explain.
3. If an event *wrought* changes, were things the same or different? Why?

4. What are some things that are *flexible*? Why are they *flexible*?
5. Is a *mutilated* forest one that has mostly healthy trees or rotting trees? Why?

Activate Prior Knowledge

1. Ask students to share what they know about dinosaurs. Ask if they believe any dinosaurs are alive today.
2. Help students find Gabon, the Congo, and Lake Tele on a world map.

Preview and Predict Ask students what clues the title of the article, the illustration, and the caption provide. What predictions about the article might students make? *(Possible answer: Some people claim to have seen a monster that looks like a dinosaur living in equatorial Africa.)*

Build Background The *Brontosaurus*, as it is commonly known, is formally classified in the *Apatosaurus* genus. This dinosaur lived during the late Jurassic time period, about 150–145 million years ago, in North America and Europe. It was one of the largest land animals of all time: about 15 feet tall, weighing more than 30 tons, and measuring 70 feet from head to tail. It had a long thin neck, a relatively small head, and legs that were straight and thick like pillars. It also had a long heavy tail, which it would use for balance. The tail may have served another function, too. Since the *Brontosaurus* was a peaceful plant eater, it needed something to defend itself against potential predators. Scientists think it may have used its long tail like a whip, to send potential attackers flying.

DURING READING

Infer An inference is a logical guess about information that the writer suggests but doesn't directly state. Making inferences helps readers find deeper meaning in what they read. Ask students to look for details that aren't fully explained. Have them combine clues from the text with their personal knowledge to identify what the writer suggests.

AFTER READING

Respond to the Article Have students write a journal or blog entry about whether they think Mokele-Mbembe is real. Ask students: Do you believe this monster is living in Africa? What facts from the article support your opinion? What could you do to prove your opinion true?

Support Individual Learners

DIFFERENTIATED INSTRUCTION

Ask students to write riddles about animals, sports, work, or other subjects of interest. Have partners take turns reading and guessing the answers to their riddles. Encourage them to discuss how clues in the riddles and their previous knowledge helped them make inferences and solve the riddles.

ENGLISH LANGUAGE LEARNERS

Picture books for older readers can be useful for helping students understand the concept of making inferences. Have students read the books in small groups and make three inferences about what happened in each book. *Hey, Al,* by Arthur Yorinks, is the story of a man named Al who works as a janitor. One morning a bird calls to Al and tells him he has a solution to all of his problems.

GRAPHIC ORGANIZERS

💻 Go to **www.mhereadingbasics.com.** Use Graphic Organizer 8 as a Venn Diagram. Make copies for each student. Have students write the heading *Mokele-Mbembe* above the left circle, *Both* above the center area, and *N'yamala* above the right circle. Then tell students to write each descriptive phrase below in a circle under the appropriate heading. Use the diagram to discuss how the monsters are alike and different.

brownish-grey	blood-red eyes
long neck	huge mouth
one tooth	smooth skin

Intermediate 2 Reader

Lesson Plan Intermediate 2 Reader

Unit 3 Lesson 3.2 🔊 "Spiritualism: Fact or Fraud," pages 93–102

Summary In March 1848 two girls, Margaret and Katherine Fox, claimed to have a conversation with a spirit, and spiritualism was born! One of the girls asked the "spirit" to do as she did. She snapped her fingers, and the spirit answered with the same number of raps. The girls, joined by their older sister Leah, took their "show" on the road. Years later, Margaret confessed to making the noises herself, but people refused to believe her. In 1884 spirits began to speak through a woman named Leonora Piper while she was in a trance. Many people studied her abilities, but no fraud was found.

Introduce

Teach Lesson Skills

BEFORE READING

Build Vocabulary List the vocabulary words and their definitions on the board. Discuss each word's meaning with students. Then write the sentences that contain the words on the board. Read the sentences aloud and discuss them with students.

cloven: divided into two parts

discredit: cast doubt on

revelation: discovery

wily: shrewd

dominate: control

1. Both deer and cattle have *cloven* hooves.
2. People wanted to *discredit* the scientist, so they looked for mistakes in his research.
3. It was a *revelation* when people learned that Earth was not flat.

4. Foxes have a reputation of being *wily* animals.
5. Which candidate do you think will *dominate* the debate?

Activate Prior Knowledge

1. Have students discuss strange noises they have heard at home. Ask what they think caused the noises.
2. Ask students to discuss times they have tried to trick someone into believing something that was not true. Have them tell if it worked.
3. Ask students if they think we can communicate with spirits.

Preview and Predict Ask students what clues the title of the article, the illustration, and the caption provide. What predictions about the article might students make? *(Possible answer: I think this article is about spiritualism and whether or not it is real.)*

Build Background According to people who believe in spiritualism, a living person can communicate with a dead person's spirit through a medium. Spiritualism began in the 1840s and spread quickly. Many mediums began charging for their services. The mediums had séances that took place in darkened rooms. People often sat around a table. Unusual things were believed to have happened, such as a cool breeze blowing or flowers suddenly appearing. The spirits then spoke through the mediums' voices. Spiritualism flourished in the mid- to late 19th century and still exists today.

DURING READING

Ask Questions Asking questions helps you to monitor your understanding of the text. Have students ask *who, what, when, where, why,* and *how* questions and look for the answers. Questions may include: What is this selection about? What do we learn about the beginnings of spiritualism? Who were the Fox sisters? Why do some people believe they were frauds?

AFTER READING

Respond to the Article Have students write a journal or blog entry about whether they believe spiritualism is a fact or a fraud. Ask students: How did reading about spiritualism make you feel? What information from the article supports spiritualism being true? What supports it being a fraud? How might you find out if people like Leonora Piper are telling the truth?

Support Individual Learners

DIFFERENTIATED INSTRUCTION

Encourage students to keep a reading log to help them become better readers. Have them answer questions like the following for articles they read: Did anything in the text remind you of an experience you have had? Did you have a positive or negative reaction to anything in the text? With what parts of the text did you agree or disagree? Which part of the text, if any, was confusing to you?

ENGLISH LANGUAGE LEARNERS

Assign proficient English-speaking partners to English language learners and ask the partners to help the English language learners form questions about what they have read. Having English language learners actively question things they don't understand in a text will help them to understand difficult text in a new language.

GRAPHIC ORGANIZERS

💻 Go to **www.mhereadingbasics.com.** Use Graphic Organizer 1 as a Characteristics Map. Make copies for each student. Ask students to write *Fox Sisters* in the center bubble of the graphic organizer and one of the adjectives about the sisters in each of the outer bubbles. Then have students add information from the article that supports each adjective. Discuss their responses.

shrewd   wily   dishonest

Intermediate 2 Reader

Introduce

Summary In 1995 in Puerto Rico, farmers began to find dead animals. Their blood had been drained primarily through puncture holes in their chests or necks. Similar reports started popping up around the world, but their worst attacks were in Puerto Rico and Mexico. The deaths were attributed to a beast that was named *Chupacabra*, which is Spanish for "goatsucker." People claimed this monster was part bat, kangaroo, insect, reptile, and armadillo. Some thought it was a beast from outer space. Although experts have shown that natural predators, such as wild dogs and coyotes, were responsible for some of the killings, some people remain uncertain and afraid. They believe Chupacabras exist and are a danger to their animals and to their families.

Teach Lesson Skills

BEFORE READING

Build Vocabulary List the vocabulary words and their definitions on the board. Discuss each word's meaning with students. Then write the sentence stems on the board. Read the sentence stems aloud and ask students to complete them.

epidemic: widespread

mutants: creatures that have been drastically changed

demon: an evil spirit

stunned: shocked

ghoulish: creepy

1. The disease reached *epidemic* proportions when . . .
2. People think the peculiar animals are *mutants* because . . .
3. Some people think the huge dog is a *demon* because . . .

4. I was *stunned* when . . .
5. We saw a lot of *ghoulish* creatures when . . .

Activate Prior Knowledge

1. Have students describe scary creatures they have seen or read about.
2. Help students find the following places on a world map: Puerto Rico, Mexico, San Francisco, Miami, San Antonio, New York City, London, Moscow.

Preview and Predict
Ask students what clues the title of the article, the illustration, and the caption provide. What predictions about the article might students make? (*Possible answer: People claim to have seen a beast named Chupacabra that kills goats and sucks their blood.*)

Build Background Legends of vampire-like creatures have been around for centuries. Many people in Eastern Europe in the 1700s believed that vampires rose from their graves at night, wandering around and sucking blood from humans. Some people believed that vampires could transform into bats. Real blood-sucking bats do exist, although they live in Central and South America, not Eastern Europe. They use their sharp incisors to puncture the skin of an animal (or human!) and then lick up the blood.

DURING READING
Determine Word Meanings from Context Think of context as the words or sentences that surround a word you don't know. This information can help you make a good guess about what the word means. Have students look for clues such as descriptions, synonyms, or examples to help them figure out the meaning of an unfamiliar word.

AFTER READING
Respond to the Article Have students write a journal or blog entry about whether they think Chupacabras really exist. Ask students: What evidence from the article supports the thinking that a Chupacabra is a real monster? What evidence supports the belief that Chupacabras do not exist? What do you believe? Which evidence convinces you?

Support Individual Learners

DIFFERENTIATED INSTRUCTION
Have students figure out what *skepticism* means in this context: "Some people were filled with skepticism when they heard about the monster. They did not believe the monster was real." Have students take turns explaining to the class how they determined the meaning of the unfamiliar word.

ENGLISH LANGUAGE LEARNERS
Show students how to use appositives to define a word within a sentence. Point out that when commas surround a phrase, the writer might be using the phrase to describe or define the word that comes before it. Provide an example, such as "Wild predators, animals that kill other animals for food, were really killing the sheep."

GRAPHIC ORGANIZERS
💻 Go to **www.mhereadingbasics.com**. Use Graphic Organizer 1 as a Concept Map. Make copies for each student. Have students write *Chupacabra* in the center bubble. Then ask them to write sentences that describe the monster in the outer bubbles. Discuss their responses.

Unit 3 Lesson 3.4 🔊 *"Challenger:* The Final Countdown," pages 111–119

Introduce

Summary In 1985 Christa McAuliffe, a social studies teacher, was chosen to be the first civilian to travel in space. After 114 hours of space-flight training, she was scheduled for the launch of *Challenger* on January 23, 1986. Due to bad weather, however, countdown didn't commence until January 28. That day was unusually cold and windy. Shortly after liftoff, the space shuttle erupted into a giant fireball. All seven crew members died. NASA was faulted for allowing the launch to proceed in such bad weather. It was two and a half years after this horrendous disaster occurred before another shuttle was launched into space.

Teach Lesson Skills

BEFORE READING

Build Vocabulary List the vocabulary words and their definitions on the board. Discuss each word's meaning with students. Then write the following questions on the board. Read the questions aloud and discuss the answers with students.

celebrated: famous

anticipation: expectation

in unison: together

jubilant: very joyous and excited

dynamic: energetic

1. Which would be a *celebrated* event—the president speaking at your school or seeing your friend at school? Why?
2. Would you feel *anticipation* before making breakfast or before starting a new job? Why?
3. If people are singing *in unison,* is everyone singing? Explain.

4. When you feel *jubilant,* are you happy or sad? Why?
5. If you want to do something *dynamic,* would you watch television or climb a mountain? Why?

Activate Prior Knowledge

1. Ask students what comes to mind when they hear the term *space shuttle.* Record their responses in a web.
2. Ask students what astronauts do in space. *(Possible answers: command and pilot shuttles, maintain spacecraft and equipment, perform experiments, explore by going on space walks)* Go to http://www.nasa.gov/worldbook and click on "Astronauts."

Preview and Predict Ask students what clues the title of the article, the photograph, and the photo caption provide. What predictions about the article might students make? *(Possible answer: I think the article will be about the* Challenger *and how it exploded right after liftoff.)*

Build Background The purpose of the Apollo space program was to land humans on the moon. On July 20, 1969, the first humans stepped on the moon. In 1970 NASA announced that it would begin researching the possibility of creating a reusable space shuttle. In 1976 the shuttle *Enterprise* was introduced as a test vehicle. *Columbia,* the second shuttle, was the first to fly into space in April 1981. *Challenger,* the next shuttle, had its first flight on April 4, 1983. *Challenger* successfully completed nine missions before it exploded on its final flight on January 28, 1986.

DURING READING

Identify Sequence Sequence is the order in which events, ideas, or things are arranged. Time order refers to the order in which events occur. Following the sequence of events helps you see how the text is organized and how events relate to each other. As students read, ask them to look for key words such as *beginning, then, later,* and *after.*

AFTER READING

Respond to the Article Have students write a journal or blog entry about this statement: "The Challenger Center is a way to talk about how the mission continues . . ." Ask students: How do you think the families felt after the disaster? Why do you think the families wanted the mission to continue?

Support Individual Learners

DIFFERENTIATED INSTRUCTION

Give students some related photographs or magazine pictures and ask them to arrange them in a logical sequence. Then have them explain why they chose to order the pictures in time order, spatial order, order of importance, or as steps in a process. Students could also use objects to create spatial-order sequences, such as arranging pens, paper clips, and books on a desk, and use signal words to describe the order.

ENGLISH LANGUAGE LEARNERS

Cut apart panels of comic strips and ask students to place the frames in a logical sequence. Have them explain to partners why they used the order they did. Encourage students to use key words such as *first, next, then, last,* and *finally.*

GRAPHIC ORGANIZERS

💻 Go to **www.mhereadingbasics.com.** Use Graphic Organizer 5 as a Sequence-of-Events Chart. Make copies for each student. Ask students to write in the boxes of the chart the following events in the order in which they happened. Discuss their responses.

The families founded the Challenger Center for Space Science Education.

President Reagan announced that a teacher would be the first civilian to travel in space.

The official countdown began, and the liftoff was spectacular.

Christa McAuliffe went through 114 hours of space flight training.

Introduce

Summary In March 1989 disaster struck Prince William Sound in Alaska. The Exxon *Valdez*, a ship loaded with oil, impaled itself on Bligh Reef. Oil spewed forth from the ship at the rate of 20,000 gallons an hour. In all, 11 million gallons of oil spilled into the sound. This was one of the biggest oil spills in the history of the United States. Wildlife died, and residents faced hardships. Captain Joseph Hazelwood, the Coast Guard, and Exxon all shared the blame for this sad event. Even after the cleanup, scientists believe it will take decades for the sound to recover.

Teach Lesson Skills

BEFORE READING

Build Vocabulary List the vocabulary words and their definitions on the board. Discuss each word's meaning with students. Then write the following questions on the board. Read the questions aloud and discuss the answers with students.

barren: dry and desolate

catastrophic: disastrous

impaled: pierced

requiem: a solemn memorial

negligent: careless

1. What word goes with "food picked up with a fork"? *(impaled)*

2. What word goes with "funeral or service for someone who died"? *(requiem)*

3. What word goes with "desert"? *(barren)*

4. What word goes with "damaging accident"? *(catastrophic)*

5. What word goes with "not paying attention and making a mistake"? *(negligent)*

Activate Prior Knowledge

1. Discuss the 2010 oil spill in the Gulf of Mexico. Ask students what they heard or read in the news about the effects of the spill.

2. Help students find the following places on a map of Alaska: Prince William Sound, Valdez, Prudhoe Bay.

Preview and Predict Ask students what clues the title of the article, the photograph, and the photo caption provide. What predictions about the article might students make? *(Possible answer: This article will probably explain why oil from the Exxon* Valdez *spilled into the ocean and how it was cleaned up.)*

Build Background In early 1968 oil was found in Alaska's North Slope. It was predicted that there were 10 billion barrels of oil below Prudhoe Bay. People proposed a pipeline to bring the oil from the frozen North Slope to market. There were legal challenges to the pipeline for years. People argued the need for energy versus protection of land and wildlife. Then in 1973 President Nixon signed the Trans-Alaska Pipeline Authorization Act, and construction began. In 1977 the first oil flowed through the pipeline, which extended 800 miles across Alaska.

DURING READING

Predict Predicting is thinking ahead to guess how events might be resolved. Predicting helps readers become involved in the text. Readers base predictions on details in the text and their own knowledge. Tell students that their predictions may change as details change or are added.

AFTER READING

Respond to the Article Have students write a journal or blog entry about their reactions to the oil spill. Ask students: What do you think was the worst effect of the spill? What do you think should have happened to Captain Hazelwood? Do you think oil should continue to flow through the pipeline?

Support Individual Learners

DIFFERENTIATED INSTRUCTION

Distribute headlines from newspaper or magazine articles. Have partners read the headlines and predict what the articles will be about. Ask them to write their predictions. Then have partners read aloud the articles that go with their headlines and discuss whether their predictions were correct.

ENGLISH LANGUAGE LEARNERS

Have students read the book *Bad Day at Riverbend*, by Chris Van Allsburg. Ask students to draw a three-column chart and make and record three predictions as they read.

GRAPHIC ORGANIZERS

💻 Go to **www.mhereadingbasics.com.** Use Graphic Organizer 9 as a Main-Idea-and-Details Map. Make copies for each student. Ask students to write the main idea below in the box on the left. Then ask them to write details that support the main idea in the boxes on the right. Discuss their responses.

Captain Hazelwood, Exxon, and the Coast Guard were all to blame for the oil spill.

Intermediate 2 Reader

INTERMEDIATE 2 READER
Unit 1 Assessment Article

Directions: Read this story. Then answer each question that follows. Circle the letter of your answer.

Lights across the Sky

Stephenville, Texas, is a small farming community about 70 miles southwest of Fort Worth, with a population of about 20,000 people. Their conversations are often about dairy farming and milk production, but on the night of January 8, 2008, people had something else to talk about.

2 At sunset that evening, many Stephenville citizens looked up at the sky and gasped. Instead of stars, they saw something they had never seen before. What it was is still being debated.

3 Most people described a huge object with very bright lights, and some said the lights were glowing red. Most agreed that the object was flying low and moving at a high rate of speed. "It was so fast," said a police officer, "I couldn't track it with my binoculars." Some witnesses said the object was only about 3,000 feet above the town.

4 A number of observers said the object remained over Stephenville for about five minutes, and then it zoomed away. A former air force worker declared, "It's an unidentified flying object." Many others agreed.

5 According to Steve Allen, an experienced pilot, the UFO was an aircraft with flashing lights. It was maybe a half-mile wide and a mile long. It streaked through the air without a sound. Allen claimed that the UFO was being chased by two fighter jets. However, the jets could not keep up with it. Allen said that the distance the craft covered in a few seconds would take him 20 minutes to travel in his plane. "It was positively, absolutely nothing from these parts," Allen said.

6 What was it that Allen and others saw? A spokesman from a naval air base in Fort Worth said that no jets were flying near Stephenville on the evening of January 8. Officials from nearby air force bases said the same thing. The UFO was nothing more than a commercial airliner, people were told. Military officials said that people were letting their imaginations get the best of them. Lights from passing airplanes could fool people's eyes. So could reflections from the setting sun.

7 Witnesses were far from convinced, however. They were sure they had seen a UFO. Even some people who had at first kept silent spoke out. As one man said, "It feels good to hear that other people saw something, because that means I'm not crazy."

8 Then, about two weeks later, something interesting happened. The air force said it had made a mistake. There *were* planes flying near Stephenville on the night of January 8. They were on a training mission. In fact, they were flying over the area at just the time that many people saw the bright lights.

9 Some people believed this new report. Others, though, wondered if the government might be hiding the truth.

Intermediate 2 Reader

INTERMEDIATE 2 READER
Unit 1 Assessment Questions

1. Which sentence best states the main idea of the article?
   a. A large UFO with bright lights landed in Stephenville, Texas, in 2008.
   b. Many people in Stephenville, Texas, believe they saw a UFO over the town in 2008.
   c. Everyone agrees that the flying object that people saw in Stephenville, Texas, in 2008 was an airplane.

2. According to the air force, the supposed UFO
   a. was being chased by fighter jets.
   b. was an airplane on a training mission.
   c. had brightly glowing red lights.

3. Which answer is probably true?
   a. Some Stephenville citizens think the government knows more than it is admitting.
   b. Witnesses were only joking when they reported seeing a UFO over Stephenville.
   c. Air force fighter jets shot down the UFO that passed over Stephenville.

4. What is the meaning of the underlined word?
   The UFO was nothing more than a commercial airliner, people were told.
   a. a colorful hot-air balloon
   b. a printed sign advertising a product
   c. a large aircraft for carrying passengers

5. The main purpose of this article is
   a. to inform readers about an event that occurred.
   b. to warn readers that UFOs are coming to Earth.
   c. to teach readers about Stephenville, Texas.

6. Which answer correctly restates this sentence from the story?
   Allen said that the distance the craft covered in a few seconds would take him 20 minutes to travel in his plane.
   a. Allen explained that the distance the craft traveled in minutes he could fly in seconds.
   b. In Allen's opinion, it would take the craft 20 seconds to travel the distance that he could fly in a few minutes.
   c. According to Allen, he would need to fly for 20 minutes to cover the same distance that the craft flew in seconds.

7. Some people were suspicious because
   a. they have pictures of the Stephenville UFO.
   b. officials changed their explanation of the event.
   c. the UFO left behind evidence of its visit.

8. From information in the article, one can predict that people in general will
   a. give little additional thought to the supposed UFO.
   b. fear the return of the UFO to Stephenville.
   c. continue to be curious about what witnesses saw in 2008.

9. Which paragraphs provide information that *best* supports your answer to question 8?
   a. paragraphs 3 and 6
   b. paragraphs 2, 7, and 9
   c. paragraphs 1 and 8

10. Into which of the following kinds of stories would this article fit?
    a. tales of imaginary people and events
    b. reports of events that may not be what they seem
    c. articles that describe interesting places to visit

Intermediate 2 Reader

INTERMEDIATE 2 READER
Unit 2 Assessment Article

Directions: Read this story. Then answer each question that follows. Circle the letter of your answer.

Godzilla, King of the Monsters

He is huge—rising up more than 160 feet and weighing 20,000 tons—with a terrifying, high-pitched roar. He has the head and body of a prehistoric reptile, complete with a long, powerful tail. His eyes are cold and blank, with no trace of pity. No guns, tanks, or missiles can harm him. He is the fearsome, dinosaur-like Godzilla, called "king of the monsters."

2 Fortunately for us all, Godzilla is a movie monster, a human-made creation designed to frighten an audience. In the 1954 Japanese movie where he first appeared, Godzilla stomps through Tokyo, trampling people and buildings, smashing bridges and trains. The massive monster with his fiery radiation breath leaves behind a trail of death and destruction as he reduces the city to smoking rubble and sends screaming victims running for their lives.

3 Godzilla was a product of the Atomic Age, the period of history associated with the use of atomic energy. Atomic, or nuclear, energy has positive uses, such as electricity production. However, it also has the power to cause great destruction. In 1945, during World War II, the United States dropped atomic bombs on the Japanese cities of Hiroshima and Nagasaki. The bombs helped end the war, but they killed many thousands of people and left the cities largely in ruins. Many more people died as a result of radiation poisoning.

4 In the Japanese movie, a scientist deduces that Godzilla is a prehistoric creature that he believes had been asleep in the sea until underwater bomb tests conducted by the United States awakened it. In this way, the movie presents Godzilla as a symbol to warn people of the dangers of atomic weapons.

5 Just as atomic bombs had destroyed Hiroshima and Nagasaki, Godzilla's rampage demolishes Tokyo. Ishiro Honda, the movie's director and a former Japanese soldier, explained the monster this way: "Most of the visual images I got were from my war experience . . . I took the characteristics of an atomic bomb and applied them to Godzilla."

6 At the end of the movie, a super weapon finally manages to kill Godzilla, but the message to viewers is clear. As one scientist comments, "I can't believe Godzilla is the only survivor of its species. If we continue testing H-bombs, another Godzilla will one day appear again, somewhere in the world."

7 Even though Godzilla died in the 1954 Japanese film, the idea for the monster did not. In fact, some 25 Godzilla movies have been made since the original, starting with a low-budget 1956 American version that blended the previous film with new scenes that were inserted. The creature continues to live on in the world's imagination.

Intermediate 2 Reader

INTERMEDIATE 2 READER

Unit 2 Assessment Questions

1. Which sentence states the main idea best?
   a. Godzilla is a movie monster inspired by the Atomic Age.
   b. Godzilla is a dinosaur-like creature who first appeared in 1954.
   c. Numerous movies have been made about the frightening monster known as Godzilla.

2. The 1954 Japanese film ends with
   a. the monster being killed.
   b. America bombing Japanese cities.
   c. Godzilla returning to the sea.

3. Which answer is probably true?
   a. Godzilla is modeled on an actual dinosaur-like creature that attacked Japan.
   b. Godzilla movies have not been very popular with the public.
   c. Ishiro Honda's wartime experiences made a big impression on him.

4. What is the meaning of the underlined word?
   In the Japanese movie, a scientist <u>deduces</u> that Godzilla is a prehistoric creature that he believes had been asleep in the sea until underwater bomb tests conducted by the United States awakened it.
   a. disproves
   b. concludes
   c. denies

5. What is the author's purpose for writing this article?
   a. to warn that Godzilla is real
   b. to describe historical events
   c. to explain the origin of Godzilla

6. Which answer correctly restates this sentence from paragraph 5?
   Just as atomic bombs had destroyed Hiroshima and Nagasaki, Godzilla's rampage demolishes Tokyo.
   a. Godzilla wrecks Tokyo in a way that reminds viewers of the bombing of Hiroshima and Nagasaki.
   b. Japanese cities were left in ruins not only by atomic bombs but also by the monster Godzilla.
   c. Attacks on Japan caused the widespread destruction of several cities.

7. As a symbol, the Godzilla monster had special meaning for Japan's people because
   a. many Godzilla films followed the original.
   b. the monster rises up from the ocean.
   c. atomic bombs took many Japanese lives.

8. What is the most likely reason for including the quotations in paragraphs 5 and 6?
   a. to show that the Godzilla film was more than just a monster movie
   b. to suggest that the author disapproves of atomic energy
   c. to express regret that Japan and the United States had fought a war

9. The main purpose of the first two paragraphs is
   a. to encourage readers to see the movie.
   b. to help readers picture Godzilla.
   c. to explain why the film was made.

10. Into which of the following categories would this article best fit?
    a. detailed accounts of World War II battles
    b. articles providing background information
    c. reports of unusual scientific occurrences

Intermediate 2 Reader

INTERMEDIATE 2 READER
Unit 3 Assessment Article

Directions: Read this story. Then answer each question that follows. Circle the letter of your answer.

A Deadly Tsunami

Walking along a Thai beach on the morning of December 24, 2004, Les Boardman was puzzled. The tide had receded drastically, revealing 200 yards of seabed. It was only when he saw fishing boats racing back to shore that he understood what was happening. He started running from the beach, a giant wave just behind him. Grabbing onto a post, he managed to survive.

2 In India's Nicobar Islands, Elsie Reuben was in her kitchen when the earth opened up under her feet. Outside, she saw water rising through the cracks in the ground. She immediately gathered up her babies and didn't stop running until she reached the higher ground of the jungle.

3 Sumatran fisherman Surya Darma bin Abdul Manaf was in a canoe off the coast of Banda Aceh when he felt an unusual wave. Looking up, he saw a flock of cranes speeding toward the inland hills. He quickly paddled toward shore and grabbed hold of a mangrove tree just as a huge wave crashed over him.

4 All over South Asia that morning, people were feeling the effects of a devastating earthquake that struck the Indian Ocean floor. The quake caused a huge volume of ocean water to shift, creating a gigantic wave called a tsunami. Coastal regions of Sumatra and other islands nearest the quake were directly in the tsunami's path. Thailand, India, and Sri Lanka were also hard hit. Thousands of miles away and many hours later, the tsunami struck the coast of east Africa.

5 Tsunami survivors described similar experiences. First, they felt the earthquake, and then they heard sounds like a jet engine or bombs exploding—probably the tsunami breaking ashore elsewhere. Some witnesses saw the tide withdraw two miles, exposing fish on the sea floor. Then, rising as high as 100 feet, the water came surging back at them. "It looked like a big, black cobra," one survivor recounted. The wave swept inland as far as five miles, swallowing everything in its path. No one could outrun the rushing wall of water, and only some were lucky enough to survive.

6 Shortly after the tsunami, photojournalist Chris Rainier said, "Banda Aceh looks like Hiroshima after the atomic bomb." This comparison says a lot about the destructive power of the disaster. In fact, the energy released by the earthquake was equal to 32,000 Hiroshima bombs. The tsunami was the deadliest in recorded history. Thousands of villages were annihilated, and two million survivors lost their homes. Nearly 230,000 people died, and numerous children were orphaned.

7 Since the tsunami, cities and villages have been rebuilt, and life has mostly returned to normal. For many survivors, however, the traumatic memories of that day and a great fear of the sea remain.

Intermediate 2 Reader

INTERMEDIATE 2 READER

Unit 3 Assessment Questions

1. Which sentence best states the main idea of the article?
   a. Cities and villages were rebuilt after the 2004 tsunami.
   b. In 2004 a tsunami caused an enormous loss of life and property in South Asia.
   c. Many survivors of the 2004 tsunami have not fully recovered.

2. A tsunami is
   a. the South Asian term for a hurricane.
   b. an earthquake on the ocean floor.
   c. a huge wave caused by an earthquake.

3. Which answer is probably true?
   a. Les Boardman was glad to see the fishermen returning to shore.
   b. Surya Darma bin Abdul Manaf was relieved when he saw the mangrove tree.
   c. Elsie Reuben was sorry she ran to higher ground.

4. What is the meaning of the underlined word?
   Thousands of villages were <u>annihilated</u>, and two million survivors lost their homes.
   a. completely destroyed
   b. mostly spared
   c. partly rebuilt

5. The main purpose of paragraphs 1–3 is to
   a. teach readers how to respond to a tsunami.
   b. describe the fear and confusion of three witnesses at the start of the tsunami.
   c. describe various parts of South Asia.

6. Which answer correctly restates this sentence from the article?
   Some witnesses saw the tide withdraw two miles, exposing fish on the sea floor.
   a. Fish withdrew two miles in the sea as observers watched.
   b. Some observers fished when the tide withdrew two miles.
   c. The tide withdrew two miles, allowing observers to see fish on the ocean floor.

7. Based on this article, you can tell that
   a. the tsunami had not been predicted.
   b. people were prepared for the tsunami.
   c. people intentionally ignored warnings.

8. Why did Surya Darma bin Abdul Manaf decide to paddle to shore when he observed the cranes?
   a. He had a superstition about seeing cranes while fishing.
   b. Their arrival meant it was time for breakfast.
   c. Their unusual flight alarmed him.

9. The survivor compared a tsunami to a cobra because
   a. he thought that both were wild and beautiful.
   b. he noticed that both rear up and then strike.
   c. he believed the tsunami was a nature spirit.

10. Into which of the following categories would this article fit?
    a. accounts of unexpected disasters
    b. reports of events not fully understood
    c. accounts of survivors

Intermediate 2 Reader

Unit 1 Language Development Activity: *Vocabulary Review*

ESL/DI Skill *Vocabulary Words:* toxic, severe, residents, publicity, defects

Activity Highlights

1. Reading sentences aloud: individual
2. Constructing word meanings from context: whole class
3. Interviewing: partners
4. Note taking: individual
5. Personal responses/summary of partner's responses: individual
6. Game: whole class

Teacher Preparation

1. Review the article "Nightmare on Chemical Street: The Love Canal Story" (Unit 1, Lesson 1.2, p. 10).
2. Write on the board or otherwise present the lesson vocabulary words: *toxic* ("poisonous"), *severe* ("serious"), *residents* ("inhabitants"), *publicity* ("attracting public interest"), *defects* ("flaws").
3. Review the interview questions below and have a copy on hand.

Interview Questions:

1. Name something you have in your home that might be <u>toxic</u> for pets.

2. Have you ever been in a <u>severe</u> thunderstorm? What happened?

3. How many <u>residents</u> in your neighborhood do you know by first name?

4. If you suddenly became a superstar, would you like or dislike the <u>publicity</u>? Explain.

5. When do you think that friends should mention each other's <u>defects</u>?

Activity Steps:

1. Review the article "Nightmare on Chemical Street: The Love Canal Story" (Unit 1, Lesson 1.2, p. 10) with the class.

2. Review the definitions of the Lesson 1.2 vocabulary words with the class.

3. The class discusses how the vocabulary was used in the article. Tell students that they will be interviewing each other using these vocabulary words in a new context.

4. Dictate the first interview question to the class. Each student writes the sentence in his or her notebook.

5. Volunteers read the sentence aloud, first as is and then substituting the definitions on the board for the underlined words. For example: *Name something you have in your home that might be <u>toxic</u> for pets. Name something you have in your home that might be <u>poisonous</u> for pets.*

6. Students pair off.

7. Partners ask each other the first interview question. As one partner answers the question, the other partner takes notes on the answer.

8. Repeat steps 4 to 7 with the other interview questions.

9. When partners have finished asking each other all the questions, the first partner summarizes the second partner's answers. The second partner suggests any corrections that may be necessary. Partners then reverse the process.

10. Each partner summarizes the other's answers to the class.

11. You may extend the activity into a game of "Who Am I?" in which volunteers give you selected interview answers to read aloud and the class tries to guess who was being interviewed in each case.

Intermediate 2 Reader

Unit 2 Language Development Activity: *Multiword Verbs*

ESL/DI Skill	*Multiword Verbs:* flew off, went on to, set off, thought up, came up, called in

Activity Highlights

1. Sequence diagram: whole class and partners
2. Visualization/sketching of sentence meanings: individual
3. Ordering sentences sequentially: partners
4. Recalling definitions: partners

Teacher Preparation

1. Review the article "Kim's Story: The Big Bubble" (Unit 2, Lesson 2.1, p. 42).
2. 💻 Go to **www.mhereadingbasics.com**. Print one copy of Unit 2 Activity Sheet: *Sequence Diagram* for each student and a copy of Unit 2 Activity Sheet Answers: *Sequence Diagram* for yourself.
3. Write on the board the sentences below this box, which are out of sequential order.
4. Draw the blank diagram from the Unit 2 Activity Sheet (from step 2) on the board.

An object rose into the air and <u>flew off</u>. Kimberly <u>went on to</u> describe the object. Allie King <u>called in</u> a reporter. Mrs. Baker doubted that her daughter had just <u>thought up</u> the experience. During King's questioning, however, something quite unexpected <u>came up</u>. Each end of the object was <u>set off</u> by red lights.

Activity Steps:

1. Review "Kim's Story: The Big Bubble" (Unit 2, Lesson 2.1, p. 42) with the class.

2. Distribute the Unit 2 Activity Sheet: *Sequence Diagram* to each student.

3. Tell students that in a sequence diagram, each event in a box happens after the one before it.

4. Read aloud the first sentence on the board: *An object rose into the air and flew off.* Ask students to visualize this sentence.

5. Students copy the sentence into box 1 in their diagrams, underlining *flew off.*

6. Guide students to give a definition of *flew off* ("flew farther away"). Students write this definition at the bottom of box 1.

7. Students draw a simple sketch of the meaning of the sentence in or near box 1.

8. Repeat steps 4–7 with the sentence *Kimberly went on to describe the object.* ("continued to")

9. Based on the article, brainstorm with the class to create definitions for the last four multiword verbs: *called in* ("invited to come"), *thought up* ("imagined"), *came up* ("came into the conversation"), *set off* ("marked in a special way").

10. Students pair off.

11. Tell students that the last four sentences on the board are out of sequential (time) order.

12. Using their books, partners collaborate to identify the order of the last four sentences and write them in the corresponding boxes of their activity sheets. (*Each end of the object was set off by red lights. Mrs. Baker doubted that her daughter had just thought up the experience. During King's questioning, however, something quite unexpected came up. Allie King called in a reporter.*)

13. Partners collaborate to recall the definitions from step 9 and write them under the corresponding sentences in the boxes.

14. You may point out that multiword verbs can have multiple meanings just as single-word verbs do: for example, *set off* a firecracker ("made a firecracker explode"), *called in* sick ("notified an employer of absence because of illness").

Intermediate 2 Reader

Unit 3 Language Development Activity: *Multiple Meanings*

ESL/DI Skill : *Multiple-meanings Words:* ordered, turn, point, direction, left

<table>
<tr>
<td>Activity Highlights</td>
<td>
1. Discussion: small group
2. Reading sentences aloud: individual
3. Writing sentences: individual
</td>
<td>Teacher Preparation</td>
<td>
1. Review the reading selection "Oil, Oil Everywhere" (Unit 3, Lesson 3.5, p. 120).
2. Write on the board or otherwise present the short passage below this box ("Hazelwood had ordered . . .").
3. For each group of 3 to 5 people, provide a dictionary.
</td>
</tr>
</table>

Hazelwood had <u>ordered</u> Cousins to make a right <u>turn</u> . . . when the ship reached a <u>point</u> near Busby Island . . . But it would be seven minutes before the *Valdez* actually changed <u>direction</u> . . . A flashing red buoy near Bligh Reef was on the ship's right side when it should have been on the <u>left</u> side . . .*

Activity Steps:

1. Review "Oil, Oil Everywhere" (Unit 3, Lesson 3.5, p. 120) with the class.

2. Volunteers read the sentences on the board aloud to the class.

3. Students form small groups.

4. Groups talk about what the underlined words mean in the context of the sentences.

5. Each student in the group chooses an underlined word from one of the sentences. If possible, there should be a different word for each student.

6. Each student writes an original sentence with his or her chosen word, unrelated to the selection, using the meaning the word has in the sentence on the board (call this meaning M1). He or she underlines the word in the sentence. For example: *The general ordered the army to march north.* Circulate to provide assistance to students as they write.

7. Students count off to determine an order for participating in the next steps.

8. Each Student 1 says his or her word (*ordered*) and reads the M1 sentence from step 6 to the group.

9. The group talks about why the chosen word (*ordered*) has the same basic meaning in Student 1's sentence as it does in the sentence on the board.

(Possible response: A ship captain and a general both give orders, or commands.)

10. Students collaborate to identify a second meaning (M2) for the word.* There may be more than two, but students should stop at two. They find or confirm the additional meaning in the dictionary. (*ordered*: "arranged to buy something and have it delivered") Circulate among groups for support.

11. Each student writes an original sentence using M2 of the chosen word. For example: *The pizza has already been ordered.*

12. Each student reads his or her sentence to the group.

13. Repeat Steps 8–12 for Student 2, Student 3, etc. If a student chose the same word as another student, the group repeats only steps 8 and 9.

14. Once everyone has taken a turn, volunteers read both of their sentences to the class.

*Multiple meanings: *ordered* ("gave a command"/ "arranged to buy something and have it delivered"); *turn* ("a move in another direction"/"a time or chance to do something"); *point* ("the condition of something"/"the form of something"); *direction* ("way in which something is pointing"/"instruction"); *left* ("opposite of right, left-hand"/"remaining").

Intermediate 2 Reader, Unit 1

Lesson 1.1: King Kong
A. Recognize and Recall Details
   1. c   2. b   3. b   4. b
B. Find the Main Idea
   1. M   2. N   3. B
C. Summarize and Paraphrase
   1. b   2. c
D. Make Inferences
   1. C   2. F   3. C   4. C   5. C
E. Recognize Author's Effect and Intentions
   1. b   2. a   3. a
F. Evaluate and Create: 1. c   2. c   3. b

Lesson 1.2: Nightmare on Chemical Street: The Love Canal Story
A. Recognize and Recall Details
   1. a   2. a   3. c   4. b
B. Find the Main Idea
   1. B   2. N   3. M
C. Summarize and Paraphrase
   1. Summaries should include these points: Hooker Chemical Company dumped chemicals in Love Canal. Later, a school and homes were built on and around the canal.
   2. b
D. Make Inferences
   1. F   2. C   3. F   4. F   5. C
E. Recognize Author's Effect and Intentions
   1. b   2. a
F. Evaluate and Create: 1. a   2. c   3. c

Lesson 1.3: An Encounter in New Guinea
A. Recognize and Recall Details
   1. c   2. a   3. b   4. b
B. Find the Main Idea
   1. M   2. N   3. B
C. Summarize and Paraphrase
   1. Summary should include these points: Gill watched the craft and then decided to go eat dinner; when he returned, the UFO had moved away and then disappeared.
   2. b
D. Make Inferences
   1. C   2. F   3. C   4. F   5. F
E. Recognize Author's Effect and Intentions
   1. c   2. b   3. a
F. Evaluate and Create: 1. a   2. b   3. a

Lesson 1.4: Ocean-born Mary
A. Recognize and Recall Details
   1. b   2. a   3. b   4. b   5. c
B. Find the Main Idea
   1. B   2. N   3. M
C. Summarize and Paraphrase
   1. Summary should include these points: at age 78, Mary went to live with her son in Henniker; she died there at age 94.
   2. b
D. Make Inferences
   1. F   2. F   3. C   4. C   5. F
E. Recognize Author's Effect and Intentions
   1. b   2. c
F. Evaluate and Create
   1. a   2. c   3. b   4. b

Lesson 1.5: Custer's Last Stand: Battle of Little Bighorn
A. Recognize and Recall Details
   1. a   2. b   3. b   4. c   5. a
B. Find the Main Idea
   1. M   2. B   3. N
C. Summarize and Paraphrase
   1. b   2. b
D. Make Inferences
   1. C   2. C   3. F   4. F
E. Recognize Author's Effect and Intentions
   1. c   2. c   3. c
F. Evaluate and Create
   1. a   2. c   3. b

Unit 1 Assessment
Lights across the Sky
1. b   2. b   3. a   4. c   5. a
6. c   7. b   8. c   9. b   10. b

Intermediate 2 Reader, Unit 2

Lesson 2.1: Kim's Story: The Big Bubble

A. Recognize and Recall Details
   1. b   2. b   3. b   4. c   5. c

B. Find the Main Idea
   1. B   2. M   3. N

C. Summarize and Paraphrase
   1. Summary should include these points: Kim and her cousins were outside; the cousins left Kim alone; Kim watched a shiny object float toward her and then fly off.
   2. b

D. Make Inferences
   1. F   2. C   3. F   4. C   5. C

E. Recognize Author's Effect and Intentions
   1. a   2. c   3. a

F. Evaluate and Create: 1. c   2. c   3. c

Lesson 2.2: Poison on the Drugstore Shelf

A. Recognize and Recall Details
   1. b   2. c   3. a   4. a   5. b

B. Find the Main Idea
   1. N   2. M   3. B

C. Summarize and Paraphrase
   1. Summaries should include these points: Adam Janus died after taking a Tylenol capsule; two of his family members died after taking Tylenol from the same bottle.
   2. b, a, c   3. a

D. Make Inferences
   1. C   2. C   3. F   4. F   5. C

E. Recognize Author's Effect and Intentions
   1. b   2. b

F. Evaluate and Create:
   1. b   2. c   3. c, b, a

Lesson 2.3: Death on the Unsinkable *Titanic*

A. Recognize and Recall Details
   1. a   2. a   3. c   4. b

B. Find the Main Idea
   1. B   2. M   3. N

C. Summarize and Paraphrase
   1. Summary should include these points: People in the lifeboats watched passengers go down with the *Titanic*. Only 711 of over 2,200 people found a seat in a lifeboat.
   2. b

D. Make Inferences
   1. C   2. F   3. F   4. C   5. C

Lesson 2.3: cont.

E. Recognize Author's Effect and Intentions
   1. c   2. b   3. c

F. Evaluate and Create: 1. a   2. a

Lesson 2.4: Sarah's Ghost House: An Architectural Fun House

A. Recognize and Recall Details
   1. c   2. b   3. a   4. b

B. Find the Main Idea
   1. N   2. B   3. M

C. Summarize and Paraphrase
   1. Summary should include these points: Coons contacted William's ghost; Coons advised Sarah to buy a house out West for the ghosts. As long as she continued to enlarge the house, she would be safe.
   2. c

D. Make Inferences
   1. F   2. F   3. C   4. F   5. C

E. Recognize Author's Effect and Intentions
   1. c   2. a

F. Evaluate and Create: 1. a   2. b   3. c, b

Lesson 2.5: Krakatoa: The Doomsday Crack Heard 'Round the World

A. Recognize and Recall Details
   1. b   2. b   3. c   4. a   5. b

B. Find the Main Idea
   1. M   2. B   3. N

C. Summarize and Paraphrase
   1. b   2. c

D. Make Inferences
   1. F   2. C   3. C   4. F   5. F

E. Recognize Author's Effect and Intentions
   1. b   2. c   3. b

F. Evaluate and Create: 1. b   2. a   3. c

Unit 2 Assessment

Godzilla, King of the Monsters
1. a   2. a   3. c   4. b   5. c
6. a   7. c   8. a   9. b   10. b

Intermediate 2 Reader

Intermediate 2 Reader, Unit 3

Lesson 3.1: The Mokele-Mbembe: Are All the Dinosaurs Gone?
A. Recognize and Recall Details
   1. c   2. a   3. c   4. a   5. b
B. Find the Main Idea
   1. M   2. N   3. B
C. Summarize and Paraphrase
   1. a, c, b
   2. b
D. Make Inferences
   1. C   2. F   3. C   4. F   5. F
E. Recognize Author's Effect and Intentions
   1. a   2. c
F. Evaluate and Create
   1. a   2. a   3. a, b *or* b, a

Lesson 3.2: Spiritualism: Fact or Fraud
A. Recognize and Recall Details
   1. b   2. c   3. a   4. b   5. c
B. Find the Main Idea
   1. N   2. M   3. B
C. Summarize and Paraphrase
   1. a, c, b
   2. b
D. Make Inferences
   1. F   2. F   3. C   4. F   5. C
E. Recognize Author's Effect and Intentions
   1. a   2. b   3. c
F. Evaluate and Create
   1. c   2. a   3. c

Lesson 3.3: Chupacabra: Bloodthirsty Beast
A. Recognize and Recall Details
   1. a   2. c   3. c   4. b
B. Find the Main Idea
   1. N   2. B   3. M
C. Summarize and Paraphrase
   1. b   2. c
D. Make Inferences
   1. C   2. F   3. C   4. F
E. Recognize Author's Effect and Intentions
   1. a   2. c   3. b
F. Evaluate and Create
   1. c   2. b

Lesson 3.4: *Challenger:* The Final Countdown
A. Recognize and Recall Details
   1. b   2. b   3. a   4. a
B. Find the Main Idea
   1. N   2. B   3. M
C. Summarize and Paraphrase
   1. a   2. c
D. Make Inferences
   1. C   2. F   3. C   4. F   5. F
E. Recognize Author's Effect and Intentions
   1. a   2. c   3. c
F. Evaluate and Create
   1. b   2. c

Lesson 3.5: Oil, Oil Everywhere
A. Recognize and Recall Details
   1. c   2. c   3. b   4. b
B. Find the Main Idea
   1. M   2. N   3. B
C. Summarize and Paraphrase
   1. b   2. c
D. Make Inferences
   1. F   2. F   3. F   4. C   5. C
E. Recognize Author's Effect and Intentions
   1. c   2. c
F. Evaluate and Create
   1. c   2. c   3. a

Unit 3 Assessment

A Deadly Tsunami
1. b   2. c   3. b   4. a   5. b
6. c   7. a   8. c   9. b   10. a

Intermediate 2 Reader Units 1–3

Lesson 1.1: King Kong

Graphic Organizer 2: Fact-and-Opinion Chart

It took one year to complete the filming of the original *King Kong* movie. *Fact*

It was heartbreaking when King Kong was killed. *Opinion*

The 1976 version of *King Kong* is better than the original. *Opinion*

Other producers made movies about giant apes. *Fact*

In the 1976 movie, King Kong climbs one of the World Trade Center Towers. *Fact*

Lesson 1.2: Nightmare on Chemical Street: The Love Canal Story

Graphic Organizer 2: Fact-and-Opinion Chart

Love Canal seemed like a great place to raise children. *Opinion*

Rusted metal barrels began to rise to the surface. *Fact*

Many residents were suffering from severe health problems. *Fact*

The federal government helped New York buy the homes closest to the dump site. *Fact*

Love Canal must be one of the safest places to live in Niagara Falls by now. *Opinion*

Lesson 1.3: An Encounter in New Guinea

Graphic Organizer 5: Sequence-of-Events Chart

A sparkling object descended toward Reverend Gill.

The UFO hovered above the ground for about four hours and then flew away.

When the UFO returned, Gill waved to the aliens, and they waved back.

Gill went inside, and the UFO disappeared.

Lesson 1.4: Ocean-born Mary

Graphic Organizer 2: Classifying Chart

Ocean-born Mary was born on a ship in 1720. *Fact*

Pedro buried a treasure in Henniker, NH. *Legend*

Mary wore a wedding dress made of green silk with embroidered flowers on it. *Fact*

Mary lived in the Ocean-born Mary house. *Legend*

Pedro gave Mary a coach-and-four to drive and took care of her children. *Legend*

Mary is buried in a cemetery in Henniker, NH. *Fact*

Lesson 1.5: Custer's Last Stand: Battle of Little Bighorn

Graphic Organizer 5: Sequence-of-Events Chart

Custer was a general in the Civil War.

Custer went to the Black Hills on an exploratory trip.

The Sioux and Cheyenne banded together near Little Bighorn River.

Terry told Custer to take the Seventh to the Little Bighorn Valley and wait there.

Lesson 2.1: Kim's Story: The Big Bubble

Graphic Organizer 1: Concept Map
Possible answers:

"like Daddy's car but higher"

"shiny, like the toaster in the kitchen"

a door and a rectangular-shaped window

red lights and a flashing green light

a man in shiny white with black buttons

Lesson 2.2: Poison on the Drugstore Shelf

Graphic Organizer 1: Cause-and-Effect Map
Possible answers:

People were afraid to buy products from stores.

Johnson & Johnson stopped making Tylenol and asked store owners to take it off their shelves.

Manufacturers made safer packaging for food and medicine.

Some cities and towns banned trick-or-treating on Halloween.

Lesson 2.3: Death on the Unsinkable *Titanic*

Graphic Organizer 3: KWL Chart
Possible answers:

Learned:

The captain held the ship to a speedy 22 knots for most of the voyage.

The iceberg left a 300-foot wound in the *Titanic*'s side.

At first, passengers did not board the lifeboats because they did not believe the ship could sink.

Only 711 of the more than 2,200 people on the *Titanic* secured places in the lifeboats and survived.

Lesson 2.4: Sarah's Ghost House: An Architectural Fun House

Graphic Organizer 4: Cause-and-Effect Chart
Possible answers:

Effects:

The spirits of people killed by Winchester rifles were seeking revenge.

Sarah saw mediums and went to séances.

Sarah moved to San Jose and continued to build onto her new house.

Work done one day would be undone the next day, such as new walls being torn down.

Lesson 2.5: Krakatoa: The Doomsday Crack Heard 'Round the World

Graphic Organizer 4: Visualizing Chart
Pictures will vary.

Lesson 3.1: The Mokele-Mbembe: Are All the Dinosaurs Gone?

Graphic Organizer 8: Venn Diagram

Mokele-Mbembe	Both	N'yamala
brownish-grey	long neck	blood-red eyes
smooth skin	one tooth	huge mouth

Lesson 3.2: Spiritualism: Fact or Fraud

Graphic Organizer 1: Characteristics Map
Possible answers:

shrewd: Leah thought of the idea of making money from the rapping.

wily: Leah continued performing even after the revelation and made a lot of money.

dishonest: Margaret made the noises herself, although she confessed to this.

Lesson 3.3: Chupacabra: Bloodthirsty Beast

Graphic Organizer 1: Concept Map
Possible answers:

The Chupacabra had fangs, spikes running down its back, and bulging red eyes.

The monster had bat wings and kangaroo legs.

The beast made puncture wounds in animals and then sucked their blood.

The Chupacabra caused fear and panic in Puerto Rico and Mexico.

Lesson 3.4: *Challenger:* The Final Countdown

Graphic Organizer 5: Sequence-of-Events Chart

President Reagan announced that a teacher would be the first civilian to travel in space.

Christa McAuliffe went through 114 hours of space flight training.

The official countdown began, and the liftoff was spectacular.

The families founded the Challenger Center for Space Science Education.

Lesson 3.5: Oil, Oil Everywhere

Graphic Organizer 9: Main-Idea-and-Details Map
Possible answers:

Hazelwood had a couple of drinks before boarding the ship and gave control of the ship to a third mate.

The Coast Guard did not track the *Valdez* by radar.

Exxon ignored Hazelwood's drinking problem.

Lesson Plan Advanced Reader

Unit 1 Lesson 1.1 🔊 "Secret Service Agents: Shield, Defend, Protect," pages 1–8

Summary On April 14, 1865, President Lincoln authorized the creation of the Secret Service to catch people who printed counterfeit money. It was not until 1901, after the assassination of President McKinley, that it became the Secret Service's responsibility to protect the President of the United States. Today, Secret Service agents accompany the president everywhere he goes. Because their job requires that they be willing to "take a bullet" for the president, agents must be able to withstand stress, anticipate danger, and react with split-second timing. Ultimately, Secret Service agents must be ready to protect the president from all danger at all times.

Introduce

Teach Lesson Skills

BEFORE READING

Build Vocabulary List the vocabulary words and their definitions on the board. Discuss each word's meaning with students. Then write the following questions on the board. Read the questions aloud and discuss the answers with students.

precautions: thoughtful plans

culmination: highest achievement

secured: made safe

sequester: withdraw from public view, isolate

apparent: obvious

1. Would you take *precautions* before hiking in a familiar area or in an area that is unknown to you? Why?

2. Would the *culmination* of your career be something you are ashamed of or proud of? Why?

3. If an area has been fully *secured* by the police, what might have happened?

4. Who would be more likely to *sequester* himself for a long time—the president or a hermit? Why?

5. Would you prefer to face danger that is *apparent* or unknown? Why?

Activate Prior Knowledge

1. Use Graphic Organizer 3 as a KWL Chart. Have students label the first column *Know* and write what they know about the Secret Service. Have students label the second column *Want to Know* and write what they want to know. This exercise will be continued after reading.

2. Challenge students to name the four presidents who were assassinated. *(Lincoln, Garfield, McKinley, Kennedy)* See http://www.infoplease.com/spot/prestrivia1.html.

Preview and Predict Ask students what clues the title of the article, the photograph, and the photo caption provide. What predictions about the article might students make? *(Possible answer: The article will give information about the Secret Service agents who protect the U.S. presidents and their families.)*

Build Background Most people know that Secret Service agents protect the president, but agents have other duties, too. Along with bodily protection, Secret Service agents also investigate any threats made against the president and vice president. One of the lesser-known responsibilities of the Secret Service is to protect the U.S. financial system. They investigate such crimes as counterfeiting, credit card fraud, computer crimes, false identification, and identity theft. During an agent's career, he or she could be appointed to any of these duties, and the agent must be ready for assignment anywhere in the world.

DURING READING

Ask Questions Questioning helps you to monitor your understanding of the text. Have students ask *who, what, where, when, why,* and *how* questions and look for the answers. Questions may include: Who did you read about in this article? What did you learn about them? Where did some events take place? When did the events take place? According to the article, why did the events happen? How were any problems resolved?

AFTER READING

Respond to the Article Have students write a journal or blog entry about Secret Service agents. Ask students: Why is being a Secret Service agent an important job? What do you think would be the hardest part of the job? Do you think you would like to be a Secret Service agent? Why or why not?

Support Individual Learners

DIFFERENTIATED INSTRUCTION

Invite students to keep a reading log to help them become better readers. Have them answer questions like the following for articles they read: Did anything in the text remind you of an experience you have had? Did you have a positive or negative reaction to anything in the text? With what parts of the text did you agree or disagree? Which part of the text, if any, was confusing to you?

ENGLISH LANGUAGE LEARNERS

Assign proficient English-speaking partners to English language learners and ask the partners to help the English language learners form questions. Having English language learners actively question what they don't understand will help them as they encounter unknown words and difficult text in a new language.

GRAPHIC ORGANIZERS

📖 Go to www.mhereadingbasics.com. Use Graphic Organizer 3 as a KWL Chart. Have students use the charts they started before reading or they can start it now. Students should label the third column *Learned* and add information they learned about Secret Service agents. They may wish to add more questions to the *Want to Know* column. Have students discuss their charts. Encourage students to find answers online or at the library.

Advanced Reader

Lesson Plan Advanced Reader

Unit 1 Lesson 1.2 🔊 "Humanitarian Aid Workers: Comfort Under Fire," pages 9–16

Introduce

Summary Humanitarian aid workers serve in areas of civil unrest to help people survive. They bring food and other life-saving supplies to people displaced by war, as well as services to help traumatized children. Being an aid worker is a dangerous job, and hundreds of aid workers do not survive. From 2000 to 2010, more than 700 aid workers were killed in places like Sudan, Iraq, and Afghanistan. There is rarely any consequence for killing aid workers, so the risk to the workers goes on. Even so, aid workers feel that the satisfaction they get from helping people makes the risks worthwhile.

Teach Lesson Skills

BEFORE READING

Build Vocabulary List the vocabulary words and their definitions on the board. Discuss each word's meaning with students. Then write the sentences that contain the words on the board. Read the sentences aloud and discuss them with students.

strife: conflict

horrific: terrifying

traumatized: wounded or distressed, often mentally

1. Soldiers often face danger in areas where there is *strife*.
2. The damage caused by the hurricane was *horrific* for the residents of the city.
3. The explosions *traumatized* the children during the war.

altruistic: generous and caring

accelerate: speed up

4. The *altruistic* volunteers helped the victims of the earthquake.
5. Once we reached the countryside, the train started to *accelerate*.

Activate Prior Knowledge

1. Ask students to discuss volunteer opportunities in their community. Ask how volunteers help people or animals in need.
2. Have students find these places on a map: Burundi, Chechnya, Afghanistan, Pakistan, Sudan, Darfur.

Preview and Predict Ask students what clues the title of the article, the photograph, and the photo caption provide. What predictions about the article might students make? *(Possible answer: Humanitarian aid workers help people in need, like those in Afghanistan, by opening schools and health clinics.)*

Build Background Sudan is Africa's biggest country. Darfur, about the size of Texas, is an area in western Sudan. About six million people lived there before 2003, when conflict arose between rebel movements and the government. More than 400 villages were destroyed as ethnic groups were targeted by government forces, and civilian casualties were huge. About 300,000 people died between 2003 and 2005. In 2008 a United Nations–African Union peacekeeping force replaced the African Union peacekeeping mission in Darfur. However, without the necessary resources, it struggled to protect the millions of displaced people. Fighting still continued, and the Sudanese government made matters more difficult by refusing to cooperate with peacekeeping forces and even expelling some groups of humanitarian aid workers.

DURING READING

Find Vocabulary in Context As students read the article, have them note the new vocabulary words. Ask them to think about each word's meaning as they read.

AFTER READING

Respond to the Article Have students write a journal or blog entry about humanitarian aid workers. Ask students: Why do you think some people choose to become humanitarian aid workers? What are the benefits of this job? What are the dangers? Do you think you would like to do this kind of work? Why or why not?

Support Individual Learners

Advanced Reader

DIFFERENTIATED INSTRUCTION

Explain that the author's purpose is the reason he or she has written something. Generally, an author will write to persuade, inform, describe, explain, or entertain. Point out that an author can have more than one purpose. Then have students work in small groups and provide each group with magazines that include a variety of topics. Ask students to name the authors' purpose for each feature.

ENGLISH LANGUAGE LEARNERS

Have students share words or phrases from their first languages that writers might use for different purposes. For example, English words that may be used to persuade include *fantastic* or *incredible*. Spanish words may include *muy bueno* and *excelente*. Descriptive words may include colors. Explanations often include words or phrases such as *because* or *the reason is*. Stories that entertain may begin with "Once upon a time . . . ."

GRAPHIC ORGANIZERS

💻 Go to **www.mhreadingbasics.com**. Use Graphic Organizer 7 as an Author's-Viewpoint Chart. Make copies for each student. Have students write the author's viewpoint given below in the bottom box of the chart. Then have them write three details from the article that provide evidence of the author's viewpoint.

Author's Viewpoint
Humanitarian aid workers have an important but dangerous job.

Lesson Plan Advanced Reader

Unit 1 Lesson 1.3 🔊 "Bomb Squad: No False Moves," pages 17–24

Summary Soldiers in a bomb squad find and disarm bombs. In Afghanistan and Iraq, these brave soldiers look primarily for IEDs (improvised explosive devices), which have killed more American soldiers there than any other weapon. Made by individuals, no two IEDs are the same. Thus IEDs are especially dangerous because they cannot all be disarmed in the same way. To reduce the dangers to the bomb squad, the army has begun to rely on robots. Even with robots, though, the bomb squad soldiers risk their own lives every day in the act of saving others.

BEFORE READING

Build Vocabulary List the vocabulary words and their definitions on the board. Discuss each word's meaning with students. Then write the following sentence stems on the board. Read the sentence stems aloud and ask students to complete them.

carnage: killing in great numbers

inoperable: not able to work; broken

virtually: almost, but not in actual fact

vulnerability: being open to harm

motivated: eager to act

1. The *carnage* from the hurricane provided an important lesson about . . .
2. My lawn mower is *inoperable* now because . . .
3. It is *virtually* impossible to solve this problem because . . .

4. The soccer goalie has a sense of *vulnerability* when . . .
5. Some people are *motivated* to exercise because . . .

Activate Prior Knowledge

1. Ask students if they have ever had to perform an important task in a hurry. How did they react to the pressure of having a time limit? What do they think are the necessary traits of someone who can work well in pressure situations?
2. Ask students to name jobs that people in the military do. (*Possible answers: soldier, health care, bomb squad, computer systems*)
3. Have students locate Afghanistan and Iraq on a world map.

Preview and Predict Ask students what clues the title of the article, the photograph, and the photo caption provide. What predictions about the article might students make? (*Possible answer: I will learn what a bomb squad is and how it uses remote control robots.*)

Build Background Shortly after the bombing of the World Trade Center Towers on September 11, 2001, the United States, together with British forces, began air strikes in Afghanistan. The offensive was part of Operation Enduring Freedom, a campaign to drive Osama bin Laden and Taliban leaders from northern Afghanistan. The Bush administration recommended that the military action be expanded to Iraq in 2002 because Iraq was not cooperating with the United Nations on inspections for weapons of mass destruction. The Second Persian Gulf War, or the Iraq War (also called Operation Iraqi Freedom), began in March 2003 with an air strike. Ground forces soon followed. In 2010 President Obama called a formal end to combat operations in Iraq. Many troops remained to train and support Iraqi forces.

DURING READING

Cause and Effect A cause is an event or action that makes something else happen. An effect is the result or the outcome of that action. Writers use clue words such as *because, so, since, if,* and *therefore* to signal cause and effect. Have students look for cause-and-effect relationships by asking: What happened? Why?

AFTER READING

Respond to the Article Have students write a journal or blog entry about being a member of a bomb squad. Ask students: What characteristics do you think most bomb squad members have? Is this a job you would apply for? Why or why not?

DIFFERENTIATED INSTRUCTION

Kinesthetic learners may benefit from using physical movements to understand cause-and-effect relationships. Have students perform actions that illustrate cause and effect; for example, have them use the "halt" hand sign to cause someone to stop, or have them turn off the light to cause the room to get darker.

ENGLISH LANGUAGE LEARNERS

Have students fold pieces of paper in half lengthwise and label the left side *Cause* and the right side *Effect*. Ask them to draw sketches or cut pictures from magazines that show cause-and-effect relationships. For example, they may place a picture of a speeding car on the left and a police officer giving a ticket on the right.

GRAPHIC ORGANIZERS

📖 Go to www.mhreadingbasics.com. Use Graphic Organizer 4 as a Cause-and-Effect Chart. Make copies for each student. Have students label the left column *Causes* and the right column *Effects*. Ask students to write each sentence below under the *Causes* column. In the *Effects* column, ask students to write an effect for each cause. Discuss responses.

Causes

IEDs are not all made the same way.

IEDs can be planted anywhere.

Enemies often plant other IEDs close to the first one.

The military is looking for ways to reduce danger to bomb squads.

Introduce

Teach Lesson Skills

Support Individual Learners

Advanced Reader

Lesson Plan Advanced Reader

Unit 1 Lesson 1.4 🔊 "Tornado Chasers: Eyes of the Storm," pages 25–32

Introduce

Summary Most people take cover when a tornado approaches, but tornado chasers will actively seek out the tornado. Some chase tornadoes for the thrill and some for the research. Chasing tornadoes dates back to the 1950s. Since then, scientific interest has increased, and equipment has become more sophisticated. First, tornado chasers used portable Doppler radar. Then, a vehicle was designed to drive into a tornado. As a result of the movie *Twister*, hundreds of people wanted to chase tornadoes. Today, some people are "twister tourists," paying thousands of dollars to go on storm-chasing tours!

Teach Lesson Skills

BEFORE READING

Build Vocabulary List the vocabulary words and their definitions on the board. Discuss each word's meaning with students. Then write the following questions on the board. Read the questions aloud and discuss the answers with students.

generated: produced

sophisticated: complicated

shards: pieces of hard or brittle substance

superficial: on the surface only

entrepreneurs: people who start and manage their own businesses

1. What word goes with "selling your own merchandise"? *(entrepreneurs)*
2. What word goes with "broken glass"? *(shards)*
3. What word goes with "scientific equipment"? *(sophisticated)*
4. What word goes with "scrapes and bruises"? *(superficial)*
5. What word goes with "electricity made from wind power"? *(generated)*

Activate Prior Knowledge

1. Ask students to discuss the movie *The Wizard of Oz*. Have them tell how Dorothy and Toto arrived in Oz. If necessary, refer them to http://www.loc.gov/exhibits/oz/.
2. Tell students that *twister* is another name for a tornado. Ask students who have seen *Twister* to discuss the movie.
3. Have students find the states that make up the Great Plains on a map. *(Montana, North Dakota, South Dakota, Nebraska, Wyoming, Kansas, Colorado, Oklahoma, Texas, New Mexico)*

Build Background Although a tornado can occur in any part of the world, some areas are more prone to tornadoes than others. The United States has the highest occurrence rate in the world. Around 1,000 tornadoes hit the United States each year. Many of the tornadoes form in an area of the Great Plains called Tornado Alley. Most tornadoes occur here between May and early June and between 4 and 9 P.M. The reason this region gets so many tornadoes is that the flat land is a good place for the cold, dry, polar air from Canada to meet the warm, moist, tropical air from the Gulf of Mexico. When the two types of air meet, conditions are ripe for a tornado to form.

Preview and Predict Ask students what clues the title of the article, the photograph, and the photo caption provide. What predictions about the article might students make? *(Possible answer: This article will tell what tornado chasers do when they chase, or track, tornadoes.)*

DURING READING

Identify Sequence Sequence is the order in which events, ideas, or things are arranged. Time order refers to the order in which events occur. Following the sequence of events helps you see how the text is organized and how events relate to each other. As students read, ask them to look for key words such as *finally, then, later, after,* and *when.*

AFTER READING

Respond to the Article Have students write a journal or blog entry about tornado chasers. Ask students: What kind of personality does a tornado chaser need to have? Why is this an important job? Do you think you would like to try chasing a tornado? Why or why not?

Support Individual Learners

Advanced Reader

DIFFERENTIATED INSTRUCTION

Explain that the most common types of sequence are time order, spatial order, order of importance, and steps in a process. Time order refers to the order in which events occur. Spatial order refers to where things are in relation to one another. Order of importance refers to events or ideas arranged from most to least important. Steps in a process refers to the order in which something is done: for example, a recipe.

ENGLISH LANGUAGE LEARNERS

Have students describe events from their past in time order or explain things they can do using steps in a process. Prompt them to use signal words in their descriptions. Have students create time lines of the events they are describing as a visual aid.

GRAPHIC ORGANIZERS

💻 Go to **www.mhereadingbasics.com.** Use Graphic Organizer 6 as a Time Line. Make copies for each student. Ask students to use the dates below as labels on the time line. Then for each date, have students write an important event in the history of tornado chasers.

mid-1950s	1989
1961	1999
1977	2009

Lesson Plan Advanced Reader

Introduce

Summary High-rise window washers wash the windows of skyscrapers. Washing windows that high above the ground is a dangerous job. Hector Estrada and Oscar Gonzalez almost lost their lives when they swung in midair for nearly 15 minutes before being rescued. Arturo Rodriquez was saved because he was wearing a safety harness. Robert Domaszowec wasn't so lucky. He plunged to his death from a 17-story building. While there are dangers to the job, there are some benefits, too. For some, the extra money they earn makes high-rise window washing worth all the dangers.

Teach Lesson Skills

BEFORE READING

Build Vocabulary List the vocabulary words and their definitions on the board. Discuss each word's meaning with students. Then write the sentences that contain the words on the board. Read the sentences aloud and discuss them with students.

testified: declared
interior: inside
hazardous: risky

diligent: careful and thorough
congested: crowded

1. The guide *testified* that those hills were the hardest to climb.
2. The painters will use yellow paint for the *interior* walls and blue paint for the outside walls.
3. Both firefighters and police officers have *hazardous* jobs.

4. The student was *diligent* and studied hard so she would do well on the test.
5. During rush hour, it is hard to get any place quickly on the *congested* city streets.

Activate Prior Knowledge

1. Have students describe and discuss tall buildings or skyscrapers they have seen or visited.
2. Ask students to describe how they wash windows. Ask students how washing inside windows would be different from washing outside windows in their homes.
3. Have students discuss how people wash skyscraper windows. Ask why that might be a dangerous job.

Preview and Predict Ask students what clues the title of the article, the photograph, and the photo caption provide. What predictions about the article might students make? *(Possible answer: This article is about the people who wash the windows of extremely tall buildings and the dangers these people face.)*

Build Background Since off-the-ground window washing is a dangerous job, it is very important for workers to follow all the necessary safety guidelines. Before a job, the window cleaners must check all equipment. They should also examine the building, assessing the risks and creating an appropriate emergency plan. Each window washer should be fully trained. Workers should secure their tools, maintain a safe working load, and wear safety harnesses as necessary. Finally, they should always check the weather conditions before beginning a job and should avoid operating if the wind is too strong.

DURING READING

Visualize Visualizing is picturing in your mind the details of the setting, events, and characters in the passage. Encourage students to draw pictures or diagrams of these images as they read.

AFTER READING

Respond to the Article Have students write a journal or blog entry about why people choose to be high-rise window washers. Ask students: How did reading this article make you feel? How do you think the workers feel before, during, and after a job? What assumptions can you make about people who decide to be high-rise window washers?

Support Individual Learners

DIFFERENTIATED INSTRUCTION

Choose a descriptive poem and read it aloud to students. Have students visualize the poem. Then, reread the poem and have students act out what they see in their mind's eye. Finally, ask students to make a sketch or drawing or write a description of their visualizations.

ENGLISH LANGUAGE LEARNERS

Have students take turns describing favorite places. As each student describes a place, have others visualize it and then draw pictures or write descriptions of the place. Encourage students to ask questions as needed to help them clarify their visualizations.

GRAPHIC ORGANIZERS

💻 Go to **www.mhereadingbasics.com.** Use Graphic Organizer 1 as a Visualizing Map. Make copies for each student. Have students write *Estrada and Gonzalez* in the center bubble. Then in each outer bubble, ask students to write a description from the article that helped them visualize what happened during Estrada and Gonzalez's window-washing accident.

Advanced Reader

Lesson Plan Advanced Reader

Unit 2 Lesson 2.1 🔊 "Tiger Trainers: Schooling the Big Cat," pages 41–48

Introduce

Summary It takes hard work, long hours, and 10 years or more to become a tiger trainer. Why does it take so long? People need to be around tigers for a long time to understand them. Tiger trainers use different approaches to training. One approach is a system of positive and negative rewards and punishments. Another is "affection conditioning." Still another is a combination of rewards and affection. Trainers must always remember, though, that even a trained tiger is not tamed.

Teach Lesson Skills

BEFORE READING

Build Vocabulary List the vocabulary words and their definitions on the board. Discuss each word's meaning with students. Then write the following questions on the board. Read the questions aloud and discuss the answers with students.

migrant: moving from place to place

bluntly: honestly but abruptly

consequence: something that follows naturally after an action

proclivities: natural preferences

mauled: battered

1. Does a *migrant* worker usually live in one place all year or travel often? Why?
2. If you answer a question *bluntly*, are you usually telling the truth or only part of the truth? Why?
3. When a teenager uses the car without permission, what might a fair *consequence* be? Why?
4. Would the *proclivities* of a tiger be to live in a zoo or in the wild? Why?
5. If one dog is *mauled* by another dog, what might have happened?

Activate Prior Knowledge

1. Have students describe tigers they have seen in captivity (*zoo, circus*) or in the wild.
2. Explain that the *Siegfried and Roy Show* was a magic show that included trained animals. Have students discuss this or other magic shows. See http://www.siegfriedandroy.com.

Preview and Predict Ask students what clues the title of the article, the photograph, and the photo caption provide. What predictions about the article might students make? (*Possible answer: Tiger trainers train tigers, including Bengal tigers. Training tigers takes many years of practice.*)

Build Background The tiger is the largest member of the feline family. Like most felines, tigers are solitary predators. They have adapted to a variety of habitats, from the cold Siberian woodlands to the tropical forests of Sumatra. Despite a common misconception, tigers do not live in the wild in Africa, since they need large areas of forest cover and water for hunting. Today, tigers are on the brink of extinction. Only six of the nine known subspecies of tigers remain, and poaching and the loss of habitat threaten their existence. In the past 100 years, the population of wild tigers has decreased dramatically, so conservation societies have formed to spread awareness and restore tiger habitats.

DURING READING

Infer An inference is a logical guess about information that the writer suggests but doesn't directly say. Making inferences helps readers find deeper meaning in what they read. Ask students to look for details that aren't fully explained. Have them combine clues from the passage with their personal knowledge to identify what the writer suggests.

AFTER READING

Respond to the Article Have students write a journal or blog entry about training tigers. Ask students: What are your thoughts about training tigers? Do you think this is something you would ever consider doing? What does the author mean by this statement: "Just because a tiger can be trained, that doesn't mean it is tamed"?

Support Individual Learners

DIFFERENTIATED INSTRUCTION

Collect passages, newspaper headlines, jokes, or cartoons that require students to make inferences in order to understand the passage fully. Place students in groups and have them work together to make inferences based on the text. The dialogue among students builds background knowledge, and those who have difficulty with this skill can learn from those who are more adept at it. Allow groups to share their inferences with the class.

ENGLISH LANGUAGE LEARNERS

Picture books for older readers can be useful for helping students understand the concept of making inferences. Have students read the books in small groups and make three inferences about what happened in each book. For example, *Why?*, by Nikolai Popov, shows how disagreements can escalate into war. *The Stranger*, by Chris Van Allsburg, tells about a mysterious stranger. The reader must use clues to figure out who he is.

GRAPHIC ORGANIZERS

💻 Go to www.mhereadingbasics.com. Use Graphic Organizer 9 as a Main-Idea-and-Details Chart. Make copies for each student. Have students write the following main idea in the box on the left. Then have them write three details from the article that support the main idea. Discuss their responses.

Main Idea

It takes a lot of hard work to become a tiger trainer.

Advanced Reader

Lesson Plan Advanced Reader

Introduce

Summary Rodeo bull riding is often called "the most dangerous eight seconds in sports." That's because while riders try to stay on the bulls, the bulls try to dump riders off their backs. When riders are thrown, they run the risk of getting stomped on. This does not stop bull riders, though. Men, women, and children participate in the sport. Is the sport cruel to bulls? Some critics, like PETA, believe it is because a flank rope is tied tightly around the bull's hips. Sometimes the bull is prodded by an electric jolt, too. Even so, bull riding remains a popular sport in which riders risk their lives for a challenge and money.

Teach Lesson Skills

BEFORE READING

Build Vocabulary List the vocabulary words and their definitions on the board. Discuss each word's meaning with students. Then write the following questions on the board. Read the questions aloud and discuss the answers with students.

in the abstract: in theory

claustrophobic: likely to cause fear by being small and closed in

recuperate: recover

agitated: deeply distressed

contradictory: opposing

1. What word or phrase goes with "small room"? *(claustrophobic)*
2. What word or phrase goes with "two different explanations"? *(contradictory)*
3. What word or phrase goes with "the way something should be"? *(in the abstract)*

4. What word or phrase goes with "angry parents"? *(agitated)*
5. What word or phrase goes with "a patient who is healing"? *(recuperate)*

Activate Prior Knowledge

1. Write *bull* on the board. Have students brainstorm words they think of when they think of a bull. Record their responses in a web. *(Possible answers: horns, steer, rodeo, matador, bull fighting)*
2. Have students share what they know about Annie Oakley's participation in rodeos. If necessary, go to http://www.pbs.org/, enter "Annie Oakley" in the search box, and click on the first result.

Preview and Predict Ask students what clues the title of the article, the photograph, and the photo caption provide. What predictions about the article might students make? *(Possible answer: I will read about bull riders and how hard it must be to stay on the bull for eight seconds.)*

Build Background Rodeos were always about competition, but they weren't always big events that people paid money to watch. Rodeos started as part of the roundup of livestock, when cowhands would compete with each other to show off their skills. The rodeo gained popularity and became a spectator sport in the late 1880s. Today, rodeos show off the riding and roping skills of cowboys and cowgirls in the spirit of the Old West. There are two types of contests: rough stock events and timed events. Rough stock events, in which contestants have a set number of seconds, include bull and bronco riding. Timed events, in which contestants see how quickly they can complete an event, include roping, steer wrestling, and barrel racing.

DURING READING

Determine Word Meanings from Context Have students think of context as the words or sentences that surround a word they don't know. This information can help them make a good guess about what the word means. Have students look for clues such as descriptions or synonyms to help them figure out what unfamiliar words mean.

AFTER READING

Respond to the Article Have students write a journal or blog entry about whether they think it's cruel to ride bulls in rodeos. Ask students: What is your opinion about the flank ropes and electric shocks used on bulls? What do you think will happen to bull riding in the future?

Support Individual Learners

DIFFERENTIATED INSTRUCTION

Ask students to bring in song lyrics or poems that contain words that may be unfamiliar to other students. Have students take turns explaining to the class how they determined the meanings of unfamiliar words using context clues.

ENGLISH LANGUAGE LEARNERS

Tell students that they can sometimes figure out the meaning of an unfamiliar word by seeing how the word relates to other words around it. Use the word *berserk* in the first sentence of paragraph 7 as an example. Then have students read the next two sentences and identify the context clues that help them identify the meaning of *berserk*. If necessary, explain that the words *buck and spin so frantically* help readers understand the meaning of *berserk*.

GRAPHIC ORGANIZERS

💻 Go to **www.mhreadingbasics.com**. Use Graphic Organizer 2 as a Fact-and-Opinion Chart. Make copies for each student. Ask students to label the columns *Fact* and *Opinion*. Have students write the following sentences in the correct column. Discuss their responses.

Bull riding is "the most dangerous eight seconds in sports."

Mike Lee competed at the Professional Rodeo Cowboys Association rodeo in Arkansas.

It took Lee four months to recuperate and ride again.

Bull riding is the greatest sport there is.

Use of the flank strap is cruel.

Sometimes bulls are prodded with an electric jolt.

Lesson Plan Advanced Reader

Introduce

Summary Sherpa guides assist climbers of the Himalayan Mountains. They carry equipment, food, and oxygen tanks; clear away ice; anchor ropes; and cook food. Sherpas also perform heroic tasks to rescue climbers who are in trouble. Why do Sherpas have so much stamina and resilience? It's partly because they are born and live in the mountains, so they are used to the conditions. Why do they go on such grueling expeditions? One reason is to make money, but they are also selfless and courageous. Every year, they prove vital in helping climbers reach the summits of some of the highest mountains on Earth.

Teach Lesson Skills

BEFORE READING

Build Vocabulary List the vocabulary words and their definitions on the board. Discuss each word's meaning with students. Then write the following sentence stems on the board. Read the sentence stems aloud and ask students to complete them.

synonymous: the same; identical
customary: routine
indispensable: absolutely necessary

stamina: ability to endure
incentive: motivation

1. A woodchuck and a groundhog are *synonymous* because . . .
2. On Saturdays, my *customary* chores include . . .
3. The doctor proved to be *indispensable* when she . . .

4. The runner has so much *stamina* that he . . .
5. One *incentive* for getting good grades is . . .

Activate Prior Knowledge

1. Ask students to share what they know about mountain climbing, either from personal experience, the movies, or books they've read. What equipment do climbers need? *(Possible answers: ropes, backpacks, boots, food)*
2. Have students find the Himalayas on a map.

Preview and Predict
Ask students what clues the title of the article, the photograph, and the photo caption provide. What predictions about the article might students make? *(Possible answer: The article is about how Sherpas assist mountain climbers.)*

Build Background
The word *Himalaya* comes from the Sanskrit language and means "the abode of snow." Located on the northern border of the Indian subcontinent, the Great Himalayas are the highest mountain range in the world. More than 100 peaks in the Himalayas have elevations above 24,000 feet. Mt. Everest, one of the peaks, is the highest mountain in the world at over 29,000 feet. The Himalayas stretch 1,550 miles from east to west and vary from 125–250 miles north to south. They cover a total area of close to 230,000 square miles. The mountains are mostly in India, Nepal, and Bhutan, but some are in Pakistan and China, too.

DURING READING

Predict Predicting is thinking ahead to guess the outcome of events. Predicting helps readers become involved in the text. Readers base predictions on details in the passage and their own knowledge. Tell students that their predictions may change as details change or are added.

AFTER READING

Respond to the Article Have students write a journal or blog entry about how climbers feel about their Sherpa guides. Ask students: Why is it important for climbers to hire Sherpa guides? If you were a climber, what would you say to your Sherpa guide before and after the climb?

Support Individual Learners

DIFFERENTIATED INSTRUCTION
Give students a comic strip with the final frame missing. Ask them to draw their predictions of what happens at the end. Remind them to use clues the cartoonist has provided. When they finish, give them the final frame of the comic and have them compare their predictions to the ending.

ENGLISH LANGUAGE LEARNERS
Have partners practice predicting the outcomes of stories. Students may read a story or tell the plot of a book or film. Have the storyteller stop periodically and ask, "What do you think happens next?" Ask the partner to make a prediction. Have students discuss if their predictions were correct or if they had to revise them. Then ask students to switch roles.

GRAPHIC ORGANIZERS
💻 Go to **www.mhreadingbasics.com**. Use Graphic Organizer 1 as a Characteristics Map. Make copies for each student. Ask students to write *Sherpa Guide* in the center bubble of the graphic organizer. Then have them write one of the adjectives about the guides in each of the other bubbles. Ask students to add a fact that they learned from the article that supports each adjective. Discuss their responses.

strong   selfless
heroic   resilient

Advanced Reader

Lesson Plan Advanced Reader

Unit 2 Lesson 2.4 🔊 "Astronaut Mechanics: Hanging in Space," pages 65–72

Introduce

Summary All astronauts face hazards in space, but astronaut mechanics face the most. Their job often includes going on a spacewalk or venturing into space. They have only a supply of oxygen and their high-pressure space suits for protection. Leaking oxygen and a puncture in their space suits are just two of the dangers they face. Another is exposure to the extreme temperatures of space. Some scientists are investigating the theory that exposure to cosmic rays makes astronaut mechanics age faster, too! In spite of these dangers, astronaut mechanics have risked their lives to repair damages to the Hubble Space Telescope and the International Space Station.

Teach Lesson Skills

BEFORE READING

Build Vocabulary List the vocabulary words and their definitions on the board. Discuss each word's meaning with students. Then write the sentences that contain the words on the board. Read the sentences aloud and discuss them with students.

lubricating: making slippery
reluctant: unwilling
sobering: serious

reflecting: thinking calmly
methodically: precisely

1. The mechanic tunes up her bicycle by putting *lubricating* oil on the chain.
2. I threw the tennis ball into the waves, but my cautious dog was *reluctant* to fetch it.
3. When the car drove through the red light, it was a *sobering* reminder to look both ways before crossing the street.

4. The scientists are not *reflecting* on what won't work because they are thinking about what will work.
5. The carpenter worked *methodically* and repaired the house perfectly by the end of the day.

Activate Prior Knowledge
1. Ask students what they know about the Hubble Space Telescope and the International Space Station. See http://www.nasa.gov.
2. Ask students what jobs astronauts do in space. *(Possible answers: command and pilot shuttles, maintain spacecraft and equipment, perform experiments, spacewalk)*

Preview and Predict Ask students what clues the title of the article, the photograph, and the photo caption provide. What predictions about the article might students make? *(Possible answer: One thing that astronaut mechanics do is install cameras on the outside of a space station.)*

Build Background Astronaut mechanics rely on their space suits for support and mobility while working in space. A modern space suit, also called the Extravehicular Mobility Unit, is a model of sophisticated technology. The inner garment, which resembles long underwear, regulates the temperature inside the suit. The outer shell maintains a pressurized atmosphere, while also protecting the astronaut from space debris and solar radiation. A separate backpack unit provides oxygen and removes carbon dioxide. Moreover, since an astronaut mechanic may spend several hours working on a repair, the space suit needs to accommodate basic food, water, and waste elimination needs. There are pockets inside the suit that contain a cereal bar and a water pouch, and a diaper-like garment is used for waste collection. The space suit is designed to be worn up to seven hours.

DURING READING
Find Vocabulary in Context As students read the article, have them note the new vocabulary words. Ask them to think about each word's meaning as they read.

AFTER READING
Respond to the Article Have students write a journal or blog entry about what they learned about astronaut mechanics. Ask students: What worries does an astronaut mechanic have? Why do you think astronaut mechanics choose to do this job? Would you do it? Why or why not?

Support Individual Learners

DIFFERENTIATED INSTRUCTION
Explain that when students summarize a passage, they determine the most important ideas and details. Tell students that thinking about who, what, where, when, why, and how will help them summarize. Then ask students to give a summary of a movie or television show they have seen or of an experience they have had.

ENGLISH LANGUAGE LEARNERS
Have students choose a short magazine or newspaper article. Help them write the main idea of each paragraph. Then ask students to use the main ideas to summarize the article.

GRAPHIC ORGANIZERS
Go to www.mhreadingbasics.com. Use Graphic Organizer 7 as a Summary Chart. Make copies for each student. Ask students to write in the top three boxes three dangers astronaut mechanics face. Then have them use those dangers to summarize the article. Write the summary in the big box at the bottom of the chart. Discuss their responses.

Advanced Reader

READING BASICS Part 3: Readers 261

Lesson Plan Advanced Reader

Unit 2 Lesson 2.5 🔊 "James Herman Banning: Pioneer Pilot," pages 73–80

Introduce

Summary James Herman Banning was an African American pioneer pilot during the early days of aviation history. Despite discrimination and prejudice, his determination led him to become the first African American aviator to be licensed by the U.S. Department of Commerce. In 1932 Banning and his mechanic set out in a two-seat biplane on a cross-country flight. After 21 days, but a total of only 42 hours of flight, Banning became the first African American pilot to complete a cross-country flight. He died during an air accident in 1933. His courage helped future African American pilots fulfill their dreams of flying.

Teach Lesson Skills

BEFORE READING

Build Vocabulary List the vocabulary words and their definitions on the board. Discuss each word's meaning with students. Then write the following questions on the board. Read the questions aloud and discuss the answers with students.

deterred: prevented from acting

craze: intense interest; fad

visionary: far thinking; dreamy

skeptics: doubters

solicited: asked for

1. If a roadblock *deterred* you from taking the highway, did it prevent or allow you to get on the highway? Why?
2. Is a *craze* a popular or an unpopular event? Why?
3. Would a *visionary* scientist more likely be interested in the past or the future? Why?

4. Would *skeptics* doubt or believe a politician's campaign promises? Why?
5. If you *solicited* advice, did you ask for advice or give advice? Why?

Activate Prior Knowledge

1. Ask students to share their knowledge of the history of flying or airplanes.
2. Invite students who have been to air shows or airplane exhibits to share their experiences.

Preview and Predict Ask students what clues the title of the article, the photograph, and the photo caption provide. What predictions about the article might students make? (*Possible answer: Banning and Allen were pilots who successfully flew an airplane cross-country.*)

Build Background From the 1880s through the 1960s, Jim Crow laws were enacted by states to enforce segregation. (The term "Jim Crow" came from a minstrel act that made an exaggerated portrayal of racial stereotypes. It became associated with a derogatory expression for African Americans.) Many states had laws that forbade interracial mixing in business and public institutions. It was not until 1950 that the tide began to turn, when the Supreme Court ordered the University of Texas to admit an African American student. In 1957 the schools in Little Rock, Arkansas, were forced to admit African American students, and in 1964, Alabama had to integrate the university system. The final end to Jim Crow laws came in the 1960s with the passage of the Civil Rights Act (1964), the Voting Rights Act (1965), and the Fair Housing Act (1968). These acts officially ended the ability of states to discriminate based on race.

DURING READING

Identify Sequence Sequence is the order in which events, ideas, or things are arranged. Time order refers to the order in which events occur. Following the sequence of events helps you see how the text is organized and how events relate to each other. As students read, ask them to look for key words such as *finally, then, when, later,* and *after.*

AFTER READING

Respond to the Article Have students write a journal or blog entry about their response to the information they read about James Herman Banning. Ask students: How did Banning show courage and determination? What can you learn about yourself from reading about his life?

Support Individual Learners

DIFFERENTIATED INSTRUCTION

Have students place photographs or magazine pictures in sequence and explain why they chose to order the pictures in time order, spatial order, order of importance, or as steps in a process. They could also use objects to create spatial-order sequences, such as arranging pens, paper clips, and books on a desk, and use signal words to describe the order.

ENGLISH LANGUAGE LEARNERS

Cut apart panels of comic strips and ask students to place the frames in sequence. Have them explain to partners why they used the order they did. Encourage them to use the key words such as *first, next, then, last,* and *finally.*

GRAPHIC ORGANIZERS

💻 Go to **www.mhereadingbasics.com**. Use Graphic Organizer 5 as a Sequence-of-Events Chart. Make copies for each student. Ask students to write the following events in time order. Discuss their responses.

Banning and Thomas Allen flew across country in a biplane.

Banning flew as a passenger at an air show.

Banning was the chief pilot for the Bessie Coleman Aero Club.

Banning ran an auto repair shop.

Advanced Reader

Lesson Plan Advanced Reader

Unit 3 Lesson 3.1 🔊 "Embedded Journalists: Writing from the Front Lines," pages 81–88

Introduce

Summary Embedded journalists have been embedded in military units in Iraq. The concept was developed in 2003 by the Department of Defense and major news organizations. While it gave journalists access to the daily activities of U.S. troops, they had to follow some rules—13 pages of them. Some people find that allowing embedded journalists to live alongside soldiers has distinct advantages. For example, they have better understanding of war and engage in eyewitness war reporting. Others point out the negatives, such as problems with perspective, loss of objectivity, and loss of autonomy. Everyone agrees on one thing, though—embedded journalists face danger.

Teach Lesson Skills

BEFORE READING

Build Vocabulary List the vocabulary words and their definitions on the board. Discuss each word's meaning with students. Then write the following questions on the board. Read the questions aloud and discuss the answers with students.

assailants: attackers

unprecedented: never before known

objectivity: ability to view without emotion or bias

autonomy: independence

compromised: endangered

1. What word goes with "a judge"? *(objectivity)*
2. What word goes with "people who hurt innocent bystanders"? *(assailants)*
3. What word goes with "freedom to be your own boss"? *(autonomy)*

4. What word goes with "a brand-new discovery"? *(unprecedented)*
5. What word goes with "at risk"? *(compromised)*

Activate Prior Knowledge

1. Use Graphic Organizer 1 to make a Concept Web for the word *journalist*. Ask students to tell what journalists do. *(write/report news; investigate issues; interview people; work for newspapers, magazines, or online media)*

2. Ask students what they think a war correspondent does. Have them tell how this job would be similar to and different from what other journalists do.

Preview and Predict Ask students what clues the title of the article, the photograph, and the photo caption provide. What predictions about the article might students make? *(Possible answer: Embedded journalists cover wars by working alongside soldiers and having daily access to their activities.)*

Build Background The concept of a professional independent war correspondent first emerged in the 1800s. The Mexican-American War in the 1840s and the Crimean War between Turkey and Russia in the 1850s were the first areas of conflict to gain widespread journalistic coverage. Until the telegraph came into broad use, reports from the front would be sent via letter and took a week to arrive. The telegraph, as well as the advent of photography, helped to make war coverage more immediate. By World War I, motion-picture film was also being used, and with World War II came the age of radio. Television broadcasting brought the Vietnam War to American living rooms, becoming the primary source of news coverage. With the arrival of the digital age, however, war journalists have been able to provide coverage with greater immediacy than ever before.

DURING READING

Determine Word Meanings from Context Tell students to think of context as the words or sentences that surround a word they don't know. This information can help them make a good guess about what the word means. Have students look for clues such as descriptions, synonyms, or examples to help them figure out what unfamiliar words mean.

AFTER READING

Respond to the Article Have students write a journal or blog entry about their opinions about embedded journalists. Ask students: How does having embedded journalists affect the objectivity of the news? Why do you think embedded journalist have to agree to follow 13 pages of rules?

Support Individual Learners

DIFFERENTIATED INSTRUCTION

Have students work in pairs to read a passage from a newspaper or magazine. Ask them to identify at least three unfamiliar words, use context clues to figure out the meanings, and discuss how the context clues helped them. Then have students check the meanings in a dictionary.

ENGLISH LANGUAGE LEARNERS

Show students how to use synonyms to define a word within a sentence. Point out that the synonym can come before or after the word. Use the word *embed* in paragraph 2 as an example: ". . . came up with a plan to insert, or 'embed,' . . ." Ask students to identify the synonym for *embed*. Point out how *insert* helps students understand the meaning of *embed*.

GRAPHIC ORGANIZERS

📀 Go to www.mhereadingbasics.com. Use Graphic Organizer 2 as a Classifying Chart. Make copies for each student. Ask students to write *Pro* at the top of the left column and *Con* at the top of the right column. Then have students write two or three pros and two or three cons of being an embedded journalist. Discuss their responses.

Advanced Reader

Lesson Plan Advanced Reader

Unit 3 Lesson 3.2 🔊 "Bush Pilots: Tough Takeoffs, Rough Landings," pages 89–96

Introduce

Summary Bush pilots fly over wilderness to remote places where commercial airplanes don't fly. They also fly into dangerous war zones. The courageous pilots bring necessary supplies or humanitarian aid to inhabitants in need. Sometimes bush pilots are like taxicab drivers in the sky. They transport sports teams to their games or campers in and out of the wilderness. Bush pilots don't have runways like commercial planes. They take off and land on anything that is flat and long enough. The fearless bush pilots risk their lives with each flight, but to them, it's "just a normal way of life."

Teach Lesson Skills

BEFORE READING

Build Vocabulary List the vocabulary words and their definitions on the board. Discuss each word's meaning with students. Then write the following sentence stems on the board. Read the sentence stems aloud and ask students to complete them.

conventional: matching accepted standards

mundane: commonplace

monitor: keep track of

hostile: warlike

adverse: unfavorable

1. We fly on *conventional* airplanes when we . . .
2. My weekend activities were *mundane* because . . .
3. Teachers *monitor* their students' progress because . . .

4. The workplace had become a *hostile* environment because . . .
5. Due to the *adverse* weather conditions, the family decided to . . .

Activate Prior Knowledge

1. Have students discuss airplane flights. Ask them to describe takeoffs, landings, and the flight itself.
2. Ask students who have lived or camped in the wilderness to describe their experiences.
3. Have students discuss or research wilderness areas. For more information, see http://www.wilderness.net.

Preview and Predict Ask students what clues the title of the article, the photograph, and the photo caption provide. What predictions about the article might students make? *(Possible answer: Bush pilots fly over the wilderness in places like Alaska. They depend on their steady hands and sharp eyesight.)*

Build Background Because bush pilots fly in adverse conditions in the wilderness, their planes are different from large commercial airplanes. A good bush plane must be rugged, and it must be able to take off and land in short distances. Most bush planes have wings high on the body, which allows for an unrestricted view for passengers and good lateral stability. Moreover, it helps the plane land on small strips that have an overgrowth of vegetation. Bush planes also often have "tail draggers," or conventional landing gear, where two main gear units are positioned near the center of gravity and a much smaller support is at the rear of the craft. This type of landing gear helps the bush plane become airborne more quickly.

DURING READING

Infer An inference is a logical guess about information that the writer suggests but doesn't directly say. Making inferences helps readers find deeper meaning in what they read. Ask students to look for details that aren't fully explained. Have them combine clues from the passage with their personal knowledge to identify what the writer suggests.

AFTER READING

Respond to the Article Have students write a journal or blog entry about bush pilots. Ask students: How would you feel about being a bush pilot? How would you compare the risks to the benefits?

Support Individual Learners

DIFFERENTIATED INSTRUCTION

Ask students to write riddles about animals, sports, classroom objects, or other subjects of interest. Have partners take turns reading and guessing the answers to their riddles. Encourage them to discuss how clues in the riddles and their previous knowledge helped them make inferences to solve the riddles.

ENGLISH LANGUAGE LEARNERS

Picture books for older readers can be useful for helping students understand the concept of making inferences. One example is *Flotsam*, by David Wiesner, in which a boy discovers a barnacle-encrusted underwater camera with many secrets to share. Have students read several books in small groups and make three inferences about what happened in each book.

GRAPHIC ORGANIZERS

💻 Go to **www.mhereadingbasics.com**. Use Graphic Organizer 8 as a Compare-and-Contrast Chart. Ask students to label the outside ovals *Daryl Smith* and *Heather Stewart*. Ask them to write each detail in the correct oval. In the middle area, have students write three ways in which the two people are alike. Discuss their responses.

Flew into war zones in Somalia and Sudan

Flew over the wilderness in Alaska

Took women to the hospital to have babies

Saved lives of refugees

Lesson Plan Advanced Reader

Introduce

Summary Today's pirates are different from the pirates of old. They use smaller, faster boats and high-tech weapons. Luckily, pirate chasers are different, too. Some are government or multinational groups from the marines, navy, or special military task forces who patrol on ships stocked with modern-day devices and missiles. Others are private security forces trained in reconnaissance, surveillance, guerilla warfare, and counterterrorism. Although pirate chasers are making progress at reducing the number of successful pirate attacks, a pirate chaser's life is still one of high adventure and high risk.

Teach Lesson Skills

BEFORE READING

Build Vocabulary List the vocabulary words and their definitions on the board. Discuss each word's meaning with students. Then write the sentences that contain the words on the board. Read the sentences aloud and discuss them with students.

converging: coming together

factor in: take into account

rampant: out of control

simultaneously: at the same time

subdued: conquered

1. The *converging* armies will meet by the river at noon.
2. We should *factor in* the weather forecast before we make our plans.
3. When there was a *rampant* attack of mosquitoes, the people moved the party indoors.

4. Two soccer players from opposing teams ran for the ball *simultaneously*, hoping to get there first.
5. After the attackers had been *subdued*, they were arrested and put in jail.

Activate Prior Knowledge

1. Have students discuss pirate movies they have seen. Ask them to describe what the pirates looked like and how they acted.
2. Ask students to discuss real pirate stories they have read or heard about in the news.
3. Have students find Malaysia, Bangladesh, Somalia, and the Morocco Strait on a map.

Preview and Predict Ask students what clues the title of the article, the photograph, and the photo caption provide. What predictions about the article might students make? *(Possible answer: This article is about how pirate chasers catch the pirates who use small speedboats to attack large ships.)*

Build Background Although pirates have been around for most of history, they were particularly active in the 17th and 18th centuries. Pirates had horrific reputations to go along with their skull-and-crossbones flags. One famous pirate, known as Blackbeard, was especially feared. Not only did he carry knives, cutlasses, and pistols, but he also had wild eyes and thick, tangled hair, which gave him a ferocious appearance. There were a few women pirates, too. They had to disguise themselves by dressing up as men, since it was against the pirates' rules to have women onboard. In the 1800s, governments sent armed naval warships to fight pirates. Many of the pirates were killed in battle. Others were captured and executed.

DURING READING

Visualize Visualizing is picturing in your mind the details of the setting, events, and characters in the passage. Encourage students to draw pictures or diagrams of these images as they read.

AFTER READING

Respond to the Article Have students write a journal or blog entry about whether a career as a pirate chaser appeals to them. Ask students: Why does John Dalby say that there is nothing pleasant about this business? Do you agree? What details from the article support your opinion?

Support Individual Learners

DIFFERENTIATED INSTRUCTION

Have students choose descriptive paragraphs from stories they have read. Have partners work together to practice visualizing. Partners take turns reading their paragraphs and visualizing the details. Ask students to draw pictures to show their visualizations.

ENGLISH LANGUAGE LEARNERS

Have students choose pictures from books or magazines. As each student describes a picture (without showing it), have others visualize it and then draw pictures or write about the description they heard. When students have finished drawing, invite them to compare their pictures to the original.

GRAPHIC ORGANIZERS

📖 Go to **www.mhereadingbasics.com**. Use Graphic Organizer 2 as a Classifying Chart. Ask students to label the columns *Pirates* and *Pirate Chasers*. Then have students write each of the following sentences in the correct column. Discuss their responses.

They use small speedboats and machine guns.

They are filled with desperation and greed.

They work in small teams to carry out dangerous missions.

They are "brutal, ruthless, and cold blooded."

They have ships with helicopter pads and missiles.

They do their riskiest work from 1 A.M. to 6 P.M.

Introduce

Summary Even with technological advances, ranching can be a difficult and dangerous job. Sometimes equipment malfunctions or unpredictable animal behavior leads to severe injuries or death. Toxic pesticides can cause health risks. Disease can kill animals, and a drop in market price can wipe out a rancher's yearly profit. With all the risks and stresses, why do ranchers still want to perform their jobs? To them, it's more than a job; it's a way of life.

Teach Lesson Skills

BEFORE READING

Build Vocabulary List the vocabulary words and their definitions on the board. Discuss each word's meaning with students. Then write the following questions on the board. Read the questions aloud and discuss the answers with students.

potential: possible

toxic: poisonous and deadly

decimate: kill a large part of

significant: important, critical

exempt: free from a rule or responsibility

1. Would you rather worry about a *potential* danger or face an immediate danger? Why?
2. Are *toxic* chemicals harmless or dangerous? Why?
3. Would a late spring snowstorm help your plants grow or *decimate* them? Why?

4. If your friend gave you *significant* information, would you ignore it or pay attention to it? Why?
5. If you were *exempt* from taking a test would you take it? Why?

Activate Prior Knowledge

1. Write *ranch* on the board. Have students brainstorm words they think of when they hear the word *ranch*. (Possible answers: *cattle, cows, horses, cowboys, range*)
2. Have students imagine they work on a ranch. Ask what they might do as part of their job. For ideas, go to http://www.collegeboard.com, enter "ranchers" in the search box, and click on "Ranchers."

Preview and Predict Ask students what clues the title of the article, the photograph, and the photo caption provide. What predictions about the article might students make? *(Possible answer: The article might be about the kind of work ranchers do and why they love their jobs.)*

Build Background Ranching is the raising or breeding of animals such as cattle, horses, or sheep. Ranching came to the United States from Latin America. In the mid-1800s, ranchers owned the animals and equipment but not the land; it was free public land. The animals grazed on the open range, and cowhands did most of the work. By the late 1800s, fencing went up, and the open ranges were divided into large ranches with many cowhands. Today, ranchers usually own their land and do most of the work themselves.

DURING READING

Cause and Effect A cause is an event or action that makes something else happen. An effect is the result or the outcome of that action. Writers use clue words such as *because, so, since, if,* and *therefore* to signal cause and effect. Have students look for cause-and-effect relationships by asking: What happened? Why?

AFTER READING

Respond to the Article Have students write a journal or blog entry about the variety of jobs that must be done on a cattle ranch. Ask students what job they would find most appealing. What are some other duties ranchers must perform that were not mentioned in the article?

Support Individual Learners

DIFFERENTIATED INSTRUCTION

Ask students to watch a news report about something that was caused by an action or event, such as a fire caused by a malfunctioning space heater or a soccer victory as a result of a last-second goal. Ask students to rewrite the report using words such as *because, as a result, since, consequently, therefore,* and *so* to help show cause-and-effect relationships.

ENGLISH LANGUAGE LEARNERS

Ask students to tell a partner a common folktale or legend that has cause-and-effect relationships in it. Have them pause to discuss the causes and effects by asking and answering questions that ask why. Model by pausing as you tell a story to ask about cause-and-effect relationships.

GRAPHIC ORGANIZERS

💻 Go to **www.mhereadingbasics.com**. Use Graphic Organizer 1 as a Concept Map. Make copies for each student. Ask students to write *Ranching* in the center bubble of the graphic organizer. Then have students write a sentence in each of the outer bubbles about why ranching can be a difficult job. Discuss their responses.

Advanced Reader

Lesson Plan Advanced Reader

Introduce

Summary Delta Force, or 1st Special Forces Detachment-Delta, is one of the premier counterterrorist units in America. The unit's mission is to fight terrorism around the world, but its operations are so secretive that no one will admit it officially exists. Since its inception in 1977, operatives have worked in the most dangerous places in the world. Who exactly are these operatives? They are the best of the best. Potential members are recruited and put through a grueling training program. If they pass, they must be ready to perform one of the toughest jobs in the U.S. military at any given moment.

Teach Lesson Skills

BEFORE READING

Build Vocabulary List the vocabulary words and their definitions on the board. Discuss each word's meaning with students. Then write the following questions on the board. Read the questions aloud and discuss the answers with students.

extracting: physically removing

indigenous: local

inconspicuous: unnoticed

elite: top-notch

covert: undercover

1. What word goes with "secret agent or spy"? *(covert)*
2. What word goes with "people who live in a country"? *(indigenous)*
3. What word goes with "highest grade-point average"? *(elite)*
4. What word goes with "blends in with the crowd"? *(inconspicuous)*
5. What word goes with "having your wisdom teeth removed"? *(extracting)*

Activate Prior Knowledge

1. Use Graphic Organizer 3 as a KWL chart. Have students label the first column *Know* and write what they know about Delta Force. Have students label the second column *Want to Know* and write what they would like to know about Delta Force. This exercise will be continued after the reading.
2. Have students find these places on a map: Mogadishu, Somalia, Iraq, Thailand.

Preview and Predict Ask students what clues the title of the article, the photograph, and the photo caption provide. What predictions about the article might students make? *(Possible answer: The Delta Force is a secret force that works with other countries to fight terrorism.)*

Build Background
Many U.S. organizations work together in counterterrorist operations. The FBI and CIA both list counterterrorism as a top priority, partnering with law enforcement, intelligence, and military agencies to root out terrorist networks. The Office of the Coordinator for Counterterrorism, which is part of the State Department, is responsible for coordinating counterterrorist efforts with foreign governments. The Department of Homeland Security, an agency that was created in response to the September 11 terrorist attacks, consolidates the efforts of various federal, state, and local departments to secure the nation. It fights terrorism by looking for explosives in public places, protecting the infrastructure, detecting agents of biological warfare, and working to help state and local law officials be prepared for potential threats.

DURING READING

Ask Questions Questioning helps you to monitor your understanding of the text. Have students ask *who, what, where, when, why,* and *how* questions and look for the answers. Questions may include: Who did you read about in this article? What did you learn about? Where did the events take place? When did the events take place? According to the article, why did the events happen? How were the problems resolved?

AFTER READING

Respond to the Article Have students write a journal or blog entry about their response to the information in the article. Ask students: Why do you think no government or U.S. Army official will acknowledge the existence of the Delta Force? Why do you think some critics argue that some operatives go beyond legal bounds?

Support Individual Learners

DIFFERENTIATED INSTRUCTION
Have students choose a newspaper article that interests them. Then have them pretend that they are the editor of the paper and they want more information about the article. Have them write at least five questions the editor can ask the writer to gain the additional information.

ENGLISH LANGUAGE LEARNERS
Have students choose a magazine article and study the pictures. Ask them to come up with three questions about the pictures that might be answered in the article. Then have partners read the article, including the headline and captions, to find the answers to their questions.

GRAPHIC ORGANIZERS
💻 Go to www.mhereadingbasics.com. Use Graphic Organizer 3 as a KWL Chart. Have students use the charts they started before reading the article. If they did not do this exercise before reading, they can start it now. Have students label the third column *Learned* and add information they learned about the Delta Force. They may wish to add more questions to the *Want to Know* column. Have students discuss their charts. Encourage them to find answers online or at the library.

Advanced Reader

ADVANCED READER
Unit 1 Assessment Article

Directions: Read this story. Then answer each question that follows. Circle the letter of your answer.

Skywalkers

Picture yourself on the 50th floor of a skyscraper. You're not inside the building, though, because it is still under construction and only the steel frame has risen this high. You are balancing on a steel beam that is only six inches wide, and it sways slightly in the wind, which is blowing much harder up here than on the ground far, far below. You're carrying heavy tools and a bag of bolts, and you must walk to the edge of the structure. If this image reminds you of a nightmare, then ironwork is not the job for you.

2 Ironworkers, who have been called "skywalkers," connect steel columns, beams, and girders into the frames that support buildings and bridges. Each piece of steel weighs tons. It dangles from a crane, and ironworkers position it and bolt or weld it into place. The work is physically challenging and dangerous and seems to require a lot more courage than the average pedestrian has.

3 "Maybe your hands are sweating, you're shaking, you got a lump in your stomach," explains ironworker Jack Doyle. "But if it's in you to do the work, that'll go away and you'll start to feel comfortable."

4 "I'm scared of heights," says David Rice, who began ironworking in 1969, helping to build New York City's World Trade Center towers, the tallest buildings of their time. "The way I was taught, you put one foot in front of the other, look straight ahead, and never look down." One time, he panicked while trying to walk across a girder. "I had a bucket of bolts on my shoulder. I don't recall how long I was up there alone. Finally, I just walked to safety. No one came out after me because you could lose two men that way."

5 David Rice is Native American—Mohawk—and for more than 100 years, Mohawk ironworkers have worked on every major structure in North America, from the Golden Gate Bridge in San Francisco to the Empire State Building in New York City.

6 Ironworking is a Mohawk tradition passed down from generation to generation. Ironworking is a tradition for other groups, too, and most ironworkers today can point to relatives who "walked iron" before them.

7 Ironwork is much safer than it was before the days of safety ropes and harnesses and strict regulations. Still, the conditions can be brutal because work goes on in sizzling heat and freezing cold. Bruises and broken bones are a common risk. Fatalities occur, too. Few jobs bring a greater sense of pride than ironwork. As one ironworker has said, "We're like the kings of construction."

8 Back on the ground, ironworkers look like ordinary pedestrians. However, there's a difference. An ironworker who looks up to see a soaring skyscraper or a magnificent bridge can say, "I built that."

Advanced Reader

ADVANCED READER
Unit 1 Assessment Questions

1. Which sentence states the main idea best?
   a. Ironworkers are proud of their traditions.
   b. Ironwork is a construction job.
   c. Ironwork is hard, dangerous, and rewarding.

2. According to the article, ironworkers work with
   a. steel beams.
   b. iron railings.
   c. metals of all kinds.

3. Which answer is probably true?
   a. Ironworkers learn to handle their fear.
   b. Ironworkers are less fearful than most people.
   c. Most ironworkers prefer to work indoors.

4. What is the meaning of the underlined word?
   Bruises and broken bones are a common risk. Fatalities occur, too.
   a. deaths
   b. injuries
   c. accidents

5. The author wrote this article mainly to
   a. persuade readers to become ironworkers.
   b. provide information about ironworkers.
   c. explain how buildings are constructed.

6. Which answer correctly restates this sentence from the story?
   Ironworking is a Mohawk tradition passed down from generation to generation.
   a. Mohawk ironworkers have had the same religious practices since the time of their ancestors.
   b. Mohawk grandparents, parents, and children are ironworkers who work together.
   c. Mohawk ironworkers teach their children about the work, and their children become ironworkers, too.

7. Which sentence expresses an opinion?
   a. Ironworkers have been called "skywalkers."
   b. Ironwork is much safer than it was before the days of safety ropes and harnesses and strict regulations.
   c. Few jobs bring a greater sense of pride than ironwork.

8. The author contrasts ironworkers and pedestrians because
   a. pedestrians stay on the ground.
   b. pedestrians are usually fearful.
   c. pedestrians can't see structures such as skyscrapers and bridges.

9. What is the most likely job requirement for ironworkers?
   a. pride in building things
   b. physical fitness
   c. fearlessness

10. What does the author seem to think of ironworkers?
    a. They take unnecessary risks.
    b. They deserve to be admired.
    c. They have the best jobs in construction.

Advanced Reader

ADVANCED READER
Unit 2 Assessment Article

Directions: Read this story. Then answer each question that follows. Circle the letter of your answer.

Working in a Coal Mine

The next time you switch on a light, consider the sacrifices that make that convenience possible. Chances are the electricity that powers your light comes from coal, a fossil fuel mined at some risk to its workers.

2 Although today's mines yield more coal with fewer workers, the image of the sweat-stained and coal-streaked miner is still accurate. The Emerald Mine in Pennsylvania uses longwall mining. The longwall method represents the peak of underground mining technology, but every day its miners still descend far below the ground through cold, dark, narrow tunnels.

3 The longwall miners' destination is a high-tech factory floor—if the factory were located in the pit of a volcano. Some 150 workers toil in the enclosed space amid stunning heat and noise. A machine of mind-bending dimensions—four football fields long—moves back and forth, chewing away at a wall of coal. The coal spews onto a conveyor belt for its long journey up.

4 When the longwall machine has covered 60 feet, the seven-mile-long belt must be moved. Doug Conklin, a miner for Emerald, says, "Imagine buying a Cadillac, taking it apart in your garage, moving it a few blocks to your buddy's garage, putting it all back together again, and then taking your family for a drive. That's what we do in here every day!" And that's just the conveyor belt. When the wall is mined out, the longwall machine itself gets reassembled farther on in a process that takes 11 days.

5 Mining safety has come a long way since West Virginia's Monongah coal mine explosion claimed 362 lives in 1907, but it remains a dangerous job. The risk of a sudden ceiling collapse is always present, as is the buildup of explosive methane gas. On average, 50 to 60 coal miners die on the job each year. Long-term health problems are another hazard, and exposure to coal dust can cause permanent lung damage.

6 Nowhere is the awareness of mining's danger more raw than in West Virginia. In April 2010 a massive explosion ripped through the Upper Big Branch mine, killing 29 miners. Still, miner James Songer echoes the attitude of many West Virginia miners when he says, "I try not to let it get to me in any way. Try not to think about it. Say a prayer before I go in."

7 In spite of the dangers, coal miners persevere, especially in areas where coal mining is the best-paying job around. Coal miners enjoy a close-knit camaraderie, joking around but always looking out for one another. Documentary filmmaker Mari-Lynn Evans says, "The people of the coal fields of West Virginia are the most inspirational, strongest people you will ever meet in this world . . . You have people whose daddies and granddaddies all worked for the mine. They're proud of that heritage." As half of our electricity comes from coal, it's a heritage we should all appreciate.

ADVANCED READER
Unit 2 Assessment Questions

1. Which sentence states the main idea best?
   a. Coal mining has become more dangerous.
   b. Coal mining remains a dangerous job.
   c. Coal mining is not as dangerous as people think.

2. According to the article, the Emerald Mine is located in
   a. Pennsylvania.
   b. West Virginia.
   c. Wyoming.

3. Which answer is probably true?
   a. Miners are not usually careful about their own safety.
   b. Mining has become as safe as it can possibly get.
   c. Miners are well aware of the risks of mining.

4. What is the meaning of the underlined word?
   In spite of the dangers, coal miners persevere, especially in areas where coal mining is the best-paying job around.
   a. worry
   b. enjoy themselves
   c. carry on

5. The author wrote this article mainly to
   a. warn job seekers away from coal mining.
   b. inform readers about a worthwhile but dangerous job.
   c. entertain readers with exciting stories about a hazardous occupation.

6. Which answer correctly restates this sentence from the story?
   Nowhere is the awareness of mining's danger more raw than in West Virginia.
   a. West Virginians are just starting to become aware of the hazards of mining.
   b. People in West Virginia are painfully aware of mining's danger.
   c. West Virginians seem unaffected by the risks of coal mining.

7. Which of the following is a fact?
   a. The longwall method represents the peak of underground mining technology.
   b. Nowhere is the awareness of mining's danger more raw than in West Virginia.
   c. Half of the electricity we use comes from coal.

8. Why would methane gas be likely to build up in a mine?
   a. The mine is like an underground factory in the pit of a volcano.
   b. Once released in an enclosed space underground, the gas can't escape.
   c. Methane gas builds up when the ceiling collapses.

9. One probable reason that coal mining has become safer since 1907 is that
   a. mining no longer takes place underground.
   b. mining has become less common, so fewer are at risk.
   c. mining technology and oversight have improved.

10. Miner Doug Conklin makes a comparison between breaking down and rebuilding a Cadillac and
    a. moving the seven-mile-long conveyor belt.
    b. reassembling the longwall machine.
    c. chewing away at the wall of coal in Emerald Mine.

Advanced Reader

ADVANCED READER

Unit 3 Assessment Article

Directions: Read this story. Then answer each question that follows. Circle the letter of your answer.

Going to Extremes for Oil

The 19-year-old Veetoune Mokhantha loved his job on one of Alaska's North Slope oil rigs. Even as an entry-level worker he was making $24 an hour. For every two weeks he spent up in the North Slope oil patch, he got two weeks off back home. In fact, he was due to head back home when he accidentally stepped into a pit containing a rotating auger. An auger, or giant corkscrew, circulates the mud that cools the drill. The drill and the mud get very hot, and when the hot mud comes in contact with the arctic air, thick vapors form. Mokhantha couldn't see where he was going and was seriously injured as a result.

2 Although the modern oil industry got its start in Texas in 1901, the popular image of the lone Texas oilman striking an oil vein in the dusty plains of West Texas no longer matches the reality of crude oil extraction. The scarcity of oil in the continental United States has forced oil companies to locate and drill for oil in increasingly extreme environments, and oil workers have followed.

3 The phrase "Warning: Contents under Pressure" applies at all times on an oil rig. In April 2010 a surge of natural gas caused an explosion on an oil rig in the Gulf of Mexico, killing 11 workers and injuring 17. Rigs have backup systems to cope with explosions, but these complex systems can fail. In particular, keeping the systems working when they're standing in several thousand feet of water is an enormous challenge.

4 In fact all the complications of drilling for oil increase in deep water. From above, the rigs are battered by hurricanes. From below, where drilling may occur at depths of 5,000 feet or more, frigid temperatures, incredible pressure, and strong currents are constant concerns.

5 Modern technology has made working on these offshore rigs as comfortable as possible. A gulf rig called *Boudreaux* is anchored in 8,000 feet of water. Highly trained technicians use joysticks and video to operate deep-water robots. With flat-screen TVs and gym equipment, the rig's living quarters can feel like a hotel, but when one of the workers has an accident or health problem, the nearest hospital is a two-hour helicopter ride away.

6 Offshore oil-rig worker Pancho Fondren of Texas says, "The wind blows, mixed with sleet and snow, but that doesn't make any difference. You keep going . . . A squall could blow through here, and you could be in some real rough trouble . . . It's really not a *nice* job, but I wouldn't change with anybody."

Advanced Reader

ADVANCED READER
Unit 3 Assessment Questions

1. Which sentence states the main idea best?
   a. Oil-rig workers in the Gulf of Mexico are well paid.
   b. Oil-rig workers set up and operate oil rigs.
   c. Today's remote oil rigs can be dangerous workplaces.

2. According to the article, deep-sea oil rigs are
   a. more difficult to operate than land rigs.
   b. unstable and uncomfortable.
   c. seldom at depths greater than 200 feet.

3. Which answer is probably true?
   a. Oil companies will look for oil in ever more remote locations.
   b. At some point, the number of land-based oil rigs will rise sharply.
   c. The United States will pump more oil than it can use.

4. What is the meaning of the underlined word?
   The image of the Texas oilman striking an oil vein no longer matches the reality of crude oil extraction.
   a. method of payment
   b. process of digging
   c. action of taking out something

5. The author wrote this article mainly to
   a. warn job seekers away from oil-rig work.
   b. explain how the location of oil affects oil workers' jobs.
   c. provide a technical explanation of how to dig for oil.

6. From the information in the article, one can predict that
   a. the oil wells will dry up soon.
   b. the rig workers will be replaced entirely by robots and computers.
   c. oil rigs will be built wherever a company thinks it can extract oil.

7. Which answer correctly restates this sentence from the story?
   The phrase "Warning: Contents under Pressure" applies at all times on an oil rig.
   a. High-pressure fire extinguishers are present everywhere on oil rigs.
   b. Oil rigs are hazardous places because of the pressure of oil and gas underground.
   c. The oil-rig workers are under constant pressure to be efficient *and* safety conscious.

8. According to the passage, how is drilling in Alaska's North Slope similar to drilling in the Gulf of Mexico?
   a. The harsh conditions in both locations make drilling a challenge.
   b. The subzero temperatures cause work to progress slowly in both sites.
   c. In both locations, workers use robots from the comfort of enclosed control rooms.

9. Why does oil-rig worker Pancho Fondren likely say he "wouldn't change [his job] with anybody"?
   a. He loves the stark beauty of Alaska's North Slope oil fields.
   b. Working on an offshore rig is exciting and well-paying.
   c. He could not find a safer, more comfortable job if he tried.

10. Why does the image of the lone Texas oilman no longer fit the reality of oil-rig work?
    a. Oil companies no longer drill for oil in West Texas.
    b. There's less oil in Texas than before, and drilling now involves advanced technology and a large crew.
    c. The conditions in Texas were much more uncomfortable than current oil-rig drilling sites.

Advanced Reader

Advanced Reader

Unit 1 Language Development Activity: *Vocabulary Review*

ESL/DI Skill	*Vocabulary Review:* testified, interior, hazardous, diligent, congested

Activity Highlights

1. Reading sentences aloud: individual
2. Substituting definitions for vocabulary words: individual
3. Oral responses to interview questions: partners
4. Note taking, summarizing: individual
5. Creation of original interview questions: individual

Teacher Preparation

1. Review the article "High-rise Window Washers: A Bird's-eye View" (Unit 1, Lesson 1.5, p. 33).
2. Write on the board or otherwise present the lesson vocabulary words: *testified* ("declared"), *interior* ("inside"), *hazardous* ("risky"), *diligent* ("careful and thorough"), *congested* ("crowded").
3. Review the interview questions below and have a copy on hand.

Interview Questions:

1. Have you seen a movie or TV show in which someone <u>testified</u> in court that they were innocent?

2. In what way do you decorate the <u>interior</u> of your house or apartment?

3. In your opinion, what is the most interesting and <u>hazardous</u> job in the world?

4. In what ways are you <u>diligent</u> about your family or social responsibilities?

5. What is the most <u>congested</u> area where you travel, and how could the situation be improved?

Activity Steps:

1. Review the article "High-rise Window Washers: A Bird's-eye View" (Unit 1, Lesson 1.5, p. 33) with the class.

2. Review the definitions of the Lesson 1.5 vocabulary words with the class.

3. The class discusses how each word was used in the article. Tell the class that they will be interviewing each other using the words in a new context.

4. Read the interview questions aloud to the class.

5. Volunteers read the sentences again, substituting the definitions on the board for the underlined words. For example: *What is the most <u>crowded</u> area where you travel, and how could the situation be improved?*

6. The class discusses possible responses to the first topic. (*Possible response: The person who declared in court that he was innocent was not telling the truth.*)

7. Students pair off.

8. Partners interview each other using the discussion topic questions on the board.

9. As one partner answers the questions, the other partner takes notes on the answers.

10. The second partner summarizes the first partner's answers to him or her.

11. The first partner suggests any corrections that may be necessary.

12. Partners reverse the process so that each partner has acted as interviewer once.

13. If time permits, partners create original questions to ask each other.

14. Partners summarize each other's answers to the class.

Advanced Reader

Advanced Reader

Unit 2 Language Development Activity: *Idioms and Common Phrases*

ESL/DI Skill	*Idiom:* last-ditch effort

Activity Highlights

1. Flashcards: individual, partners
2. Substituting definitions for vocabulary words: individual
3. Reading sentences to the class: individual
4. Writing original sentence pairs: partners
5. Sharing aspects of personal experience and culture: individual

Teacher Preparation

1. Review the article "Sherpas: Helpers in High Altitudes" (Unit 2, Lesson 2.3, p. 57).
2. Provide four blank index cards per student.
3. Write the following sentence on the board: *A fellow Sherpa named Dawa agreed to go back up the mountain in a* <u>last-ditch effort</u> *to save Tolo.*

Activity Steps:

1. Review the article "Sherpas: Helpers in High Altitudes" (Unit 2, Lesson 2.3, p. 57) with the class.

2. Talk about what *last-ditch effort* means in the context of the article. Had anyone made a previous effort to save Tolo? Was it successful?

3. Write a simple definition of *last-ditch effort* on the board: "a final and desperate attempt." Students write the idiom on one side of an index card and its definition on the other.

4. Read aloud the sentence on the board. A volunteer comes to the board and erases *last-ditch effort* and writes the definition in its place. He or she reads the new sentence aloud: *A fellow Sherpa named Dawa agreed to go back up the mountain in a* <u>final and desperate attempt</u> *to save Tolo.*

5. Volunteers describe a last-ditch effort they once made to save or fix something.

6. Write additional idioms and their definitions on the board, for example: *the last straw* ("the offense that makes someone completely lose their patience"), *have the last laugh* ("gain the advantage in a conflict after being down"), *famous last words* ("a confident conclusion that was later proven wrong").

7. Students write each additional idiom on one side of an index card and its definition on the other.

8. Students pair off.

9. Partners practice silently with their own cards for several minutes. Then they quiz each other.

10. Model a sentence pair for one of the additional idioms presented. For example: *When she lost my keys for the third time,* <u>it was the last straw</u>. / *When she lost my keys for the third time,* <u>it made me lose my patience completely</u>.

11. Partners write original sentence pairs for the other idioms.

12. Tell the class that *the last straw* comes from an Arabic story in which a camel's owner kept loading more and more straw onto its back. The camel stayed on its feet until one final piece of straw was added. That "last straw" caused the camel to fall to the ground.

13. Partners talk about other idioms they know and what their origins might be. Circulate to give students examples. You may search the Internet using the phrase *English idioms* to find examples.

Advanced Reader

Advanced Reader

Unit 3 Language Development Activity: *Multiple Meanings*

ESL/DI Skill	*Multiple-meaning Words:* piracy, smoking, deck, plank, chests

Activity Highlights

1. Discussion/analysis: small group
2. Writing sentences: individual
3. Reading sentences aloud: small group, whole class

Teacher Preparation

1. Review the article "Pirate Chasers: Crime Waves on the High Seas" (Unit 3, Lesson 3.3, p. 97).
2. Write on the board or otherwise present the short passage below this box. ("Piracy has changed significantly . . .")
3. For each group of 3–5 people, provide a dictionary.

Piracy has changed significantly . . . Pirates roamed the seas in sailing ships . . . with dozens of smoking cannons on deck. Pirates were famous for . . . forcing victims to walk the plank, making off with chests of jewels . . .*

Activity Steps:

1. Review "Pirate Chasers: Crime Waves on the High Seas" (Unit 3, Lesson 3.3, p. 97) with the class.

2. Volunteers read the sentences on the board aloud to the class.

3. Students form small groups.

4. Groups talk about what the underlined words mean in the context of the sentences.

5. Each student chooses an underlined word from one of the sentences. If possible, there should be a different word for each student in a group.

6. Each student writes an original sentence with his or her chosen word using the meaning the word has in the sentence on the board (call this meaning M1). He or she underlines the word in the sentence. For example: *Modern piracy requires motor boats.*

7. Students count off to determine an order for participating in the next steps.

8. Each Student 1 says his or her word (*piracy*) and reads his or her "M1" sentence from step 6 to the group.

9. Students collaborate to identify a second meaning (M2) for the word.* There may be more than two meanings, but students should stop at two. They find or confirm the additional meaning in the dictionary. (*piracy:* "the unauthorized use of another person's intellectual work") Circulate among groups to support students' work.

10. Each student writes an original sentence using M2 of the chosen word. For example: *The manufacturing company was sued for piracy of another company's plans.*

11. Each student reads his or her sentence to the group.

12. Repeat Steps 8–11 for Student 2, Student 3, etc. with the words they chose in step 5.

13. Once everyone has taken a turn, volunteers read both of their sentences to the class.

*Multiple meanings: *piracy* ("robbery at sea"/"the unauthorized use of another person's intellectual work"); *smoking* ("emitting smoke after having fired ammunition"/"breathing smoke from cigarettes"); *deck* ("the top floor of a ship"/"pack of cards"); *plank* ("wooden 'diving board' used by early pirates to make people jump into the sea"/"thin, long board used for construction"); *chests* ("large containers used by early pirates to store gold and other treasures"/"people's upper front body area")

Advanced Reader, Unit 1

Lesson 1.1: Secret Service Agents: Shield, Defend, Protect

A. Recognize and Recall Details
   1. c   2. b   3. a   4. b   5. b

B. Find the Main Idea
   1. M   2. N   3. B

C. Summarize and Paraphrase
   1. a   2. b

D. Make Inferences
   1. F   2. C   3. C   4. F   5. C

E. Recognize Author's Effect and Intentions
   1. b   2. a   3. b

F. Evaluate and Create   1. c   2. b

Lesson 1.2: Humanitarian Aid Workers: Comfort Under Fire

A. Recognize and Recall Details
   1. b   2. a   3. a   4. b

B. Find the Main Idea
   1. N   2. M   3. B

C. Summarize and Paraphrase
   1. b, c, a   2. a

D. Make Inferences
   1. F   2. C   3. F

E. Recognize Author's Effect and Intentions
   1. c   2. b   3. a   4. c

F. Evaluate and Create
   1. a. O   b. F   c. O   2. c, a

Lesson 1.3: Bomb Squad: No False Moves

A. Recognize and Recall Details
   1. c   2. b   3. b   4. c   5. a

B. Find the Main Idea
   1. B   2. N   3. M

C. Summarize and Paraphrase
   1. Summaries should include these points:
      Terrorists often plant two or three bombs close together. Bomb squad members worry about snipers.
   2. a   3. b

D. Make Inferences
   1. F   2. C   3. C   4. C   5. F

E. Recognize Author's Effect and Intentions
   1. b   2. a   3. c

F. Evaluate and Create
   1. a   2. a, b or b, a

Lesson 1.4: Tornado Chasers: Eyes of the Storm

A. Recognize and Recall Details
   1. b   2. a   3. c   4. b   5. c   6. a

B. Find the Main Idea
   1. N   2. M   3. B

C. Summarize and Paraphrase
   1. c   2. c, a, b

D. Make Inferences
   1. C   2. C   3. F   4. F   5. C

E. Recognize Author's Effect and Intentions
   1. a   2. b   3. b

F. Evaluate and Create
   1. a. F   b. O   c. O   2. b, c

Lesson 1.5: High-rise Window Washers: A Bird's-eye View

A. Recognize and Recall Details
   1. c   2. b   3. a   4. c

B. Find the Main Idea
   1. M   2. N   3. B

C. Summarize and Paraphrase
   1. b
   2. Summaries should include these points:
      The platform hit the building several times, breaking about two dozen windows. Pedestrians were afraid they would see the two men die.

D. Make Inferences
   1. F   2. C   3. F   4. F   5. C

E. Recognize Author's Effect and Intentions
   1. a   2. c   3. b

F. Evaluate and Create
   1. a   2. b, a

Unit 1 Assessment

Skywalkers
   1. c   2. a   3. a   4. a   5. b
   6. c   7. c   8. a   9. b   10. b

Advanced Reader, Unit 2

Lesson 2.1: Tiger Trainers: Schooling the Big Cat
A. Recognize and Recall Details
   1. b   2. a   3. c   4. c   5. a
B. Find the Main Idea   1. N   2. M   3. B
C. Summarize and Paraphrase
   1. b, a, c
   2. Summaries should include these points:
   To become a tiger trainer, expect to spend 10 years on the job. First you clean tiger cages and then gradually work your way up to apprentice trainer. Apprentice trainers work long hours every day for at least two years.
   3. c
D. Make Inferences
   1. C   2. F   3. F   4. C   5. C
E. Recognize Author's Effect and Intentions
   1. b   2. b
F. Evaluate and Create
   1. c   2. b   3. a, b or b, a

Lesson 2.2: Bull Riders: Ride or Run!
A. Recognize and Recall Details
   1. a   2. c   3. b   4. c   5. a   6. b
B. Find the Main Idea   1. N   2. B   3. M
C. Summarize and Paraphrase
   1. a   2. b
D. Make Inferences
   1. F   2. C   3. F   4. C   5. C
E. Recognize Author's Effect and Intentions
   1. c   2. c   3. b   4. b
F. Evaluate and Create   1. a   2. b, a

Lesson 2.3: Sherpas: Helpers in High Altitudes
A. Recognize and Recall Details
   1. c   2. b   3. b   4. c
B. Find the Main Idea   1. N   2. M   3. B
C. Summarize and Paraphrase
   1. b, a, c   2. a
D. Make Inferences
   1. C   2. F   3. F   4. C   5. F
E. Recognize Author's Effect and Intentions
   1. b   2. a   3. c
F. Evaluate and Create   1. b, a   2. c   3. b

Lesson 2.4: Astronaut Mechanics: Hanging in Space
A. Recognize and Recall Details
   1. b   2. b   3. c   4. b   5. a   6. c
B. Find the Main Idea   1. N   2. B   3. M
C. Summarize and Paraphrase
   1. b
   2. a
   3. Summaries should include these points:
   Astronaut mechanics were trying to replace a camera on the Hubble Space Telescope. All astronauts face dangers, but astronaut mechanics face additional risks when they spacewalk.
D. Make Inferences
   1. C   2. C   3. F   4. C   5. F
E. Recognize Author's Effect and Intentions
   1. c   2. c
F. Evaluate and Create   1. a   2. c   3. a

Lesson 2.5: James Herman Banning: Pioneer Pilot
A. Recognize and Recall Details
   1. a   2. c   3. a   4. b   5. c   6. a
B. Find the Main Idea   1. B   2. N   3. M
C. Summarize and Paraphrase
   1. a   2. a, c, b
   3. Summaries should include these points:
   James Banning and Thomas Allen fixed up an old biplane and flew it 3,300 miles on a 21-day journey across the United States. They had to ask for money for food and fuel along the way.
D. Make Inferences
   1. C   2. F   3. C   4. F
E. Recognize Author's Effect and Intentions
   1. c   2. b   3. b   4. a
F. Evaluate and Create   1. b   2. b

Unit 2 Assessment
Working in a Coal Mine
   1. b   2. a   3. c   4. c   5. b
   6. b   7. c   8. b   9. c   10. a

Answer Key Reader Lessons and Unit Assessment

Advanced Reader, Unit 3

Lesson 3.1: Embedded Journalists: Writing from the Front Lines
A. Recognize and Recall Details
   1. a   2. c   3. b   4. c
B. Find the Main Idea   1. B   2. N   3. M
C. Summarize and Paraphrase
   1. c   2. a
D. Make Inferences
   1. C   2. F   3. C   4. F   5. C
E. Recognize Author's Effect and Intentions
   1. b   2. c   3. a
F. Evaluate and Create
   1. a   2. b, c *or* c, b

Lesson 3.2: Bush Pilots: Tough Takeoffs, Rough Landings
A. Recognize and Recall Details
   1. b   2. a   3. a   4. c
B. Find the Main Idea   1. M   2. N   3. B
C. Summarize and Paraphrase
   1. b
   2. Summaries should include these points:
      Bush pilots earn less than airline pilots and have poorer equipment. They crash more often.
D. Make Inferences
   1. F   2. C   3. C   4. C   5. F
E. Recognize Author's Effect and Intentions
   1. a   2. b   3. a
F. Evaluate and Create
   1. b.   2. c

Lesson 3.3: Pirate Chasers: Crime Waves on the High Seas
A. Recognize and Recall Details
   1. a   2. c   3. b   4. b
B. Find the Main Idea   1. N   2. B   3. M
C. Summarize and Paraphrase
   1. c, b, a   2. c
D. Make Inferences
   1. F   2. C   3. F   4. F   5. C
E. Recognize Author's Effect and Intentions
   1. b   2. c   3. b   4. a
F. Evaluate and Create
   1. c   2. b

Lesson 3.4: Ranching: You've Got to Love It
A. Recognize and Recall Details
   1. b   2. c   3. a   4. b
B. Find the Main Idea
   1. B   2. M   3. N
C. Summarize and Paraphrase
   1. a   2. a
D. Make Inferences
   1. F   2. F   3. C   4. C
E. Recognize Author's Effect and Intentions
   1. b   2. a   3. b
F. Evaluate and Create
   1. a.   2. b   3. c

Lesson 3.5: Delta Force: Under Cover and Out of Sight
A. Recognize and Recall Details
   1. b   2. a   3. b   4. b
B. Find the Main Idea
   1. N   2. B   3. M
C. Summarize and Paraphrase
   1. Summaries should include these points:
      Delta Force candidates must be in excellent physical shape and have the ability to shoot accurately. They undergo a tough selection course and an Operators Training Course.
   2. b   3. c
D. Make Inferences
   1. C   2. C   3. C   4. F
E. Recognize Author's Effect and Intentions
   1. a   2. c
F. Evaluate and Create
   1. c   2. a   3. c, a

Unit 3 Assessment
Going to Extremes for Oil
   1. c   2. a   3. a   4. c   5. b
   6. c   7. b   8. a   9. b   10. b

Advanced Reader, Units 1–3

Lesson 1.1: Secret Service Agents: Shield, Defend, Protect

Graphic Organizer 3: KWL Chart
Possible answers:

Learned:

President Lincoln authorized the creation of the Secret Service.

At first, an agent's job was to catch people who printed fake money.

In addition to the president, agents protect other people, such as the president's family, the vice president, and major presidential candidates.

After President Kennedy's assassination, the Secret Service tightened its rules so presidents could not ride in open cars.

Lesson 1.2: Humanitarian Aid Workers: Comfort Under Fire

Graphic Organizer 7: Author's-Viewpoint Chart
Possible answers:

Humanitarian aid workers have been killed.

The author gives reasons, like making a positive difference in the world, that humanitarian aid workers persist.

The author uses words and phrases like the following to describe aid workers and what they do: *strong, noble motives, brave, altruistic, incredible risks, immense satisfaction.*

Lesson 1.3: Bomb Squad: No False Moves

Graphic Organizer 4: Cause-and-Effect Chart
Possible answers:

Effects:

They cannot all be disarmed in the same way.

Bomb squad members must constantly be on the lookout for anything that looks out of the ordinary.

Defusing one bomb doesn't mean you are in the clear.

The army has begun to use robots to check anything that looks suspicious.

Lesson 1.4: Tornado Chasers: Eyes of the Storm

Graphic Organizer 6: Time Line
Possible answers:

mid-1950s: People started chasing tornadoes.

1961: Neil B. Ward radioed a description of a tornado he was chasing to a local weather bureau.

1977: David Hoadley published the first journal, *Storm Track*, for storm enthusiasts.

1989: *Life Magazine* published Warren Faidley's photo of a lightning bolt. The term *storm chaser* was used for the first time.

1999: Tornado chasers measured a tornado's wind speed of 318 miles per hour, the fastest ever recorded.

2009: Reed Timmer and two others drove a Dominator into the path of a strong tornado.

Lesson 1.5: High-rise Window Washers: A Bird's-eye View

Graphic Organizer 1: Visualizing Map
Possible answers:

Estrada and Gonzalez could only hang on for dear life.

The platform became nearly vertical as it swung furiously back and forth in the strong wind.

Each time the swaying platform slammed into the building, it knocked out an office window or two.

Paper and debris floated out of the windows and began drifting like confetti before settling on the street.

Lesson 2.1: Tiger Trainers: Schooling the Big Cat

Graphic Organizer 9: Main-Idea-and-Details Chart
Possible answers:

You will spend at least 10 years learning on the job.

You will clean cages for about two years before you become an apprentice trainer.

As an apprentice trainer, you will be expected to work all day, every day.

Lesson 2.2: Bull Riders: Ride or Run!

Graphic Organizer 2: Fact-and-Opinion Chart

Bull riding is "the most dangerous eight seconds in sports." *Opinion*

Mike Lee competed at the Professional Rodeo Cowboys Association rodeo in Arkansas. *Fact*

It took Lee four months to recuperate and ride again. *Fact*

Bull riding is the greatest sport there is. *Opinion*

Use of the flank strap is cruel. *Opinion*

Sometimes bulls are prodded with an electric jolt. *Fact*

Lesson 2.3: Sherpas: Helpers in High Altitudes

Graphic Organizer 1: Characteristics Map
Possible answers:

strong: The Sherpa guides carry all the equipment and food.

Answer Key Graphic Organizers

heroic: One Sherpa guide climbed down the steep, icy slope without ropes to get help for the climbers.

selfless: A Sherpa guide will risk his life to save injured or sick climbers.

resilient: Sherpa guides can keep climbing when many climbers have collapsed in exhaustion.

Lesson 2.4: Astronaut Mechanics: Hanging in Space

Graphic Organizer 7: Summary Chart
Possible answers:

top box 1: There are extreme temperatures in space, so astronaut mechanics can get burned or frostbitten.

top box 2: Sharp objects from the spaceship or from space can puncture space suits and cause oxygen to escape.

top box 3: Astronaut mechanics are exposed to cosmic rays, which may cause them to age more quickly.

bottom box: Summaries will include the points above.

Lesson 2.5: James Herman Banning: Pioneer Pilot

Graphic Organizer 5: Sequence-of-Events Chart
Banning ran an auto repair shop.
Banning was the chief pilot for the Bessie Coleman Aero Club.
Banning and Thomas Allen flew across country in a biplane.
Banning flew as a passenger at an air show.

Lesson 3.1: Embedded Journalists: Writing from the Front Lines

Graphic Organizer 2: Classifying Chart
Possible answers:
Pros:
They have access to the daily lives of the troops.
Journalists can get the truth directly from the troops.
They gain a better understanding of the war.
Journalists can give their readers or viewers a clearer sense of what it's like in the field.
Cons:
It might be hard to develop a broad view of the war.
Journalists cannot send stories without the approval of the commander.
They cannot objectively cover both sides of the war.
If they break a rule, they can become "disembedded."

Lesson 3.2: Bush Pilots: Tough Takeoffs, Rough Landings

Graphic Organizer 8: Compare-and-Contrast Chart
Daryl Smith:
Flew over the wilderness in Alaska
Took women to the hospital to have babies
Heather Stewart:
Flew into war zones in Somalia and Sudan
Saved lives of refugees
Both:
Helped people in need
Had a job that involved risk
Landed and took off from makeshift strips

Lesson 3.3: Pirate Chasers: Crime Waves on the High Seas

Graphic Organizer 2: Classifying Chart
Pirates:
They use small speedboats and machine guns.
They are filled with desperation and greed.
They are "brutal, ruthless, and cold blooded."
Pirate Chasers:
They work in small teams to carry out dangerous missions.
They have ships with helicopter pads and missiles.
They do their riskiest work from 1 A.M. to 6 P.M.

Lesson 3.4: Ranching: You've Got to Love It

Graphic Organizer 1: Concept Map
Possible answers:
Ranchers work with large, complex machines that can malfunction.
Animals can be unpredictable and hurt ranchers.
Bad weather or diseases can decimate the herds.
The market price can drop and wipe out a year's profit.

Lesson 3.5: Delta Force: Under Cover and Out of Sight

Graphic Organizer 3: KWL Chart
Possible answers:
Learned:
Delta Force's mission is to combat terrorism.
Operatives rely on secrecy, which is why they use indigenous weapons and try to be inconspicuous.
Candidates for Delta Force are selected by invitation only and then must go through grueling tests and training.